OBJECTIVE

IELTS

Michael Black
Annette Capel

Self-study Student's Book

Advanced

YORK

CAMBRIDGE
UNIVERSITY PRESS

PUBLISHED BY THE PRESS SYNDICATE OF THE UNIVERSITY OF CAMBRIDGE
Cambridge, New York, Melbourne, Madrid, Cape Town, Singapore, São Paulo

CAMBRIDGE UNIVERSITY PRESS
The Edinburgh Building, Cambridge CB2 2RU, UK

www.cambridge.org
Information on this title: www.cambridge.org/9780521608831

First published 2006

Printed in Italy by Eurografica (part of the LEGO group)

A catalogue record for this book is available from the British Library

ISBN-13 978-0-521-60883-1 Self-study Student's Book
ISBN-10 0-521-60883-X Self-study Student's Book

ISBN-13 978-0-521-60884-8 Student's Book
ISBN-10 0-521-60884-8 Student's Book

ISBN-13 978-0-521-60879-4 Workbook
ISBN-10 0-521-60879-1 Workbook

ISBN-13 978-0-521-60878-7 Workbook with Answers
ISBN-10 0-521-60878-3 Workbook with Answers

ISBN-13 978-0-521-60875-6 Teacher's Book
ISBN-10 0-521-60875-9 Teacher's Book

ISBN-13 978-0-521-60876-3 Class Cassette Set
ISBN-10 0-521-60876-7 Class Cassette Set

ISBN-13 978-0-521-30877-0 Audio CD Set
ISBN-10 0-521-60877-5 Audio CD Set

Designed and produced by Kamae Design, Oxford

Map of Objective IELTS Advanced Student's Book

TOPIC		TEST SKILL AC = Academic GT = General Training	TASK TYPE	LANGUAGE FOCUS V = Vocabulary, G = Grammar, P = Pronunciation
Unit 1 Information overload 8–11 Studying	1.1	Listening Speaking	Multiple choice Note completion Part 1	V Compound nouns
	1.2	Reading (GT)	Reading quickly	G Modality
Test folder 1 12–13		Reading	**Headings**	
Unit 2 Only a game 14–17 Sport	2.1	Reading (AC / GT) Style extra	Headings Time adverbials	G Perfect tenses
	2.2	Listening Speaking	Note completion Part 3	P Numbers and letters V Intensifying adverbs
Writing folder 1 18–19		Academic and General Training Writing Task 2	**Planning an essay**	
Unit 3 Brands 20–23 Marketing	3.1	Listening Style extra	Multiple choice Matching Academic style	V Word building P Stressed vowels
	3.2	Reading (AC / GT) Speaking	Global multiple choice Yes / No / Not given Part 2	G Cleft sentences
Test folder 2 24–25		Reading	**True / False / Not given** **Yes / No / Not given**	
Unit 4 Spotlight on communication 26–29 Human and animal communication	4.1	Reading (AC / GT) Speaking	Locating information Part 3	V Language terms
	4.2	Listening	Summary completion Matching	G Adverbial clauses P Vowels
Writing folder 2 30–31		Academic Writing Task 1	**Commenting on graphs**	
Revision Units 1–4 32–33				
Unit 5 Is plastic fantastic? 34–37 Plastic products	5.1	Listening Speaking	Sentence completion Note completion Part 2	V Collocations related to packaging and waste P Lists
	5.2	Reading (AC / GT) Style extra	Sentence completion Comparative structures	G Passive forms
Test folder 3 38–39			**Speaking Parts 1, 2 and 3**	
Unit 6 Music matters 40–43 Music	6.1	Reading (AC) Style extra	Multiple choice Quoting	V Word building
	6.2	Listening Speaking	Classification Part 3	P Two words with only one difference G Concessive clauses
Writing folder 3 44–45		Academic and General Training Writing Task 2	**Reporting ideas**	
Unit 7 Worlds to explore 46–49 Exploration	7.1	Reading (AC / GT)	Global multiple choice Multiple choice with multiple answers Summary completion	V Personal qualities
	7.2	Listening Style extra Speaking	Matching Labelling a diagram *It* replacing a clause Part 3	P How the letter 'a' is pronounced
Test folder 4 50–51		Reading Listening	**Sentence and note completion**	

TOPIC		TEST SKILL AC = Academic GT = General Training	TASK TYPE	LANGUAGE FOCUS V = Vocabulary, G = Grammar, P = Pronunciation
Unit 8 **Culinary tools 52–55** Food technology	8.1	Reading (AC / GT)	Global multiple choice Deducing meanings of words from context Matching	V Phrasal verbs with *up*
	8.2	Listening	Flow-chart completion	G Modals in conditional sentences
Writing folder 4 56–57		Academic Writing Task 1	**Describing a process**	
Revision Units 5–8 58–59				
Unit 9 **Old and new 60–63** Cities	9.1	Speaking Reading (AC / GT) Style extra	Part 2 Sentence completion Linking words	
	9.2	Listening	Summary completion	V Word building G Inversion
Test folder 5 64–65		Listening Reading	**Multiple choice**	
Unit 10 **In your dreams 66–69** Dreams	10.1	Reading (AC) Style extra	Headings True / False / Not given Academic and journalistic styles	V Collocations in academic writing
	10.2	Listening Speaking	Matching Multiple choice Part 3	G Modal verbs of speculation and deduction P Vowel changes in related words
Writing folder 5 70–71		Academic and General Training Writing Task 2	**Developing an argument**	
Unit 11 **The physical world 72–75** The earth's natural features and forces	11.1	Listening Speaking	Labelling maps Sentence completion Part 2	V Geographical terms
	11.2	Reading (AC)	Short-answer questions Locating information	G Non-finite clauses
Test folder 6 76–77		Listening Reading	**Labelling diagrams and maps**	
Unit 12 **Nature or nurture? 78–81** Genetic inheritance and learning	12.1	Reading (AC) Speaking	Yes / No / Not given Matching Part 3	V Phrasal verbs with *on*
	12.2	Listening Style extra	Short-answer questions (lists) Matching Short-answer questions Features of spontaneous speech	G Infinitives
Writing folder 6 82–83		Academic Writing Task 1	**Comparison and contrast**	
Revision Units 9–12 84–85				
Unit 13 **Cosmic debris 86–89** Space	13.1	Reading (AC) Style extra	Summary completion Academic style	V Cause and result
	13.2	Listening Speaking	Sentence completion Part 2	P Word stress – adverbs G The future
Test folder 7 90–91		Listening Reading	**Matching**	
Unit 14 **Trends in society 92–95** Social change	14.1	Reading (AC) Speaking	Classification Sentence completion Part 3	V Adjective–noun collocations
	14.2	Listening Style extra	Matching Multiple choice Signalling intentions	G Pronouns clinic
Writing folder 7 96–97		Academic and General Training Writing Task 2	**Appropriate style and tone**	

Content of the IELTS Test

Each candidate takes four IELTS test modules, one in each of the four skills, Listening, Reading, Writing and Speaking. All candidates take the same Listening and Speaking Modules. There is a choice between Academic and General Training in the Reading and Writing Modules.

Listening 40 questions approximately 30 minutes

There are four sections to this part of the test and they are always in the same order. Each section is heard ONCE only. During the test, time is given for you to read the questions and write down and check your answers. Ten minutes is allowed at the end of the test for you to transfer your answers from the question paper to an answer sheet.

Section	Format	Task types	Objective Test folder
1 and 2	The first two sections are concerned with social needs. There is a conversation between two speakers, followed by a monologue.	Questions are chosen from the following types: • multiple choice • short-answer questions • sentence completion • note completion • summary completion • labelling a diagram • table/flow-chart completion • classification • matching	TF 5 TF 4 TF 4 TF 10 TF 6 TF 9 TF 7
3 and 4	Sections 3 and 4 are concerned with situations related to educational or training contexts. There is a conversation between up to four people and then a further monologue.		

Reading 40 questions 60 minutes

There are three reading passages in the Reading Module, with a total of 2,000 to 2,750 words (Academic) or 2,000 to 2,500 words (General Training). All answers must be entered on an answer sheet during the test. No extra time is allowed to transfer answers.

Academic	General Training	Task types	Objective Test folder
Texts are taken from magazines, journals, books and newspapers, which have been written for a non-specialist audience. They deal with issues which are interesting and accessible to candidates entering undergraduate or postgraduate courses or seeking professional registration. At least one text contains detailed logical argument. One text may contain non-verbal materials such as diagrams, graphs or illustrations.	Texts are taken from notices, advertisements, official documents, booklets, newspapers, instruction manuals, leaflets, timetables, books and magazines. The first section, 'social survival', contains texts relevant to basic linguistic survival in English. The second section, 'training survival', focuses on the training context – either training itself or welfare needs. This section involves a text or texts of more complex language. The third section, 'general reading', involves reading longer, more complex texts.	Questions are chosen from the following types: • multiple choice • short-answer questions • sentence completion • note completion • summary completion • labelling a diagram • table/flow-chart completion • headings • Yes/No/Not given • True/False/Not given • locating information • classification • matching	TF 5 TF 4 TF 4 TF 10 TF 6 TF 1 TF 2 TF 2 TF 8 TF 9 TF 7

Writing 2 tasks 60 minutes

Task	Academic	General Training	Objective Writing folder
Task 1 Allow about 20 minutes for this	Describing graphic data / a diagram You will be assessed on your ability to: • organise, present and compare data • describe a process • describe an object, event or sequence of events • explain how something works You must write at least 150 words.	Writing a letter You will be assessed on your ability to: • write a personal or formal letter • ask for and provide factual information • express needs, wants, likes and dislikes • express opinions, complaints You must write at least 150 words.	**Academic** WF 2 WF 4 WF 6 WF 8 WF 10 **General Training** WF 8
Task 2 Allow about 40 minutes for this	Writing an essay You will be assessed on your ability to: • present the solution to a problem • present and justify an opinion • compare and contrast evidence • evaluate and challenge ideas You must write at least 250 words.	Writing an essay You will be assessed on your ability to: • provide general factual information • outline a problem and present a solution • present, evaluate and challenge ideas You must write at least 250 words.	**Academic and General Training** WF 1 WF 3 WF 5 WF 7 WF 8 WF 9 WF 10

Speaking approximately 11–14 minutes

The Speaking Module consists of an oral interview between you and an examiner.

Part	Format	Timing	Objective Test folder
Part 1 Introduction and interview	The examiner introduces him/herself and asks questions about familiar topics, for example, your home, family, job and interests.	4–5 minutes	TF 3
Part 2 Individual long turn	The examiner gives you a card, which contains a topic and some prompts, and asks you to speak for 1–2 minutes on the topic. The examiner asks one or two questions to round off the long turn.	3–4 minutes (including 1 minute preparation time)	TF 3
Part 3 Two-way discussion	The examiner invites you to take part in a discussion of a more abstract nature, based on questions thematically linked to the Part 2 topic.	4–5 minutes	TF 3

Information overload

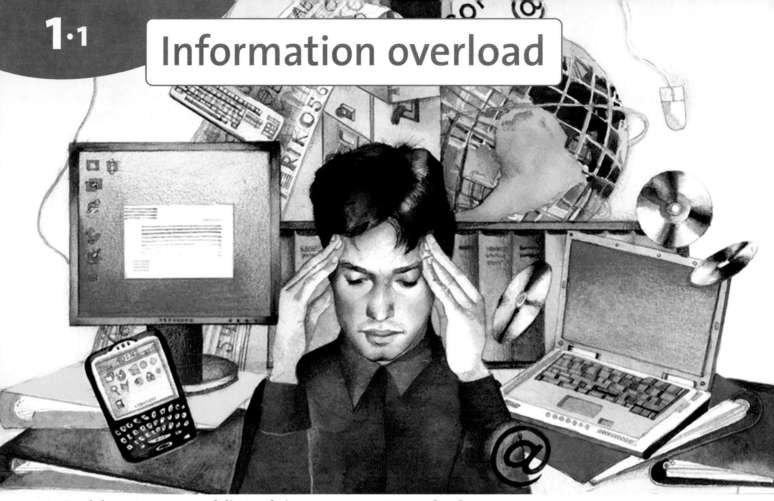

1 Read these statements and discuss their implications for academic work and studying.

> As much new information will be available in the next decade as has been discovered in the whole of human history.
>
> It is estimated that it would take around seven hundred years for one person to read a single year's output in the field of chemistry.
>
> In 2003, the World Wide Web contained 170 terabytes* of information on its surface; the 'deep Web' was at that time thought to be up to 540 times larger (91,850 terabytes).

* One terabyte of information is roughly equivalent to the amount of text printed on 40.25 million sheets of paper.

2 Based on this information, do you have a terror of terabytes, or do you think they're terrific? How does 'information overload' affect you personally, in your studies or your daily life?

Vocabulary Compound nouns

3 The word *overload* is a compound noun, formed from a preposition and a verb. Make more compound nouns by combining a word from column A with a word from column B to fill the spaces in sentences 1–5 below.

A	B
in	come
out	kill
over	put
	work

1 My tutor wants me to expand the introduction of my paper, but I think that would be complete .... !
2 The reading .... for the course consists of a core textbook and additional photocopied articles.
3 The .... of this study is very confusing because the results differ from one sample to another.
4 Our .... of new titles has increased this year, although we are producing fewer journals.
5 Lynn is suffering from .... , with two essay deadlines this week.

4 *Overload* is an uncountable noun – you cannot add -*s* to it and it takes a singular verb. Which of the compound nouns in exercise 3 are also uncountable?

5 Select two words from the box that are similar in meaning to each of the words (1–8) below. Most of these words will come up in the listening task, so use a dictionary to check on their meaning if necessary.

There are four extra words that you won't need. What part of speech are they and what do they mean?

biased	confident	critical	efficiently
evaluate	false	inundated	judge
locate	means	overwhelmed	
periodical	productively	resources	
retrieve	review	spine	support
sure	virtually		

1 overloaded   5 certain
2 tools   6 journal
3 inaccurate   7 proficiently
4 find   8 assess

Listening

6 🎧 You are going to hear a conversation between a university tutor and two students about studying and research methods. To help you, the recording will be separated into four parts and you will hear some focus questions at the beginning of each one. Read the Test spot and then close your book, to concentrate on your listening.

Test spot

In IELTS Listening Section 3, you will hear a conversation between up to four speakers, who will be talking about an aspect of academic work or studying. Work out who the speakers are at the beginning of the recording and remember to check which speaker is focused on in each question. There may be a variety of task types within the section, for example multiple choice and note taking.

7 🎧 Read the instructions and questions below, noting which speakers are referred to. Then listen to Parts 2–4 again and answer the questions as you listen.

Part 2

*Choose the correct letter, **A**, **B** or **C**.*

1 What was Mark's biggest challenge when he started at university?
   A the method of teaching history
   B the length of the core textbooks
   C the amount of information available

Part 3

Complete Jenny's notes.

Write NO MORE THAN TWO WORDS *for each answer.*

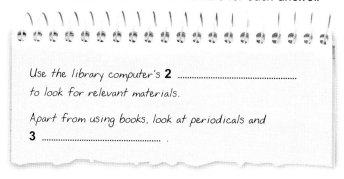

Use the library computer's **2** ....
to look for relevant materials.

Apart from using books, look at periodicals and
3 ....

Part 4

*Choose the correct letter, **A**, **B** or **C**.*

4 Dr Lucas advises Jenny
   A to avoid using the Internet as an essay source.
   B to be critical of information taken off the Internet.
   C to limit how much time she spends on the Internet.

8 🎧 Listen to the whole conversation to check your answers. You can ask your teacher for a copy of the recording script.

Speaking *Part 1*

Test spot

In Part 1 of the Speaking Module, the examiner will ask you questions about yourself – for example, your work or studies, your home, or your family. Make sure you revise relevant vocabulary for these familiar topics and practise ways of extending your answers, to show your language range.

9 With a partner, ask and answer the questions below, giving as much detail as you can.
   1 Why are you preparing for IELTS?
   2 How much time do you spend studying each week?
   3 What do you see as essential in your learning of English?
   4 Do you think it's better to study full-time or part-time?

10 🎧 Now listen to recorded answers A–H. Each time, decide which question (1–4 above) has been asked, and write the question number 1–4 below letters A–H.

A   B   C   D   E   F   G   H
....

11 🎧 Listen again and decide which answer to each question is better. Be ready to give reasons for your choices.

1 Answer this questionnaire about studying. Then compare your answers with another student and discuss your own approaches to studying.

Reading

2 Texts **A–D** below, written by four university students, represent different approaches to essay writing. Focus on the groups of words as you read text **A**. Use the highlighted words in text **B** to train your eyes to move more quickly from left to right. Time yourself as you read texts C and D in a similar way. An efficient reader would read each text within 30 seconds.

A ⏱ about 150 words

For years I was confused about my writing because I simply could not carry out my teachers' instructions. They were always telling me, 'You must make a plan' and kept saying that my essays needed to 'be more organised'. I found it very difficult to make an outline and then stick to it. My mind didn't seem to work that way. I always had to start writing and sometimes write quite a lot before I knew where I might be going. That meant I usually had to cut and do different drafts. Sometimes I would find that I had to start writing one section even if it was in the middle of the assignment, and then build up the whole thing slowly, in bits. In the end it worked out, and now I seem to have found my own mix of a method.

B ⏱ about 150 words

When I **write** I try to get down some **headings** that seem to **relate** to the question. At least they give me an **idea** of what **topics** and **divisions** my writing should have. But I am **not** yet exactly **sure** if I have an **argument**. I start to **write** what I can under these **headings** and, as I go, I am trying to **find** a way of **joining** all these parts **together**. When I have got my first **draft** like this, I will go **back** and put in bits that **improve** the **links** between the different **parts**. I may **move** some material **around** at this stage. Sometimes I have to **cut** out quite a lot because now that I am much **clearer** about my **argument**, I realise that **not everything** I originally thought was **interesting** is actually **relevant** or important. Gradually I **fit** the bits **together** to produce a **well-structured** argument.

Do you ...

		YES	NO
1	need a deadline to motivate you?	☐	☐
2	find it easier to study sitting at a desk?	☐	☐
3	think of yourself as a fast reader?	☐	☐
4	use a dictionary to check spellings?	☐	☐
5	make visual diagrams of your ideas?	☐	☐
6	prepare a plan before writing an essay?	☐	☐
7	write anything in longhand instead of using a computer?	☐	☐
8	keep a diary about your studies?	☐	☐

Test spot

There is a lot to read in the IELTS Reading Module (between 2,000 and 2,750 words) and you only have one hour, so you may need to improve your reading speed. By the end of this course, you should be able to read up to 300 words per minute. Time yourself and use the approximate word count given with this symbol ⏱ to work out your reading speed, dividing the number of words by the time taken. One way of reading more efficiently is to train your eyes to process groups of words, rather than reading every word separately.

C ⏱ about 125 words

In my opinion, you mustn't start writing until you're ready. I spend a great deal of time reading and making notes, trying to absorb it all thoroughly. I find I have to read much more than I eventually use. Then I think about what I have read. I needn't be sitting at my desk, because I can think as I'm doing other things. Finally I just sit down and write it out in longhand, and it's as though it has all come together in my inner mind. Sometimes I add an introduction once I have finished, and I will read the whole assignment through, but really, I have never found I could write down a plan and I don't usually have to do any redrafting.

D ⏱ about 150 words

First I write down some notes. These focus on important content and I include possible headings. I like to use a whole page so that I can space out my ideas in a diagram-like fashion. At this stage, I also think about the things I ought to do before I start. Sometimes I have a column on one side to note down ideas that I might use later on. I keep this list to one side so that I can add to it as I am trying to develop my overarching idea on the main part of the page. When I have finished I have some notes which all relate to this 'central idea' so that I have an outline for the whole piece of writing. Sometimes I like to use visual diagrams for my planning. I think and plan before I even begin to think about starting to write.

3 Now match these cartoons and headings to texts A–D. Briefly explain each person's approach to essay writing. Which type of writer are you?

1 The grand plan writer   2 The patchwork writer

3 The architect writer   4 The diver writer

Grammar Modality

4 Underline the modal and semi-modal verbs in 1–12 and match them to uses a–h below.

EXAMPLE: 1 c

1 I simply could not carry out my teachers' instructions.
2 You must make a plan.
3 They kept saying that my essays needed to be more organised.
4 I may move some material around at this stage.
5 You mustn't start writing until you're ready.
6 I find I have to read much more than I eventually use.
7 ... before I knew where I might be going.
8 I needn't be sitting at my desk.
9 I can think as I'm doing other things.
10 I don't usually have to do any redrafting.
11 I also think about the things I ought to do before I start.
12 At least they give me an idea of what topics and divisions my writing should have.

a possibility (2 forms)
b ability
c inability
d prohibition
e strong obligation (2 forms)
f weak obligation (2 forms)
g necessity
h lack of necessity
i lack of obligation

G ···⟫ page 138

5 Complete the second sentence so that it means the same as the first, using a suitable modal or semi-modal verb.

EXAMPLE: It'd be useful to read the next two chapters as well.
You ....*should*........ read the next two chapters as well.

1 It isn't necessary to include footnotes in your report.
You .... include footnotes in your report.
2 I'm unable to meet the essay deadline this week.
I .... meet the essay deadline this week.
3 It is essential for all students to carry identity cards.
Every student .... carry an identity card.
4 It's possible that the missing page is in the bin.
The missing page .... be in the bin.
5 Harry wasn't able to come to the seminar.
Harry .... come to the seminar.
6 I found it was essential to read each chapter twice.
I found I .... read each chapter twice.
7 It would be a good idea for you to read this article.
You .... to read this article.
8 Students aren't allowed to email their assignments.
Students .... email their assignments.

OBJECTIVE IELTS IS CORPUS-INFORMED

A corpus is a very large collection of texts held on computer, which can be sorted and searched electronically. To make sure that *Objective IELTS* focuses on useful language and deals with typical areas of learner error, the authors have consulted both the *Cambridge Academic Corpus* and the *Cambridge Learner Corpus*. The latter corpus contains over 20 million words of Cambridge ESOL examination scripts, including many IELTS answers.

6 The *Cambridge Academic Corpus* shows that modal verbs are common in academic writing for speculation and deduction. Look at these corpus examples and decide how certain the writer is each time.

1 The contamination could be due to industrial waste but it will be difficult to prove this.
2 Other cell types may also be affected.
3 From these results it must be concluded that there are no tangible benefits.
4 This supports the view that sunlight couldn't have been a significant factor.

Test folder 1

Headings

(Academic Reading and General Training Reading Modules only)

You may be asked to choose suitable headings for some paragraphs or sections of the passage, which will be labelled alphabetically.

For each paragraph you must choose a different heading. There are always more headings than you need.

The headings are given Roman numerals, where i = 1, v = 5 and x = 10. The numbers one to twelve are: i, ii, iii, iv, v, vi, vii, viii, ix, x, xi, xii. Although you don't need to know this number system, you must copy the numbers correctly.

When this task is used, it is always the first one on a particular passage, and the headings are given before the passage.

1   This is a relatively easy introduction to the headings task. The passage, written by an American university, is about 500 words long. (See *Content of the IELTS Test* on pages 6–7 for the length of reading passages in the test.)

The reading passage has eight paragraphs A–H. Choose the correct heading for each paragraph from the list of headings below.

List of Headings

i   Use the lecture to help you plan assignments
ii   Certain words will guide you
iii   Speaking is a slow form of communication
iv   Co-operate with other students
v   The number of key points will be limited
vi   Choose your seat carefully
vii   Make sure you know something about the topic
viii A time to listen and a time to write
ix   We may have the wrong idea about listening
x   Process what you hear
xi   Interact with the speaker

Example: Paragraph **A** .....*ix*......

1   Paragraph **B**   5   Paragraph **F**   ....
2   Paragraph **C**   6   Paragraph **G**   ....
3   Paragraph **D**   7   Paragraph **H**   ....
4   Paragraph **E**   ....

Advice

- Skim the passage quickly to get a general idea of its meaning.
- Re-read the first labelled paragraph or section, and decide what it's about. Read all the headings, and write beside the paragraph the number of all those that might be suitable. Make sure they fit the meaning of the whole paragraph and don't simply use some of the same words.
- Do the same with the other paragraphs, in each case reading *all* the headings.
- Where you have chosen more than one heading, decide which one fits best. Remember that every paragraph or section will have a different heading and there will always be more headings than paragraphs. If you are given an example, make sure you don't use that heading for other questions.

Are you listening effectively?

A   Listening is a very neglected communication skill. Many students feel that because they can hear, they are listening. Allowing words to pour into your ear is not listening. Yet listening is the most used method of learning.

B   Lead rather than follow. Leading involves two steps: read assignments you're given before you come to class. If you read before you hear the lecture you will be more alert to important ideas. And set up questions to keep yourself in the lead. These are not questions that you ask your instructor, but ones around which you plan your listening.

2 This is to give you practice in choosing headings for part of a harder passage such as you might find in the Academic Reading Module. At about 325 words, the passage is much shorter than a full reading passage in the Test.

The reading passage has three paragraphs A–C. Choose the correct heading for each paragraph from the list of headings below.

List of Headings
i How musicians use their brains
ii Anticipated medical benefits
iii Students show interest in the technique
iv A measurement of what can be achieved
v An explanation of the results
vi Using video in the experiment
vii Variations in performance

1 Paragraph **A** ....
2 Paragraph **B** ....
3 Paragraph **C** ....

STIMULATING THE BRAIN

A While most students attempt to soak up fact after fact, not many would consider improving memory capacity as an exam tactic. However, according to Tobias Egner, a researcher from Imperial College, London, who has used 'neurofeedback' to examine the way people use their brains, 'If the brain has greater ease to shift between different states of focus … the individual is then able to adjust to any kind of challenges in everyday life more.' Dr Egner's researchers used the technique to help young musicians from the Royal College of Music. The results showed musical performance was improved by an average of up to 17%.

B The technique is a feedback loop. Each person has their brain waves collected from electrodes and fed into a computer, which converts the electrode readings into a format similar to a retro video game. The object is to change the length of coloured bars on the screen – with your mind alone. Dr Egner and his colleagues encourage people to score points by changing the length of the bar during a course of training sessions. But not everyone appears to react in the same way. 'Some people pick this up quite quickly and find their own strategy to score points and to enhance a particular frequency. To others it is a very long process or they might not really be able to do it very much at all.'

C The Royal College of Music has now integrated such methods into its courses – psychology of performance is now a component of the curriculum. But Dr Egner's main interest is not in easing the workload of students: 'Even though this sort of thing may be worthwhile, I think it's still more interesting to do it in a clinical context.' Using neurofeedback to control the unconscious functions of the brain has potential to help people suffering from brain function problems such as epilepsy, attention-deficit hyperactivity disorder (ADHD) and chronic fatigue syndrome.

C Look for the important ideas. Most lecturers will introduce a few new ideas and provide explanation, examples, or other support for them. Your job is to identify the main ideas. The instructor may come back to the same few ideas again and again. Be alert to them.

D Listen for the signals. Good speakers use signals to telegraph what they are going to say. Common signals are: to introduce an example: 'for example' 'There are three reasons why…'; to signal support material: 'For instance…' 'Similarly…' 'In contrast…' 'On the other hand…'; to signal a conclusion or summary: 'Therefore…' 'In conclusion…' 'Finally…' 'As a result…'; to signal importance: 'Now this is very important…' 'Remember that…'.

E Listening is not just soaking up sound. To be an effective listener, you must be active. It will help if you place yourself close enough to the instructor to see and hear easily. The further away you are from him or her, the greater the chance of sound being distorted, or of interference from normal classroom noises, overhead projector fans, heating blowers, or noises from outside the room.

F Another key to active listening is to maintain eye contact. The eyes truly tell all. An instructor can tell whether you're 'getting it' or not, simply by looking at you, specifically, your eyes. Furthermore, it is almost impossible to fall asleep when looking someone directly in the eyes, so your ability to concentrate will improve! And respond to the instructor. This can be anything from asking and answering questions to nodding in understanding or smiling appropriately at your instructor's attempts at humor. Ask questions for active listening.

G You should also use thought speed. Your mind works many times faster than the instructor can talk; some studies report findings that the rate of the brain is almost four times that of normal speech, which often explains why daydreaming during a lecture occurs so frequently. Anticipate where the instructor is going with the lecture.

H Take notes. In ordinary conversation we mentally interpret, classify, and summarize what is said. In classroom learning, we do this more effectively by keeping written notes. Note taking helps us to listen by providing a logical organization to what we hear. It is very difficult to listen to and remember disorganized, unrelated bits of information. Organization is the key to effective listening and remembering.

2·1

Only a game

1 Identify the sports shown in the pictures and say what you know about each one, using some of these words to help you.

amateur / professional   indoor / outdoor
individual / team   local / national / international

2 Which sports are televised (broadcast on TV) where you live? Is it better to see whole matches or events on TV, or just edited highlights? Why?

Reading

3 Read this passage quickly, thinking about the content of each paragraph. Time yourself as you read.

⏱ about 650 words

A Software that can identify the significant events in live TV sports coverage should soon be able to compile programmes of highlights without any human intervention. When this technology becomes commercially available, it will save
5 millions in editing costs.

B Picking out the key moments from a game – whether it be snooker, rugby, baseball, football or basketball – is extremely labour-intensive at present. As the footage streams into a TV station or outside-broadcast truck, someone has to watch the
10 action and keep notes on what happens and when. Only after that are the clips retrieved and put together to form a highlights package, which will probably amount to less than five minutes' viewing per game when it is finally broadcast.

C However, as sports follow fixed rules, and take place in
15 predictable locations, computers ought to be able to pick out the key pieces of play and string them together. Anil Kokaram and colleagues at Trinity College in Dublin, Ireland, are among the research teams trying to turn the idea into reality. They have decided to analyse table-based ball games like
20 snooker and pool. These are the sports that a computer should find relatively easy to handle as the action is slow, the lighting is fairly consistent and cameras mostly shoot from fixed positions.

D The Trinity team uses the edges of the table and the
25 positions of the pockets to work out where the balls are on the table. The software has the rules of the game programmed in,

so it can track the moving balls and work out what has happened. For example, if a ball approaches a pocket and then disappears from view, the program assumes it has been potted. By working out how to detect foul shots – when a   30
player hits the wrong ball – the team hopes to find a way to create a compelling highlights package for the sport.

E Until recently, the chances of getting similar software for football were not high. Involving a far greater number of moving objects (22 players and a ball) on a playing field   35
whose appearance can vary with the weather and lighting, football had been proving an impossible challenge to developers, but then Carlo Colombo and his colleagues at the University of Florence in Italy started to approach the task in another way. They have found that they can compile   40
highlights from footage without tracking either the ball or the moving players. Instead, they have looked at the position of the players in set pieces. Their software detects the position of the pitch markings in a shot to work out which area is in the frame (see graphic). Then, by checking the positions the   45
players adopt in relation to the markings, the software can decide whether a player is about to take a penalty, free kick or corner, and whether a goal is scored as a result.

F The Florence team has not yet worked out how to enable the computer to determine when a goal is scored in open   50
play. However, Ahmat Ekin, a computer scientist from the University of Rochester in New York, may be close to solving that problem. He has designed software that looks for a

4 The reading passage has seven paragraphs **A–G**.

Choose the correct heading for each paragraph from the list of headings below.

Write the correct number **i–x** next to questions 1–6.

List of Headings

i	The development costs of highlights software
ii	Commercial applications for the home
iii	Tackling a fast-moving outdoor team sport
iv	Good news for efficiency-minded broadcasters
v	The attraction of indoor sport for software developers
vi	Considering both visual and audio input
vii	Job prospects in the broadcasting industry
viii	One team's innovative processing of snooker
ix	Challenging the public's TV viewing habits
x	The current approach to sports editing

Example: Paragraph **A** ....*iv*....

1 Paragraph **B** ....
2 Paragraph **C** ....
3 Paragraph **D** ....
4 Paragraph **E** ....
5 Paragraph **F** ....
6 Paragraph **G** ....

Camera view   Software analysis

Camera angle

specific sequence of camera shots to work out whether a
55 goal has been scored. For example, player close-ups
often indicate a gap in play when something important
has happened, and slow-motion footage is another useful
cue. Ekin also includes sound analysis so it is
conceivable that the software could hunt for the
60 commentator's extravagant shouts of 'Goooooaaal!'

G A Japanese electronics company has been trialling a
simple highlights package that can cut down an hour of
American football to around 14 minutes and an hour's
baseball to 10 minutes. Eventually, the firm wants to
65 develop highlights software for a new generation of video
recorders, which would allow people to customise their
own sports highlights packages from the comfort of their
living rooms.

Style extra

5 Match each time adverbial in these sentences from the reading passage with a time adverbial chosen from a–h.

1 At present, picking out the key moments from a game is labour-intensive.
2 Until recently, the chances of getting similar software for football were not high.
3 Eventually, the firm wants to develop highlights software for a new generation of video recorders.

a Shortly after that
b At some time in the future
c During this period
d At the moment
e In the meantime
f Within months
g Up to a short time ago
h Over the last five years

This form of linking helps to structure a text and indicates the time sequence. Try to use it in your writing.

Grammar Perfect tenses

6 Explain why the present perfect is used rather than the simple past in the underlined examples in paragraphs C and D of the reading passage.

7 Explain why a past perfect tense is necessary in paragraph E (consider the events and time reference within the sentence). Why is the continuous form used here?

G ⋯⟩ page 138

8 Complete the sentences with a verb from the box in a suitable simple or continuous perfect tense.

build	do	expect	injure	test	win

1 The winning athlete .... positive for the drug Nandrolone. She will no doubt be disqualified.
2 .... those fitness exercises regularly enough, Angela?
3 They .... the new stadium for three years but it's still not ready.
4 Although he .... his knee in training the night before, Jon still came to the match to support the team.
5 Real Madrid .... all their home matches recently.
6 The swimming competition was not as exciting as Jan ....

1 Have you ever taken part in a sports competition? Does your school or college compete in any national or international student events?

Listening

> ### Test spot
> In the IELTS Listening Module, everything is heard only once. The Section 1 task is always a conversation between two people. The topic is social or general and one speaker usually requires information from the other.
>
> Look at the questions before the recording starts and predict what you will hear.
>
> Write no more than three words or a number for each question. Don't write any numbers out as words, as this is unnecessary and takes too long. Make sure you can pronounce all the letters of the alphabet, as you may have to write down a spelled name.

2 You are going to hear a conversation between a Scottish student called John and a Finnish student called Pirkko about the Tampere Student Games in Finland. Before you listen, look at John's notes and decide what is needed in the spaces: numbers or words. Predict possible answers in pairs.

3 🎧 Listen to the conversation and fill in the missing information.

*Complete the notes below. Write **NO MORE THAN THREE WORDS AND/OR A NUMBER** for each answer.*

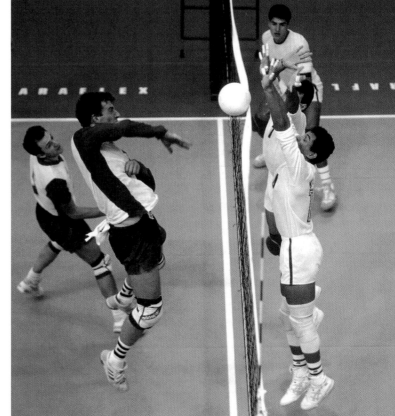

Tampere Student Games

Dates of the games **1** ....

Cost of taking part **2** .... euros per day each

Entry fee includes competition entrance, meals and **3** ....

Hotel **4** .... has a special rate during the games

Hotel is close to **5** ....

Website address **6** ....

Pronunciation *Numbers and letters*

4 🎧 Sometimes it is difficult to hear the endings of numbers correctly. Listen again to two examples from the recording. Then circle the numbers you hear.

EXAMPLES: It's the 80th anniversary of Finnish student sport.
It's 18 euros a day.

1 15th / 50th
2 1914 / 1940
3 9.13 / 9.30
4 6° / 60°
5 19% / 90%
6 $\frac{1}{7}$ / $\frac{1}{70}$

5 🎧 Practise spelling out these famous names. Then listen to the recording to check your pronunciation.

MICHAEL SCHUMACHER
SERENA WILLIAMS
TIGER WOODS
LANCE ARMSTRONG
PARK JI-SUNG

6 With a partner, think of some other famous people and take turns to spell out their names. Your partner should write down what you say. Check each other's spelling.

Vocabulary Intensifying adverbs

In the recording, Pirkko said that the Games would be a *really special event*. The adjective (*special*) is made stronger by the adverb (*really*) that precedes it. While this use of *really* is typical of informal spoken language, many intensifying adverbs are used in academic writing. Try to learn which adverbs collocate with certain adjectives and verbs, to sound natural.

7 Choose the adverb that collocates with each adjective or verb in these sentences.

1 The number of entrants for the competition is *highly / surprisingly* low in comparison with last year's figures.
2 Support for the rugby team has been *noticeably / bitterly* thin on the ground.
3 The athletes had to run in *extremely / bitterly* high temperatures and were worried about the effects of dehydration.
4 It was a *bitterly / significantly* cold winter and the skaters enjoyed their longest season ever on the frozen lake.
5 Sports facilities in and around the city are *surprisingly / significantly* better as a result of a local government initiative.
6 The 18-year-old player is *highly / noticeably* rated for his ability to score goals.

8 In the following sentences IELTS candidates have used adverbs that do not collocate with the verb. Replace each one with an adverb from the box.

Use each adverb once only. Change the word order if necessary.

carefully	closely	considerably	extremely
highly	severely	~~significantly~~	

EXAMPLE: Medicine has improved and life expectancy has therefore ~~highly increased~~. *increased significantly*

1 In fact, food is deeply related to a country's culture.
2 It is really recommended that an assistant is appointed as soon as possible.
3 The air conditioning failed and my illness got terribly worse because of this.
4 It is absolutely important to introduce new technology in order to compete effectively.
5 This is another fact that should be highly considered when planning similar events in the future.
6 People have not respected the environment enough and as a result have bitterly disturbed the ecosystem.

Speaking *Part 3*

9 Brainstorm the questions below with a partner, writing down your ideas and any useful vocabulary. Then discuss the questions with a different partner. Try to use intensifying adverbs in your discussion. This will help you in Part 3 of the IELTS Speaking Module.

- What are the benefits of becoming a member of a sports club?
- Do you think enough sport is taught in schools nowadays?
- Why do international sports competitions sometimes encourage strong nationalism?
- Is it always important to win at sport? Why, or why not?

Writing folder 1

Task 2 Planning an essay

In Task 2 of both the General Training and Academic Writing Modules candidates have to write an essay of at least 250 words. You should spend about 40 minutes on this task and it is a good idea to take up to five minutes planning your essay before you start writing.

1   Read the two tasks, A and B. Which task would appear on the Academic Writing Module and which on the General Training Writing Module? Why?

A

Write about the following topic.

> *Some people believe that professional sportsmen and women are paid too much money nowadays in relation to their usefulness to society.*
> *Do you agree or disagree?*

Give reasons for your answer and include any relevant examples from your own knowledge or experience.

Write at least 250 words.

B

Write about the following topic.

> *The amount of sport shown on television every week has increased significantly and this is having an impact on live sports events.*
> *Do you think the benefits of having more televised sport are greater than the disadvantages?*

Give reasons for your answer and include any relevant examples from your own knowledge or experience.
Write at least 250 words.

2   Here are two possible ways of designing an essay plan. Match each plan to its task in exercise 1.

Mind map:

Paragraph plan:

3 Read this essay and divide it into paragraphs corresponding to the paragraph plan in exercise 2. Cross out any material you consider to be irrelevant or inappropriate. For any paragraph that looks too short, decide what needs to be added, by checking against the plan.

How useful are sports players to our society? Do they earn too much money? This essay will discuss these questions. If we consider the top sports players, it is true that they are paid huge salaries. For example, the footballer David Beckham earns millions with his club and then he is paid more money to endorse the products of various sports companies. I wish I could earn a million dollars by wearing a pair of football boots! Sportsmen tend to earn a lot more money than their female equivalents. In tennis, Martina Navratilova has won more titles than the greatest male players but her earnings are probably significantly less. The most useful jobs in society are those that help people: doctors make people better when they are sick and teachers prepare a new generation for entry into society. Perhaps the most useful job of all is that of the firefighter, who saves lives and property on a regular basis. Yet firefighters are paid very little and often have to do a second job to earn enough money to live on. Other people in society apart from sports players earn a lot of money. Some businessmen are millionaires. Sport is undoubtedly one of our main forms of entertainment today. Even if people don't go to live matches, they watch sport on television, either broadcast live or the highlights afterwards. However, this doesn't justify such large salaries, in my opinion.

4 The essay in exercise 3 opens with two 'rhetorical' questions. Used sparingly, rhetorical questions can be an effective way of introducing the topic or raising a new point in an essay. Turn these notes for task B into rhetorical questions, starting with the word given and adding any other words necessary.

1 so much sport broadcast   *Why … ?*
2 in the best interests of sport   *Is … ?*
3 effects of this on players   *What … ?*
4 tickets sold at matches   *How many … ?*
5 viewers cope with sport overload   *Can … ?*

5 Look back at the Style extra on time adverbials (page 15). Expressions like these are useful for task B. Why?

6 Write the following sentences under the three task B headings below. Then add your own ideas.

1 Ticket prices have risen dramatically.
2 Sport has become an important form of entertainment.
3 Smaller clubs have suffered financial losses.
4 Top players can ask for large salaries.
5 Fewer people attend live football matches nowadays.
6 There are more TV channels than ten years ago.
7 Larger football clubs benefit financially from TV revenue.
8 More people have developed an interest in sport.

Reasons for growth of televised sport

Benefits

Disadvantages

7 Now write the first draft of an answer to task B. Try to include some of the information you have just worked on in exercises 4, 5 and 6. Your essay should contain five paragraphs, including an introduction and a conclusion.

8 Use the checklist below to make any changes necessary and then write your final answer.

Checklist
Have you
- answered all aspects of the task?
- included an introduction and a conclusion?
- made your paragraphing clear and logical?
- checked all your material is relevant?
- used any rhetorical questions?
- checked your spelling and grammar?
- written at least 250 words?

1 In pairs, think of some well-known brands of cars, clothes and accessories – that is, products identified by a particular name. Some should be international and some from your own country. Then discuss these questions:

  • Are you loyal to any brands: that is, do you always try to buy that particular brand?
  • Do you want other people to know you buy a particular brand?
  • Do you buy any products without considering the brand name?

Listening

2 You are going to listen to a monologue similar to section 4 of the Listening Module. It is in two parts.

🎧 **Questions 1 and 2**

Choose the correct letter, A, B or C.

1 What does the speaker say about the term *product*?
  A It should be applied only to manufactured goods.
  B The general public often misunderstand it.
  C The way it is used has changed.

2 According to the speaker, it is becoming more common for people to
  A apply for jobs as if they have something to sell.
  B place adverts when they are looking for a job.
  C identify similarities between themselves and various products.

🎧 **Questions 3–9**

Look at the following companies (questions 3–9) and the list of statements below. Match each company with the statement made about it.
*Choose your answers from the box and write the letters **A–K** next to questions 3–9.*

> A created one of the earliest brands
> B was the first company to realise the value of advertising
> C has increased the number of brands it produces
> D has lost its dominance of the market
> E makes brands which compete with each other
> F makes products that are unrelated
> G sells several variations of the same basic product as one brand
> H may not manufacture its own brands
> I only sells products using its company name
> J sells through the Internet
> K uses something visual to identify its brand

Example: *Answer:*
0 Levi Strauss   ...D...

Although some of the other options are also true of Levi Strauss, only D reflects what the speaker *says* about the company.

Test spot

Remember that this is a test of your listening, rather than of what you know about the topic, so answer the questions according to what you hear. The questions are in the order in which you will hear the information on the recording.

In matching tasks the words and phrases in the box are usually all mentioned, but not in that order, and you will not need to use them all. It may be helpful to underline the key words in the rubric, questions and options before you listen. ···⟫ **TF 7**

3 Pears   ....   **7** Yamaha   ....
4 Microsoft   ....   **8** Tesco   ....
5 Procter & Gamble ....   **9** Coca Cola   ....
6 Ford   ....

Vocabulary Word building

3 Complete this table with words related to the ones given, most of which you heard in the recording. Use an English–English dictionary if necessary.

verbs	nouns	adjectives
....	product, productivity, ... , ... , ...	(un)....................
....	consumer, ...	
....	competition, ...	(un)....................

4 Complete each sentence using a word from the table in exercise 3 in the correct form.

1 Many manufacturers these days are trying to appeal to the growing number of .... who are concerned about environmental issues.

2 The meeting was very .... as the chairperson was ineffective.

3 As countries grow more prosperous, the .... of non-essential goods rises.

4 Manufacturers try hard to ensure their .... don't get ahead of them.

5 Oil will soon run out if we continue to .... it at the current rate.

6 In order to remain .... , many companies move production to regions or countries with lower labour costs.

7 There is an increasing demand for organically grown agricultural ....

Pronunciation *Stressed vowels*

5 🎧 Mark the stressed syllable in each of these words, then listen to the recording and check your answers. The first one has been marked.

0 pro'duce (v)	6 productivity
1 producer	7 compete
2 product	8 competitor
3 produce (n)	9 competitive
4 production	10 competition
5 productive	

Style extra

The language of lectures and academic writing is typically fairly formal and impersonal, with, for example:

- fairly complex sentence structures
- passive sentences
- technical expressions
- relatively formal, often long, words
- a tendency to use nouns rather than verbs (for example, *The mass production of most consumer goods results in there being few differences between them*, rather than the less formal *Most consumer goods are mass-produced, and so they aren't very different from each other.*)

6 The a and b sentences below have very similar meanings, but the b sentences are written in a more formal style.

Complete each b sentence with a noun (singular or plural) formed from one of the verbs in the box.

consume	deduce	perceive	purchase
recognise	reduce		

1 a People mostly buy things to use themselves.
   b People make most of their .... for their own ....

2 a A 'brand image' is how people think of the brand; for example, one brand might be thought of as young and fashionable.
   b A 'brand image' is made up of consumers' .... and beliefs concerning the brand.

3 a Companies often use a logo to help keep a brand in people's minds.
   b Companies often use a logo to strengthen brand ....

4 a Cutting prices can be bad for sales of luxury goods with an image of being exclusive.
   b Price .... can harm sales of luxury goods with an image of being exclusive.

5 a The production manager thought hard, and worked out why some goods were faulty.
   b Through a process of .... , the production manager identified the reason why some goods were faulty.

7 In small groups, imagine that you're going to launch a new line of clothing. Discuss what image you want the clothes to have, and how you would advertise them.

Useful language

Image
luxury, upmarket, downmarket, sporty, casual, smart

Advertising
TV and radio commercials, magazines, billboards, sponsorship, target market

Reading

1 Think of pop groups who are famous in your country. Do you know how they were formed? Can you think of other ways of forming a pop group?

2 As you read this article, decide which of the four statements A–D best sums up the writer's main point.

A The general public do not fully understand business methods.
B There is something wrong with present-day values.
C Hear'Say was a unique phenomenon.
D Television is essential for success in pop music.

⏱ about 550 words

Hearts for sale

First there were simply goods that we could buy, and services we could pay someone else to provide. Then came brands, first of all for manufactured goods, and later for services, too. In the next stage even people became brands. Drawn from the world of business, and in particular of marketing, branding would have
10 been an alien concept to Leonardo da Vinci or Beethoven, or most other self-respecting artists and musicians, and one
15 that the vast majority would have rejected.

What's happening now, however, is that the creativity displayed
20 by an artist – or more often a musician – is turned into a brand, something to be marketed and sold,
25 as though there were no difference between a talented and internationally renowned singer and a bar of chocolate.
30 At least in most cases the singer or the artist has proved their worth, and branding takes place on the back of their talent and success. But now we have gone one step further: the brand
35 comes first, and the mere human beings are chosen to fit. A classic example of the manufactured pop group is Hear'Say.

More than five thousand people
40 auditioned to join the yet-to-be-formed group, and ten of them were

Hear'Say

shortlisted to take part in Popstars, a talent show on British television. Here they performed in front of three
45 judges, who chose the five people they considered best embodied their concept of the group – two young men and three young women, all able to sing, dance, and handle press
50 conferences and interviews, and all good-looking. The perfect pop group.

Out came an official video of the TV series, dolls, posters, a line of clothing – all ways of turning music into a
55 business, and making money from the brand. Within a few weeks of being created in a television contest, Hear'Say had gone from obscurity to having a number-one single, video,
60 and other merchandise – and there was even an hour of prime-time television about their short lives and breathtakingly brief careers. The Hear'Say phenomenon became

unstoppably self-fuelling – the faster
65 their fame increased, the more the audience wanted of them.

Within two years of its formation, however, the group split up, blaming public hostility – which certainly
70 existed, alongside the mass adulation – and the pressures of music industry life.

Other groups have been branded and marketed as aggressively as Hear'Say; none as quickly. As their licensing
75 manager admitted, they were marketing the group before they even knew who was going to be in it. Hear'Say succeeded because they brilliantly exploited marketing's Big Idea – namely, the
80 quickest way to your customers' wallets is through their hearts.

The marketing lore is that the consumer is swamped with
85 products and the only brands which will succeed are those that make an emotional connection.
90 Increasingly, what we want is to buy our values – we need products to bring meaning and purpose
95 into our lives.

The danger is that this commercialisation of our private world breeds cynicism and emotional
100 detachment: happiness is reduced to no more than having the latest mobile phone. Emotional exploitation ultimately generates a pessimism about human nature which assumes that
105 everyone is a brand, with some failing and some succeeding, and that everyone is out to 'sell themselves' in life's great talent contest. It is as a reflection of our times, rather than as
110 musicians, that Hear'Say have their greatest significance.

3 Answer these questions.

Do the following statements agree with the views of the writer?

Write

YES   *if the statement agrees with the views of the writer*

NO   *if the statement contradicts the views of the writer*

NOT GIVEN *if it is impossible to say what the writer thinks about this*

Example: The introduction of brands for goods and services was an undesirable development.

Answer: *Not given. (The relevant section of the text is underlined. It does not indicate the writer's opinion of the introduction of brands.)*

1 Beethoven would probably have accepted the idea of branding.

2 The judges on Popstars were well qualified for their roles.

3 The people chosen to form Hear'Say lacked talent.

4 Hear'Say's licensing manager built his success on his experience of marketing other groups.

5 Appealing to people's emotions is an effective way of selling products.

6 The most successful products are those that are best at what they are designed to do.

7 The general public is becoming concerned about the increase in cynicism.

8 Commercialisation is affecting our attitude towards other people.

Grammar Cleft sentences

Cleft sentences are often used in academic language to focus attention on the key message of a sentence. They are divided into two sections (*cleft* means *divided*), each with its own verb.

Look at these sentences from the reading passage, paying particular attention to the underlined sections. These contain the writer's key idea.

What's happening now, however, is that <u>the creativity displayed by an artist – or more often a musician – is turned into a brand.</u>

It is <u>as a reflection of our times</u>, rather than as musicians, that Hear'Say have their greatest significance.

G···⫶ page 139

4 Underline the key idea in each sentence.

1 What the success of Hear'Say shows is that fame can be manufactured.

2 It was in a talent contest that the members of Hear'Say met.

3 It is because our emotions affect our behaviour that advertisers appeal to them.

4 What surprised many people was that the group was marketed before it existed.

5 These cleft sentences are being used to correct mistakes. Underline the key idea, and complete each sentence with some incorrect information.

EXAMPLE: It was <u>business</u> that started advertising in the nineteenth century, not ... *the government.*

1 It was in the 19th century that advertising first became common, not ...

2 It was to increase their sales that businesses started using brand names, not ....

3 What was new in the nineteenth century was the use of brand names, not ....

4 What most consumers want is low prices, not ....

5 It is the power of marketing that Hear'Say's success demonstrates, not ...

Speaking *Part 2*

6 Spend a minute thinking about the topic below and making brief notes, then talk to a partner for a minute. What you say doesn't have to be true. If you can't think of an effective logo, invent one.

Describe a logo that you think is effective.

You should say:

what brand or company the logo is used for
where you have seen the logo
what the logo looks like

and explain what makes the logo effective.

Useful language
eye-catching   well-designed   colourful   stylish
memorable   intriguing

Test folder 2

True / False / Not given and Yes / No / Not given

(Academic Reading and General Training Reading Modules only)

You will be given some sentences which relate to the reading passage. The sentences follow the order of the passage.

You must decide whether each sentence agrees with the text or contradicts it, or whether there is not enough information in the passage for you to decide.

True / False / Not given is used to test your understanding of factual information. *Yes / No / Not given* is used to test your understanding of the writer's opinions.

Advice

- Skim the whole passage before you start working on any of the tasks. Then read the instructions, so that you know what you need to do. They are not always phrased in the same way.
- Read the first statement. It may help to underline key words.
- Look through the passage to find the relevant information, and think carefully about what it means. Underline the part of the text that contains the answer. Decide if the statement agrees with or contradicts the passage or is *Not given*. Remember you must base your answer on what is in the passage, not on your own knowledge or what you think is likely to be true. *Not given* means that there isn't enough information in the passage to decide if the statement is *True* or *False* (or *Yes* or *No*).
- Continue with the other statements in turn. If you can't find the relevant part of the passage, it probably means that the statement is *Not given*.
- Always give an answer – you won't lose any marks if it's wrong. If you're not sure, choose *Not given*.

Both these reading passages are similar to those in the Academic Reading Module and Section 3 of the General Training Reading Module, except that they are shorter.

1 The first passage is about 400 words long.

How Product Placement Works

Have you ever watched a television show or a movie and felt like you were watching a really long commercial? If so, then you've been the victim of bad product placement. Clever marketing folks want their products to be visible within a scene, but not the focus. When done correctly, product placement can add a sense of realism to a movie or television show that something like a can simply marked 'soda' cannot.

Product placement dates back to at least the early 1950s when a drinks company paid to have a character in the movie *The African Queen* toss loads of their product overboard. Since then, there have been countless placements in thousands of movies.

Sometimes product placement just happens. A set dresser might think of something to boost the level of credibility or realism of the story. One example is the use of a can of ant killer in a violent fight scene in the popular television programme *The Sopranos*. A spokeswoman for the manufacturer said the company was not approached about the use of their product and they would not have given it a thumbs-up.

Then there are arranged product placement deals. The most common type is a simple exchange of the product for the placement. A deal is made; in exchange for the airtime, the cast and crew are provided with an ample supply of the company's products.

Sometimes, a gift of the product isn't an appropriate form of compensation, so money powers the deal. Someone from a manufacturer's marketing team hears about a movie project, and approaches the set dresser with a financially attractive proposal. They come to an agreement, and the product makes a number of seemingly casual appearances. Both teams are happy.

Before product placement really saw a surge in the mid 1980s, it was pretty much a do-it-yourself effort. Now there are entire agencies that can handle the job. Some larger corporations will dedicate personnel to scout out opportunities for product integration or placement within films, television shows – even games and music.

The next time you watch a movie, keep an eye out for products or brand names you recognize. It's highly likely that you'll see one of the major soft drink companies represented. 'And how,' you'll wonder, 'can the actor hold the can just the right way every time so that the logo is perfectly visible?'

Do the following statements agree with the information given in the reading passage?

Write

TRUE   if the statement agrees with the information

FALSE   if the statement contradicts the information

NOT GIVEN   if there is no information on this

Example: Good product placement draws the viewer's attention to the product.

Answer: False *(Clever marketing folks want their products to be visible within a scene, but not the focus.)*

1 The first instance of product placement was the idea of a movie company.
2 Product placement may be intended to make a movie more convincing.
3 The manufacturer of ant killer allowed its product to be used in *The Sopranos*.
4 Arranged product placement generally results in the movie personnel receiving supplies of the product.
5 Film makers would rather be paid than receive goods.
6 Product placement has always been the responsibility of specialist teams.
7 Certain brands of soft drinks can be seen in many movies.

2 In the next set of questions, based on the reading passage below (about 300 words long), you are being tested on your understanding of the writer's *opinions* or *claims*, whether or not you think they are correct.

Do the following statements reflect the claims of the writer in the reading passage?

Write

YES   if the statement reflects the claims of the writer

NO   if the statement contradicts the claims of the writer

NOT GIVEN   if it is impossible to say what the writer thinks about this

1 When establishing a Personal Brand Identity, you should compare yourself with your competitors.
2 It is necessary to understand the network of relationships in which your customers are situated.
3 The best form of personal branding involves using the skills you enjoy, whatever the response of your 'customers'.
4 The organizations in which we are involved can affect our behaviour.
5 It is useful to emphasise contrasts between ourselves and our competitors.
6 The way we speak contributes to the image we present.
7 Personal Branding provides an ideal type of person that everyone should try to copy.

Building a Personal Brand Identity

Your Personal Brand Identity is created by finding the intersection of who you are, who you want to become, and what your 'organization' and 'customers' want from you, all relative to any competitors.

All brands have customers, products, and competitors. Your 'customer' may be a boss, friend or relative. The goal of Personal Branding is to build and/or improve your trust relationship with the target customer.

You are a 'product' with features and benefits, certain skills and special talents that other people value. In creating your Personal Brand, ideally you want to use those skills and talents that are highly valued by your 'customer' and that you enjoy using.

You are part of a larger 'organization'. We all live and work in these, whether it is our family or the place we work. These organizations have written or unspoken values and cultures that have a big impact on how we act. They are important to our success and happiness.

Whether we are competing for a job or a mate, we all have 'competitors', in business and in our personal lives, that we need to be aware of. By finding the best 'position' to take relative to these competitors, we can make ourselves seen as not only different to them, but better.

Your Personal Brand identity is the image that surrounds you. Just like brand-name clothing, our personal identity is a 'package' consisting of ourselves as a 'product' that is part of a larger 'organization' with 'customers' and 'competitors'. Your brand image is communicated by what you wear, your hairstyle, your personality, and your physique.

The goal of Personal Branding is not about being someone we aren't. It is not about exaggeration or egotism. It is simply about becoming the best 'You'. It is about finding your own personal essence that, at the same time, is valued by people in your organization.

Spotlight on communication

The Complexity of Animal Communication

A Communication is by no means a human monopoly, although our languages make possible by far the most detailed and subtle forms of communication that we know of. Most vertebrates (that is, mammals, fish, birds, reptiles and amphibians) can distinguish the sounds made by
5 different individuals, so they are able to tell whether a sound is made by a parent or offspring, another member of their species, or a stranger. Virtually all owners of cats and dogs can provide evidence of their pet's skills at communicating: not just with their own species – to warn off an intruding cat or dog, say – but also with their owners: demanding food,
10 asking to be let out, greeting them when they return home.

B Apes, monkeys and many other primates have evolved fairly elaborate systems of calls for communicating with other members of their species. These sounds can be placed in three main categories: food calls, warnings of the presence of predators, and calls for help. The 'vocabulary' of most
15 species amounts to only a handful of distinct sounds. However, the vervet monkeys of the Rift Valley in Kenya appear to have developed many more calls, each with its own meaning, making theirs by far the most complex communication system of any animals other than human beings.

C The monkeys spend most of their time in the treetops, where they are
20 generally safe from predators. However, every morning at first light they climb down to search for food at ground level. Here they are far more exposed, and so at greater risk from predators. In order to minimise that risk, one of the vervets acts as a guard.

D If the guard sees a leopard approaching, it emits a loud barking call
25 and the monkeys run into the trees, where the leopard can't follow them. When an eagle is sighted, the warning is a double-syllable cough. Other vervets respond by looking up into the air, then seeking shelter among the dense branches of trees or bushes, where the eagle won't follow them for fear of damaging its wings. The warning that a snake is approaching is a
30 noise which the researchers who first studied vervet communication called a 'chutter' sound (apparently from the noise made by a motorcycle engine that is getting a lot of fuel). The monkeys stand up on two legs and look in the grass, then run to safety.

E Each sound is only used in its own precise situation. In effect, it means
35 'There's a leopard – or eagle, or snake – coming.' Experiments using recordings of the alarm calls when no predators are present show the same responses. The monkeys understand and respond to the call itself.

F Young vervets imitate the calls, and, like young children, at first overgeneralise their meaning. A toddler brought up in an English-speaking
40 environment will come to the conclusion that the past tense of all verbs ends in -ed, and will use *goed* and *runned* as the past of *go* and *run*, before discovering that not all verbs follow that 'rule'. Similarly, infant vervets also use the leopard warning call when they see various other mammals,
45 the eagle alarm for other birds, and the snake cry for anything similar to a snake. As they mature and gain experience, they begin to use the calls correctly.

G Eagles are not only a danger to vervet monkeys: they also prey on small birds, such as the superb
50 starling. This species has its own alarm call for eagles, which vervets recognise. When a starling squeaks the warning 'danger in the air', nearby monkeys repeat it – translating it into their own term – and all the birds and monkeys rush for
55 safety.

---

1 In small groups, discuss these questions.

• How many different ways of communicating can you think of, for example, speaking face-to-face, facial expressions? What can be communicated using these methods?

• How do animals and birds communicate?

Reading

2 Skim this passage. Don't worry about anything you don't understand. Either in your head or on paper, summarise the main topic or point of each paragraph in a single sentence.

⏱ about 625 words

Test spot

In both Academic Reading and General Training Reading, you may be asked which paragraph of a passage contains various pieces of information. You may find it helpful to underline the key words in the question (as in the example below). You should look for something that fits the whole piece of information, so in the example it is not just something about *protection*, but about *how* it is *organised*. ···▷ **TF 8**

3 The passage has seven paragraphs labelled **A–G**. Which paragraph contains the following information?

Write the correct letter **A–G**.
NB You may use any letter more than once.

Example: **0** how a species organises protection for itself
Answer: ....C......
(The relevant section of text is underlined.)

1 evidence that animals react to warnings even when they are not in danger
2 why animals place themselves in a dangerous position
3 examples of communication between animals and human beings
4 an account of different reactions to different sounds
5 an instance of one non-human species understanding sounds made by another
6 a classification of all animal sounds according to their function
7 an explanation of the reason for using a particular term
8 a comparison between the numbers of sounds used by different species
9 a classification of sounds according to who produces them
10 evidence of a learning process in animals

Vocabulary Language terms

4 Here are nine words and phrases to do with communication. Complete each definition with the right ending from the box opposite. Use the examples to help you.

EXAMPLE: 1 e

1 accent – the way ...
2 acronym (e.g. *UNESCO*) – a word ...
3 nonverbal communication – communication ...
4 collocation (e.g. *on speaking terms*) – a phrase ...
5 false friend (e.g. English *gift* [= a present] in relation to German *Gift* [= poison]) – a word ...
6 idiom (e.g. *to talk the hind legs off a donkey*) – a phrase, ...
7 jargon (e.g. *Wi-Fi*, in information technology) – technical vocabulary ...
8 proverb (e.g. *Least said, soonest mended*) – a short saying ...
9 slang (e.g. *kisser* [= mouth]) – informal words ...

a used primarily to show membership of a particular group
b mainly used in a specific field
c made up of the initial letters of a phrase
d consisting of words that are frequently used together
e in which people in a particular area, country or social group pronounce words
f the meaning of which can't be worked out from the individual words
g expressing a general belief
h resembling a word in another language, but with a different meaning
i using gestures and movement

5 Label the words and phrases in *italics* below with one of the words and phrases (1–9) from exercise 4.

1 My newspaper's gone up to a *quid*.
2 Despite its name, *NASA* not only carries out research into space, but also into the earth.
3 Would you like to listen to my *brand new* CD?
4 I'm going to have to buy a new computer – my old one's *on its last legs*.
5 Not all *semantic phenomena* can be handled by *binary features*.

Speaking Part 3

6 In small groups, discuss these questions.

- What makes some people sound boring when they are speaking?
- Can you give some examples of effective speakers, perhaps a salesperson, or one of your friends?
- How do effective speakers keep the attention of their listeners?
- How important is non-verbal communication, such as facial expressions and gestures, when speaking?

1 Think about how your language is spoken in different regions. Are some accents regarded as more attractive than others? Are judgements made about people's education or intelligence on the basis of how they speak?

Listening

2 Our attitudes towards different accents and other varieties of our language are affected by our attitudes towards the groups of people who speak them.

You are going to hear part of a lecture about this relationship between language and social values. This is typical of Section 4 of the Listening Module. Make sure that your answers reflect what the speaker says. The lecture is in two parts. Read the summary carefully and then listen to the first part of the recording and answer questions 1–4.

Test spot

In the Listening Module, you may be asked to choose words from a box (as below), or to write words that you hear. Words in a box are usually different from those you hear. First read through the box of words and the summary. Try to work out what information is missing. When you have listened and completed the summary, check that your answers fit both the meaning and the grammar. Make sure that your answers reflect the meaning of what you hear. ···⁝ **TF 10**

Questions 1–4

Complete the summary below, using words from the box. There is one example.

accuracy	~~behaviour~~	conformity	convention
evaluation	identity	membership	norm
quality	status		

How different varieties of a language acquire different social values

Social groups develop their own patterns of **0** *behaviour* , and a high degree of **1** .... is usual. One area in which a distinctive pattern evolves is language, and the language variety's **2** .... differs from group to group. National varieties are generally taken as a **3** .... Attitudes towards a language variety usually reflect a particular **4** .... of the people who speak it.

Questions 5–7

What point does the speaker want to illustrate with each example?
*Choose your answers from the box, and write **A**, **B**, **C** or **D** next to each question.*

A Accents can help to identify someone's personal characteristics.
B People's attitude towards their accent may reflect their attitude towards their place of origin.
C Persuasiveness may depend on the speaker's accent.
D Judgements of attractiveness may actually be disguised social judgements.

5 research using rural and urban accents
6 the Yorkshire dialect
7 research concerning capital punishment

3 What are the advantages and disadvantages for a foreign learner of sounding like a native English speaker?

Grammar Adverbial clauses

4 Read these sentences, which are based on the reading passage on page 26.

1 *Where vervet monkeys live*, they are at risk from leopards, eagles and other predators.
2 There is always a monkey on guard *because they are more vulnerable on the ground than in the trees.*
3 *When a snake comes close*, the guard gives a call which means 'snake'.
4 *If the guard sees an eagle approaching*, it gives a call that means 'danger from the air'.
5 The guard gives a warning *so (that) the other monkeys can escape.*
6 *Although vervet monkeys and superb starlings are different species*, the monkeys can understand the starlings' warnings.

The sentences illustrate some of the main functions of adverbial clauses.

What is the function of each adverbial clause (printed in *italics*) in sentences 1–6 above? Choose your answers from the box.

time
place
reason
purpose
condition (used when one circumstance depends on another)
concession (used to contrast two different ideas)

G ···⁝ page 139

5 Now choose a word or phrase from the box to complete these sentences so that they match the ideas in the passage. Decide on the function of each adverbial clause (in *italics*).

although	once	since
so (that)	unless	while

1 Researchers visited the Rift Valley .... *they could study vervet monkeys.*
2 .... *there were no predators present in the researchers' experiments,* the vervets reacted as though they were in danger.
3 .... *children overgeneralise language rules that they learn,* they often make errors.
4 Vervets don't make a barking call .... *they see a leopard nearby.*
5 Young vervets don't always use warning calls correctly .... *they are growing up.*
6 .... *vervets have grown up,* they fully understand the different warning calls.

6 Rewrite these pairs of sentences as one sentence, turning one of them into an adverbial clause.

EXAMPLE: Experiments in teaching chimpanzees to communicate using their voices failed. Their vocal organs are incapable of speech. (as)

Experiments in teaching chimpanzees to communicate using their voices failed, as their vocal organs are incapable of speech.

1 Attempts were made to communicate with chimps in sign language. Dramatic progress was claimed. (when)
2 It was postulated that chimps would not be able to combine signs appropriately except in one case. This was that they understood at least some of the rules of human language. (unless)
3 A female chimpanzee, Washoe, was taught sign language. The reason for this was to enable her to communicate by using her hands. (so that)
4 At first her progress was slow. She learned 132 signs in just over four years and could combine them in short sentences. (although)
5 Two more chimps, Moja and Pili, were taught to sign and made faster progress than Washoe. Their training started when they were younger than she was. (because)
6 Chimps have proved themselves able to communicate by using signs. There is disagreement as to how far they understand the nature and grammatical rules of language. (although)

7 Complete these sentences with an adverbial clause.

1 It is probably easiest to learn a foreign language while ...
2 Being able to communicate with animals is less important than communicating with other people, because ...
3 Considerable research has been carried out into animal communication, although ...
4 Several chimpanzees were taken to live at the Chimpanzee and Human Communication Institute so that ...
5 Research into animal communication is unlikely to be useful unless ...

Pronunciation *Vowels*

Most English–English dictionaries can help you to improve your pronunciation by showing how words should be said.

This is how the Cambridge Advanced Learner's Dictionary shows the pronunciation of the word *dictionary*: /ˈdɪk.ʃ³n.³r.i/ ⒰ /–er.i/. The symbols and the sounds that they represent are given on the last page of the dictionary. The stressed syllable, /ˈdik/, is shown by the ' in front of it, and the superscript ³ means that the sound can be pronounced or not pronounced. This entry also shows that the British and American pronunciations are slightly different.

8 The table below shows the symbols of some English vowel sounds. Write the words below in the correct part of the table, to show the pronunciation of the underlined letters. If you aren't familiar with the symbols, use an English–English dictionary that shows pronunciation.

/ɪ/	/e/	/ʌ/	/ɒ/	/iː/

/ɑː/	/eə/	/ɪə/	/əʊ/	/aʊ/

after	although	air	come	ear
found	heart	here	instead	key
language	laugh	no	not	now
quality	receive	run	see	set
sit	there	wanted		

You might find it useful to make a list of words and sounds that you have difficulty pronouncing, and practise them often.

Writing folder 2

Task 1 Commenting on graphs

In Task 1 of the Academic Writing Module you may be given one or more graphs or charts and asked to explain the information shown in around 150 words. You should only spend about 20 minutes on this task, as Task 1 carries fewer marks than Task 2.

1   Identify graph/chart types A–C and complete their descriptions, 1–3 below, using words and phrases from the box.

A   Sales of three product lines for last year ('000s)

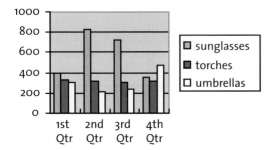

B   Main forms of communication used by the Marketing Department

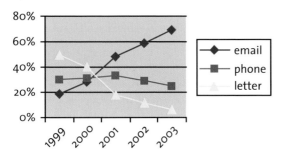

C   Market share of four brands of tomato paste

accounting for	accounts for	constant
high	horizontal axis lines	low
lowest	peaked period	relative
single	unit vertical axis	volumes

1   The line graph (graph ....) shows changes in the use of different forms of communication – email, telephone and letter – over a five-year
1 .... , from 1999 to 2003. The
2 .... of the graph gives percentage use of the three forms of communication. While the choice of telephone as the preferred means of communication remained fairly **3** .... , communication by letter fell significantly, to a
4 .... of around 10% in 2003. Conversely, use of email increased dramatically,
5 .... around 70% of all communication in the department in 2003.
(94 words)

2   The pie chart (graph ....) illustrates the
6 .... market share of four brands of tomato paste. Brand C **7** ....
approximately half of all sales, whereas brand D has the **8** .... market share. Brands A and B have a similar share of the market, in the region of 20% each.
(54 words)

3   The bar chart (graph ....) gives
9 .... sales of three product
10 .... over a **11** ....
year. The **12** .... plots quarter-year periods. During the first quarter, sales
13 .... of the three products were fairly similar. However, in the second and third quarters, sales of sunglasses were considerably higher than the other two products, reaching an all-time **14** .... in the second quarter. Sales of umbrellas **15** .... in the fourth quarter. Sales of torches were steady throughout the year.
(84 words)

2 What is the function of the adverb *Conversely* in description 1? Choose from a–c below.

   a summarising the content
   b introducing contrasting information
   c suggesting a reason or result

3 Classify the adverbs in *italics* below according to a–c above.

   1 Turnover has risen dramatically in the last year and our costs have been driven down. *Consequently*, our profits have increased.
   2 Company performance worldwide has *generally* been satisfactory, apart from a disappointing start to our Spanish joint venture.

4 Underline the examples of intensifying adverbs in descriptions 1 and 3. For each one, decide whether the following adverbs could be substituted, basing your decision on both meaning and appropriate register.

   amazingly   noticeably   surprisingly

5 Which adverb in description 2 has a similar meaning to *roughly*?

6 Choose the better conclusion for description 1. How could the other one be improved?

   a It can be seen from the information contained in the graph that from 1999 to 2003 email was used in a certain way, letters were used in another way and the telephone was also used in the department.
   b This data reflects the growth of email in business use and consequent decline of letter-writing during the period in question, with the telephone continuing as a fairly important form of communication.

7 The graph below shows the percentage sales of trainers made by a sportswear company in one year. The 'Flying Boots' trainers were launched at the beginning of that year. Write a description for the graph, commenting on the sales performance of each style of trainer. Use vocabulary from the box in 1 and intensifying adverbs. Try to write at least 100 words.

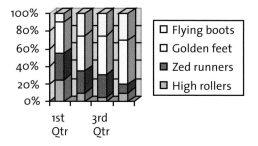

Advice

When describing graphs and other visual data …
- look at the visual information carefully
- summarise for yourself what the material is illustrating
- think about any trends or unusual features shown
- decide on the most important observations to include
- write an opening sentence that explains the content clearly; do NOT lift (copy) language from the question
- include only the salient (most important) points rather than describing all the information repetitively
- use adverbs to make a point more forcefully
- link your writing by means of adverbs or adverbial phrases.

Units 1–4 Revision

Topic review

1 Discuss these sentences with a partner and say which are true for you, giving more information about each one.

1 Although I can understand the language of academic texts, I have to concentrate hard while I'm reading them.
2 In my opinion, it's always best to buy the cheapest products, whatever brand they are.
3 I ought to spend more time studying at the weekends than I currently do.
4 Over the last couple of years, I've been playing more and more sport.

5 I don't think anyone should negotiate a business deal in a foreign language unless they can communicate effectively.
6 I believe that many people have become too dependent on luxury consumer goods.
7 Achieving a suitable IELTS score is essential because of my plans for the future.
8 My mobile phone is a vital form of communication and I can't imagine life without it.

Grammar

2 Read this newspaper article about the launch of a new hand-held electronic product. Complete each space with one word only.

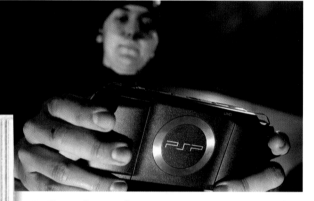

Hand to hand

Certain shops opened their doors at one minute past midnight this morning to satisfy demand for 0 ......*the*...... latest consumer craze, Sony's PlayStation Portable. 1 .... is expected that we will purchase at least a million of these hand-held PSPs in Britain within four months of the launch, and maybe more. 2 .... this sales forecast illustrates is that we 3 .... become a nation of incurable consumers, perpetually eager for the next new gadget.

The PSP is just another stage in a cultural revolution that 4 .... seen entertainment move from outside (cinemas and concert halls) into the home (TV sets and music systems), and is now attaching 5 .... to people on the move. A typical PSP buyer 6 .... well already own an iPod, a mobile phone and a digital watch, so will now need 7 .... carry a fourth electronic device around – for the time being, anyway.

In the longer term, consumers 8 .... prefer to buy a single multifunctional device, 9 .... this is far from certain. After all, even 10 .... there is a clock built into virtually every mobile phone, most people still wear watches. Sometimes, it would appear, old technologies are simply too difficult to dislodge.

3 In each set of sentences, one or two are incorrect. Tick the correct sentences and put a cross by any incorrect ones and rewrite them.

1 a Essays must to have adequate paragraphing for clarity.
  b Essays should to be properly planned before being written.
  c Essays ought to be thoroughly checked for errors in punctuation.

2 a The athletics team had been training at a higher altitude for the past five days and are now ready to compete.
  b Following their five days of high-altitude training, the athletics team now appear ready to compete.
  c Every athlete has recently attended a five-day training session at high altitude in order to be ready to compete.

3 a Training documents are much easier to process when they contain little or no jargon.
  b While it is true that specialist documents contain some technical terms, every effort should be made to avoid using unnecessary jargon.
  c Jargon shouldn't be used in training documents unless it isn't absolutely essential.

Vocabulary

4 Insert an appropriate intensifying adverb from the box into each sentence below. Use each adverb once only.

> bitterly ~~closely~~ considerably excessively increasingly surprisingly widely

EXAMPLE: Brad has been *closely* involved in the introduction of the new company logo.

1 Reviews of the new generation DVD player have been .... poor.
2 A .... bigger budget has been set aside for this year's marketing campaign in Asia.
3 The sales director was .... disappointed by her team's failure to increase market share.
4 It is looking .... likely that the product will have to be withdrawn from sale.
5 The instructions for the product are .... complicated and this has contributed to a number of returns.
6 It is .... believed that the ex-chairman was given a seven-figure payoff.

5 Use a word related to one in the box to complete each sentence. Sometimes you need to use a negative prefix.

> classify consumer efficient ~~face~~ imitate predict respond

EXAMPLE: Sometimes the most effective communication takes place without words, such as through changes in *facial* expression.

1 Domestic animals can be very .... to voices they recognise as familiar.
2 The .... of parental distress calls by juvenile birds is a vital step in their development.
3 Fieldwork in particular can yield extremely .... results, which may necessitate the complete redesign of a research project.
4 One .... system uses a ten-point scale to describe the relative hardness of rocks.
5 The .... of organically produced vegetables in Britain has increased substantially over the last five years.
6 Our .... in terms of resources management is unacceptable.

6 Choose the correct compound noun, a, b or c. Use a dictionary to check any words that are unfamiliar.

1 Whatever the .... of the enquiry, there will be some far-reaching changes in policy.
   a outflow   b outset   c outcome
2 To go into so much detail on what is a peripheral point seems complete .... to me!
   a overkill   b overwork   c overload
3 A player's .... of energy drinks during a match can improve performance considerably.
   a input   b intake   c income

7 Classify each sentence according to the term from the box that each one exemplifies. Underline the relevant word or phrase, or tick the whole sentence.

> acronym   collocation   idiom
> proverb   slang

EXAMPLE: The enemy of my enemy is my friend. ✓
proverb

1 Instead of wasting money as you do, why not put it in a bank?
2 FIFA has just released details about next year's championship.
3 You seem to have bitten the bullet regarding your workload.
4 Every cloud has a silver lining.
5 What you said has given me food for thought.
6 Have you got any change for a quid?
7 This movie director is highly rated, you know.

Style extra

8 Choose the correct time adverbial in these sentences from the *Cambridge Academic Corpus*.

1 By any stretch of the imagination, Dean Acheson was a significant figure worldwide, yet *within days / up until recently*, he did not receive the attention he deserved.
2 *Over the two-year period / At some point in the future* we observed students in the lab on almost 100 separate occasions.
3 In 1973 the rise in retail prices was under 10%; but in 1974 it was 20% and still accelerating. *At the moment / In the meantime*, the rise in wage rates was also gathering pace and had already reached 28% by the end of 1974.
4 It is first explicitly described as a shire in 1065. Its western boundaries at, before and *shortly after that date / eventually* are uncertain.
5 *Once upon a time / From time to time*, the core in the centre of the cut is struck with a hammer and broken off and removed.

5·1 Is plastic fantastic?

1 How would our daily lives be without plastic?
List six objects made of plastic that you use
regularly. Then decide with a partner whether each
object could be made from another material, such
as metal, glass or paper.

2 Why are so many products made of plastic?
Discuss this question in groups of four, considering
the factors below.

   Cost
   Weight
   Safety
   Versatility

3 Each choose one of the factors from exercise 2 and
make some notes, which you will use in a brief
presentation later in this lesson. Include examples
of plastic products to illustrate your ideas.

Vocabulary Collocations

4 Check you understand the words in the box.
Then select words that collocate with verbs 1–8 below.
(Two words aren't used.) List all possible collocations.
You will hear some in the next listening task.

accidentally	consumption	corrosion
efficiently	energy	fresh	functional
healthier	needs	quietly	resources

EXAMPLE: keep (+ adjective) *keep fresh*

1 conserve (+ noun)
2 make (+ adjective)
3 resist (+ noun)
4 satisfy (+ noun)
5 operate (+ adverb)
6 waste (+ noun)
7 run (+ adverb)
8 cut (+ noun)

Listening

5 You are going to hear two separate recordings about the uses of plastics. Before you listen to each recording, identify what kind of information is missing, and predict possible answers with a partner. Then listen carefully and fill in the spaces.

🎧 **Questions 1–5**

Complete the sentences below.

Write **NO MORE THAN THREE WORDS AND/OR A NUMBER** *for each answer.*

1 According to the speaker, the three factors contributing to the success of plastics today are safety, ... and ....

2 .... and other food products are wrapped in plastic to protect them from contamination.

3 The use of plastics in major appliances ensures that they will .... corrosion.

4 Experts have calculated that a kilo of plastic packaging can lead to a reduction of .... in wasted food.

5 Plastic parts have made air conditioners as much as .... more efficient since the 1970s.

Check your answers with a partner. Were any of your predictions correct?

🎧 **Questions 6–10**

Complete the notes below.

Write **NO MORE THAN THREE WORDS AND/OR A NUMBER** *for each answer.*

A history of the plastic bag	
1957:	Introduction of **6** ....
1966:	Around one third of packaging in **7** .... consists of plastic bags
1969:	'New York City Experiment': **8** .... collected in plastic bags
9 ....:	Plastic grocery bags first manufactured commercially
2002:	New Irish tax of **10** .... per carrier bag

Pronunciation *Lists*

6 🎧 When giving a list of three or more things or qualities, you may want to put more stress on the final one, as in this example from the first recording. Listen to it again. How does the speaker emphasise the last word?

In each case, plastics help to make your life easier, healthier and, of course, safer.

7 🎧 Now say the following lists, including the phrase in brackets before the final item in the list. Then listen to check your pronunciation.

1 For the walk, you'll need to bring sandwiches, chocolate and plenty of water. (most importantly)

2 The product comes in four colours: red, green, blue and purple. (unusually)

3 During the experiment, you should monitor your temperature, pulse and heart rate. (last but not least)

4 In August, the weather will be a bit windy, dry and sunny. (without a doubt)

5 Plastics are used in computers, televisions and mobile phones. (naturally)

Speaking *Part 2*

8 Look again at the notes you made in exercise 3. Can you add any more ideas or product examples from the recordings?

9 Present your ideas to the class, focusing on the factor you chose (cost, weight, etc.). Use some of the sentence openers below to structure your ideas. Try to keep talking for at least one minute.

Useful language

Introducing
I'm going to talk about ...
The aspect/factor/issue I've looked at is ...
What I'm going to cover is ...

Explaining
The main reason why ...
Most importantly, ...
Last but not least, ...

Exemplifying
Consider ..., for example.
Take ... as one example of ...
In the case of ... ,

1 Read the diary entries below and say which everyday problem is being illustrated. Does this happen to you? Why, or why not?

MONDAY Buy pair of shoes, get one thick, shiny bag. Add to 'reusable' collection at bottom of wardrobe. (running total this week = 1; grand total = 78)

TUESDAY Do weekly food shop, gain seven supermarket carriers. Put in cupboard under sink. (running total = 8)

WEDNESDAY Re-use one carrier taking DVDs round to a friend, but gain two buying vegetables on the way home. (running total = 9)

THURSDAY Buy sandwich and chocolate at service station on motorway journey, gain one bag. Bin it straight after lunch. (running total = 9)

FRIDAY Boss lends me some books, bag they came in goes under sink with the others. (running total = 10)

SATURDAY Re-use two carriers as rubbish bags. Go clothes shopping and bring home four more, stash in wardrobe. (running total this week = 12; grand total = 90)

2 With a partner, take turns to describe the process shown in this diagram, using the underlined words as part of the present simple passive.

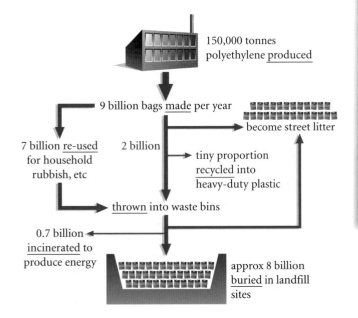

150,000 tonnes polyethylene <u>produced</u>

9 billion bags <u>made</u> per year

become street litter

7 billion <u>re-used</u> for household rubbish, etc

2 billion

tiny proportion <u>recycled</u> into heavy-duty plastic

<u>thrown</u> into waste bins

0.7 billion <u>incinerated</u> to produce energy

approx 8 billion <u>buried</u> in landfill sites

BATTLE OF THE BAG

For a growing number of people, the humble plastic bag has become an unnecessary evil that must be stopped. Discarded carrier bags litter our towns and countryside, <u>they kill wildlife</u> and hang around in the environment for
5   decades. Landfill operators dislike them for their annoying habit of being blown away from their intended burial site. The only people who have a good word to say about them are those in the plastic-bag industry. Big surprise, you might say, but in fact, the industry's arguments do make
10 some sense. Objectively, plastic bags are nowhere near the world's worst environmental problem. The reason they are being picked on, the industry claims, is because they are an easy and emotive target.

Like it or not, the plastic bag has become a part of our
15 lives, and today most people around the world don't use anything else to carry their shopping in. Depending on who is asked, the UK gets through somewhere between 9 billion and 17 billion plastic bags a year. Globally, we carry home between 500 billion and a trillion annually,
20 which is 150 bags a year for every single person on Earth, or, to put it another way, a million a minute and rising. Shocking as these statistics are, they don't explain why plastic bags have become so hated.

Given that there are far more voracious uses of fossil fuels
25 than the production of high-density polyethylene used to make the bags, the argument is possibly more about aesthetics than wasting resources. After they have been carried home, bags may be re-used once, but most end up at landfill sites. A proportion will try to escape somewhere
30 along the way, blustering around the streets or flapping annoyingly in trees. This irritating habit has earned them a variety of nicknames round the world, such as 'white pollution' in China, and the 'national flower' in South Africa.

Plastic bags can also have a devastating effect on sea
35 creatures. There have been a number of cases recently where they have been ingested by turtles and whales, leading to internal obstruction and death. The Planet Ark Environmental Foundation in Sydney, Australia, estimates that tens of thousands of whales, seals, turtles and birds
40 are killed every year from plastic bag litter, far out at sea. Yet at the seaside, plastic bags make up only a tiny

Reading

3 Read the above article about the plastic bag. How serious a problem does the writer consider this form of pollution to be?

⏱ about 600 words

proportion of actual litter, with plastic bottles featuring higher in the list.

According to the Carrier Bag Consortium, a group of UK suppliers which was set up in 2002 to fight the anti-bag campaign, measures like the Irish bag tax have done nothing to reduce the consumption or solve the problem of disposal of plastic bags. The Consortium likes to point out that plastic bags have among the highest re-use rates of any disposable product and, what is more, they are more energy-efficient to manufacture and transport than bulkier, heavier alternatives like paper or cardboard. Unsurprisingly, the industry takes issue with being blamed for general environmental irresponsibility. 45 50

So if plastic bags aren't as bad as they are made out to be, are governments and green campaigners jumping on the wrong bandwagon? Well, yes and no. While the plastic carrier may have been made a scapegoat, it is also true that if you want people to think about sustainability, an everyday object that most of them already feel guilty about is a good place to start. Governments have realised that by focusing on something so symbolic, they can get messages across to people about their behaviour and how the environment is and will continue to be affected by it, unless we all undertake some lifestyle changes. 55 60 65

4 Answer questions 1–8. To locate the information, underline key words and match them to a word or phrase in the passage that is similar in meaning. The words for 1 have been underlined for you.

Test spot
If you are asked to complete notes or sentences with words from the reading passage, you must use these words, rather than other words that mean the same. Make sure you copy the words correctly, as you will lose marks for incorrect spelling.

Complete the sentences below with words taken from the reading passage.
Use **NO MORE THAN TWO WORDS** for each answer.

1 The writer states that plastic bags can be <u>deadly</u> to ....

2 Plastic bags are unpopular with those dealing with waste management because they have a tendency to be ....

3 The writer suggests that apart from environmental concerns, another reason for disliking plastic bags may be based on ....

4 Plastic bags have caused fatal .... in some sea creatures.

5 According to the writer, ... are a more serious litter problem on beaches.

6 The Carrier Bag Consortium claims that the Irish bag tax has not achieved a cut in the .... of bags.

7 Nor has the Irish bag tax helped the .... of plastic bags.

8 The writer believes that the plastic bag has become .... of a way of life that is unsustainable.

Grammar Passive forms

5 Underline all the passives in the reading passage. Then find an example of each tense 1–7 below.

   EXAMPLE: modal present passive (obligation) *must be stopped*

   1 modal present passive (possibility) ....
   2 modal perfect passive (possibility) ....
   3 present continuous passive ....
   4 present simple passive ....
   5 present perfect passive ....
   6 past simple passive ....
   7 passive infinitive ....

6 Complete these sentences using the passive form of the verbs in brackets.

   1 At present, plastic bags (*see*: present simple) .... as an unnecessary evil.
   2 Bags that (*throw away*: present perfect) .... often end up littering the environment.
   3 As many as 17 billion bags (*use*: modal present, possibility) .... per year in Britain.
   4 In China, bag litter (*know*: present simple) .... as 'white pollution'.
   5 The plastic bag often seems (*see*: infinitive) .... as a symbol of an unsustainable way of life.
   6 Consumption of plastic bags (*not reduce*: present perfect) .... by the Irish bag tax.

 G ⋯⋮ page 140

Style extra

7 The writer uses comparative structures to emphasise the scale of the problem:
   far more voracious uses of fossil fuels than ...
   plastic bags are nowhere near the world's worst environmental problem

   The tone of these examples is inappropriate to academic writing. However, the *Cambridge Academic Corpus* shows that comparatives are often used in academic writing.

   Choose the correct ending (a–e) for each sentence.

   1 The drug has in fact been shown to be
   2 A simple soil bacterium could become
   3 Most of the prototypes being exhibited are
   4 Unlike cardboard, plastic is waterproof and
   5 The long-term effects on the environment are

   a by far the best solution to dealing with toxic waste.
   b not nearly as heavy to transport, either.
   c a good deal more serious than first claimed.
   d far more effective than expected in its early trials.
   e slightly smaller than the final products will be.

Test folder 3

Speaking

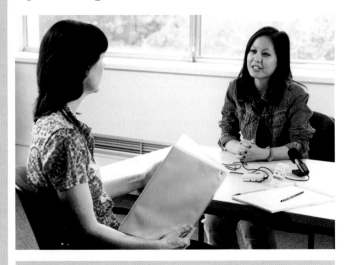

Advice

- The Speaking Module gives you the opportunity to show how well you can speak English. Show what you know. Make sure you use as wide a range of grammar and vocabulary as you can.
- It is in three parts, so don't worry if you feel you have done badly in one – you can make up for it in the other parts.
- Your English is being assessed, not your intelligence or imagination. So don't worry if you think your answers aren't very clever, or if you say something that isn't true.
- Try to behave in a friendly, relaxed way, as that will help you to do your best. Don't expect the examiner to comment on what you say: this isn't like a normal conversation.
- If you don't understand what the examiner asks you, ask him or her to repeat it, or say that you don't understand.
- Don't leave long silences, as they don't show how good your English is.

Part 1

The examiner will ask you some questions about yourself, your opinions and everyday topics.
Make sure your answers are of a reasonable length. Saying just a word or phrase doesn't show how good your English is, and a very long answer won't allow enough time to go through the whole Module.

1 🎧 Listen to these five questions and answers. Decide which comment from the box applies to each answer.

1 ....
2 ....
3 ....
4 ....
5 ....

A	The answer is the right length and appropriate.
B	The answer is too long.
C	The answer is too short.
D	The answer is appropriate, but the candidate does not make the most of the opportunity to speak.
E	The answer is hard to understand.
F	The answer does not deal with the question.

2 Think of an appropriate answer to each of these questions. Make sure you use a suitable tense. Practise asking and answering with a partner.

1 Are plastic goods popular in your country? Why? / Why not?
2 What do you think are the benefits of having a mobile phone?
3 How important do you think packaging is for food and other goods?
4 Is there much pollution in your country?
5 Do you do anything to try and reduce the amount of pollution?

Part 2

You are given a topic to speak about for one to two minutes. The topic is based on your own experience. Quickly think of something that is relevant to the topic. If you can't think of anything suitable, invent something.

You have one minute to prepare. Write down three or four key words, to remind you of what you want to say. Don't write whole phrases or sentences: if you simply read out what you have written, you will get a low band score.

The first three points are usually quite factual. Speak about them in turn, fairly briefly. Allow yourself enough time to talk about the last line. This often asks for an explanation, so it gives you the opportunity to use a wider range of language.

Make sure you keep to the topic. Don't worry if the examiner stops you before you have finished. This won't affect your band score.

3 🎧 Look at this card. Then listen to the talk by a native speaker of English, and notice how much she says about each point on the card.

> **Describe an occasion when you were pleased that an object was made of plastic.**
>
> **You should say:**
>
> > **what the object was**
> > **how you were using it**
> > **what happened**
>
> **and explain why you were pleased that the object was made of plastic.**

Notice that the examiner asks one or two questions after the talk. These should be answered briefly.

4 Now read this topic card, and spend one to two minutes planning a talk. Make notes if you want to. Then speak for one to two minutes.

> **Describe an occasion when you couldn't pay for something you wanted.**
>
> **You should say:**
>
> > **what you wanted to pay for**
> > **why you weren't able to pay**
> > **what you did**
>
> **and explain how you felt about the situation.**

When you have finished speaking, think of short answers to these questions.

- Do you think other people would feel the same in that situation?
- Have you had a similar experience since then?

Part 3

The examiner will ask you questions related to the topic of Part 2. The questions will use verbs like the ones in **bold** in exercise 5 below.

Your answers should be at least one or two sentences long. Expand them, for example by considering both sides of an argument.

Speculate about possibilities; for example, *If shops weren't open late in the evening, it would be easier for shop workers to spend time with their families and friends.*

If you can't immediately think of an answer, say something to give yourself time to think, for example *I haven't thought about that before.*

5 🎧 Look at these questions and make sure you understand them. Then listen to the answers and assess them.

1 Could you **describe** how people use plastic credit cards?
2 Can you **contrast** carrying credit cards with carrying cash?
3 Can you **identify** ways in which credit cards have changed our spending habits?

Now answer these questions.

4 How would you **account for** the popularity of credit cards?
5 Can you **outline** the methods used to encourage people to borrow money?
6 Can you **suggest** ways of educating people about the dangers of borrowing a lot of money?
7 Could you **speculate** on whether people will change their attitudes towards borrowing money?
8 Could you **outline** changes in the types of goods and services available in your country?
9 How would you **assess** the impact on our lives of having a greater choice of goods?

Music matters

1 Quickly list as many situations as you can where you might hear music playing – for example, in a restaurant, swimming in a pool. Do you find background music pleasant or irritating?

2 Check your understanding. Which is the odd word out in each set? Why?

1 carefree	2 depressed	3 confident
cheerful	elated	excited
light-hearted	gloomy	hypnotised
miserable	sorrowful	optimistic

3 🎧 Listen to three very different extracts of music – A, B and C. How does each one make you feel? Tick the words in exercise 2 that best describe your feelings.

4 🎧 Compare your reactions with a partner. Then listen again and say which extract, A, B or C …

1 has the most regular rhythm.
2 is an orchestral piece.
3 makes you most want to dance.
4 engenders a feeling of sadness.
5 has the strongest melody.

Reading

5 Read this passage quickly to get a general idea of its meaning. Don't worry if you don't understand every word. Then suggest an appropriate title.

⏱ about 600 words

It was the Greek philosopher Plato who said that music gave 'soul to the universe, wings to the mind, flight to the imagination, and charm and gaiety to life'. According to the Russian writer Leo Tolstoy, it was the 'shorthand of
5 emotion'. From our earliest societies, we have filled our lives with music. Nowadays, we are increasingly surrounded by music of all kinds, which we sometimes cannot escape. The difference in our modern world is that while we *listen* to more music, we *make* less.

10 Why does music affect us so powerfully? Professor of Psychology John Sloboda believes that there are three reasons for this. Firstly, music is a strong source of personal associations. Research into the psychology of memory and the psychology of emotion suggests that close
15 to events of high emotion, your brain takes a 'recording' of all the other things that were going on at that heightened moment. So, a piece of music linked to an emotional event in your life may well bring it flooding back when you hear it again. However, this reaction is unpredictable and, by
20 virtue of its individual nature, idiosyncratic.

A second important reason is rooted in our physiology, which dictates the range and organisation of the sounds we call music. Some of the most popular rhythmic patterns in music reflect rhythms in our own bodies, especially heartbeat and breathing. This mimicry extends to emotional 25 signals, such as the manipulation of human speech: if you speak very slowly, pitching your voice down at the end of words and sentences, anyone listening will assume you are pretty depressed. In the same way, slow music with a falling cadence engenders a feeling of sadness. Sloboda observes 30 that this is an 'iconic connection': when you listen to music, you make links to innate human vocalisations of excitement, depression, anger, and so on. This might explain the universal appeal of many forms of music, since basic human emotions are common to all cultures. 35

For Sloboda, the third reason is the most interesting one. He points out that a key aspect of our emotions is that they are tuned to detect change. The change may be positive (falling in love, winning the lottery) or negative (sickness, bad luck), but either way, the message of 40 change is: pay attention now! In general, patterns are easily recognisable to us humans and, more to the point, so are deviations in patterns. Since music is essentially pattern in sound, it is easy to see how it can 'hook' its

Test spot

An IELTS reading task will often include three or four multiple-choice questions. They are likely to follow the order of the text.
- Read the question or 'stem' only and decide what part of the text it refers to.
- Read the relevant text carefully, underlining any key phrases.
- Try to answer the question or complete the stem in your own words.
- Look at choices **A–D** and decide which is the closest to your answer.
- Check that the other three choices are incorrect by re-reading the text.

···> TF 5

6 Read the passage again more carefully and answer questions 1–3, following the advice given in the Test spot.

Choose the correct letter, A, B, C or D.

1 What explanation is given for why a certain piece of music can bring back memories?
 A Music making is still of central importance to our lives.
 B If music is playing during a period of emotion, we register this.
 C Our recall of music is highly predictable and universal.
 D We remember music more readily than other experiences.

2 According to Sloboda, it is possible for music to
 A mirror universal emotions.
 B reproduce bodily sounds.
 C reflect individual cultures.
 D mimic the human voice.

3 Why is the notion of change important to Sloboda's work?
 A It is easier to recognise musical patterns if they change.
 B His subjects prefer to listen to music that is unpredictable.
 C Listeners show better concentration when music varies.
 D People never fail to react to the unexpected in music.

45 listeners with subtle variation in melody, structure or rhythm. People pick up on the patterns and make predictions about what will come next, without needing any formal music training. When musical surprises happen, emotional responses are guaranteed.

50 In recent experiments, Sloboda has been plotting emotional highs and lows by having his subjects move a joystick while they listen to music. In this way, he has been able to record a trace of their emotional reaction. Interestingly, unlike the associative memories, these reactions are not idiosyncratic, 55 and by and large, people experience higher or lower emotion at the same point in the music. This is scientifically useful because the investigator can isolate those points and question what's going on.

So we may in fact have little control over the roller-coaster 60 ride from sorrow to joy that music seems to take us on. Some melodies are quite manipulative, working on our emotions very effectively, and composers have often exploited this to the full: take an orchestral piece by the Austrian composer Gustav Mahler, for example, which for most listeners is a 65 gripping and totally involving experience. Such is the raw power of music, which should never be underestimated.

Vocabulary Word building

7 There are many examples of affixation in the reading passage – that is, words formed from another word by the addition of prefixes or suffixes (or both). Underline words in the passage which are related to 1–10 below.

EXAMPLE: imagine *imagination* (line 3)

1 increase
2 associate
3 predict
4 manipulate
5 universe
6 recognise
7 react
8 science
9 effect
10 involve

8 Write the words from exercise 7 and other words in the same family in your vocabulary notebook, noting the part of speech each time.

EXAMPLE:

philosophy (noun)
philosopher (noun)
philosophise (verb)
philosophical (adjective)
philosophically (adverb)

Style extra

9 Explain the two different uses of quotation marks in examples 1–3.
 1 *According to the Russian writer Leo Tolstoy, it was the 'shorthand of emotion'.*
 2 *... your brain takes a 'recording' of all the other things that were going on at that heightened moment.*
 3 *Sloboda observes that this is an 'iconic connection'.*

10 When you need to refer to someone else's ideas, you can use a variety of reporting verbs, such as *observe* in example 3 above. Find four other reporting verbs in the passage (one is a phrasal verb).

11 Can the four verbs you found in exercise 10 be replaced by any of the ones below? Note that all these verbs can be followed by *that*.

argue claim consider emphasise
maintain presume suspect

···>WF 3

1 Have you ever seen any of these instruments being played live in concert or on television? What do you know about them? Which one do you think is the most difficult to play? Why?

Listening

> **Test spot**
>
> In the Listening and Reading Modules you may be asked to classify pieces of information. There are normally three options. In the Listening Module the questions follow the order in which you will hear the information, but in the Reading Module the questions are not in the same order as the information in the passage. You will be asked to write letters – either **A**, **B**, **C**, or others. Don't write anything else. ⋯⟫ **TF 9**

2 🎧 You are going to hear two students planning a performance for their college project. Read the task below. Then listen to the section of the recording that goes with the example.

Then listen to the rest of the recording and answer questions 1–8.

What will accompany each piece of music?

A images on screen
B live movement
C live speech

Example: 1812 Overture
Answer: A

1 gamelan orchestra ....
2 steel band ....
3 sitar music ....
4 pan pipes ....
5 Mahler's 5th symphony ....
6 music from Mali ....
7 didgeridoo ....
8 electronic music ....

Pronunciation *Two words with only one difference*

3 Talk to a partner. Which English sounds do you find most difficult to pronounce correctly, for example, vowels (as in *sit*, *run* or *make*), consonants (like the *l* and *r* in *land* and *room*), or consonant clusters (like *th+s* in *months*)?

4 🎧 In each pair of words below, only one sound is different, and some people find it difficult to hear the difference. Listen to the recording. You will hear *one* word from each pair, said twice. Tick (✓) the word that you hear.

1	sit	set	7	ear	air
2	said	sad	8	no	now
3	ran	run	9	eat	heat
4	sung	song	10	long	wrong
5	not	note	11	worse	worth
6	get	gate	12	so	show

Now listen to each pair of words above, and repeat them. Each pair is said once.

5 With a partner, take turns to say one of the words in each pair while your partner identifies which word you have said.

Grammar Concessive clauses

6 What is the difference in the use of *while* in these two examples?

a *So now we need to decide what should be happening while each piece is being played.*
b *The difference in our modern world is that while we listen to more music, we make less.*

7 Which sentence in each pair contains a concessive clause?

  1 a Kim used to love playing the cello, even though he wasn't very good!

    b Even if you aren't sure you can come to the concert, please buy a ticket.

  2 a Ellen can play the tenor saxophone as well as the flute.

    b Much as I've tried, I can't master the correct breathing technique for the clarinet.

> Some linking words can be used in front of an *-ing* form, or a noun or adjective group without a verb, to make concessions.
> *Despite practising regularly, I made little progress on the piece.*
> *It was an uneven concert, although quite a lively one.*
> *Though fairly straightforward to play, the guitar needs careful tuning.*

G ⋯⋗ page 140

8 Choose the correct ending (a–f) for sentences 1–6.

  1 I really enjoyed Todd Rundgren's live concert, although

  2 You should keep practising the guitar even if

  3 The pianist played all the pieces perfectly, despite

  4 Violins and violas are held against the chin, whereas

  5 CDs are often on sale at around £15, while

  6 Everyone enjoyed going to the jazz club in spite of

  a cellos and double basses are played upright.

  b having no printed music in front of her.

  c you can download a whole album for half of that.

  d the band you're in isn't performing at the moment.

  e its smoky atmosphere and high prices.

  f the quality of the sound wasn't very good.

9 The following sentences show common errors that IELTS candidates have made with linking words. Correct them either by replacing the linking word or by changing what follows it.

  1 The music classes were satisfactory, despite there was not any individual tuition.

  2 Nobody likes jazz more than I do, but although its promising title, this is a disappointing album.

  3 The concert was supposed to last for at least an hour, while it was only forty minutes.

  4 In spite of I've been playing the trumpet for three years, I found this piece too difficult.

  5 As can be seen from the chart, despite the USA has the highest percentage employed in this area, only 10% are women.

  6 There was a general feeling that inspite the friendly atmosphere the entertainment was rather dull.

7 In conclusion, even though, there are some advantages the problems are too great.

8 My daughter is not allowed to watch TV after 8.30 in spite of that some programmes would be interesting for her.

10 Rewrite 1–5 as single sentences with a concessive clause, using the linking words in brackets and making any other changes necessary. There may be more than one possible answer.

  EXAMPLE: The singer was excellent. The backing group was poor. (while)
      While the singer was excellent, the backing group was poor.

  1 I'm not keen on the band's latest CD. I love their earlier ones. (although)

  2 With a guitar the hand movement is downwards. With a sitar you also pull the strings. (whereas)

  3 The musician lives in New York. He performs mainly in Europe. (despite)

  4 Orchestral concerts involve many performers. Not every performer is needed throughout the concert. (even though)

  5 The song is over 100 years old. The song is still popular today. (in spite of)

Speaking *Part 3*

11 In preparation for Part 3 of the Speaking Module, have a class debate on the following statement.

Every child should know how to play a musical instrument by the age of 10.

Decide whether you agree or disagree by thinking about these questions. Discuss your ideas with a partner. Then join in the debate.

♪ Is there enough time in the primary school curriculum to introduce music?

♪ Does every school have the financial resources to support such a programme?

♪ What are the benefits of learning a musical instrument at a young age?

♪ What are the challenges in teaching music to young children?

Writing folder 3

Task 2 Reporting ideas

In the Task 2 essay, you may want to support your argument or offer a balanced view by reporting other people's opinions or ideas. The *Cambridge Academic Corpus* shows that reporting verbs are used extensively in academic English.

1   Read these opinions that were voiced in a survey on recycling.
Complete each statement below reporting their ideas.

> There should be a heavy fine imposed on people who fail to recycle glass and paper.

> It costs more to recycle plastic than to bury it in landfill.

1 Several people argued for ....
....

2 A few people suggested that recycling plastic ....
....

> We should be given separate containers; this would make it easier for us to recycle different materials.

> I don't see the need to recycle anything!

3 Someone claimed that if we ....
....

4 One person maintained that there ....
....

2   Rewrite each sentence below, putting the reporting verb into the passive and making any other changes necessary. The agent can be omitted, but include one of these adverbs if many people are involved.

commonly   generally   universally   widely

EXAMPLE: Most people think that his arguments against a tougher recycling policy are seriously flawed.

His arguments against a tougher recycling policy are widely thought to be seriously flawed.

1 A lot of people believe that the recycling of plastic is too costly a process.
2 Many people now see air travel as the biggest threat to the environment.
3 Someone has suggested a new tax on non-returnable bottles.
4 Environmental campaigners everywhere view the latest international agreement as insubstantial.
5 Most people feel that excess supermarket packaging is at the heart of the landfill problem.
6 Newspapers report that government measures on household recycling are imminent.

3 Complete the second sentence so that it means the same as the first, using a modal passive.

   EXAMPLE: It would be possible to persuade most citizens to participate in household collection schemes.
   Most citizens _could be persuaded_ to participate in household collection schemes.

   1 It is crucial for us to conserve valuable natural resources.
      Valuable natural resources .... at all costs.
   2 You can reduce the amount of domestic rubbish by taking bottles to a bottle bank.
      The amount of domestic rubbish .... by taking bottles to a bottle bank.
   3 The government would in theory impose this higher target by 2012.
      In theory, this higher target .... by 2012.
   4 Unfortunately, it is impossible to produce recycled paper of a high quality.
      Recycled paper of a high quality .... unfortunately.
   5 They might offer a tax rebate to people who recycle enough of their rubbish.
      A tax rebate .... to people who recycle enough of their rubbish.

4 Use some of the ideas above and others of your own to answer the following essay task. You could also look back at Unit 5 for more ideas and useful language. You should give a balanced argument, reporting the views of both those in favour of and those against recycling.

Write about the following topic.

   Recycling is now an essential measure: it is time for everyone in society to become more responsible towards the environment.
   To what extent do you agree or disagree with this statement?

Give reasons for your answer and include any relevant examples from your own knowledge or experience.

Write at least 250 words.

Worlds to explore

1 Read these comments about space exploration and discuss how far you agree with each opinion.

1 Space exploration is ridiculously expensive, considering how little we get for the money wasted on it.

2 It's stimulating to think about what exists beyond, but what are the chances of getting something useful out of space exploration? It should be scaled down.

3 We've got our priorities wrong. It's about time science turned its eye back to this planet and set about doing something about poverty, disease and pollution. Once we've sorted out our own problems, let the exploration continue.

Reading

2 This passage is adapted from a web page of the Astronomical Data Center, which used to be a branch of the American space agency, NASA. Skim through it, and choose the best sentence A, B, C or D to summarise it.

A Space exploration can encourage collaboration on earth.

B Space exploration is justified by the gains we have already made from it.

C Space exploration may help us to avoid potential problems on earth.

D Space exploration provides better value for money than most people realise.

⏱ about 625 words

Why do we explore space?

Why should mankind explore space? Why should money, time and effort be spent exploring, investigating and researching something with so few apparent benefits? Why should resources be spent on space rather than on conditions and people on Earth?
5 These are questions that, understandably, are very often asked.

Perhaps the best answer lies in our genetic makeup as human beings. What drove our distant ancestors to move from the trees into the plains, and on into all possible areas and environments? It appears that we are driven to ensure the success and
10 continuation of not just our own genes, but of the species as a whole. The wider the distribution of a species, the better its chance of survival. Perhaps the best reason for exploring space is this genetic predisposition to expand wherever possible.

Nearly every successful civilisation has explored, because by doing so, any dangers in surrounding areas can be identified 15 and prepared for. These might be enemies in neighbouring cultures, physical features of the area, a change in the area which might affect food supplies, or any number of other factors. They all pose a real danger, and all can be made less threatening if certain preparations are made. Without 20 knowledge, we may be completely destroyed by the danger. With knowledge, we can lessen its effects.

Exploration also allows minerals and other potential resources to be located. Additional resources are always beneficial when used wisely, and can increase our chances of survival. Even if we have 25 no immediate need of them, they will perhaps be useful later.

Resources may be more than physical assets. Knowledge or techniques acquired through exploration, or preparing to explore, filter from the developers into society at large. The techniques may have medical applications which can improve 30 the length or quality of our lives. Techniques may be social,

3 Questions 1–3

*Choose **THREE** letters, A–F.*

Which **THREE** of the following reasons for exploring space are mentioned by the writer?

A It is natural for us to do so.
B We may find new sources of food.
C It will help us to prevent earthquakes.
D It has side-effects that improve the quality of our lives.
E It may enable us to find alternative homes.
F We will discover whether other planets are inhabited.

Questions 4–11

Complete the summary below.
*Choose **NO MORE THAN TWO WORDS** from the passage for each answer.*
One example is given.

Test spot

When you are asked to complete a summary by choosing words from the passage, you must use the exact words that are given, and must write no more than the maximum number of words. The answers usually follow the order of the passage, but may not. Read the summary before you start completing it. ⋯⟐ **TF10**

Reasons for exploring space

One reason for exploring space is that we have a **0** ..*genetic*. tendency to ensure the **4** .... of the species into neighbouring regions. Exploration will allow us to make suitable **5** .... for dealing with any **6** .... that we might face, and we may be able to find physical resources such as **7** .... , for present or future use. It is possible that new knowledge and techniques will provide social or **8** .... benefits. Further, exploration might one day enable us to prevent impact by a **9** .... or .... , making the **10** .... of the human race less likely. It will make it possible for us to live on other **11** .... and .... , should the need arise.

allowing members of society better to understand those within or outside the culture. Better understanding may lead to more efficient use of resources, or a reduction in competition for
35 resources. We have already benefited from other spin-offs, including improvements in earthquake prediction – which has saved many lives – in satellites used for weather forecasting and in communications systems. Even non-stick saucepans and mirrored sunglasses are by-products of technological
40 developments in the space industry!

While many resources are spent on what seems a small return, the exploration of space allows creative, brave and intelligent members of our species to focus on what may serve to save us. While space may hold many wonders and explanations of how
45 the universe was formed or how it works, it also holds dangers. The chances of a large comet or asteroid hitting the Earth are small, but it could happen in time. Such strikes in the past may account for the extinction of dinosaurs and other species. Human technology is reaching the point where it might be able

Vocabulary Personal qualities

4 In a small group, imagine that you have answered this advertisement, and been chosen for the mission.

> **Volunteers wanted for one-month manned mission to the moon, so that doctors can research the effects of space travel on human beings. You must have plenty of stamina, and show initiative. You should also be determined, self-confident and co-operative, and keep calm under pressure.**

Beside each of the following questions, write the relevant personal quality from the advert. Then discuss whether you have these qualities.

Expressing opinions, expanding your ideas and responding to each other's comments will help you to do well in the Speaking Module.

1 Do you avoid panicking in an emergency?
2 Can you do what is necessary without being told?
3 Are you a team player?
4 Can you endure long periods of hard work?
5 Are you sure of your ability to perform well?
6 Do you make sure you achieve what you set out to do, without giving up?

5 Here are adjectives describing other personal qualities. In your group, choose the five that you consider most important for an astronaut and put them in order.

well-organised   resourceful   obedient
conscientious   a good leader   decisive
brave   optimistic   supportive

to detect the possibility of this happening, and enable us to
50 minimise the damage, or prevent it completely, allowing us as a species to avoid extinction. The danger exists, but knowledge can help human beings to survive. Without the ability to reach out across space, the chance to save ourselves might not exist.

In certain circumstances, life on Earth may become impossible:
55 over-population or epidemics, for instance, might eventually force us to find other places to live. While Earth is the only planet known to sustain life, surely the adaptive ability of humans would allow us to inhabit other planets and moons. It is true that the lifestyle would be different, but human life and
60 cultures have adapted in the past and surely could in the future.

The more a culture expands, the less chance there is that it will become extinct. Space allows us to expand and succeed: for the sake of everyone on the Earth, now and in the future, space exploration is essential.
65

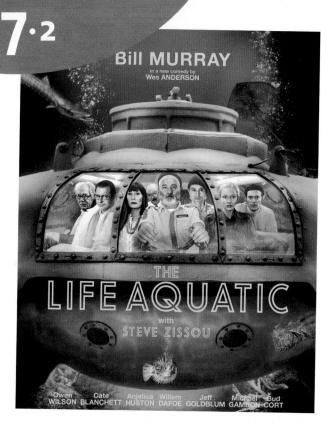

1 *The Life Aquatic* is a film set at sea. Would you like to travel under water, as in the poster?

Listening

2 You are going to hear part of a lecture, as in Section 4 of the Listening Module. It is a brief history of submersibles – that is, vessels for carrying people under water.

As you listen to the first part of the lecture, answer questions 1–4. Each question should have a different answer.

🎧 *Questions 1–4*
What is said about the following people's underwater vessels?
Choose your answers from the box and write the letters
A–F *next to questions 1–4.*

A A mechanism was built into it to move it forwards.
B A supply of air was carried inside the vessel.
C Air was supplied from external containers.
D It may or may not have existed.
E It was moved forwards by human physical effort.
F Power for moving it was transmitted from a surface vessel.

1 Alexander the Great   ....
2 Van Drebbel   ....
3 Halley   ....
4 Beebe and Barton   ....

Now listen to the second part of the lecture, which describes Alvin, the vessel shown in the diagram below.

🎧 *Questions 5–9*
Label the diagram below.
Choose five answers from the box and write the letters
A–H *next to questions 5–9.*

A camera
B current meter
C forward and reverse thruster
D hatch
E pressure sphere
F rotation thruster
G stowage basket
H vertical thruster

Alvin – side view

Style extra

It replacing a clause

Look at these sentences, which contain a clause (underlined) as the subject or object of the main verb in the sentence.

Holding your breath under water for more than a few minutes is impossible.
Until he met Barton, Beebe found raising enough money to construct a vessel difficult.

Although these sentences are grammatically correct, it is more usual to place the clauses later in the sentence, and to use *it* in the subject or object position. Notice the change from the *-ing* form to the infinitive.

It is impossible to hold your breath under water for more than a few minutes.
Until he met Barton, Beebe found it difficult to raise enough money to construct a vessel.

In similar structures when the object is a *that-*clause, *it* **must** be used, for example:

Beebe thought **it** *unlikely that Barton's design would work.*
(NOT Beebe thought ~~that Barton's design would work~~ *unlikely.)*

Structures like these are particularly common in academic writing.

3 In each sentence, underline the clause which is acting as the subject or object of the main verb in the sentence. Then rewrite the sentence, using *it*, and moving the clause to the end. Make any other changes you think necessary.

  1 The lack of sunlight under water makes seeing deep-sea fish without artificial lighting impossible.
  2 That Alexander the Great descended in a diving bell is said. (*ungrammatical*)
  3 Early inventors found making submersibles watertight difficult.
  4 That Van Drebbel's boat was able to travel under water must have astonished the people of seventeenth century London. (*ungrammatical*)
  5 Beebe left raising finance for the bathysphere to Barton.
  6 Carrying out unmanned tests of the bathysphere took some time.
  7 Because Beebe had studied deep-sea fish caught in fishing nets, he found identifying the creatures he saw from the bathysphere easy.

4 Complete the sentences in any suitable way.

  1 It is never easy to …
  2 It was once thought that …
  3 It seems unlikely that …
  4 It has sometimes been claimed that …
  5 Many people find it difficult to …

Pronunciation *How the letter 'a' is pronounced*

5 Unlike some other languages, in English the same written letters – particularly the vowels – can be used to represent many different sounds.

The words in the box below are all used in this unit. In pairs, decide how each word is pronounced in standard British English, then write it in the correct line, to show the pronunciation of the letter 'a'. The words *damage* and *aquatic* should be written twice, to show how the different 'a's are pronounced. *Advantage* has been done for you.

able	~~advantage~~	after	aquatic	also
answer	any	because	can't	chance
change	damage	expand	many	
prepare	quality	small	space	what

short vowels	
1 /æ/ as in *cat*:	
2 /ə/ as in 2nd syllable of *mother*: *advantage*	
3 /ɪ/ as in *sit*: *advantage*	
4 /e/ as in *get*:	
5 /ɒ/ as in *dog*:	
long vowels	
6 /ɑː/ as in *car*: *advantage*	
7 /ɔː/ as in *saw*:	
diphthongs	
8 /eɪ/ as in *race* or *day*:	
9 /eə/ as in *fair* or *care*:	

6 🎧 Now listen to the table being read aloud, and check your answers.

Speaking *Part 3*

7 In small groups, discuss these questions.

  1 Can you identify ways in which human beings use the oceans?
  2 Do you consider that life is less interesting, now that a great deal is known about the Earth, the oceans and space?
  3 How would you account for the fact that explorers used to be willing to take great risks, by sailing across the sea without navigational instruments?

Useful language

leisure activities	deep-sea diving	transportation
storage	underwater	motives
familiarity	courageous	endurance

Test folder 4

Sentence and note completion

(Academic Reading, General Training Reading and Listening Modules)

Notes usually focus on one part of the passage. *Sentences* in the Reading Modules may relate to different parts of the passage.

The questions follow the order of information in the passage.

The sentences or notes normally use different words from the words in the passage to express the same ideas.

If you have to choose words from the passage, you will be told the maximum number of words to use for each answer.

If you have to choose words from a box, there will be more words than spaces, and they are usually different from the words in the passage. In the Reading Modules a box may contain the endings of sentences.

Words must be spelt correctly to gain marks.

Advice

Reading Modules
- Skim the whole passage before you start working on any of the tasks and work out what it is about.
- Read the first sentence or note. Then find the relevant part of the passage, and look for something that means the same. Find the words (in the passage or box) that fit the question. Consider *all* the words in the box, or all the words in the relevant part of the passage. Think about both the *meaning* and the *grammar*.
- Remember that you must use the exact word(s) from the passage or box. Copy your answer carefully.

Listening Module
- You will be given time to read the sentences or notes before you listen. Consider what information is likely to fit each space. Think about both the *meaning* and the *grammar*.
- Listen for each answer in turn. If you miss one, go on to the next question or you may miss that too.

All modules
- Check that your answers fit both the meaning and grammar, that the spelling is correct, and that you haven't written more than the maximum number of words.

Reading

1 This passage is about 625 words long and is similar to those in Section 3 of General Training Reading and in Academic Reading.

Exploration through the ages

One of the key reasons for early explorations was probably the need to find food or to move away from areas where climate change caused environmental changes. While modern technology allows water to be stored so that people can stay in areas for longer periods of time, this would not have been so in prehistoric times. When the water ran out, it would be time to move on.

Many of the earliest explorations were therefore probably accidental. As the hunters followed a source of food, they may have finished in a previously unvisited area. If the new area had adequate supplies, the hunters may even have decided to stay there.

More organized exploration began in the Middle East. The first recorded voyage into unknown seas was a four-year expedition around 4,500 years ago, to search for and buy valuable goods, including gold, incense and myrrh.

Some of the earliest sea voyages were undertaken by the Polynesians. The island areas they occupied were relatively small and they also had immediate and easy contact with the ocean. As they spread from island to island, their navigational skills and knowledge of the area grew.

While the original Vikings – from Norway – were initially prepared to loot and plunder throughout Northern Europe, others soon demonstrated a desire to settle in the new lands. Settlements were soon established throughout Europe, and it was found that the previously aggressive settlers were quite the opposite once they had some land and security.

One of the areas that the Vikings explored and settled was Iceland. As they spread through the island, they came across Irishmen who had beaten them there, but who moved away, as they were not willing to share the place with the newcomers.

Although the Vikings managed to set foot in North America, they had little idea of what exactly they had achieved. They, like many others, stumbled there thinking they had in fact found just another small island.

Often the explorations of a curious traveller would open the eyes of others to new things that might then be used in their home country. Marco Polo travelled from Italy, spending a considerable period of time in Asia, and reaching as far as China. He had a head for business, and an eye for the novel and unusual while on his journeys. He encountered and reported on many unusual plants and animals as well as the use of petroleum-based oils in the Middle East. The success of his expeditions inspired many others to follow in his footsteps.

Trade has provided one of the key reasons for exploration throughout the years. Much of the exploration by Europeans in the 15th and 16th centuries was motivated by commerce and trade in exotic goods, as well as by the need to find faster trade routes. Several governments negotiated treaties so that their nationals could trade in other countries.

Massive changes were now taking place in Europe, with new ideas affecting many traditional areas of life. Politics, economics, religion and social organisation were all undergoing huge upheavals. The population grew rapidly, creating an increased demand for food. Among the workforce, there was a trend towards developing a particular expertise, which included a rapid growth in the number of merchants. With growing wealth, the old barter economy was no longer efficient. Instead, there was a demand for gold and other precious metals, some of which was turned into coins and used for buying and selling.

Probably even more prized at this time were spices, which were used for preserving and flavouring meats. This was important at a time when even fresh food, if available, could be rather tasteless. These items, such as pepper, cinnamon, nutmeg and cloves, were only found growing naturally in India and certain areas of the east.

Questions 1–7

*Complete each sentence with the correct ending **A–J** from the box below.*

1 Prehistoric exploration often took place because of
2 Exploration in the Middle East appears to have been caused by
3 Polynesian exploration was encouraged by
4 Viking travellers illustrate
5 Viking settlers in Iceland were not
6 The Vikings of North America showed
7 Marco Polo's travels encouraged

A imitation by others.
B a change from warlike to peaceful behaviour.
C the people's geographical location.
D a misunderstanding of what they had found.
E settlers in the normal sense of the word.
F a lack of the basic necessities of life.
G the first people to reach the area.
H a suspicious attitude towards the local population.
I improvements in the design of boats.
J a desire for trade.

Questions 8–13

Complete the notes below.
*Choose **NO MORE THAN ONE WORD** from the passage for each answer.*

Some factors in European exploration of 15th and 16th centuries
- desire to find better **8** .... to use when trading
- need for states to sign **9** .... permitting trade
- need for **10** .... for increasing population
- increasing specialisation of **11** ....
- need for raw materials for production of **12** ....
- need for various **13** .... to use in cooking

Listening

2 🎧 This listening passage, which is typical of Section 4, continues the history of European exploration from the passage opposite.

Complete the sentences below using words from the box.

endurance	fame	knowledge	nationalism	nature
religion	research	ships	technology	wealth

1 For perhaps the first time, many explorers of the 15th and 16th centuries were interested in acquiring ....
2 Exploration in the 15th and 16th centuries was helped by improvements in ....
3 The 18th century saw an interest in gaining ....
4 Many 18th century voyages were intended to make .... possible.
5 A newly significant factor in 20th century exploration was ....
6 In the 21st century, exploration is often concerned with ....

Culinary tools

Reading

1 Discuss these questions in small groups.

- Who prepares the meals you eat? Do you ever cook? What do you think makes cooking easy, and what makes it difficult?
- What is your opinion of time-saving kitchen equipment, such as a dishwasher or food processor?
- What types of kitchen appliances and gadgets do you think will be useful in the future?

2 Skim this newspaper article about high-tech kitchen appliances and gadgets and answer this question:

What is the Counter Intelligence Group's main aim?
A to find alternatives to cooking
B to produce and sell kitchen gadgets
C to encourage people to cook more
D to explain why fewer people cook

⏱ about 600 words

Chips with everything

Scientists at MIT aim to ease culinary fears

Deep inside MIT – the Massachusetts Institute of Technology - lies a room full of cutting-edge gizmos. The room belongs to the Counter Intelligence Group, an international team of experts
5 brought together to invent gadgets to combat one of the biggest threats to modern America: that people are frankly hopeless in the kitchen.

This is counter intelligence with a difference. Think kitchen counters with built-in computers and you get the gist. It's about
10 software that trawls the Internet to find recipes for delicate pastries. It's about electronic knives that raise the alarm if you're hurrying your dinner. It's about using cameras to spy on food, not an enemy.

By pooling its expertise, Counter Intelligence hopes to reverse a
15 depressing trend that before long will make the kitchen obsolete. Many people are too busy to cook, so they eat on the move or get a take-away. Following recipes can be an exercise in frustration. And then there's the thought of washing up afterwards.

To address this problem, Counter Intelligence built a kitchen of
20 its own and started making gadgets to fill it with. One idea that could take a lot of the drudgery out of cooking is the appropriately named Dishmaker, designed to do away with cupboards full of crockery and the endless cycle of washing and drying up. With the Dishmaker you can create the right number
25 of plates, bowls and cups only when they're needed, simply by pressing a button. When the meal is over, the crockery is fed back into the machine, where it is crushed and melted down, ready to be used again. The Dishmaker works by forcing granules

of polymer, often acrylic, between twin hotplates to produce thin plastic sheets. Each sheet is then suspended briefly over an   30
infrared lamp and blow-moulded to shape.

Inevitably, the Internet has a role to play in the kitchen. By installing an Internet-ready computer fitted with a camera in their kitchen, Counter Intelligence has created a system to help overcome the 'What on earth can I make with this lot?'   35
dilemma. Wave the ingredients you have at the camera and, with luck, the computer will recognise them and search cyberspace for suitable recipes.

It's all well and good knowing *what* to cook, but successfully following a recipe is not always easy. The group has developed a   40
smart spoon that analyses whatever it is being used to stir. The spoon can be connected to a computer and programmed to follow a certain recipe. By taking readings from tiny temperature and pressure sensors, and salinity and acidity detectors, it can warn at each stage if whatever is being made is too hot or too   45
cold, or if too much salt has been added.

For those of you who know how to cook, there are still tedious necessities, such as regularly checking the oven to make sure you haven't incinerated your culinary masterpiece. Why bother peering through a clear door, when you can put a camera in the   50
oven to broadcast snapshots of the activities in the oven to a screen in another room?

The kitchen has long been at the forefront of technology, the first room in the house to harness everything from fire and water to refrigeration and microwaves. But disturbing figures, like the fact   55
that 20% of food consumed in the US is now eaten in the car, suggest modern life is eroding kitchen culture. Counter Intelligence hopes to redress the balance by making the kitchen more appealing: that way, people are more likely to spend time there.

3 Work out the approximate meaning of these words from the passage *in the context*. For each word write the word class and a brief definition.

EXAMPLE:

0 cutting-edge (line 3) *adjective: very modern, with all the latest features*

1 combat (line 5)
2 pooling (line 14)
3 obsolete (line 15)
4 address (line 19)
5 granules (line 28)
6 suspended (line 30)
7 dilemma (line 36)
8 sensors (line 44)
9 incinerated (line 49)
10 harness (line 54)

4 *Look at the list of gadgets **A–I** below.*
Match each action (1–5) with the gadget which can perform it.

1 indicates if incorrect quantities of ingredients are used
2 finds suitable recipes to use what's available
3 uses the same materials several times
4 conveys information about what is happening inside the stove
5 warns against eating too quickly

List of Gadgets

A kitchen counter
B electronic knife
C fridge
D dishmaker
E cupboard
F bowl
G computer with camera
H smart spoon
I camera in oven door

Vocabulary Phrasal verbs with *up*

One of the most common particles used in phrasal verbs is *up*. If the main verb has its normal meaning, *up* can function in three main ways:

a *up* means an upward movement, increase or improvement, for example, *speak up* (= speak more loudly)
b *up* means *very much* or *fully*, for example, *eat up* (= eat all the food)
c *up* has no specific meaning, for example, *make up* (in the meaning to *invent*)

5 Decide how *up* is functioning in each of these sentences, choosing among a, b and c above.

1 At the end of the banquet, the chef was invited in, and everyone stood up and applauded him.
2 If you often use the same recipe you probably don't need to keep looking it up.
3 If you often cook Indian or Chinese food, you'll need to build up a large collection of spices.
4 Some people use a lot of utensils and saucepans when they cook, so it takes them a long time to clear up afterwards.
5 A friend has just rung me up to invite me to dinner.
6 When someone feels a bit down, a good meal can sometimes cheer them up.
7 I've nearly run out of salt, so I'd better buy some more before I use it up.

6 Match each phrasal verb in *italics* with the best definition from the box. If you don't know the meaning, think about what meaning would fit the context, and make an intelligent guess.

1 Counter Intelligence was *set up* to improve the standard of cooking in American homes.
2 Check you've got all the ingredients you need, because if you have to go shopping in the middle of cooking, it will *hold* you *up*.
3 Too many people *give up* learning to cook because of one bad experience.
4 If you invite someone for a meal at a particular time, you probably won't want them to *turn up* very late.
5 I'm sorry to *bring* this *up*, but I thought you'd offered to pay for this dinner.

---

a to arrive
b to delay
c to establish
d to start to talk about a particular subject
e to stop doing something before completing it, usually because it's too difficult

---

1 Discuss these questions.

- Have there been any changes in the type of food eaten in your country? If so, can you say why?
- Can you suggest what types of food we would eat if chopsticks, knives, forks and spoons hadn't been invented?

Listening

Test spot

Completing a flow chart is very similar to completing notes or sentences. The answers come in the same order as in the recording, and come either from the recording or from a box. Remember to write no more than the maximum number of words. Before listening, read the flow chart and predict words that might fit each space. ⋯⋗ TF 4

2 You are going to hear a talk about the history of knives, forks and spoons. The talk is in two parts.

🎧 **Questions 1–7**
Complete the flow chart below.
Write **NO MORE THAN ONE WORD** for each answer.

A history of cutlery (flatware)

Prehistoric times: knife and spoon invented
Spoons generally made of **1** .... in Southern Europe, and of **2** .... in Northern Europe

↓

Ancient Greece: kitchen forks used when serving
3 ....

↓

7th century: forks used in Middle East for
4 ....

↓

Middle Ages: in Europe **5** .... were a common alternative to knives
Kings and queens frequently used **6** ....
spoons. From 14th century, most spoons were made of various **7** ....

🎧 **Questions 8–14**
Complete the flow chart below using words from the box.

affected	blunt	commonplace	curved
illegal	laughable	luxurious	ornamental
pointed	refined	simple	widely spaced

16th century: forks introduced into France, their use regarded as **8** ....

↓

17th century: forks introduced into England, initially regarded as **9** .... , later used to show that owners were **10** ....

↓

late 17th century: new forks with four **11** .... tines, **12** .... knives banned

↓

18th century: Americans used knives with **13** .... tips, and spoons

↓

20th century: growing preference for **14** .... styles

Grammar Modals in conditional sentences

3 Read these instructions for using chopsticks and follow them, using two pens. Are the instructions clear?

① Place the first chopstick in the hollow between thumb and index finger and rest its lower end below the first joint of the third finger. This chopstick remains stationary.

② Hold the other chopstick between the tips of the index and middle fingers, steady its upper half against the base of the index finger, and use the tip of the thumb to keep it in place.

③ To pick things up, move the upper chopstick with index and middle fingers.

- ➋ Don't wave chopsticks around.
- ➋ Don't spear food with chopsticks.
- ➋ To avoid spilling food, pull dishes towards you with your hand, not with chopsticks.
- ➋ You can lift your dish towards your mouth to eat small pieces of food.
- ➋ Ignore food dropped on the table.
- ➋ To use chopsticks like an expert, you just need a little practice!

First conditional

If + present tense is used to refer to *recurring* events in the present or *likely* events in the future.

4 Complete these sentences, using information from the instructions in exercise 3. Use a modal verb, such as *should, will, can, may, might* or their negatives, and any other words you need. More than one answer may be possible.

1 If you want to pick up some food, you .... the upper chopstick.

2 If you want to pick up some food, you .... spear it.

3 You .... spill your food if you .... it towards you with chopsticks.

4 If you want to eat small pieces of food, you .... towards your mouth.

5 If you drop food on the table, you ....

6 You .... chopsticks like an expert if you ....

5 Read this article, which speculates about chopsticks replacing knives and forks.

Could chopsticks replace knives and forks?

Unless you're an expert, eating with chopsticks takes time and patience, which are in short supply these days. Fast food loses its point if you can only eat it slowly, and eating on the move is tricky: imagine walking along the street, chopsticks in one hand, food in the other – how would you hold your mobile phone? Also, chopsticks were designed for picking up small pieces of food, so steak and hamburgers are out of the question. And in the hands of an amateur, there's a danger of poking someone in the eye with them.

Of course losing knives and forks wouldn't be all bad news. If switching to chopsticks forced people to eat more slowly, they might eat less, which would do quite a lot of us some good. Maybe they'd be too embarrassed to be seen struggling with the chopsticks, so they'd be less likely to eat in the street or on buses and trains. And for chopstick manufacturers, a new market of millions of people – business would boom!

Second conditional

If + past simple tense is used to refer to *unreal* situations in the present, and *unlikely* or *impossible* ones in the future.

6 Complete this summary with information from the article in exercise 5. Use a modal verb and any other words you need. More than one answer may be possible.

If people who use knives and forks switched to chopsticks, fast food **1** .... and eating on the move **2** ....
Holding a mobile phone while eating steak or a hamburger with a pair of chopsticks **3** .... , and people **4** .... each other in the eye.
On the other hand, people **5** .... more slowly, they **6** .... so much or in public places. Also, business **7** .... for chopstick manufacturers.

7 Read this article about the history of chopsticks.

A Short History of Chopsticks

Chopsticks were developed about 5,000 years ago in China. It is likely that people cooked their food in large pots which retained heat well, and hasty eaters then broke twigs off trees to retrieve the food. By 1,600 years ago, a large population and dwindling resources had forced people to conserve fuel. Food was chopped into small pieces so it could be cooked more rapidly, thus needing less fuel.

The pieces of food were small enough that there was no need for knives at the dinner table, and chopsticks became staple utensils. It is also thought that the philosopher Confucius, a vegetarian, advised people not to use knives at the table because knives would remind them of the slaughterhouse. Before long, chopstick use had spread from China to present-day Vietnam, Korea and Japan.

Third conditional

If + past perfect tense is used to refer to *unreal* situations in the past.

8 Complete the sentences with information from the article above. Use the past perfect in the *if* clause. In the main clause, use *would have, might have, wouldn't have* or *might not have*, and the verbs in brackets. Some of the answers will be in the passive.

1 If food (cook) .... in large pots, people (use) .... twigs to pick it up.

2 If pressure (put) .... on resources, people (force) .... to conserve fuel.

3 People (cut) .... food into small pieces if there (be) .... a shortage of food.

4 If food (chop) .... into small pieces, knives (need) .... at the dinner table.

5 Confucius (advise) .... people to use knives at the table if he (be) .... a meat eater.

G ⋯⋗ page 140

Writing folder 4

Task 1 Describing a process

In Task 1 of the Academic Writing Module candidates may have to describe a process, by referring to a labelled diagram. Remember that for this task you should write at least 150 words. (The description and explanation in 1 and 2 below total 155 words.)

1   This cut-away diagram shows the inside of a self-cooling drink can, designed by a specialist company. Read the description of the diagram to complete the missing labels.

drink

1

3

4

5

2

6

twistable base

heat sink

Description

The diagram shows a design for a self-cooling drink can. The can consists of two separate sections, with a seal between the two. The drink is held inside the upper section, and the lower section contains a desiccant (or drying material) in a vacuum. The upper section has two compartments: the drink is held within an inner one, and is surrounded by an outer compartment, containing a watery gel.

2   Now read the explanation opposite of how the cooling process works, choosing suitable verbs from the box to fill the spaces. You will need to use three passive forms.

absorb	build	cause	cool	evaporate
lead	prevent	result	twist	

Explanation

When the lower part of the can
1 .... , the seal breaks.
This 2 .... a drop in pressure in the upper section of the can and the water in the outer compartment's gel 3 .... quickly, cooling the drink. Excess water is soaked up by the desiccant, and any heat 4 .... by a sink in the bottom of the can, which 5 .... the can from feeling warm. The company claims that a can of drink 6 .... by 16.7° C in just three minutes.

3 Tick any of the grammatical areas below that have been used in the explanation in exercise 2. All these areas are relevant to Writing Task 1. If necessary, revise their form and use by looking at the Grammar folder.

Concessive clause ☐
Conditional structure ☐
Passive with agent ☐
Reference pronoun (to given information) ☐
Relative clause ☐

4 Another useful structure for Writing Task 1 is the *-ing* form, which follows several verbs, such as the one in space 5 of exercise 2: … *the can from feeling warm*. Here are some more verbs that can be followed by an *-ing* form. Use each verb once only to complete the sentences. The first one is done for you.

| go on | involve | ~~mean~~ | start | stop |

EXAMPLE: A twistable base ....*means*............ having a can in two sections.

1 The cooling process .... breaking a vacuum seal.
2 The drink .... cooling down as soon as the seal is broken.
3 The desiccant .... soaking up the water until there is none left.
4 A heat sink .... the can from feeling warm.

5 An *-ing* form can also be used in place of a relative clause to describe an effect, as in *cooling the drink* in the second sentence of the Explanation in exercise 2. Find three more examples of this use in the diagram below.

SpaceShipOne, a prototype re-usable spacecraft, transported by a specially designed aircraft, White Knight, to launch height. The diagram shows how it is designed to gain and lose altitude.

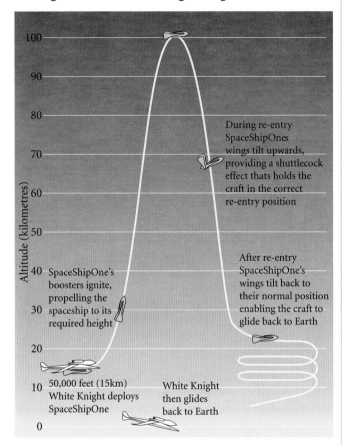

6 Write a paragraph describing the launch and re-entry process for *SpaceShipOne*, using the information provided in the diagram. You should begin with an opening sentence about the craft and its launcher, *White Knight*. Then write a sentence on each stage in the diagram. Write between 100 and 150 words.

Advice

- Spend a minute looking at the diagram carefully.
- Think about any stages in the process shown.
- Decide on key vocabulary you will need to use.
- Write an opening sentence that introduces the topic clearly. Do NOT lift language from the question.
- Remember to use passive structures and *-ing* forms.
- Use time or sequence markers to organise your writing.

Units 5–8 Revision

Topic review

1 Take turns to answer these questions with a partner, giving your opinions in detail.

1 How important is music in your life?
2 What is the most useful kitchen tool, in your opinion?
3 Why is plastic so commonly used in today's world?
4 Is it important to find out more about our oceans? Why, or why not?
5 Which gadgets in your home are made of plastic?
6 What information can the robotic exploration of Mars give us?

Grammar

2 Complete the second sentence so that it means the same as the first, using the words given. Add any other words that are necessary.

EXAMPLE: Although space exploration is informative, its excessive cost cannot be justified.
in spite of
The excessive cost of space exploration is unjustifiable ....*in spite of how*.......... informative it is.

1 Even though I have a lot of kitchen gadgets, I prefer to do food preparation by hand.
despite
I prefer to do food preparation by hand .... a lot of kitchen gadgets.

2 While music is considered an important part of the curriculum, there are few resources available for it.
even though

.... be an important part of the curriculum, there are few resources available for it.

3 Many people simply view plastic as a pollutant, yet it is a very useful material.
whereas
It is a commonly held view that plastic is a pollutant, ... that is very useful.

4 Although a brilliant performer on stage, his albums aren't very exciting.
while

.... brilliantly on stage, his albums aren't very exciting.

3 Read this text about the ocarina, a simple wind instrument. Then choose from passive structures b–k to fill the spaces.

The Ocarina

For centuries, the ocarina has been part of global music culture, for example the *hsuan* in China and the *cou-cou* in France. The word 'ocarina' means 'sweet little goose' in Italian, alluding to the birdlike sounds that
0 ....*are created*.......... by blowing into it.

In fact, ocarinas are ancient instruments, which
1 .... in some form for tens of thousands of years. Nearly every society has had a vessel flute of some kind, and in their basic form, they go back to the Stone Age. Some of the earliest examples
2 .... in Central Africa.

Traditionally made of clay, ocarinas 3 ....
from recycled plastic nowadays, in a variety of bright colours. The plastic ocarina 4 .... in sound quality to the ceramic one and additionally, 5 ....
from modern materials, has the durability required for an instrument that is likely 6 .... by young children.

The ocarina works on the following principle: when the mouthpiece 7 .... , a smooth flow of breath 8 .... out of the slit and onto the 'lip' of the instrument, giving rise to oscillations which
9 .... as musical tones. The tones
10 .... simply by covering different finger holes in the chamber.

a are created
b are heard
c to be played
d have been made
e is blown into
f can be compared
g have been uncovered
h are also produced
i can be changed
j is forced
k being made

4 Complete these sentences with the verbs in brackets, using a past perfect form in the *if* clause and a modal form in the main clause. Sometimes a negative verb (N) and/or a passive form (P) is needed. Which conditional structure is being practised here?

EXAMPLE: If I (see, N) ....*hadn't seen*.... the poster in town, I (know, N) *wouldn't have known* about the concert.

1 If the pasta sauce (contain) .... more garlic, it (taste) .... much better.

2 If the composer Mozart (live) .... in the 21st century, he (sing) .... in a rock band.

3 If astronauts (visit) .... Mars, scientists (find out) .... a lot more about the planet by now.

4 If the explorer Magellan (sail, N) .... around southern Chile, the Magellan Straits (call, P) .... something else.

5 If the supermarket (build, NP) .... here, we (have to) .... drive twenty kilometres to do our shopping.

6 If plastic (invent, NP) ...., it (be, N) .... possible to produce many everyday products.

Vocabulary

5 Match the phrasal verbs with *up* in 1–6 to definitions a–f.

EXAMPLE: Jack has just rung me up to ask for some advice. *g*

1 Helen gave up the idea of studying music and chose a course in biochemistry instead.

2 It's very important to back up all your files in case the server goes down.

3 The office was set up last year to deal with applications from other countries.

4 I'm afraid his concert in the stadium didn't live up to the CD.

5 Could I just bring up the issue of the forthcoming enquiry?

6 The percussionist Evelyn Glennie has built up a personal collection of over 1500 instruments.

a be as good as something (as it was expected to be)

b cause something to gradually increase in size or quantity

c make a copy of something

d start to talk about something

e establish

f drop or stop (doing) something

g phone

6 Sort these nouns and adjectives into four topic groups.

Scientific processes   Moods

Culinary equipment   Personal qualities
appliance

~~appliance~~ brave carefree conscientious contamination corrosion crockery cutlery decisive disciplined elated fuel gloomy microwave oven refrigerator sorrowful tolerant

7 Complete this character reference, using the adjectives from exercise 6 and the reporting verbs in brackets in a suitable tense.

To whom it may concern

Alexander the Great

I have known Alexander professionally for many years, since I accompanied him on his expedition against Persia. His army was very **0** ....*disciplined*.... during that campaign, reflecting a fundamental quality of the man himself. Furthermore, I **1** (consider + always) .... Alexander to be a **2** .... leader, in that he researches his campaigns in meticulous detail beforehand. It goes almost without saying that Alexander is tremendously **3** .... in battle, often risking his own life before that of others. As a military commander, he is utterly **4** ...., an essential quality in the heat of battle, when instant action can be the difference between victory and defeat.

Alexander is generally **5** .... of the cultures and civilisations of those he has conquered, although I **6** (suspect) .... that many residents of Thebes **7** (argue) .... against this view.

Alexander is almost a legend in his own lifetime. Only the other day, his court historian Callisthenes **8** (observe) .... that even the sea has been known to draw back at Alexander's command. It **9** (believe) .... that this extraordinary event took place in Cilicia, but I cannot personally vouch for this.

I have no doubt that, at the age of 32, Alexander has a long and distinguished career ahead of him and I am happy to recommend him to you without any reservation.

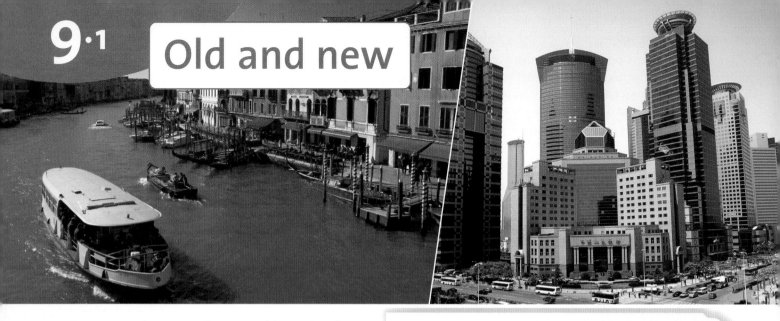

1 Compare and contrast these two cities, using the photos for ideas. Focus on architecture, transportation and demography (changes in the population).

Speaking *Part 2*

2 🎧 Read the Part 2 prompt card and listen to the recording. Is everything the candidate says relevant to the task? Is her register appropriate?

> Describe a city that you know well.
>
> You should say:
>
>> how big the city is
>> what kind of buildings it has
>> what transportation is available
>
> and explain what you particularly like or dislike about this city.

3 🎧 Listen again and tick the words you hear. Check you understand all the words, using a dictionary if necessary.

construction	☐	outskirts	☐
foundations	☐	rapid transit system	☐
infrastructure	☐	subsidence	☐

4 After class, prepare brief notes about a city of your choice for the Part 2 task in exercise 2. Practise talking for at least a minute, and try to use some of this useful language from the recording.

Useful language

By ... I mean ...	That is to say ...
How can I put it?	To put it another way ...
Of course ...	It goes without saying that ... Obviously ...

SHANGHAI: THE PRESENT AND THE FUTURE

Shanghai is now the world's most densely populated city, according to Wu Jiang, deputy director of the city's urban planning administration bureau. 'Ten million people are living in central
5 Shanghai and another ten in the suburbs. We made mistakes and now we are establishing several plans that will control the development of new skyscrapers and deal with the problems they have created.' Shanghai has been rising faster and
10 higher than any city in the history of the world, but this is proving too much for the ground beneath to bear. 'Shanghai's ground condition is very soft,' says architect Kuo-Liang Lee. 'The rock bed is about 300 metres from the surface and the
15 underground water table is higher, only 1.5 metres at most from the surface. There are now more than 4,000 buildings over 100 metres tall in Shanghai. That results in extremely severe ground settlement.'

This is just one of the reasons why Wu Jiang and
20 his colleagues are trying to halt the annexation of Shanghai's skies. Other factors are dearth of greenery, serious pollution, inadequate transport and overcrowding on the streets of the city. Among the planned solutions are a metro system, a huge
25 motorway network and an attempt at massive greening of the choking and dusty streets.

Several of the existing skyscrapers are among the tallest human constructions ever built and some of them are also among the most impressive in
30 architectural terms. The 420-metre-high Jin Mao Tower, for example, is an extraordinary skyscraper, emblematic of the successful mingling of western and eastern styles. It reflects Chinese pagoda design,

Reading

5 Read the passage quickly without stopping. Underline any words or phrases that are unfamiliar to you as you read. When you have finished, compare your underlinings in groups and discuss possible meaning.

⏱ about 675 words

6 *Complete each sentence with the correct ending **A–J** from the box.*

Example:

0 According to Wu Jiang, the population of Shanghai is around 20 million, ...*E*....

1 The architect Kuo-Liang Lee explains that high-rise construction is unsustainable in Shanghai ....

2 Wu Jiang's department has already discussed proposals ....

3 The writer approves of the Jin Mao Tower ....

4 Thomas Chow criticises recent roadbuilding in Pudong ....

5 Thomas Chow believes the imitation of western architecture has been a mistake ....

6 One aim behind Wu Jiang's plans for the orbital development of Shanghai is ....

A because of its hybrid architectural style.
B for failing to slow down construction rates.
C to improve the city's infrastructure.
D because of its impact on public transport.
E with half of these living downtown.
F to persuade city dwellers to relocate.
G for being alien to residents' needs.
H because of the subsidence caused.
I to negate its effect on pollution levels.
J due to its lessening of Shanghai's identity.

Style extra

7 Study the way these linking words are used in the passage. There is practice of them in the Workbook.

Other factors   Alongside   One ... another ... a third
Among   Worse yet   Thus

---

while at the same time echoing the art deco style of
35 Manhattan's most beautiful skyscrapers. A hotel occupies its upper 36 floors and spectacular views are offered on the 88th floor observation deck, both of the city outside and looking down the hollow insides of the building – not recommended for those suffering from vertigo!

40 Alongside these architectural wonders, however, are the less attractive results of the 21st-century building boom. Thomas Chow, co-director of the Shanghai-based Surv architecture and design practice, recently presented a paper to the Shanghai Design Biennale
45 entitled 'Five Ways to Ruin a City'. In it, he suggested that the city's ill-considered and rapid growth had made it barely habitable. 'In downtown Lujiazhui in Pudong, the scale is hostile and everything appears to have been enlarged on a photocopier; towers are
50 towering, boulevards are 12 lanes wide (and uncrossable), without any relationship to human scale,

activity or urban life,' he wrote. Worse yet, he argued, Shanghai's character was being obliterated in favour of cheap and tacky design solutions without creativity or soul. In Chow's view, 'The market's rapid pace of 55 wholesale importation of foreign imagery has resulted in a scary, perverse and at times ridiculous trend of turning modern cities into Disney-lands. The urban landscape is being littered with wholesale copies and replications of foreign styles.' 60

Wu Jiang wants to change all that. He talks excitedly of reducing plot ratios and making central Shanghai green and pleasant. 'If we want Shanghai to be the best city in the world, it's impossible to carry on with this kind of building. You can't reduce that density through 65 political power. You have to make it attractive for people to leave and live in new cities nearby.' And so, on the outskirts of Shanghai, connected by massive new motorways and rapid transit railways, ten new cities, each of one million people and each with ten 70 satellite towns of 200,000 people, are being built. One, New Harbour City, will have the biggest docks in the world; another, An Ting, will be a huge car manufacturing city; a third, called Song Jiang, will be a university centre. 75

Thus Shanghai hopes to build itself out of the problem that it has built itself into. At a pace unparalleled in the rest of the world, it is again racing down the track to a brighter future.

9·2

1 Where were the world's first cities established? Using the pictures above and the words below, describe favoured locations and explain their advantages to early settlers.

agriculture   defensive position   invader   irrigation   livestock
resources   trading centre

Listening

2 You are going to hear part of a lecture on the ancient Sumerian cities of Ur and Uruk. Before you listen, read the summary below and decide what information you need to listen for to fill the spaces.

🎧 Then listen and answer questions 1–9 with words you hear in the recording.

Complete the summary below.
Write NO MORE THAN ONE WORD AND/OR A NUMBER for each answer.

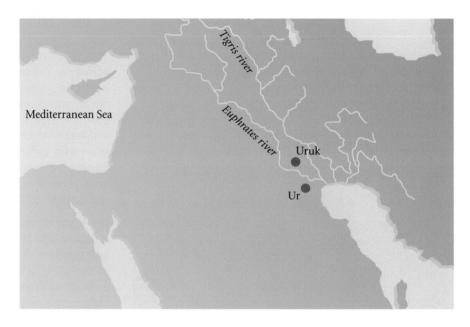

Ur

The excavations of Ur led by Leonard Woolley (1922 – **1** ....) revealed that Ur was founded over **2** .... years ago. Its inhabitants were among the earliest people to bring water and **3** .... under their control.

Away from the river, conditions made it difficult to **4** .... everyone. As the population increased, the inhabitants needed to get more supplies through **5** ....

The world's first writing system arose in Ur to record how much **6** .... they had.

Uruk

Population exceeded **7** .... (compared to 34,000 in Ur at the same time).

Uruk was known as the **8** .... city.

Uruk was actually two cities combined: Kullab and Eanna, the **9** .... centre.

Vocabulary Word building

3 Complete these extracts from the recording with a word related to a word from the box.

> archaeology   culture   ~~extend~~   settle
> strategy   surround

EXAMPLE: From the ....*extensive*.......... work of Woolley and his team ...

1 One of the most important .... projects ever undertaken ...
2 Ur was .... located close to the Euphrates and Tigris rivers.
3 Its first .... would have been self-sufficient.
4 Ur was an important .... , religious and commercial centre.
5 Ur-Nammu established his kingship in Ur and its ....

Grammar Inversion

4 The beginning of this sentence from the recording contains 'inversion'.

Hardly had the Third Dynasty begun when it was brought to an abrupt end by invaders.

What is the stylistic effect of starting the sentence in this way, instead of saying:

The Third Dynasty had hardly begun when ...

Here are some more examples of inversion. Underline the subject and describe its position in each sentence.

1 Not only was Ur the world's first city, it was also the home of the earliest writing system.
2 Little did I know Chris had already bought tickets for the match as a surprise for me.
3 In front of the ancient doorway stands a stone lion.

G ⋯⟩ page 140

5 Put the following sentences in order, starting with the adverbs given in brackets.

EXAMPLE: the new bridge / had to be declared / before / unsafe / had been used / it (Barely)
Barely had the new bridge been used before it had to be declared unsafe.

1 Tom wanted to / than / we / walk to the castle / had got back to the hotel (No sooner)
2 I / walking around a city / as safe as this / late at night / had felt (Seldom)
3 they / the office / had entered / the phone started ringing / when (Scarcely)

4 the ticket price rise / would be imposed / it was announced / had been implemented / when / a further 5% increase (Hardly)

6 Join the ideas in 1–7 and a–g using *Not only* ... and adding a word or phrase from the box.

> a further   also   as well   too

EXAMPLE: 1 c *Not only did Paris put in a bid for the 2012 Olympics, Madrid did too.*

1 Paris put in a bid for the 2012 Olympics.
2 The city of Bogotá has got an excellent bus service.
3 10 million inhabitants live in the centre of Shanghai.
4 There are a lot of art galleries in London.
5 High-rise buildings can lack style and originality.
6 The ancient city of Ur was built beside the Euphrates river.
7 Siena offers visitors a historic centre.

a 10 million live in its suburbs.
b It was close to the Tigris.
c ~~Madrid did~~.
d The countryside nearby is very beautiful.
e There are several museums.
f They are sometimes poorly constructed.
g It encourages the use of bicycles wherever possible.

7 Instead of the example in exercise 6, we could say:

*Paris put in a bid for the 2012 Olympics and **so did** Madrid.*

Join these sentences in the same way.

1 The train drivers are on strike. The bus drivers are on strike.
2 The Tokyo flight took off on time. The Taipei flight took off on time.
3 Madrid has a metro. Bilbao has a metro.
4 I can take the metro. You can take the metro.
5 John should walk to work. I should walk to work.
6 Kiosks sell bus tickets. Subway stations sell bus tickets.

8 If the first half of the sentence contains a negative verb form, you must use *neither* or *nor*. Form sentences using the information in brackets.

EXAMPLE: The Pisa flight wasn't full. (Rome)
The Pisa flight wasn't full and neither was the Rome one.
The Pisa flight wasn't full, nor was the Rome one.

1 I hadn't been to Prague before. (Dominic)
2 The school can't provide parking spaces. (the sports centre)
3 You won't be in time for the next train. (I)
4 Fortunately, the car wasn't damaged. (my bike)

Test folder 5

Multiple choice

(Academic Reading, General Training Reading and Listening Modules)

If you have to choose *one* answer, there will be three options (in the Listening Module, and occasionally in Reading) or four options (only in Reading).

If you have to choose *more than one* answer, there will be more options. In this case, the order of your answers isn't important: for example, if the answers are A, C, D, and you write D, A, C, they will still be counted as correct.

Each question normally focuses on one part of the passage. However, in the Reading Modules you may be asked one multiple-choice question about the whole passage.

The questions follow the order of information in the passage.

The options usually do *not* follow the order of information in the passage.

The questions and options are normally paraphrases of the passage.

Advice

All modules
- Read the instructions carefully. Note how many answers are required for each question.
- Read the first question. Look or listen for the relevant part of the passage. Read or listen carefully, considering *all* the options.
- Consider the options *in relation to the question*. In some cases an option may be true, but does not answer the question. Eliminate options by putting a cross (X) beside them when you are sure they are wrong.
- Always choose only the required number of options for each question.
- Make sure you answer every question – you won't lose marks for wrong answers.

Listening

1 🎧 This passage is similar to those in Section 4 of the Listening Module.

Questions 1–6
Choose the correct letter, A, B or C.

1 Rich people have been known to live in suburbs
   A at least since the 6th century BC.
   B since the 1st century BC.
   C only in modern times.

2 During the Middle Ages and Renaissance, London
   A encouraged poor people to move to the edge of the city.
   B expanded by incorporating nearby towns.
   C rebuilt its walls to contain a larger area.

3 In the 19th century, the development of suburbs was encouraged by
   A the high quality of suburban housing.
   B improvements in public transport.
   C a wish to own weekend homes.

4 European suburbs, unlike those in North America,
   A consist largely of low-density housing.
   B are well planned.
   C have individual characters.

5 Suburban sprawl is said to destroy
   A town centres.
   B business activity.
   C human relationships.

6 A major reason for the development of suburban sprawl in the USA was
   A improvements in car manufacture.
   B the availability of money to buy homes.
   C people's unwillingness to live in high density housing.

Questions 7–11
Choose FIVE letters A–J.
Which FIVE claims does the writer make about suburban sprawl?

A Housing and other components are usually separated from each other.
B There are insufficient controls over the actions of developers.
C Life in housing districts is more limited than in traditional towns.
D The residents have no input into the names of new suburbs.
E Names may give a false impression of suburbs.
F The design of school buildings tends to be old-fashioned.
G The size of schools creates problems for their students.
H The location of schools encourages the use of cars.
I The population is too small to support shops serving a small area.
J One reason for heavy traffic in suburbs is that a car is likely to contain only the driver.

2   This passage is similar to those in the Academic Reading Module and Section 3 of the General Training Reading.

The Invention of the Garden City

The garden city was largely the invention of the British social visionary Ebenezer Howard (1850–1928). After emigrating to the USA, and an unsuccessful attempt to make a living as a farmer, he moved to Chicago, where he saw the reconstruction of the city after the disastrous fire of 1871. In those pre-skyscraper days, it was nicknamed 'the Garden City', almost certainly the source of Howard's name for his proposed towns. Returning to London, Howard developed his concept in the 1880s and 1890s, drawing on notions that were circulating at the time, but creating a unique combination of proposals.

The nineteenth-century slum city was in many ways an horrific place; but it offered economic and social opportunities, lights and crowds. At the same time, the British countryside – now too often seen in a sentimental glow – was in fact equally unprepossessing: though it promised fresh air and nature, it suffered from agricultural depression and it offered neither sufficient work and wages, nor adequate social life. Howard's idea was to combine the best of town and country in a new kind of settlement, the garden city.

Howard's idea was that a group of people should establish a company, borrowing money to establish a garden city in the countryside, far enough

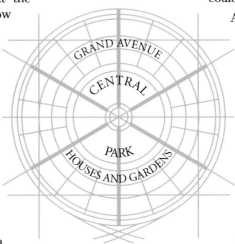

Howard's design for a garden city

from existing cities to ensure that the land was bought at rock-bottom, depressed-agricultural, land values. They should get agreement from leading industrialists to move their factories there from the congested cities; their workers would move too, and would build their own houses.

Garden cities would follow the same basic blueprint, with a high proportion of green spaces, together with a central public open space, radial avenues, and peripheral industries. They would be surrounded by a much larger area of permanent green belt, also owned by the company, containing not merely farms, but institutions like reformatories and convalescent homes, that could benefit from a rural location.

As more and more people moved out, the garden city would reach its planned limit – Howard suggested 32,000 people; then, another would be started a short distance away. Thus, over time, there would develop a vast planned agglomeration, extending almost without limit; within it, each garden city would offer a wide range of jobs and services, but each would also be connected to the others by a rapid transit system, thus giving all the economic and social opportunities of a giant city.

Choose the correct letter, **A**, **B**, **C** or **D**.

1 Howard's concept of garden cities was influenced by
  A the style in which Chicago was rebuilt.
  B other people's ideas.
  C his observations of rural life.
  D the life he had led.

2 What does the writer claim about nineteenth century life?
  A Agriculture offered more work than cities did.
  B On balance, urban life was easier than rural life.
  C Our view of rural life is more positive than the reality.
  D Too many people moved from the countryside to cities.

3 Howard proposed that garden cities should be located
  A where employment opportunities already existed.
  B in areas where people wished to live.
  C as far as possible from existing cities.
  D where cheap land was available.

4 Garden cities were planned
  A to integrate institutions within the city area.
  B to keep industrial activity to a minimum.
  C to be similar to each other in layout.
  D to provide buildings for public gatherings.

5 What is said about garden cities in the last paragraph?
  A Each one would contain a certain type of business.
  B The number would continue to rise.
  C Residents would live and work in the same place.
  D Each one would continue to expand.

In your dreams

1 How often do you have dreams? What do you dream about?

2 Why do some people have more nightmares than others? Is dreaming important to our health and well-being? Why, or why not?

Reading

3 Read the headings below and discuss the likely topic of the reading passage. Then read the passage as quickly as you can and check if you were right.

⏱ about 650 words

Now do the headings task.

Test spot
If you are asked to choose the correct heading for paragraphs, first read the paragraph carefully, then read all the headings before deciding on your answer. Do this for each paragraph in turn.

Questions 1–6
*The reading passage has six paragraphs **A–F**. Choose the correct heading for each paragraph from the list of headings below.*

List of Headings
i Interacting with others in your dreams
ii A competitor exploiting the commercial side
iii Scepticism within the specialist field
iv Dream to improve your technique!
v Not just a modern-day phenomenon
vi The product to enhance your dreamtime
vii Undermining rumours in the press
viii A bridge between sleeping and waking
ix Current research priorities

1 Paragraph **A** ....
2 Paragraph **B** ....
3 Paragraph **C** ....
4 Paragraph **D** ....
5 Paragraph **E** ....
6 Paragraph **F** ....

DEMYSTIFYING OUR DREAMWORLD

A

As a teenager, Brenda Giguere went ice skating with her friends every week, but they improved much faster than she did. She could only go round in circles and got fed up with watching her friends effortlessly switching from
5 backward skating to forward. Lying in bed one night, she thought she would try to practice those backward moves in her sleep. 'Before long I was dreaming I was skating, and I got very excited. It was so realistic. I felt the sensation of skating backward – the movement of my
10 legs, the cool air, the feeling of propelling myself this way. Suddenly it all made sense as a set of logical, fluid, sequential body movements.'

B

Brenda later found out she had experienced what is called a 'lucid dream'. Lucid dreaming is one of the most
15 controversial areas of dream research, partly because of misperceptions over how much individuals can influence their dreams – or indeed, whether they should. Those in favor say that lucidity is an important step in understanding dreams and argue that lucid dreams can take the horror
20 out of nightmares, inspire new ideas, promote self-healing of physical ailments and unravel mysteries of the psyche that can improve a person's well-being.

C

Lucid dreaming is a technique that has been practiced by Tibetan Buddhist priests for more than a millennium.
25 Writings by the ancient Greek philosopher Aristotle also refer to the conscious exploration of dreams. And when the discovery of rapid eye movement (REM) sleep 50 years ago opened up new avenues of sleep research, it also strengthened the argument for lucidity. Today, the
30 leading guru in this field is Stephen LaBerge, who founded the Lucidity Institute in 1987.

D

LaBerge believes that the state of awareness reached during lucid dreaming is akin to that of being awake.

Questions 7–13

Do the following statements agree with the information given in the passage?
Write

TRUE   *if the statement agrees with the information*
FALSE   *if the statement contradicts the information*
NOT GIVEN *if there is no information on this*

7 Brenda Giguere was able to put what she had experienced into practice.

8 Advocates of lucid dreaming claim that it may contribute to a person's thought processes.

9 According to the writer, the detection of REM sleep has been the most important breakthrough in sleep research for half a century.

10 The NovaDreamer operates purely in relation to the user's eyes.

11 According to LaBerge's findings, wearers of the NovaDreamer are three times more likely to experience a lucid dream.

12 Cartwright criticises lucid dreaming for being an unnatural practice.

13 LaBerge's latest tests focus on subjects who have never experienced lucid dreams.

With colleagues, he has developed electronic devices that give the dreamer a reminder during REM sleep to try to become lucid. The 'NovaDreamer' is a sleep mask that emits a flashing light or sound cues when the user is dreaming (detected by eye movement). LaBerge claims that this increases the dreamer's chances of becoming lucid threefold, as evidenced by research he has carried out. Ed Wirth, who has used the NovaDreamer, says the flashing light becomes incorporated into his dreams, like the flickering image of a TV screen. Of the 600 or so dreams a year that Wirth recalls, only five or six are lucid, but their effect is powerful and overwhelming. He flies in his dreams, and walks through walls: 'You can turn a threatening situation into a funny situation. It eliminates the whole nightmare. They, in effect, have changed my life. For me, it's an exploration.'

E
Not everyone shares this enthusiasm. Rosalind Cartwright, the grande dame of sleep medicine research, believes the whole concept has been overblown. Cartwright, director of the Sleep Disorders Service and Research Center at Rush University Medical Center in Chicago, says: 'It's a wish to control things out of their usual function and time. It is trying to redesign the mind in a way I don't think is necessarily helpful. It gives people false hope.'

F
LaBerge admits he doesn't have all the answers yet, but feels lucky to be able to work in such a fascinating field. His goals are simple: to learn more about lucid dreaming and to make it more accessible to the public. At the moment, he's experimenting with chemical inducements to increase the release of acetylcholine, the main neurotransmitter in REM sleep, in order to encourage seasoned lucid dreamers to have more of them. He's also testing herbal supplements such as galantamine, which is extracted from daffodil bulbs, to promote a similar effect. But LaBerge laments that more isn't being done. Research funds are not exactly pouring in for lucid dreaming, and his business operates on a shoestring with a six-member staff, lots of volunteers and funding from grants, donations and sales.

Vocabulary Collocations

4 The verbs below occur frequently in the *Cambridge Academic Corpus*. Find phrases containing these verbs in the passage. For each verb, cross through any word or phrase (a–c) that does *not* collocate with the verb. For two verbs, all three options collocate.

1 inspire (paragraph B)
   a confidence   **b** an ailment   **c** admiration

2 promote (paragraphs B and F)
   a a product   **b** unity   **c** its own interests

3 strengthen (paragraph C)
   a connections   **b** a relationship   **c** an error

4 develop (paragraph D)
   a links   **b** results   **c** strategies

5 share (paragraph E)
   a a view   **b** power   **c** concerns

6 operate (paragraph F)
   a potentially   **b** independently   **c** effectively

Style extra

5 The reading passage comes from an American newspaper, and its style is generally less suited to academic writing. Take, for example, the terms *the leading guru in this field* and *the grande dame of sleep research*. Both are used in journalism to mean 'expert'. The main collocates for *guru* are to do with lifestyle (*fitness guru, exercise guru, diet guru*) or business (*management guru, PR guru*).

Decide which of the following terms for people would be more appropriate in academic writing. If you are unsure, check in a dictionary first.

1 bit-part / minor character
2 pundit / specialist
3 children / kids
4 punter / customer
5 manager / boss

1   Look at pictures A–H and decide what each one might represent in a dream. Compare your ideas.

Listening

2   You are going to hear a conversation between a university tutor and three psychology students. The conversation is in two parts.

🎧 **Questions 1–4**

*Which picture (**A–H**) is each person talking about? Write the letters **A–H** next to questions 1–4.*

1   Carla   ....
2   Jason   ....
3   Helen   ....
4   Tutor   ....

🎧 **Questions 5–7**

*Choose the correct letter, **A, B** or **C**.*

5   In the dream that Helen describes, the central character gets
   A   as far as the summit of a mountain.
   B   nearly halfway up a mountain.
   C   close to the top of a mountain.

6   According to Helen's interpretation, the man
   A   sees himself as an outsider.
   B   is pleased to be rejoining society.
   C   needs something beautiful in his life.

7   Carla suggests that the woman looking into the mirror is
   A   positive about her situation.
   B   disappointed in some way.
   C   secretive and shy of others.

Grammar

Modal verbs of speculation and deduction

3 How certain is the speaker in these examples?

a This one must be all about limits.
b It could be an insight or a new idea.
c The dreamer may/might be experiencing some problems at work.

Modal verbs are used in this way in academic discussion and argument. How would example *a* be expressed in the negative, to mean the opposite? How does the meaning change if we say *couldn't* instead of *could* in example *b*?

4 Complete these sentences with *must, may/might/ could* or *can't/couldn't*.

1 My dream about the tower .... mean that I have to take better care of myself, though I'm not sure.
2 This quote .... be from Jung! It's much closer to Freud's thinking.
3 The article suggests that each floor of a house .... represent a different aspect of the mind in a dream.
4 They .... be at a lecture because all lectures have been cancelled today.
5 I never remember dreams. I .... sleep too deeply.

5 How certain is the speaker in these two question forms? Could these forms be used in written English? Why, or why not?

a Mightn't it be something to do with a dual life?
b He couldn't be seen as friendly, could he?

G···⟶ page 141

6 Talk about dreams 1–4 below using modal verbs and the verb in brackets. Show your level of certainty in what each symbol represents. Add your own ideas too.

EXAMPLE: Dreaming about a fire that is out of control = excessive ambition. (indicate) *Dreaming about a fire that is out of control could indicate that the dreamer has excessive ambition. Mightn't it also indicate anger or another strong emotion?*

1 A dream about a forest = the need to escape from everyday life. (display)
2 Books in dreams = wisdom and knowledge. (symbolise)
3 Being involved in some form of accident in a dream = a state of anxiety. (suggest)
4 Sitting on the wrong train = making a wrong choice in life. (represent)

Pronunciation   *Vowel changes in related words*

7 🎧 There is often a vowel shift in related words, as from the verb *decide* to the noun *decision*. Listen to the following words and write the phonetic symbol for each of the underlined vowel sounds. Choose from the following phonetic symbols:

/iː/   /e/   /juː/   /ʌ/

EXAMPLE: conc<u>e</u>de   */iː/*

1 conc<u>e</u>ssion
2 ded<u>u</u>ce
3 ded<u>u</u>ction
4 perc<u>ei</u>ve
5 perc<u>e</u>ption
6 cons<u>u</u>me
7 cons<u>u</u>mption
8 rep<u>ea</u>t
9 rep<u>e</u>titive

Speaking   *Part 3*

Test spot

In Part 3 of the IELTS Speaking Module, develop your ideas and be ambitious in your use of structures and vocabulary. Use modal verbs to speculate on possible reasons or likely advantages/disadvantages.

8 Discuss some of these Part 3-type questions with a partner.

- What can dreams tell us about ourselves?
- Do you think it is helpful to interpret someone's dreams for them?
- Why are dreams considered important in many cultures?
- Are psychological issues more prevalent in modern society? Why, or why not?
- How far should we try to investigate our inner selves?
- Is psychological well-being more or less important than physical fitness?

Writing folder 5

Task 2 Developing an argument

In the Task 2 essay, you need to present a clearly argued piece of writing, where your ideas are fully developed and exemplified. Remember that you will need to write at least 250 words (answers shorter than this are penalised).

1 Read the task and spend a few moments thinking about your own views on the statement.

Write about the following topic.

> *City living in the 21st century is stressful and offers no advantages.*
> *To what extent do you agree or disagree with this statement?*

Give reasons for your answer and include any relevant examples from your own knowledge or experience.

Write at least 250 words.

---

2 Read the two answers, A and B, which are exactly 250 words. Does each answer agree or disagree with the statement? Which answer contains the clearest argument, in your opinion? Why?

A

You always have noise in a city and it is very stressful. I agree because I live in a large city and it can be stressful. But I can do lots of things in my city, like going to the cinema and seeing rock concerts, so I might disagree with the statement too. Nowadays, more people have to live in cities. Most of the jobs you find are in cities and it takes too long to travel there each day. That is stressful, the same as living in a city.

There are some advantages to city living. A large city has too many people and there is traffic all the time so it is very stressful. I have recently visited Bilbao in northern Spain, which has an excellent transport system. There are trams and an underground network so you can go from one part of the city to another very quickly. I don't call that stressful, and it doesn't cost much either.

If I had the choice I would still live in a city because I like it. There is a lot of live entertainment and many cultural things on offer. Shops are good and every city has many shops. In other words, it must be an advantage to have shops and there aren't many shops in smaller places. With Internet shopping, it doesn't matter where you live any more.

There's no green in the city and it makes us stressed. I agree with the statement because it is stressful.

B

The percentage of the world's population domiciled in cities is increasing and because of this, some of the largest cities must be fairly oppressive places in which to live if you are short of money or unemployed. At the same time, for those with disposable income, a city provides a lively environment, with many cultural benefits and other opportunities. Thus, the advantages of contemporary urban living far outweigh any disadvantages, in my opinion. .

In terms of entertainment, city residents are often spoiled for choice, and on any night of the week could probably visit anything from small jazz venues to theatres, clubs and numerous cinemas. Cities also generally offer wonderful museums.

Another obvious benefit is the diversity of shops and specialist stores in any city of a reasonable size. While it may be the case nowadays that some people do most of their shopping over the Internet, for myself, it is essential to have the chance to browse and windowshop, and a city gives me that.

It has been said that one of the least attractive aspects of city living is transport, and I would certainly never dream of using my car to travel across town. However, most cities nowadays have developed excellent and affordable public transport systems, taking all the stress out of getting around. What is more, the cities of the 21st century often look good, with unusual modern architecture.

In short, today's cities can support a rich, varied and exciting lifestyle, which is stimulating rather than stressful.

3   Tick which points are included in each answer (A
    and B in exercise 2) and rate the development and
    clarity of each one from 1–3.

    1 unclear and/or barely addressed
    2 reasonably clear with some exemplification
    3 clearly developed and exemplified

Live entertainment	**A**	**B**
Open spaces	**A**	**B**
Transport	**A**	**B**
Cultural benefits	**A**	**B**
Noise / crowds	**A**	**B**
Shopping	**A**	**B**
Architecture	**A**	**B**

4   Underline any useful linking phrases in answers A
    and B and add them to the table below.

Introducing / referring to a point	*As far as … is concerned* *Regarding* *With reference to*
Adding another related point	*Secondly* *Additionally*
Contrasting previous information	*Conversely* *Then again* *On the other hand*
Clarifying what has been said	*To put it another way* *That is to say*
Linking to the argument	*Therefore* *For this reason* *Consequently*
Concluding / summarising	*All in all* *To sum up*

5   Try to think of different vocabulary you can use to
    say the same thing. Repetition of key words from
    the task must be avoided (as in the use of 'stressful'
    in A). Find words and phrases in answer B that
    relate to the words below from the task statement.

    city living ....
    21st century ....
    stressful ....
    offers ....
    advantages ....

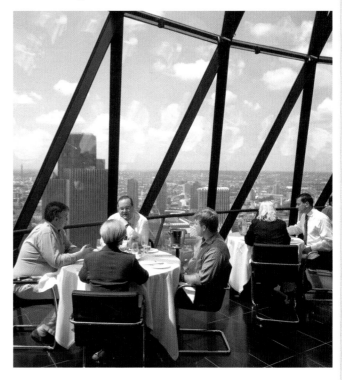

6   Now answer the task in exercise 1, following the
    advice below. Write at least 250 words.

Advice

- Read the task carefully.
- Underline key words and think of different ways
  of saying the same thing.
- Make a plan, including each new point in a new
  paragraph.
- State your overall opinion in the introduction.
- Use linking phrases to make your argument
  clearer.
- Develop and exemplify each of your main points.
- Restate your opinion in a conclusion.
- Leave time to check your answer for accuracy.

The physical world

How well do you know the geography of the world we live in?

Answer this quiz and find out!

Complete these names with a word from the box, and decide which country or region each place is in. Use each word only once.

1 the Grand .... (*above centre*)
2 the Great Rift .... (*above right*)
3 Dover ....
4 the Mesopotamian ....
5 Iguaçu .... (*above left*)
6 the .... of Bengal
7 the .... of Tonkin
8 .... Chad

Bay	Canyon
Cliffs	Falls
Gulf	Lake
Marshes	Valley

Match each definition with a word from the box.

9 the wide part of a river where it meets the sea
10 the movement of water (in a river or sea) in a particular direction
11 an area of sea water separated from the sea by a reef (a line of rocks or sand)
12 a large mass of slow-moving ice
13 a long channel of water that has been constructed
14 gradual wearing away, for example of land, often caused by the action of wind or water
15 a sudden violent movement of the Earth's crust
16 a slow movement, usually resulting from outside forces

canal	current
drift	earthquake
erosion	estuary
glacier	lagoon

What geographical features are these? Each dash represents one missing letter.

17 Everest: m _ _ _ _ _ _ _
18 Krakatoa: v _ _ _ _ _ _
19 Africa: c _ _ _ _ _ _ _ _

20 What do you think are the two main materials that form the spits in these two photographs?

Spurn Head

Chesil Beach

Listening

2 You are going to hear part of a geography lecture about two natural features of the English coast. The lecture is in three parts.

🎧 **Questions 1–5**

Label the map opposite.

*Choose five answers from the box and write the letters **A–I** next to questions 1–5.*

A area of erosion	**F** original coastline
B dunes	**G** salt marsh
C estuary	**H** spit
D headland	**I** tide
E longshore drift	

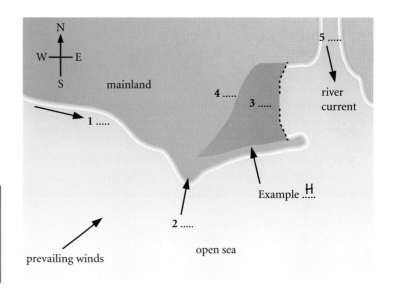

Example: ...H...

The speaker identifies the relevant part of the diagram by saying *A long, narrow accumulation of sand and/or stones, with one end joining the mainland*, before giving the name *spit*.

🎧 **Questions 6–10**

Complete the sentences below.

Write **NO MORE THAN ONE WORD AND/OR A NUMBER** for each answer.

6 Spurn Head is situated between the North Sea and a ....

7 The material of Spurn Head is produced from land further north by a process of

....

8 Longshore drift .... the material on Spurn Head.

9 The spit lasts for about .... years.

10 Eventually the sea breaks through the .... of the spit.

🎧 **Questions 11–15**

*Write the correct letter **A–I** next to questions 11–15.*

11 area of smallest stones: ....
12 lagoon: ....   14 coast erosion: ....
13 mine: ....   15 harbour: ....

Can you think of any other landscapes that have been created by the sea or rivers?

Speaking *Part 2*

3 With a partner, take turns to talk about this topic for at least one minute each.

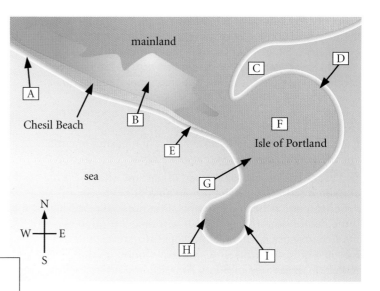

Describe the natural features of an area or country that you know.

You should say:

which area you are going to describe
what natural features the area has
what the natural features look like

and explain how you feel about the natural features of that area.

Useful language

located   situated   consists of   varied   impressive
landscape   forest   prairie   desert   vegetation
fertile

1   In small groups, try and answer these questions.

- Why do the east coast of South America and the west coast of Africa seem to fit each other?
- As coal is formed from plants that need a warm climate, why is there coal in an island near the Arctic?
- Can volcanoes and earthquakes occur anywhere in the world?

Reading

2   Now skim this article and check your answers to the questions above.

⏱ about 600 words

Moving continents

A   The belief that continents have not always been fixed in their present positions was first suggested as early as 1596 by the Dutch map maker Abraham Ortelius. Ortelius suggested that the Americas were 'torn away from Europe
5   and Africa … by earthquakes and floods', and went on to say, 'The vestiges of the rupture reveal themselves if someone brings forward a map of the world and considers carefully the coasts of the three [continents].' However, it was not until 1912 that the idea of moving continents was
10 seriously considered as a full-blown scientific theory, when the theory of continental drift was introduced in two articles by a 32-year-old German meteorologist named Alfred Lothar Wegener. He contended that all the present continents used to form one 'supercontinent', which he
15 called 'Pangaea' (the Greek for 'all lands' – the second syllable is usually pronounced 'jee' or 'gay'), and that this began to split apart around 200 million years ago. The parts drifted across the Earth, eventually breaking into the various smaller continents that exist today.

20 **B**   Wegener's theory was based in part on what appeared to him to be the remarkable fit of the South American and African continents, first noted by Ortelius three centuries earlier. Wegener was also intrigued by the occurrences of unusual geologic structures and of
25 fossils – of both plants and animals – found on the matching coastlines of South America and Africa, which are now widely separated by the Atlantic Ocean. He reasoned that it was physically impossible for most of these creatures to have swum or have been transported
30 across the vast ocean. To him, the presence of identical fossils along the coastal parts of Africa and South America was the most compelling evidence that the two continents were once joined.

C   In Wegener's mind, the drifting of continents after the break-up of Pangaea explained not only the matching   35 fossil occurrences but also the evidence of dramatic climate change on some continents. For example, indications that there were once glaciers in regions of South Africa led to the conclusion that this land must once have been situated much further away from the   40 tropics. Other mismatches of geology and present-day climate included the occurrence of coal – the product of ancient temperate or tropical forests – in Spitzbergen, an island that is now close to the North Pole.

D   At the time Wegener introduced his theory, the   45 scientific community firmly believed the continents and oceans to be permanent features on the Earth's surface. Not surprisingly, his proposal was not well received, even though it seemed to agree with the scientific information available at the time. A fatal weakness in Wegener's   50 theory was that it could not satisfactorily answer the most fundamental question raised by his critics: what kind of forces could be strong enough to move such large masses of solid rock over such great distances?

E   After Wegener's death in 1930, new evidence from   55 ocean floor exploration and other studies rekindled interest in his theory, ultimately leading, in the early 1960s, to the development of the theory of plate tectonics. This scientific concept has revolutionised our understanding of the dynamic planet upon which we live. The theory states that   60 the Earth's outermost layer is fragmented into a dozen or more plates of various sizes that are moving relative to one another as they ride on top of hotter, more mobile material.

F   The theory has provided explanations to questions that scientists had speculated upon for centuries – such   65 as why earthquakes and volcanic eruptions occur in very specific areas around the world, and how and why mountain ranges like the Alps and Himalayas formed.

3 This is how Pangaea may have looked around 225 million years ago. Can you identify the present-day continents and sub-continents?

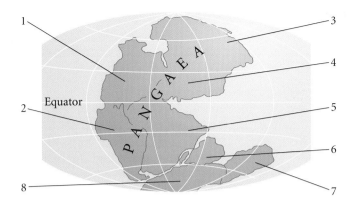

4 Questions 1–6

Answer the questions below using **NO MORE THAN THREE WORDS** *from the passage for each answer.*

> ### Test spot
> The task in questions 1–6 is similar to sentence and note completion. The questions normally follow the order of information in the passage. ⋯⟶ TF 4

1 In Ortelius's opinion, what caused continents to be separated?

2 In the theory of continental drift, what was given the name 'Pangaea'?

3 Apart from shape and geological structures, what similar phenomena are found in South America and Africa?

4 What do indications of glaciers in South Africa and coal in Spitzbergen provide evidence of?

5 According to the 1960s theory, what does the top layer of the Earth consist of?

6 What natural phenomena may have been created by movement on the Earth's surface?

Remember that in the following task the questions don't follow the order of information in the passage.

Questions 7–12

*The reading passage has six paragraphs labelled **A–F**.*

Which paragraph contains the following information?
NB *You may use any letter more than once.*

7 how later developments revived consideration of the theory of continental drift

8 evidence that some areas used to be situated in much warmer or cooler regions

9 something that Wegener's theory could not explain

10 a reason why living organisms can't have moved from one continent to another

11 an apparent contradiction in the reaction to the theory of continental drift

12 an outline of a theory that explains how continental drift occurs

Grammar Non-finite clauses

Non-finite clauses contain a verb in the form of an infinitive (e.g. *to do, to have done*), present participle (*doing*) or past participle (*done*). These clauses are normally used as part of complex sentences, which are particularly common in academic English.

5 Underline the non-finite clauses in these sentences, based on ones in the reading passage.

EXAMPLE:

0 Parts of Pangaea drifted across the Earth, <u>gradually breaking into smaller continents</u>.

1 A meteorologist working in Germany wrote two articles about continental drift.

2 Finding similar fossils on both sides of the Atlantic was strong evidence of continental drift.

3 Wegener was intrigued by fossils found in South America and Africa.

4 It is impossible for coal to form in a cold climate.

6 In which sentence(s), 0–4 above, is the non-finite clause

1 ... a relative clause?

2 ... the subject?

3 ... an adverbial clause?

7 Complete the following rules by choosing the correct alternative.

In relative clauses and adverbial clauses,
1 *-ing* generally has *an active / a passive* meaning.
2 *-ed* generally has *an active / a passive* meaning.

When a non-finite clause is the subject,
3 at the beginning of the sentence it uses *-ing / -ed / infinitive*.
4 at the end of the sentence it uses *-ing / -ed / infinitive*.

8 Choose the correct form of the verb in brackets.

1 The theory .... by Wegener has answered some age-old questions. (propose)

2 .... the two coastlines led Ortelius to his idea. (Compare)

3 Earthquakes are caused by tectonic plates .... against each other. (move)

4 It was difficult for scientists of Wegener's time .... his theory. (accept)

5 The theory has been accepted, ... our understanding of the planet. (revolutionise)

G ⋯⟶ page 141

Test folder 6

Labelling diagrams and maps

(Academic Reading, General Training Reading and Listening Modules)

In the Academic and General Training Reading Modules, you may be asked to label a diagram with words from the passage. In the Listening Module, you may be asked to label a diagram or map.

In the Reading Modules, you will be told the maximum number of words for each answer. The questions may not follow the same order as the information in the passage.

In the Listening Module the questions follow the order of information in the passage. You may need to choose words from a box, or choose parts of a drawing or map labelled alphabetically (as in exercise 1 below).

If you have to choose words from a box, there will be more words than questions.

Words must be spelt correctly to gain marks.

Listening

1 🎧 This is similar to Section 1 of the Listening Module.

Label the map below.
*Write the correct letter **A–L** next to questions 1–7.*

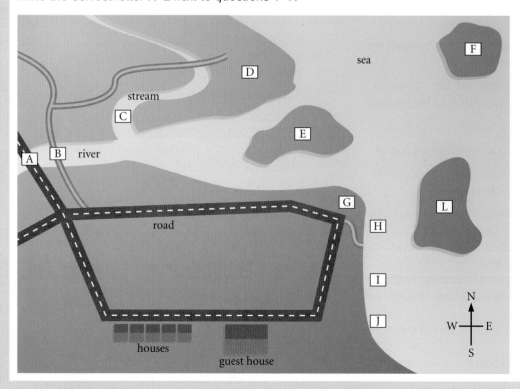

1	lighthouse	....
2	fossils	....
3	caves	....
4	footbridge	....
5	salt marsh	....
6	bird sanctuary	....
7	ruins	....

Reading

2 This text is similar to those in the Academic Reading Module, but much shorter, about 225 words.

The Floor of the South Atlantic Ocean

The surface of the ocean floor is extremely complicated. Seaward from the coast there is usually a gently sloping area called the continental shelf. This varies considerably in extent between different parts of the world: off the coast of Africa, for instance, it is relatively narrow. Its seaward edge is marked by the continental slope, which is considerably steeper. This adjoins the continental rise, an almost vertical area running down to the abyssal plain, which lies at an average depth of about 5 km.

The South Atlantic is divided into two major areas by an ocean ridge, 2–4 km in height. It sometimes breaks the ocean surface as islands such as Iceland and Tristan da Cunha. In the centre of the ridge, at the highest point away from land, there is a trenchlike feature called the axial rift. Here material from the interior of the earth rises into the void between the receding African, Eurasian and American plates.

Finally, the ocean floors, and especially the floor of the Pacific Ocean, are characterised by deep, furrow-like trenches, reaching to depths in excess of 7 km. The deepest place on earth lies in one of these trenches in the Pacific, where the greatest depth below sea level so far determined is over 11 km.

Label the diagram below.

*Choose **NO MORE THAN TWO WORDS** from the passage for each answer.*

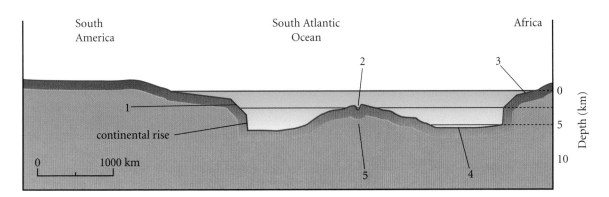

1 ....
2 ....
3 ....
4 ....
5 ....

Nature or nurture?

1 In small groups, discuss this question.

What makes somebody good at a particular activity, such as running, learning foreign languages, or singing? Consider the roles of nature (what's been passed on to them in their genes), and nurture (their upbringing).

Reading

2 Now read this article quickly, and decide what the writer's view is on the question above.

⏱ about 675 words

Nature/Nurture: An Artificial Division?

Often in the news, we see stories asking the question, 'Is this due to nature or nurture?' Certain diseases, traits, and behaviours are said to be 'genetic', while others are due to 'environment'.

5 There is no doubt that specific genes cause particular problems in certain cases. Parkinson's Disease and colour blindness both run in families because of their genetic origins. But the news reports we see cover a much wider subject area. We wonder if some people have 'natural' talent in music or sports without which any training they receive is useless. Some people assert that children living with

10 adults given to certain controversial behaviours will gain those ways from 'environmental influences'. The implication is always that behaviour is either genetic or environmental.

The concept of dividing everything into these two mutually exclusive groups is not the right way to think about diseases or

15 behaviours, because genes and environment are not independent. They influence each other greatly, and their effects can almost never be disentangled.

A creature's genes will in general cause it to seek certain environments and avoid others. That environment then influences

20 the creature's development, and plays a role in whether or not its genes are passed on. Wild dogs, for example, live in packs because their genes tell them to organise that way socially. However, the pack is also where each dog learns proper dog behaviour, practises the skills to survive, and ultimately finds a mate. The pack – the

25 dog's environment – is what makes it into a successful dog with a good chance of passing its genes on. So a well socialised, successful pack dog is the result of both genes and environment.

Humans are also social creatures. We seek other humans to live with, and, in general, do not like to be alone for long periods.

30 Newborn babies respond favourably with lower heart and respiration rates to having people nearby. So we are 'naturally' driven to live in social groups, and these very social groups provide the environment that we need to become successful humans. Genes and environment work together.

In contrast, the environment can also influence which genes are 35 expressed in a creature, and to what degree. Every organism has a unique genetic code. But a given set of genes doesn't determine exactly how a creature will be physically; instead, there is a range of possibilities. The environment plays a major role in determining how the genes will be expressed. 40

A simple example is the fact that height, a largely inherited trait, has been steadily increasing in humans over the past few centuries. Presumably this is due to better nutrition, since it is too short a time span for evolutionary changes to have occurred. So your height is a combination of your genes and various external factors. 45

A more complicated example involves brain development. Rats who live in dark, crowded, dirty cages grow fewer neural connections than rats raised in spacious cages with toys and varied diets. The disadvantaged rats learn more slowly and perform more poorly on memory tests, although the rats were related 50 genetically. It is always dangerous to extrapolate from animals to humans, so I won't draw any sweeping conclusions, but at the very least, this experiment shows that environmental factors can produce very different outcomes from similar genetic materials.

So by changing purely external factors, we can influence which 55 genes are expressed and to what degree. Your behaviour, likes and dislikes, and way of thinking are an inseparable combination of your genes and the experiences you have had growing up.

The genetic and environmental factors in a creature's life mutually influence each other and, except in a few very specific 60 cases, cannot be separated or considered in isolation.

In summary, the nature/nurture debate is outdated. We now realise that the either/or choice is too simple, and continuing to think in that way will restrict our understanding of humans and limit our ability to solve the problems we face today. Next time you 65 see a news story asking if something is 'genetic' or 'environmental', you will know the real answer is – both.

3 Answer these questions. In questions 1–6 the statements are in the order in which you will find the information in the passage. In the matching task, questions 7–10, the questions are *not* in the order of the passage.

Questions 1–6

Do the following statements reflect the claims of the writer? Write

YES   if the statement reflects the claims of the writer

NO   if the statement contradicts the claims of the writer

NOT GIVEN if it is impossible to say what the writer thinks about this

1 The effects of genetic and environmental factors can usually be distinguished.
2 The claim that human beings need to live in groups is supported by the behaviour of newborn babies.
3 A person's height has a purely genetic cause.
4 Living conditions affect the brain development of people more than of rats.
5 Our genes influence our personal preferences.
6 A desire to identify causes as either genetic or environmental may make it difficult to solve certain problems.

Questions 7–10

Look at the following examples (questions 7–10) and the list of influences that they illustrate below.
Match each example with the influence that it illustrates.
*Write the correct letter, **A**, **B** or **C** next to questions 7–10.*
***NB** You may use any letter more than once.*

7 Human babies   ....   9 Rats   ....
8 Parkinson's Disease ....   10 Wild dogs   ....

> **List of Influences**
> **A** the impact of genes alone
> **B** genes providing the conditions for an environmental effect
> **C** environment affecting how genes are expressed

Speaking *Part 3*

4 With a partner, answer these questions. Remember to develop your answers. Note that having a skill doesn't necessarily mean that you're an expert!

- Can you identify some of the skills you have?
- Could you describe how you developed one of your skills?
- Can you assess the value of having that skill?
- Could you comment on the idea that children shouldn't waste time trying to develop a skill if they lack natural ability?

Vocabulary Phrasal verbs with *on*

Transitive phrasal verbs (those that take an object) fall into two grammatical categories:

1 **Inseparable**: the object must come *after* the phrasal verb.
   - verb + preposition
     The writer touched on the subject of musical talent.
   - verb + adverb + preposition
     I'm looking forward to my holiday.

2 **Separable**: verb + adverb
   - If the object is a noun phrase, the object can come *before* or *after* the adverb particle. Usually only short objects come before the particle.
     A successful dog is likely to pass on its genes.
     A successful dog is likely to pass its genes on.
   - If the object is a pronoun, it must come *before* the particle.
     A successful dog is likely to pass them on.

A good dictionary, such as the *Cambridge Advanced Learner's Dictionary*, uses different labels for the two categories. Checking the example sentences given in the dictionary will help you learn how to use phrasal verbs in sentences.

5 Complete each sentence with the most suitable verb from the box, in the correct form. Use each verb once only.

bring on	call on	check up on	decide on
hit on	lay on	switch on	take on

1 Before .... electrical equipment, make sure it has been properly installed.
2 Some scientists have .... the idea of measuring brain activity in sleeping birds.
3 The university is going .... a coach from the airport to the conference venue.
4 Have you .... your field of research yet?
5 As we are overworked, we must .... an assistant.
6 We need .... our lab assistant quite often, as he is new to the job.
7 It is now my pleasure .... Professor Jarvis to propose a vote of thanks.

6 In which of the sentences in exercise 5 can the particle follow the object?

7 Rewrite the clauses containing phrasal verbs in exercise 5, using a pronoun as the object.

EXAMPLE: **1** *Before switching it on*

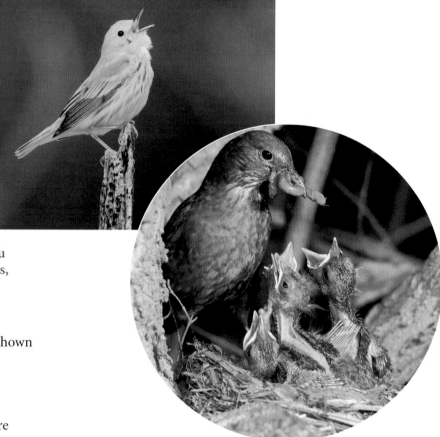

1 In small groups, discuss these questions. If you don't know much about the behaviour of birds, speculate about it, and consider alternative answers. This will help you in Part 3 of the Speaking Module.

   1 List some activities that birds do: some are shown in the photographs above. Are they done by males, females or both?

   2 Do you think birds learn how to do those activities from their parents, or is some knowledge innate (that is, something they are born knowing)?

   3 Can a bird only sing the song of its own species?

   4 Are parrots the only birds that can reproduce sounds that they hear?

Listening

2 You are going to hear a radio interview with a specialist in animal behaviour about what makes birds behave as they do. The interview is in two parts (questions 1–7 and 8–12).

🎧 Questions 1–3

List **THREE** activities that animals and birds can do instinctively (that is, without needing to learn how to do them).

Write **NO MORE THAN TWO WORDS** for each answer.

Test spot

Listen for the clue that the speaker is about to answer the question. They will probably use different words from the question. Write down only the number of activities you're asked for. The speaker will only give that number of answers, so don't leave any of them out. Don't write more than the maximum number of words you're asked for. Write only words that you hear, without changing them. It doesn't matter if you write your answers in a different order from the recording.

1 ....

2 ....

3 ....

Questions 4–7

What does the animal behaviour specialist say about each category of bird?

Choose your answers from the box and write the letters **A–F** *next to questions 4–7.*

A can only produce simple messages
B does not produce any sounds
C learns simple outline of song of its own species
D learns song of its own species in full
E learns song that its own species does not sing
F makes sounds of its own species without learning

---

4 dove ....

5 chick hearing many varieties of birds ....

6 chick growing up in isolation ....

7 chick brought up by a different species ....

🎧 Questions 8–12

Answer the questions below.

Write **NO MORE THAN THREE WORDS AND/OR A NUMBER** for each answer.

8 Where do zebra finches come from?

9 What evidence suggests that birds practise singing in their sleep?

10 By approximately what age does a male zebra finch sing its song perfectly?

11 What do some species' songs develop into?

12 What have some starlings in Oxford been known to imitate?

Grammar Infinitives

Particularly in academic English, clauses are often connected by infinitives – the **active** forms: *to do, to be doing, to have done, to have been doing,* and the **passive** forms: *to be done, to have been done,* and the rarely used *to be being done.*

3 Complete the second sentence of each pair with the infinitive matching the verb form of the first sentence (in *italics*).

   EXAMPLE:

   a A zebra finch will sing its song perfectly if it *has heard* other finches before it is 60 days old.
   b When a zebra finch is 60 days old, it will sing its song perfectly, but it needs _to have heard_ other finches before then.

   1 a We are taller than the people of a few hundred years ago, but it is unlikely that an evolutionary change *has occurred* in such a short time span.
   b We are taller than the people of a few hundred years ago, but this is too short a time span for an evolutionary change ....

   2 a I don't expect that I'*ll have finished* my research by the deadline.
   b I don't expect .... my research by the deadline.

   3 a I'm lucky that I'*ve been doing* a job I enjoy all my working life.
   b I'm lucky .... a job I enjoy all my working life.

   4 a A bird making a certain sound *is* probably *warning* other birds of danger.
   b A bird making a certain sound is likely .... other birds of danger.

   5 a It is known that colour blindness *is caused* by genetic factors.
   b Colour blindness is known .... by genetic factors.

   6 a It is known that birds *were studied* in the 18th century.
   b Birds are known .... in the 18th century.

4 In infinitives, only the main verb is stressed: *to, have, be* and *been* are all weak. Listen to the infinitives in the *b* sentences of exercise 3, and repeat them.

G ⸱⸱⸱❖ page 141

Style extra

5 The paragraph below comes from a recording of a man talking about wildlife around the power station where he works. It is unscripted, and is difficult to understand when it is written. Read it quickly, and decide which of the following is the main point:

   A Power stations can suffer problems because of wildlife.
   B Power stations are more attractive to wildlife than farms or gardens.
   C Power stations attract the same sorts of wildlife as farms and gardens.

They're, they're built in remote places so you've got all the, the er wild life around them and then you've got er farmland which uses pesticide and stuff like, which kills off the insect life and to birds all young and stuff like that. Erm, by having know that the land grows the weeds and no pesticides not disturbed, there's no shooting, they're never shot around here, the birds can come in sheltered, you know, they, they're just like a little nature reserve, protected area, game park you know, nothing shot at just left and er they like it obviously, I mean it's like anything once it learns that er it's gonna be left alone it comes again and again. People scrub up the weeds in the garden and things like that, here they're allowed to grow, the butterflies come in, insects, great you know just, just love it.

6 Now turn the passage into sentences that could be part of a fairly formal written report for a wildlife organisation. Start each sentence with the words and phrases below.

   1 Power stations ...
   2 Farmland ...
   3 Birds ...
   4 The land around power stations is protected ...
   5 Once a bird learns ...
   6 Weeds ...

7 What is your opinion of the skills that birds show?

NATURE OR NURTURE?   81

Writing folder 6

Task 1 Comparison and contrast

In Task 1 of the Academic Writing Module you may be given graphs or charts to compare and contrast. You need to write at least 150 words (but don't waste time writing much more than this, as Task 2 carries more marks). It should take you around nine minutes to physically write 150 words, allowing you some time to plan and check your answer.

1 Look at the graphs below, taken from a scientific journal. They show fluctuations in temperature during the period 1856–2000. The top graph shows data for the world as a whole, whereas in the other two graphs, the data is split for the Northern and Southern Hemispheres.

Global and Hemispheric Annual Temperature Anomalies 1856 – 2000

2 Read the following extract from the journal, which is a commentary on the top graph, just over 150 words long. Then, using the information given in the commentary and its graph, decide whether statements 1–4 below are true or false.

Trends in annual mean temperature anomalies for the globe show relatively stable temperatures from the beginning of the record until about 1910, with fairly rapid and steady warming through to the early 1940s, followed by another period of relatively stable temperatures through the mid-1970s. From this point onward, another rapid rise similar to that in the earlier part of the century is observed. 1998 was the warmest year of the global mean temperature series to date, followed by 1997. The most recent year of the record, 2000, also saw a significant positive temperature anomaly (0.29°C), but represents a cooling compared to the recent very warm years of 1997 and 1998. Even so, 2000 ties with 1991 for the sixth warmest year in the global record, and the eight warmest years of the global record have all occurred since 1990. Overall, the average surface air temperature of the globe has warmed by approximately 0.5°C since the middle of the nineteenth century.

1 Average temperatures in 1910 were warmer than in 1940.
2 It was not as warm in 2000 as it was in 1998.
3 The average temperature in 1991 was the same as in 2000.
4 The warmest year in the global record was 1997.

3 Statements 1–4 above contain examples of comparative structures. Quickly check your knowledge of comparative and superlative forms by completing this table.

wet		
dry		
rapid		
gradual		

4 When comparing and contrasting, we often use the qualifiers below to point up similarities or differences. Select appropriate ones to complete the text describing the bottom two graphs in exercise 1. More than one answer is possible.

exactly/just the same (as)
almost/nearly/practically/virtually the same (as)
not entirely/quite the same (as)
completely/entirely/totally different (from/to)

a little / hardly / only just (warmer than)
rather / somewhat (warmer than)
a great deal / considerably / substantially (warmer than)

The graphs for the Northern and Southern Hemispheres show certain similarities. There is **1** .... the same peak temperature in the early 1940s, and in both graphs the highest temperatures occur after 1980. However, there are several notable differences. The warming trend observed for the Northern Hemisphere from about 1910 through to 1930 is **2** .... as that of the Southern Hemisphere, where there is a dip in average temperatures after 1920. Here, there was more rapid warming from about 1930 through to the early 1940s. From the early 1940s to the late 1950s, the Northern Hemisphere record shows **3** .... more gradual cooling than the Southern Hemisphere, which indicates an abrupt shift to cooler temperatures after 1945, followed by a gradual increase over several decades, and a general levelling off since the late 1980s. The 1990s in the Northern Hemisphere show a very different picture, where temperature fluctuations are **4** .... more marked than in the Southern Hemisphere.

5 Now answer the task below, following the advice given at the bottom of the page.

You should spend about 20 minutes on this task.

The graphs below show average monthly temperature and rainfall in two places in South Africa.
Summarise the information by selecting and reporting the main features, and make comparisons where relevant.

Write at least 150 words.

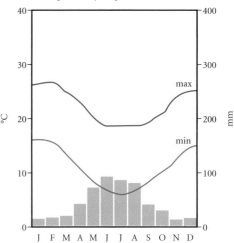

Cape Town, South Africa
Average monthly temperature and rainfall

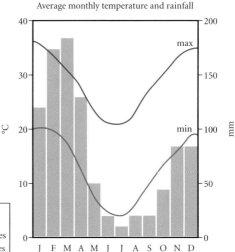

Upington, South Africa
Average monthly temperature and rainfall

Key
■ = rainfall in millimetres
— = maximum temperatures
— = minimum temperatures

Advice

- Look at the graphs carefully.
- Check you understand what each axis shows.
- Make quick notes of similarities and differences in two columns.
- Introduce the subject of the graphs in your opening sentence.
- Focus on the main trends and avoid repetition.
- Use comparative structures with qualifiers where appropriate.
- Aim to write 150–160 words in a little less than 10 minutes.
- Read through your answer to check everything is clear.
- Check spelling and grammar.

Units 9–12 Revision

Topic review

1 Compare and contrast the paired subjects including as much information as possible.

1 an estuary and a canal
2 a dream and a nightmare
3 high-rise and low-rise buildings
4 human and animal behaviour
5 a volcano and a mountain
6 natural talent and acquired skills

Grammar

2 Reorder these sentences to begin with the words in *italics*, making any other changes necessary.

EXAMPLE: Ruth had *no sooner* got to sleep than she was woken by a thunderstorm.
No sooner had Ruth got to sleep than she was woken by a thunderstorm.

1 New Orleans was *not only* hit by a severe hurricane but by disastrous flooding as well.
2 We had *hardly* checked into our hotel on the bay when we were taken on yet another boat trip.
3 Babies *no sooner* learn to crawl than they start walking.
4 There are *not only* genetic factors to consider but also environmental ones.
5 I *little* thought that I would be visiting the city of Rosario for work.
6 The torrential rain did *not* ease up *until* the following night.

3 Complete the sentences by forming a suitable active or passive infinitive of the verb in brackets.

EXAMPLE: The river is unlikely (change) ..._to have_.. ..._changed_.... its course since Wallace's time.

1 The city authorities claim (do) .... everything possible to improve the current situation.
2 The methods used in this research into sleep patterns seem rather questionable and may need (investigate) .... further.
3 The engineer professed not (contact) .... by the authorities until three days after the building's collapse.
4 Smith and Cochrane are almost bound (deal with) .... the same subject in their talk last year.
5 Toxic waste appears (build up) .... unchecked in the lake for the last decade.
6 Other primitive settlements are known (establish) .... in the same area of grassland.
7 Aspects such as these would continue (monitor) .... at both local and national level.
8 The baby's low birth weight seems (cause) .... more by the conditions of pregnancy than by genetic inheritance.

4 Finish the second sentences to make them more speculative than the first ones.

EXAMPLE: The city must be attracting tourists because of its excellent amenities.
The excellent amenities in the city *could be the reason why so many tourists are visiting it.*

1 The beach can't be vulnerable to flooding given the sea wall is so high.
In spite of the height of the sea wall, the beach
....
....
2 The animal's poor diet can be explained by the restrictions of its habitat.
The restrictions of the animal's habitat ....
....
3 Your nightmare must be due to your eating so much cheese late last night.
One reason for your nightmare ....
....

Style extra

5 Rewrite this report about a company in a more formal style. Use the words and phrases below to replace the underlined parts, making any other changes necessary. The formal version is started for you below.

> additionally   assist   clients   consultancy work
> Dr   field   ~~have a discussion~~   have a PhD
> impressive   investigate   managing director
> presentations qualified   reputation   specialist
> views on the matter

Yesterday I <u>chatted to</u> the <u>boss</u> of the company Dreams-U-Like, Janet Stephenson. I think she<u>'s a doc</u> in psychology and she seems to know her <u>stuff</u>. <u>Plus</u> there's a <u>leading guru</u> in dream analysis, Barry Whitehead, doing some <u>bits of work</u> for her. We should <u>check out</u> BW's <u>fame</u>, maybe he could <u>sort us out</u> too? <u>Doc</u> Stephenson says he's <u>brilliant</u> with <u>punters</u>, you know, gives good <u>shows</u>. What <u>do you think</u>?

Yesterday I had a discussion with ...

Vocabulary

6 Complete the sentences below using a phrasal verb with *on* from the box, in the correct form.

> bring on   decide on   expand on   hit on
> lay on   pass on   touch on

EXAMPLE   The mayor ......*has laid on*...... a special reception for the winning football team, whose flight is expected to land at midday.

1 Your essay barely .... the reasons for rural depopulation – it would have been better if you .... these at length.
2 We .... our preferred office location yet, but it will need to be close to the city centre.
3 Usually, this type of inherited condition .... by the male parent.
4 After following many false trails, the chemist in the group finally .... a solution to the problem, quite by chance.
5 Her asthma attack .... by pollution in the atmosphere.

7 Read the definitions of words to do with urban and geographical features and complete the crossword.

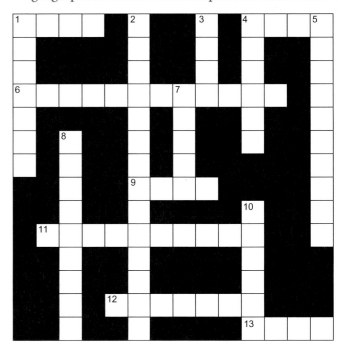

Across

1 a large area of sea beside the coast, e.g. the ——— of Mexico (4)
4 a large area of fresh water, surrounded by land (4)
6 building work (12)
9 The Great ——— Valley (4)
11 a very tall building in a city (10)
12 wearing away of land by wind or water (7)
13 a hill of sand by the sea or in a desert (4)

Down

1 a large mass of slow-moving ice (7)
2 basic facilities such as transport, communications, or power supplies (14)
3 a long, flat, narrow piece of land jutting out into the sea (4)
4 an area of calm sea water separated from the sea by a reef or sandbank (6)
5 sudden violent movement of the Earth's crust (10)
7 a high area of coastal land with one very steep side (5)
8 the parts of a city that are farthest away from its centre (9)
10 the soil and rock on the Earth's surface (6)

1 Dinosaurs became extinct 65 million years ago. Do you know why?

2 In this context, decide what opposing theories a *catastrophist* and a *gradualist* might have.

Reading

3 Read this article to check your ideas about catastrophists and gradualists. Don't worry about the underlined parts yet.

⏱ about 600 words

KILLER BLOW

A meteor as big as the city of San Francisco hurtles towards the Earth at 20 km per second, smashes into the tropical lagoons of the Gulf of Mexico and gouges a fathomless hole. As a result, a tidal wave surges outwards. Fires sweep
5 across North and South America and fallout blocks the sun and plunges the Earth into permanent gloom.

This catastrophic event is the <u>classic answer</u> as to why dinosaurs <u>were wiped out</u> 65 million years ago, but does the theory <u>hold water</u>? Everyone agrees that the Earth suffered
10 a large meteor strike towards the end of the Cretaceous period, yet more than 20 years after the Chicxulub impact was proposed as the cause of mass extinction, scientists are still arguing over what really killed the dinosaurs.

On one side are the 'catastrophists', who <u>say</u> the impact
15 <u>snuffed out</u> the majority of life on Earth in a matter of months or a few years. On the other are 'gradualists', who point out that the fossil record shows a steady decline in the number of species, starting several hundred thousand years before the end of the Cretaceous period. This is
20 known as the K/T mass extinction, when some 70% of the world's species died out. The gradualists don't deny the Chicxulub impact happened, but maintain that it wasn't responsible for the mass extinction.

The debate between the two sides has been polarised
25 and acrimonious, but thanks to a feat of engineering, scientists may finally be able to <u>find out</u> exactly what happened to our planet on that fateful day 65 million years ago. By boring through solid rock, drilling contractors have pulled out a core, 1112 metres long and 7.6 cms in

diameter, which records the full story of the impact and its 30 aftermath. Geologists (<u>mainly</u> catastrophists, <u>of course</u>) are <u>queuing up</u> to analyse the core. In so doing, they hope to confirm whether the impact was devastating enough to kill the dinosaurs. As Jan Smit, a geologist at the Free University of Amsterdam, says, 'The rocks are excellently 35 preserved and certainly promise some scientific fireworks!'

For the catastrophists, however, there are two big problems. First, they don't know how intense and widespread the meteor's effects were and would have to provide evidence of an extreme global change that lasted 40 for at least a year. Secondly, it <u>wasn't just</u> meteors that were <u>stirring up unrest</u>. At that time, an area known as the Deccan Traps in what is now Western India was enduring one of the most intense spells of volcanism in Earth's history. A 'hot spot' deep in the mantle was 45 producing plumes of superheated lava that burst through the crust, inundating 2.5 million square km of land.

Greenhouse gases and water vapour emerged with the lava and, in 1981, Dewey McLean proposed that the Deccan Traps triggered severe global warming and a mass 50 extinction. In support of this theory, the gradualists point out that this is not the only episode of supervolcanism that has occurred simultaneously with a mass extinction. At the Permian-Triassic boundary 250 million years ago, over 90% of marine species became extinct just as the 55 region that is now Siberia was being flooded with lava.

More evidence emerged in support of a gradual extinction in 2002, when a team of geologists in China discovered dinosaur eggshells in rock layers above the K/T boundary, showing that some species of dinosaur survived 60 for a further 250,000 years after the Chicxulub impact. One thing is clear: both catastrophists and gradualists still have plenty to investigate; the rest of us can just sit back and enjoy the fireworks.

4 *Complete the summary below using words from the box.*

The Chicxulub meteor strike created a deep **1** ....
and gave rise to a period of total darkness as the sun was obscured
by **2** .... Catastrophists believe this led to the
3 .... of the dinosaurs, but gradualists don't agree,
pointing to the significant loss of **4** .... prior to the
Chicxulub **5** .... There has been a long-running
6 .... between the two sides. Catastrophists need
7 .... of the precise **8** .... of the
adverse atmospheric **9** .... Moreover, gradualists
are drawing attention to the **10** .... of intense
volcanic activity, which released vast **11** .... of the
gases that cause global warming. Their **12** .... have
been further strengthened by dinosaur fossils recently unearthed in
strata laid down after the meteor strike.

arguments	biodiversity	coincidence	conditions
controversy	crater	debris	dispute	duration
eradication	hypothesis	incident	meanings	outcomes
proof	quantities	research	

Style extra

5   Replace the underlined parts of the article with the phrases below to create a more serious, academic style. Make any other changes necessary.

became extinct
contributing to an unstable environment
claim
establish
led to the extinction of
most commonly held explanation
most of whom
naturally
other factors apart from
tenable
waiting eagerly

Vocabulary

Cause and result

6   Here are various ways of expressing cause and result. Use some of these phrases in the sentences below, paying attention to any prepositions following the spaces.

Noun phrases:
cause (of), effect/effects (of ... on), explanation (for), outcome/outcomes (of), reason, result

Verb phrases:
affect, be caused (by), cause ... (to + inf), be responsible (for), contribute (to), lead (to), result (in), suffer (from), trigger

Linking words:
as a result, in so doing

1   One of the immediate .... of the meteor strike was a tidal wave.

2   The extensive fires that .... by the impact .... to a long period of darkness.

3   Catastrophists believe that the Chicxulub impact .... in the extinction of the dinosaurs.

4   Gradualists refuse to believe that the impact .... for the end of the dinosaurs.

5   Dewey McLean's theory suggests that the Deccan Traps .... the Earth's temperature to rise and, ... , there was a mass extinction.

6   Some researchers are convinced that the volcanic activity which formed the Deccan traps .... in part to the end of the dinosaurs.

7   Up until now, many scientists have seen these eruptions as being too infrequent to .... extreme environmental change.

8   However, new research by Chenet et al suggests that this volcanic activity could provide a watertight .... for the dinosaurs' extinction, as it shows the Deccan Traps were formed more quickly than previously thought.

13·2

1 Do this quiz with a partner.

What do you know about comets?

True or false?
1 The name 'comet' comes from the Greek and means 'long-haired'.
2 'Asteroid' is another name for 'comet'.
3 Comets follow circular orbits around the sun.
4 The nucleus of a comet is made solely of icy matter.
5 When a comet gets closer to the sun, it changes its shape.
6 The tail of a comet consists solely of dust and debris.

Listening

2 🎧 You are going to hear a lecture about the Rosetta mission. Before you listen, look at the sentences and try to work out what kind of information you need to listen for.

Complete the sentences below.
*Write **NO MORE THAN TWO WORDS** for each answer.*

1 The ESA Rosetta Mission was also called the 'comet ....'.
2 The mission was delayed in 2003 because of a problem with the ....
3 The revised flight plan includes several flybys – one of Mars and three of ....
4 The indirect route will allow Rosetta to visit the main asteroid ....
5 Rosetta will arrive at its final destination (the comet Churyumov-Gerasimenko) in .... 2014.
6 Once in orbit, it will carry out its .... exercise.
7 The Rosetta Lander will remain in one place, attached to the comet's ....
8 Comets' tails are made up of .... and ....
9 As well as giving us information about comets, data from Rosetta may help us to understand how .... are created.

Pronunciation *Word stress – adverbs*

3 🎧 The adverbs below are useful in the prepared talk and discussion (Parts 2 and 3) of the Speaking Module, because they will help to show your range of language. Listen to these adverbs and mark the main stress for each one by putting a stress mark before the stressed syllable.

EXAMPLE: 'actually

actually   basically   certainly
eventually   fundamentally   hopefully
increasingly   initially   originally
typically

4 🎧 Now listen to how some of the adverbs in exercise 3 were used in the recording.

5 🎧 Add the correct adverb to each sentence. The ⅄ mark shows you where to put it. Say each sentence with its adverb. Then listen to check your pronunciation and stress.

1 I ⅄ know one of the scientists working on the Rosetta mission. (actually / fundamentally)
2 The launch was planned for 2003 ⅄ . (completely / originally)
3 It ⅄ took place a year later. (hopefully / eventually)
4 ⅄ comets develop bright tails as they get nearer the sun. (Originally / Typically)
5 Scientists will ⅄ be given a lot of data by the end of the mission. (certainly / initially)

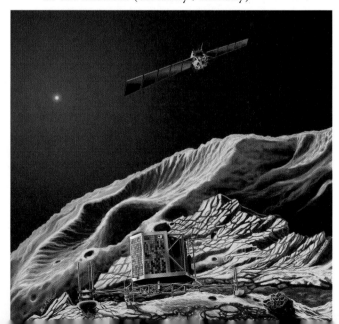

Grammar The future

6 Match these extracts from the recording to tenses a–e and explain why each tense is used.

1 Today I'm going to be talking to you about the European Space Agency Mission Rosetta.
2 46P/ Wirtanen will have travelled far beyond Rosetta's flight path.
3 Rosetta will be tracking a comet known as …
4 The lander will anchor itself to the crust …
5 Meanwhile, the orbiter will have been transmitting radio signals through the nucleus to the lander.

a future with *will*
b future with *going to*
c future continuous
d future perfect simple
e future perfect continuous

G ⤳ page 141

7 Complete the text, using a suitable simple or continuous future tense of the verb in brackets. Remember to use a negative form or a passive where necessary.

On March 2 2009, Rosetta **1** (travel) .... for five years but it **2** (reach) .... the comet Churyumov-Gerasimenko until August 2014. At this time, the comet **3** (approach) .... the sun, whose warmth **4** (cause) .... gas and dust to be ejected from the comet's nucleus. This is how the tail **5** (form) ....

Once in orbit around the comet, Rosetta's on-board cameras **6** (take) .... photographs constantly, to survey the entire surface. In this way, a suitable site **7** (find) .... for the lander.

In December 2015, the mission **8** (terminate) .... By then, the comet **9** (pass) .... its closest proximity to the sun and **10** (make) .... its way towards colder regions again.

Speaking *Part 2*

8 Read the Part 2 task and the two sets of notes below. Decide which set of notes would be the more useful (remember there is only one minute allowed for preparation in Part 2). What else could be said?

> Describe an ambition you have for the future.
>
> You should say:
>
> what this ambition is
> when you expect to be able to achieve it
> how it will change your life in the future
>
> and explain why this ambition is important to you.

A

Ambition = own business (give details)
When? 5 yrs (studying 7 yrs)
Change = responsibility, decisions, long hours
BUT earning!
Why important? Work for myself, please parents, …

B

I'd like to set up a business of my own. I'll achieve this within 5 years. By then, I'll have been studying for 7 years. It will change my life because I'll be taking all the decisions. I'll be working long hours but I'll be earning a lot of money, hopefully. This ambition is important to me becau

9 Now spend exactly one minute making notes about your own future ambition. Then give your talk to a partner, who will time you. Try to keep talking for two minutes. Use some of the adverbs in exercise 3 and a range of future forms (see B's notes above).

Test folder 7

Matching

(Academic Reading, General Training Reading and Listening Modules)

You may be asked to match questions with options from a box in all three modules. In the General Training Reading Module *only*, you may need to match questions with parts of the passage.

In the Listening Module, the questions follow the order of what you hear. In the Reading Modules they don't.

Sometimes there are more options than questions, and you must choose a different option each time.

Sometimes there are more questions than options, and you will see the instruction '**NB** You may use any letter more than once'.

If you have to write any words, they must be spelt correctly to gain marks.

Advice

Reading Modules
- Skim the whole passage before you start working on any of the tasks. Then read the instructions and the task carefully. It may help to underline the key words in the questions.
  Matching questions with options in a box
- If the options in the box are names, underline them in the text.
- Read the first option in the box and then find the part of the passage that mentions it. Read what is written about it. Look through the questions. If you find one that matches what is in the passage, write your answer. If nothing matches, it may be one that you don't need to use, so go on to the next option.
- You might find it helpful to underline the part of the text that contains the answer.
- Remember that the words in the questions or in the box may be paraphrases of words in the passage.
  Matching questions with parts of the reading passage (GT only)
- Read each part of the passage in turn, and see which of the questions match it before going on to the next part of the passage.

Listening Module
- Read the task before you listen.
- If you miss an answer, stop thinking about it when you hear the speaker going on to talk about the next question, or you'll miss that one too.

All modules
- Check that all your answers are different, unless you read the instruction '**NB** You may use any letter more than once'.
- Always give an answer – you won't lose any marks if it's wrong.

Listening

Wolf Creek Crater, Australia

1 🎧 You might find a task like this in Section 4 of the Listening Module.

What does the lecturer say about each meteorite or crater?
*Choose your answers from the box and write the letters **A–I** next to questions 1–6.*

A	crater first identified from the air
B	it was used to prove where meteorites come from
C	meteorite damaged by humans
D	meteorite destroyed part of forest
E	meteorite has become tourist attraction
F	meteorite landed in uninhabited region
G	meteorites sometimes revealed by natural forces
H	story invented about it
I	thought to be largest known crater

Example: Ensisheim
Answer: ....C....
(The speaker says *people began chipping off pieces*.)

1 Krasnojarsk   ....
2 Antarctica   ....
3 Cape York   ....
4 Siberia   ....
5 Vredefort Crater   ....
6 Wolf Creek Crater   ....

Reading

2 This passage is similar to those in the Academic Reading Module and Section 3 of the General Training Reading. It is about 600 words long.

Understanding the Milky Way

The Solar System in which the Earth is situated is part of the Milky Way galaxy, the pale band of light crossing the night sky. This is one of a vast number of galaxies in the universe, each consisting of billions of stars (such as our Sun) bound together by gravity. The ancient Greek philosophers speculated on the nature of the Milky Way, and around 2,500 years ago Pythagoras appears to have believed that it was composed of a vast number of faint stars. The astronomer Hipparchus is thought to have created the earliest known catalogue of the stars in the 2nd century BC. But it was only with the development of the telescope in the 17th century, making far more stars visible, that the nature of the Milky Way could really begin to be understood. When Galileo first turned his telecope on the sky, in 1609, he found proof that, as Pythagoras had suggested, the Milky Way indeed consisted of innumerable stars.

The idea that the Milky Way is a vast disc-shaped aggregation of stars comprising all the stars seen by the naked eye or with a telescope was first put forward by Thomas Wright in 1750. William Herschel and his sister Caroline set out to map the structure of the Milky Way by counting the numbers of stars they could see in different directions. Their efforts were severely hampered by the dimming effect of the dust between the stars. William Herschel at first believed that there were other galaxies besides the Milky Way, a theory that had been advanced earlier by Christopher Wren. However he later came round to the view that the universe consisted solely of the Milky Way system, and by the end of the 19th century this was the prevailing view.

In the early 20th century the Dutch astronomer Jacobus Kapteyn used star-counts to derive a model of the Milky Way in which the sun lay close to the centre of a huge disc, a mistake that Herschel had also made. This work, like Herschel's, was flawed by neglect of the role of interstellar dust, which Edward Barnard was beginning to uncover. In a 1922 debate in the USA, Harlow Shapley argued that the Milky Way included all known structures in the universe, while Heber Curtis advocated the theory that other galaxies existed. The core of the debate was the issue of the size of the Milky Way system. Shapley arrived at a size about three times too great. Curtis, on the other hand, used Kapteyn's star-counts to derive a size about three times too small. In both cases it was interstellar dust which caused the error.

An important development in our understanding of the galaxy came in 1933, when Karl Jansky detected radio waves from the Milky Way. He was working for Bell Telephone Labs on the problem of the hiss on transatlantic telephone lines. He built an antenna to try to locate the origin of this noise, and found to his surprise that it arose from the Milky Way. Radio astronomy made a new start in 1942, during World War II, when John Hey started monitoring German jamming of British radar. For two days there was a remarkably intense episode of radar jamming which knocked out all the coastal radar stations. Hey realised that the direction of the jamming followed the sun, and learnt from the Royal Greenwich Observatory that an exceptionally active sunspot had crossed the solar disc at that time. Hey had discovered radio emission from the sun.

Look at the following descriptions (1–9) and the list of people below.
Match each description with the appropriate person.

Examples:

A Pythagoras: *mentioned twice in the first paragraph. Description 4 might at first seem to apply to him, but although he **believed** the Milky Way to be made up of a large number of stars, there is nothing in the passage to suggest he found evidence for this. **A** is not the answer to any of the questions.*

B Hipparchus: *mentioned in the first paragraph. 'Created the earliest known catalogue of the stars' matches description 7.*

1 changed his mind about the number of galaxies in the universe ....
2 discovered noise coming from the Milky Way ....
3 overestimated the size of the Milky Way ....
4 was the first to find evidence that the Milky Way is made up of a large number of stars ....
5 identified an effect of solar activity ....
6 originated the idea that every visible star is part of the Milky Way ....
7 identified and listed a number of stars *B*
8 found that dust between stars affected understanding of the Milky Way ....
9 first proposed the idea that there are a number of galaxies ....

List of People		
A Pythagoras	**B** Hipparchus	**C** Galileo
D Thomas Wright	**E** William Herschel	**F** Christopher Wren
G Jacobus Kapteyn	**H** Edward Barnard	**I** Harlow Shapley
J Heber Curtis	**K** Karl Jansky	**L** John Hey

Trends in society

1 What do the charts suggest about the future demography of Australia? What implications does this have for Australian society?

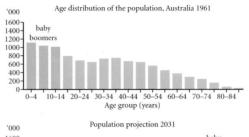

Age distribution of the population, Australia 1961

Population projection 2031

Reading

2 Read this article quickly, to confirm your ideas.

⏱ about 625 words

THE LEGACY OF THE BABY BOOM IN AUSTRALIA

The period from the end of the Second World War in 1945 until around the mid-1960s has come to be known as the *baby boom* in Australia and in several other countries such as New Zealand, Canada and the USA. After the war, these were all relatively prosperous, industrially advanced countries with rapidly expanding economies, enhanced living standards and serious labour shortages. In 1961, the total fertility rate in Australia peaked at 3.6 babies per woman. Twenty years later, it had fallen to half that level and has continued to decline, though at a much slower rate.

Based on assumptions of continued low fertility, combined with the fact that people are generally living longer with each generation, Australia's population is projected to continue ageing. Between 2011 and 2031, baby boomers will make a significant contribution to the number of people aged 65 years and over. During this period, the population aged 65 and over is projected to grow from 3 to 5 million. By 2031, all surviving baby boomers will be between 65 and 84 years of age. In the years immediately beyond this, baby boomers are projected to swell the population aged 85 and over from 612,000 to 1.1 million.

Structural ageing has many implications for society. In 2031, if not before, 27% of all Australians of voting age (18 years and over) will be aged 65 or older. This has implications both for the level of social expenditure that might be required in future and the level of resources that might be available to fund it. For example, as the population aged 65 and over increases in size, associated social expenditure on income support and health services can be expected to increase. However, since the potential labour force is projected to expand at a slower rate from 2011, it may be more difficult to generate the level of resources and public support needed to maintain a large aged population with an acceptable standard of living and quality of life.

In addition to changing demographics, there are many other factors, both social and economic, which could also have an important bearing on future levels of social expenditure and how it is distributed. Future rates of economic growth, productivity improvements and taxation levels will affect the level of resources potentially available. At the same time, the circumstances of future older generations, such as labour force participation, level of private income and asset holdings, health status, and availability of family and community support networks, will influence the extent to which resources will be needed for care of the elderly, health, housing and income support.

On the other hand, future trends in education, labour force participation, unemployment rates and income distribution among the younger age groups will influence the level and nature of competing demands such as university spending, employment programmes, unemployment benefits and support for low-income families.

Changes in social values, attitudes and government policy will also have an impact on the level of support provided for older people, as well as shaping the respective roles of government, private business, community groups, families and individuals in providing it. While much of the current research and policy on ageing tends to focus on the potential 'burden' to society of a large older population, the likely economic stimulus created by a growing market for home help, specialised housing, and financial advice has been largely overlooked. Better educated and more affluent than their parents' generation, baby boomers are currently an influential market sector and could remain so well into their retirement years. In addition, as the population ages, it is to be expected that public debate and government policy on ageing will be increasingly influenced by the views of older people.

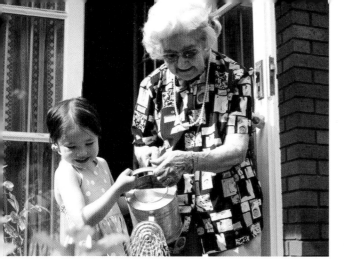

3 Now read the article again and carry out the tasks below.

Questions 1–5

Classify the following information as referring to

A 1961
B 2011
C 2031

*Write the correct letter, **A**, **B** or **C**.*

1 more than a quarter of the Australian electorate over 65
2 highest recorded number of births per female
3 3 million aged 65 or older
4 the elderly (85+) exceed 1 million soon after this
5 less growth in the numbers seeking employment

Questions 6–10

Complete the sentences below with words taken from the passage.
*Use **NO MORE THAN TWO WORDS** for each answer.*

6 The declining proportion of younger age groups in society and consequent increase in older age groups is known as ....

7 There are likely to be higher levels of public spending on .... and medical care.

8 Future developments affecting the young are expected to have an effect on .... for resources.

9 Researchers and policy makers have tended to see a larger older population as a ....

10 One aspect that has been forgotten is the .... to the economy caused by an increased demand for care and other services.

Vocabulary Adjective–noun collocations

4 Check your understanding of these nouns and noun phrases from the reading passage.

1 *living standards* (line 7)
2 *labour shortages* (lines 7–8)
3 *social expenditure* (line 31)
4 *standard of living* (line 36)
5 *roles* (line 59)
6 *market sector* (line 68)

5 In the reading passage, underline the adjective that comes before each noun or noun phrase above.

6 Where possible, choose an adjective from the box that has a similar meaning to each adjective you have underlined.

acute	corresponding	crucial	declining
frivolous	inadequate	ineffectual	negligible
powerful	related	~~rising~~	satisfactory
thriving	unconnected		

EXAMPLE: *enhanced* (living standards) – *rising*

7 Which of the remaining adjectives in the box mean the *opposite* of the underlined adjectives in the passage? One underlined adjective doesn't have an opposite. Some adjectives aren't needed.

EXAMPLE: *enhanced – declining*

Speaking *Part 3*

8 You are going to hear a strong IELTS candidate being asked the questions below by an examiner. Before you listen, discuss each question with a partner.

- Can you explain why the birth rate is falling in many countries?
- What impact does an ageing population have on society?
- Should the state provide completely free care for the elderly?
- In the future, will working people have to retire at a later age than they currently do?
- What can young people learn from their grandparents and great-grandparents?
- Why are people generally living longer nowadays, in your opinion?

9 As you listen, notice how the candidate uses the language below.

I'm not an expert, but ...	Yes, in theory ... but in practice ...
I read somewhere that ...	I suppose so.
That's a real possibility.	Speaking personally ...
It has many implications.	That's crucial.
There's a question mark over ...	

1 Identify some of the ways in which life in your country has changed since your grandparents were children.

Listening

2 You are going to hear an extract from a lecture about social change and what causes it. The lecture is in two parts.

 Questions 1–5

According to the lecturer, what impact on society (**A–G**) did each event (**1–5**) have?
Choose your answers from the box.

A Agricultural production improved.

B Newcomers were absorbed into the receiving community.

C People gained a better understanding of the cultures of other countries.

D Tensions arose between communities.

E The receiving community adopted some aspects of the newcomers' culture.

F There was a lack of development in the local community.

G There was an increase in social equality.

1 the Irish potato famine
2 immigration to the UK by French Protestants
3 immigration to the UK from Asia
4 the increase in air travel
5 the First World War

 Questions 6–10
*Choose the correct letter **A**, **B** or **C**.*

6 What is the speaker's opinion of political factors in social change in Britain?
   A They have tended to have little impact.
   B They are more significant than economic factors.
   C Their significance is less than is usually claimed.

7 Many people moved to towns in the 19th century because of
   A a decline in agricultural production.
   B the availability of a wider choice of housing.
   C changes in how goods were made.

8 One result of education becoming compulsory was that
   A more women went out to work.
   B people had a greater choice of jobs.
   C changes took place in family structure.

9 What has been an effect of people moving into the countryside recently?
   A More and more facilities are provided in rural areas.
   B Rural life is far more oriented towards towns than in the past.
   C There are tensions between traditional village dwellers and new residents.

10 What does the lecturer regard as the main characteristic of an 'urban village'?
   A The area has a clear boundary.
   B People know each other.
   C The housing is of a low standard.

Style extra

3 In the following spoken examples, the lecturer is signalling the level of detail he is going to go into:

I now want to look briefly at ...
Just to give you an idea of ...

In the written examples below, from the *Cambridge Academic Corpus*, is the writer

a signalling brief or concise treatment of content?
b referring to information coming later?
c explaining a content omission?

1 In a nutshell, it is impossible to prove or disprove the theory at present.
2 Such considerations are beyond the scope of this work.
3 In short, this is an interesting and densely written book, but it has problems.
4 Some of these articles receive only very cursory coverage here.
5 These developments are considered in more depth in Chapter 10.
6 I have written extensively on this subject elsewhere, so do not propose to give it any space whatsoever.
7 However, as discussed in more detail in the Appendix, in two classes students worked in pairs rather than individually.

Grammar Pronouns clinic

4 All the words in *italics* in these extracts from the recording are pronouns. Explain what they refer to in each case.

1 We'll be looking at some of the causes of social change around the world, and we'll have one or two examples of *each*.
2 The Irish potato famine of the 1840s led vast numbers of individuals and whole families to emigrate from rural areas of Ireland to cities, particularly in Britain and the USA. As is usually the case, *those* who went away were the most active and ambitious.
3 Immigrants usually make a massive contribution to the culture of the receiving country, and Britain has benefited a great deal from *this* over the centuries.
4 New methods of production meant that, for the first time, most items were manufactured in big factories, instead of in people's homes, and *these* required a large number of workers living nearby.
5 Just to give you an idea of how one change can lead to a succession of *others*, ...
6 ... the nuclear family – that is, *one* consisting of husband, wife and children.

5 Reference pronouns are used a lot in academic writing, but the *Cambridge Learner Corpus* shows that they can be problematic for IELTS candidates. In the essay extract below, replace the underlined phrases with suitable pronouns, and use a relative clause where marked.

Today's students have to deal with a number of problems. <u>The problems</u> include an acute shortage of affordable accommodation and rising debt. To supplement their finances, students are often forced to work long hours and <u>working long hours</u> will more often than not affect the quality of their college work. Even if the students manage to get a good degree, <u>the students</u> then face declining job prospects. <relative> <u>Job prospects</u> are particularly poor for <u>the students</u> in arts and humanities.

G ⋯⋗ page 142

6 Correct the errors that IELTS candidates have made with pronouns in these sentences.

1 This is the basic requirement in both big companies and small one.
2 The number then declined sharply to 42 million holidays with a total of 8 million of it taken abroad.
3 Combined efforts by the government and the individuals itself could make it possible for everyone to learn how to use a computer.
4 When the woman works, she gets a salary, which makes herself independent.
5 Somebody claim there should be no government restrictions but other disagree.
6 In contrast, 70% of males got a postgraduate diploma, it was more than twice the number of females.
7 For their who do not have the strength to work until 65 years, it would be best to retire.

Writing folder 7

Task 2 Appropriate style and tone

For both parts of the Writing Module, the language you use must be consistently appropriate in style and tone. The Cambridge Learner Corpus shows that IELTS candidates are not always able to do this, especially for Task 2.

1 Tick the features you consider appropriate to academic writing from this list.

- ☐ impersonal style
- ☐ aggressive tone
- ☐ colloquial language
- ☐ neutral to formal language
- ☐ serious tone
- ☐ informal language
- ☐ humorous style

2 Read the task and the answer below. Underline examples in the answer of any inappropriate features listed in exercise 1.

Write about the following topic.

> *Because of falling birth rates and better healthcare, the world's population is getting steadily older and this trend is going to cause serious problems for society.*
> *To what extent do you agree or disagree with this statement?*

Give reasons for your answer and include any relevant examples from your own knowledge or experience.

Write at least 250 words.

I cannot agree with your views concerning an ageing population, which I find totally ridiculous and untenable. You really should not paint a picture of the future that is as negative as this! I mean we'll all be old one day, won't we?

It is true without a doubt that folks are living longer, due to a healthier diet, rising living standards and better medical treatment. And they say we're all gonna be even older in the future! Apart from leading to huge sales of false teeth and walking sticks, what will be the main issues of having a larger percentage of older people in our society? First and foremost, it'll cost a packet in terms of looking after the elderly and forking out for their pension payments. Such an imbalance in the population will place an added burden on younger people, through higher taxation levels and more substantial family commitments. Do you think we'll all have to slave away until we're 90? It is highly likely, given the current statistics.

As for there being fewer babies on the scene, that's certainly the case in my country at the moment. However, governments should not be encouraging people to have larger numbers of kids, because our planet is already packed out.

In the final analysis, it will be up to all of us to support each other, whether through additional taxation or by showing a greater awareness of the different generations at a personal level. Some aspects of daily life that are currently taken for granted may have to change fundamentally. For example, instead of enjoying their much-deserved retirement, grandparents could find themselves taking on the role of main childcarers while the parents work longer hours to maintain their family's standard of living.

Come on, it won't be that bad!

3 Choose phrases from those below to replace some of the inappropriate language in the second and third paragraphs. There may be more than one possible choice.

children
continue to be employed
contributing to
declining birth rate
funding
lower fertility
overpopulated
people
projected to continue ageing
remain in the job market
result in increased expenditure

4 Cross out any inappropriate language remaining in these paragraphs and then rewrite the paragraphs, using the phrases from exercise 3 and making any other changes necessary.

5 The first paragraph of the answer in exercise 2 is unusable. Complete the new opening sentence below with some of these words. Two aren't needed.

actually   corresponding   impossible   provided   questionable   unlikely

Although it is 1 .... to argue with the facts 2 .... in the first half of the statement, it remains 3 .... whether society is 4 .... under threat due to its ageing population.

Now add the necessary verb forms to the sentence below, which completes the replacement first paragraph.

Nonetheless, it 5 .... (negative modal passive + *deny*) that radical social reform 6 .... (future passive + *require*) in the near future.

6 Read the examiner comments under the final sentence. Then write a replacement sentence to include at the end of the fourth paragraph.

Come on, it won't be that bad!

This light-hearted ending in very informal language is completely inappropriate and leaves a very negative effect on the reader. A pity, because the fourth paragraph contains elements of a conclusion and just needs a suitable closing sentence. Throughout the answer, the language is inconsistent and there is an unhappy mix of styles. There are some good ideas, but only a few have been expressed in academic English.

7 Now answer the task below, following the advice given.

Write about the following topic.

There are fewer and fewer employment opportunities for graduates entering the job market and this will have serious implications for higher education.
To what extent do you agree or disagree with this statement?

Give reasons for your answer and include any relevant examples from your own knowledge or experience.

Write at least 250 words.

Advice
- Underline key words in the task and think of appropriate paraphrases.
- Make a plan, putting each new point in a new paragraph.
- State your overall opinion in the first paragraph.
- Use an impersonal style unless you are mentioning your own experience.
- Produce consistently neutral to formal language.
- Maintain a serious tone throughout.
- Develop and exemplify each of your main points.
- Restate your opinion in a conclusion.
- Leave enough time to check your answer for grammatical accuracy and stylistic consistency.

Risk and reality

1 In small groups, list some of the risks that we take in everyday life.

Reading

2 Skim the passage, and think about how far it reflects your own attitude towards risk.

⏱ about 700 words

How rational are we when we assess risks?

A One of the many design faults in humans is our startling unwillingness to measure consequences. We become so mesmerised by one particular risk that we cannot see beyond it. So, for instance, convinced that our children are in perpetual danger from strangers (though statistically the risks are tiny), we refuse to let our kids walk to school and instead trigger obesity, which is far more likely to harm them.

B And what happened after the Hatfield rail crash in the UK in 2000, which killed four people? The cause was identified as a broken rail and an immediate slowdown was ordered on 500 sections of suspect track. Frustrated by delays, a third of rail passengers switched to the roads, where the accident rate per kilometre is 12 times that of rail. The resulting growth in road traffic probably resulted in five additional fatalities – compared with only six caused by broken rails over the last 30 years. Meanwhile, train drivers operating on a railway with no timetable were having to consult up to 16 pages of special directions on speed instructions, increasing the likelihood of passing a signal at red – 10 times more likely to result in death than a broken rail.

C Then there are seatbelts. If you have the misfortune to be in a crash, there is no doubt that a seat belt will reduce your risk of dying, but overall, there has been no discernible effect of seatbelt legislation on fatalities for car drivers and passengers. Why not? Because no one foresaw the consequences of people changing their behaviour once they were securely belted up – driving faster and more recklessly. Similarly, sports researchers have found that protective aids, such as body armour, lead to more injuries because players take greater risks.

D Human behaviour is fuelled by perceptions, not the 'facts' or what scientists present as 'real' risks. Research has identified several ways in which we perceive and assess risk, including the following.

E In many areas of technology, such as nuclear power generation, major accidents involving safety system failures can have catastrophic effects, and risk is seen as a fatal threat. Such an event could, theoretically, occur at any time, although the likelihood of its occurrence is extremely low. A look at the perception of rare random events shows, however, that probability plays hardly any role at all in how people perceive danger: it is the random nature of the event that poses the feeling of threat.

F Natural disasters like earthquakes are usually seen as unavoidable events with catastrophic effects, but because they are natural, they are beyond control – unlike accidents caused by human error. In such cases, the relative rarity of the event provides psychological reinforcement for risk denial, as shown by the large numbers of people who choose not to move away from earthquake zones.

G When, despite the considerable risk, people climb the world's highest mountains without breathing apparatus, or throw themselves off a cliff-top with nothing more than a pair of artificial wings to save them, and do so in the name of sport, the meaning of risk takes on a new dimension. The attraction of such activities is the fact that they involve risk. People take risks in order to test their own strength and to triumph over natural forces.

H In recent times, reports on environmental pollution and its long-term impact on health, life and nature have forced scientific risk assessment to adopt a role as early warning indicators. In this risk perception model, scientific studies contribute to the early detection of lurking danger and the discovery of causal relationships between activities or events and their latent effects. This definition of risk is used, for example, in assessing food additives and genetic modification of plants and animals.

I Probability and severity of adverse effects are not the only – and certainly not the most important – components that people use as yardsticks for perceiving and evaluating risks. There are also the emotional distortions mentioned above. The question is, should officials take these into account when making decisions about genetically modified crops, or the siting of a new airport, or try to change them by providing more information?

3 Think about the title and the four subheadings in the notes below to help you do the following task.

Questions 1–10
Complete the notes below.

*Choose **NO MORE THAN TWO WORDS** from the reading passage for each answer.*

How rational are we when we assess risks?

<u>Problem:</u>
- people's **1** .... to consider effects of actions

<u>Examples of unexpected effects:</u>
- driving children to school leads to increase in **2** ....
- response to Hatfield rail crash probably caused five extra **3** .... on roads
- protection for sports players has increased number of **4** ....

<u>Ways of perceiving risk include:</u>
- fearing fatal threats that are very unlikely, because their occurrence is **5** ....
- minimising risk of natural disasters because they are not the result of **6** ....
- taking personal risks when seen as **7** ....
- using scientific assessment with the intention of providing **8** .... of potential harmful effects of new processes.

<u>Conclusions:</u>
- People's assessment of risk is affected by **9** ....
- **10** .... need to find a response to irrational assessments of risk

Questions 11–15
*The passage has nine paragraphs labelled **A–I**.*
Which paragraph contains the following information?
*Write the correct letter **A–I**.*

11 why people may deliberately seek out risks
12 a form of assessment that overestimates risks
13 a suggestion that the response to a specific event was over-cautious
14 a type of risk that is generally disregarded
15 how safety measures can have unexpected effects on risk-taking behaviour

Pronunciation *Intonation*

4 In pairs, discuss this question: how do people speak when they feel happy or enthusiastic, and when they feel sad or bored?

5 🎧 Intonation is a way of communicating mood and meaning. Listen to these four short exchanges. In all of them the second speaker says *Yes*, but the speakers mean different things. Decide what they are doing when they say *Yes*, from the functions a–e.

a expressing uncertainty
b inviting another person to speak (possibly by asking a question), or saying something incomplete
c expressing enthusiasm
d making a statement, saying something complete or definite
e showing lack of interest

1 .....   2 .....   3 .....   4 .....   5 .....

6 🎧 Listen to the exchanges again, and decide which of the intonation patterns f–j is used for *Yes* in each one. You may find it helpful to imitate the second speakers.

f (rise)   **g** (fall-rise)   **h** (level)   **i** (fall)   **j** (rise-fall)

1 .....   2 .....   3 .....   4 .....   5 .....

Speaking *Part 3*

7 🎧 Listen to this person answering a question in Part 3 of the Speaking Module. You will hear him twice. Does the speaker sound more interested in what he is saying the first or the second time? He is answering the question: *Could you describe any risks that you take in your hobbies?*

(Potholing is a sport that involves climbing in and around underground caves.)

8 In small groups, discuss these questions. Make sure you use intonation to sound interested.

- What is your attitude towards taking risks at work or in your hobbies?
- Evaluate the importance of considering the risks before choosing a means of travelling.
- Explain the attitudes of people in your country towards nuclear and non-nuclear power stations.

Useful language

to take a risk	to run the risk of	a dilemma
a drawback	fossil fuels	side-effects
likewise	on the other hand	as a consequence/result

1 What different forms can classes at college or university take?

Listening

2 🎧 Listen to a university teacher talking about a number of sessions that will take place during two study days on Philosophy.

In what form will each of the following sessions begin?

A lecture by one person
B seminar with a teacher
C small-group workshop without a teacher

*Write the correct letter, **A**, **B** or **C**.*

Example: 'Language and how we see the world'
Answer: ..A..

> The speaker says 'I'll spend the first half hour giving you an overview of the main theories, and then we'll divide into discussion groups.' So the class will *begin* as a lecture by one person.

1 'Is it ever right to break the law?' ....
2 'Political ideologies' ....
3 'Philosophy in medicine' ....
4 'What is time?' ....
5 'The philosophy of coincidence' ....

3 Which of these factors form part of the definition of a coincidence?

> A at least two events occur
> B each event is unusual
> C the events are closely related in time
> D both events have the same cause
> E people are surprised
> F there doesn't seem to be a rational explanation

Can you think of some coincidences that you've experienced?

4 Match the three examples of apparent coincidences and their explanations (1–3 below) to the correct option, A, B, or C in exercise 5.

1 *Coincidence:* If you ask ten people to choose a whole number between 1 and 100, it's quite likely that two of them will pick the same number. *Explanation:* The odds are more than one in three that this will happen, but most people wrongly assume that there's only a one in ten chance.
2 *Coincidence:* Children with larger hands are better readers than children with smaller hands. *Explanation:* As children get older, their hands grow and their reading improves.
3 *Coincidence:* You talk about someone you haven't seen for years, and they phone you the next day. *Explanation:* There are millions of opportunities for coincidence in each of our lives, so some are bound to happen. We notice the ones that do, but not those that don't.

5 🎧 Now listen to part of a seminar about coincidences.

What explanation is given for us finding the following situations (questions 1–5) surprising?
A We do not consider the true cause of the events.
B We underestimate the mathematical chances of the events coinciding.
C We ignore other events which don't seem like coincidences.

*Write the correct letter, **A**, **B** or **C**.*

1 two children in a class having the same birthday
2 receiving correct predictions of football results
3 accurately describing someone's personality
4 an increase in people eating ice cream and in attacks by sharks
5 someone winning a lottery twice

Vocabulary Abstract nouns

> Nouns can be either *concrete* or *abstract*. Concrete nouns refer to physical objects, such as *house*, and are usually (but not always) countable. Abstract nouns refer to something abstract or mental, such as *hope*. They tend to be uncountable, and are particularly common in academic English.

6 In each pair of sentences 1–3, an abstract noun (in *italics*) is countable in one sentence and uncountable in the other, with slightly different meanings. Which one is countable and which is uncountable? How does the word differ in meaning in each pair of sentences?

  1 a We become mesmerised by a *risk*, such as children being attacked on the way to school.
    b Research has identified several ways in which we perceive and assess *risk*.

  2 a Some people have a *perception* of academic study in which sciences are much more serious and demanding than arts.
    b Few people show outstanding powers of *perception*.

  3 a It is often difficult to distinguish a decision which was good but turns out to be a *failure* from a bad decision.
    b During its first five years, the company seemed doomed to *failure*.

7 Complete these two rules by circling the right alternative in each case.

  a Abstract nouns are generally *countable/ uncountable* when they refer to the concept in general.
  b Abstract nouns are generally *countable/ uncountable* when they refer to specific examples of the concept.

8 Now decide whether or not to put *a(n)* in each space. You might find it helpful to use an English–English dictionary.

  1 The ruins had become ... danger to visitors, so access was restricted.
  2 With so much construction going on, the city seems to have ... transitional nature.
  3 Linguists can measure the degree of ... attraction between two words that often collocate, such as 'lend' and 'money'.
  4 The sudden resignation of the financial director forced the company to make ... appointment very quickly.
  5 The prime minister issued ... denial of the report that she was about to resign.
  6 Some philosophers attempt to relate urban culture to the laws of ... nature.
  7 We are in ... danger of not meeting government safety requirements.
  8 The opportunity to travel is ... major attraction of my new job.
  9 We need to make ... modification to the engine so that it uses less fuel.
  10 I have been trying to interest a manufacturer in my invention, but so far without ... success.

Style extra

9 Paragraphs A and B present the same ideas in slightly different ways, where B is in a more academic style. Read paragraph A, then complete paragraph B using nouns related to the corresponding verb or adjective in A.

A

What is reality?

Normally when we are conscious we naïvely accept that the objects around us exist and rarely reflect on how real they are. Like breathing, the nature of reality is something we do not normally have to consider. We can usually live through events and interact with objects without thinking of the fact that there could be significantly different ways of experiencing them. Only in fairly extreme circumstances, such as waking from a nightmare, do we become less certain about what is real and what might be illusion or fantasy. When we are fully conscious we typically try to avoid suspecting that reality may be more precarious than it seems.

B

During states of normal **0** ......*consciousness*...... we live in naïve **1** .... of the **2** .... of objects around us and rarely reflect on their reality. Like breathing, the nature of reality is something that normally does not require **3** .... We can usually live through events and interact with objects without giving any **4** .... to the fact that there could be significantly different ways of experiencing them. Only in fairly extreme circumstances, such as waking from a nightmare, do we experience less **5** .... about what is real and what might be illusion or fantasy. When we are fully conscious, we typically try to avoid the **6** .... that reality may be more precarious than it seems.

10 Have you ever discovered that something you thought was real was actually a dream or illusion?

Am I dreaming?

Test folder 8

Locating information

(Academic Reading and General Training Reading Modules only)

You might be asked which paragraph or section of a passage contains certain information.

The answers only come from those paragraphs or sections that are labelled alphabetically.

The information in the questions doesn't come in the same order as in the passage.

The questions generally say what *type* of information you must find, such as an explanation, an example, a recommendation, how, why, etc. They are not *paraphrases* of the information itself.

A Tale of Two Towns

How the entire social life of a community and the well-being of its members are dependent on their interpretation of a particular situation

A There were once two small communities that had very different ways of seeing the world. They had this problem in common, however: both were hard hit by recession, so that in each of the towns about one hundred people were unemployed. They tried hard to find work, but the situation did not improve.

B The town councillors of Town A had been brought up to believe that there is always enough work for everyone, if you look hard enough. Comforting themselves with this doctrine, they could have turned their backs on the problem, except for the fact that they were genuinely kind-hearted people. They felt they had to prevent the unemployed from suffering, but their principles told them that if people were given something for nothing, it would ruin their moral character. This made the councillors very unhappy, because they were faced with the horrible dilemma of letting the unemployed starve, or destroying their moral character.

C After much debate, they eventually decided to give the unemployed monthly 'relief payments'. To make sure these payments were not taken for granted, however, they decided that the 'relief' would be made so difficult and humiliating to obtain that there would be no temptation for anyone to go through the process unless it was absolutely necessary. Further, the moral disapproval of the community would be turned upon the recipients of the money, so that they would try hard to get 'off relief' and 'regain their self-respect'. The councillors expected those who received payments to be grateful, since they were getting something for nothing, something which they hadn't worked for.

D When the plan was put into operation, however, the recipients of the relief seemed ungrateful. They resented the cross-examinations by the 'relief investigators', who determined whether they should receive money. When they permitted themselves a rare luxury, such as going to the cinema, their neighbours who still had jobs looked at them sourly as if to say, 'I work hard and pay my taxes just to support loafers like you in idleness and pleasure', an attitude which increased their resentment. The relief policy averted starvation, but to the surprise and disappointment of the councillors it also led to quarrels, unhappy homes, class hatred and crime.

E The story of the other community, B-ville, was entirely different. One of the councillors explained that unemployment, like sickness and accidents, hits unexpectedly, irrespective of the victim's merits. He argued that B-ville homes, parks, and industries had been built in part by the work of the people who were now unemployed. He then suggested that if the work that these unemployed people had done for the community could be regarded as a form of 'insurance premium', payments now made to them could be regarded as 'insurance claims'. Eventually he convinced the other councillors.

F B-ville's 'claims adjusters' had a much better time than Town A's 'relief investigators'. The latter had been resentfully regarded as snoopers, because of their somewhat aggressive way of making their demands. The former, however, having no moral lesson to teach but simply a business transaction to carry out, treated their clients with business-like courtesy and found out as much as the relief investigators had, with considerably less difficulty.

G The councillors held a civic ceremony, at which the governor of the region presented the first insurance cheques. There were speeches, photographs, and cheering. All the recipients felt, therefore, that they had been personally honoured, and that they could face their unemployment with greater courage, since their community was behind them. All in all, B-ville's unemployed, unlike those in Town A, were not haunted by a sense of failure, did not turn to crime, did not manifest personal maladjustments, and did not develop class hatred, as the result of their monthly payment.

*The reading passage has seven paragraphs labelled **A–G**.*
Which paragraph contains the following information?
***NB** You may use any letter more than once.*

Example: Read paragraph A, then read the nine questions. Only number 4, *a similarity between the two towns*, matches the information in paragraph A.

1 reference to a claim that people are not to blame for becoming unemployed ....
2 an account of a difficult choice that some people had to make ....
3 what one town did to turn the giving of money into a special occasion ....
4 a similarity between the two towns ....*A*....
5 a contrast between different ways of gaining information ....
6 details of a policy for discouraging the unemployed from applying for money ....
7 an example of actions by the unemployed that aroused hostility ....
8 an outline of a proposal that took into account people's previous work ....
9 how a town's actions had unexpected consequences ....

The human mind

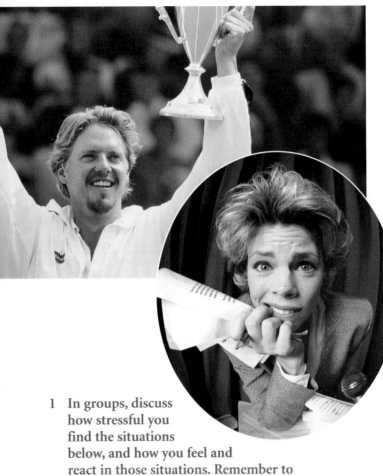

1 In groups, discuss how stressful you find the situations below, and how you feel and react in those situations. Remember to develop your comments.

- meeting new people
- being the centre of attention
- in a crisis
- not being able to find something important
- winning a competition
- when somebody else needs assistance

Speaking *Part 2*

2 With a partner, talk for at least one minute about the following topic.

> Describe how you behaved in a stressful situation.
>
> You should say:
> what the situation was
> how you behaved
> how other people might have behaved
>
> and explain how you felt about your behaviour afterwards.

Reading

3 **Questions 1–6**

*The reading passage has seven paragraphs **A–G**. Choose the correct heading for each paragraph from the list below.*

List of Headings
i   A degree of control
ii   Where research has been carried out into the effects of family on personality
iii Categorising personality features according to their origin
iv   A variety of reactions in similar situations
v   A link between personality and aspects of our lives that aren't chosen
vi   A possible theory that cannot be true
vii Measuring personality
viii Potentially harmful effects of emotions
ix   How our lives can reinforce our personalities
x   Differences between men's and women's personalities

Example:
0 Paragraph **A** ...*iv*....

1 Paragraph **B** ....
2 Paragraph **C** ....
3 Paragraph **D** ....
4 Paragraph **E** ....
5 Paragraph **F** ....
6 Paragraph **G** ....

⏱ about 650 words

What is *personality?*

A   We are all familiar with the idea that different people have different personalities, but what does this actually mean? It implies that different people behave in different ways,
5   but it must be more than that. After all, different people find themselves in different circumstances, and much of their behaviour follows from this fact. However, our common experience reveals that different people
10   respond in quite remarkably different ways even when faced with roughly the same circumstances. Alan might be happy to live alone in a quiet and orderly cottage, go out once a week, and stay in the same job for
15   thirty years, whilst Beth likes nothing better than exotic travel and being surrounded by vivacious friends and loud music.

Questions 7–13

Do the following statements reflect the claims of the writer?

Write

YES if the statement reflects the claims of the writer

NO if the statement contradicts the claims of the writer

NOT GIVEN if it is impossible to say what the writer thinks about this

7 Alan and Beth illustrate contrasting behaviour in similar situations.

8 As we grow older, we become more able to analyse our personalities.

9 Nervousness is an example of a learned characteristic.

10 The discovery of differences in temperament has changed the course of psychological research.

11 Adopted children provide evidence that we inherit more of our personality than we acquire.

12 The rational behaviour of different people shows greater similarity than their emotional behaviour.

13 Most psychologists agree on the five major dimensions of personality.

Vocabulary Synonyms

4 Replace each word or phrase in *italics* with a word from the passage which is similar in meaning. You may need to change the form of the word. (Some of the words in italics are also in the passage.)

1 (paragraph A) People can *react* quite differently to similar situations.

2 (paragraph B) To some extent, our behaviour in various situations is *controlled* by genetic factors.

3 (paragraph B) The *effects* of our decisions may not be those we had expected.

4 (paragraph C) The ability to use language appears to be an *innate* characteristic of human beings.

5 (paragraph D) Differences in people's emotional systems lead to considerable variation in their behaviour when facing a *difficult choice*.

6 (paragraph F) Artistic talent usually first *shows* itself when the artist is very young.

5 People's personalities are often described in one or two adjectives, for example we may say that somebody is *reserved and selfish*, or *considerate and conscientious*. How useful do you think it is to define personality in this way?

B In cases like these, we feel that it cannot be just the situation which is producing the differences in behaviour. Something about the way the person is 'wired up' seems to be at work, determining how they react to situations, and, more than that, the kind of situations they get themselves into in the first place. This is why personality seems to become stronger as we get older; when we are young, our situation reflects external factors such as the social and family environment we were born into. As we grow older, we are more and more affected by the consequences of our own choices (doing jobs that we were drawn to, surrounded by people like us whom we have sought out). Thus, personality differences that might have been very slight at birth become dramatic in later adulthood.

C Personality, then, seems to be the set of enduring and stable dispositions that characterise a person. These dispositions come partly from the expression of inherent features of the nervous system, and partly from learning. Researchers sometimes distinguish between temperament, which refers exclusively to characteristics that are inborn or directly caused by biological factors, and personality, which also includes social and cultural learning. Nervousness, for example, might be a factor of temperament, but religious piety is an aspect of personality.

D The discovery that temperamental differences are real is one of the major findings of contemporary psychology. It could easily have been the case that there were no intrinsic differences between people in temperament, so that given the same learning history, the same dilemmas, they would all respond in much the same way. Yet we now know that this is not the case.

E Personality measures turn out to be good predictors of your health, how happy you typically are – even your taste in paintings. Personality is a much better predictor of these things than social class or age. The origin of these differences is in part innate. That is to say, when people are adopted at birth and brought up by new families, their personalities are more similar to those of their blood relatives than to the ones they grew up with.

F Personality differences tend to manifest themselves through the quick, gut-feeling, intuitive and emotional systems of the human mind. The slower, rational, deliberate systems show less variation in output from person to person. Deliberate rational strategies can be used to override intuitive patterns of response, and this is how people wishing to change their personalities or feelings have to go about it. As human beings, we have the unique ability to look in at our personality from the outside and decide what we want to do with it.

G So what are the major ways personalities can differ? The dominant approach is to think of the space of possible personalities as being defined by a number of dimensions. Each person can be given a location in the space by their scores on all the different dimensions. Virtually all theories agree on two of the main dimensions, neuroticism (or negative emotionality) and extroversion (or positive emotionality). However they differ on how many additional ones they recognise. Among the most influential proposals are openness, conscientiousness and agreeableness. In the next section I shall examine these five dimensions.

Vocabulary Adjectives

1 The adjectives in the table are used in the lecture you are going to listen to. In small groups, make sure you understand those adjectives and also those in the box opposite. Then, under each heading in the table, write the adjectives from the box that have a similar meaning. Two adjectives fit under two headings.

certain	complicated
crucial	dissimilar
distinct	diverse
essential	exceptional
extraordinary	indispensable
intricate	involved
key	particular
remarkable	special
unlike	unusual

vital	specific	complex	different (from each other)	striking

Listening

2 🎧 Now listen to part of a lecture about what happens in our brains when we recognise something or someone. Answer the questions as you listen.

Scans show that electrical activity occurs in different areas of the brain, depending on what we are doing. The active regions are indicated here by the red, orange and yellow patches.

*Choose the correct letter, **A**, **B** or **C**.*

1 When people suffer from agnosia
   A they are normally unable to recognise man-made objects.
   B in each case the same area of the brain has been damaged.
   C the location of the brain damage determines what objects they cannot recognise.

2 The trombone is used to illustrate the claim that
   A where an object is remembered in the brain depends on our experience of it.
   B everything connected with music is remembered in a particular part of the brain.
   C we can only remember an object if we know what it is called.

3 Our recognition of a trombone
   A focuses on one of its qualities more than on the others.
   B combines recognition units from different parts of the brain.
   C suggests that everyone's concept of an object is identical.

4 Face recognition is an ability that
   A shows our similarity to other animals.
   B has developed because of its value to us.
   C becomes more useful as we grow older.

5 We recognise people we haven't seen for a long time if
   A they have an unusual face.
   B we have thought about them.
   C we have strong feelings about them.

6 Our first impressions of people are likely to
   A give an accurate insight into their personalities.
   B depend on how we feel immediately before seeing them.
   C be affected by our feelings towards other people.

Grammar Verb patterns

3 Study these examples of five of the patterns that can follow various verbs. Match each sentence (1–5) with the grammatical description (a–e) of the pattern that follows the verb in *italics*.

1 Psychologists *know* (that) we are born with certain characteristics, such as nervousness.
2 I *attempted* to carry out research into memory.
3 The success of the experiment *enabled* the student to complete her assignment.
4 The scientists at the conference were surprised when they *saw* some reporters arrive.
5 If you spend too long reading you *risk* being late for class.

> Verb followed by
> a object + *to* infinitive
> b object + bare infinitive
> c finite clause
> d *-ing* form
> e *to* infinitive

In academic writing, the pattern '+ object + *to be*' is particularly common after verbs such as *believe, consider, think*, for example
*Psychologists **believe** our personalities **to be** the product of both our genes and our life experiences.*
It is often used in the passive:
*Our personalities **are thought to be** the product of both our genes and our life experiences.*

G ⋯⟶ page 142

4 Complete each sentence with the correct ending a–g below. Consider both grammar and meaning.

1 Measuring someone's personality allows
2 The researcher considered
3 My research involves
4 Being rather cautious, my sister intends
5 People's odd reactions on seeing the man made
6 By observing people's behaviour for a week, I realised
7 The human brain has evolved in a way that enables

a to stay in the same job indefinitely.
b that there is a great deal of variation in even the most common situations.
c some of the criticism of her work to be wrong.
d us to predict how healthy they are likely to be.
e him wonder what was wrong.
f babies to recognise faces.
g making some very complicated calculations.

5 Correct the errors that IELTS candidates have made with verb patterns in these sentences. Make as few changes as possible. Two sentences are correct.

1 Life forced them to work and growing up before their time.
2 I am an outgoing person. I like talking to customers to make them feeling comfortable.
3 Nowadays, people seem have a better material life than before.
4 It is very good to let children to do some paid work.
5 I enjoy watching people doing a strenuous activity such as running.
6 Nowadays, lack of money makes that people to spend too much time working.
7 A good education enables them getting jobs in the future.
8 I would like to suggest you to build a small storeroom outside the house.
9 Should parents expect schools to teach children good behaviour?
10 I want that our newspaper to help me to solve this problem.

6 Complete each sentence with a verb from the box in the correct form. In some cases more than one answer is possible. You may use any verb more than once.

> argue   consider   contend   demonstrate
> encourage   intend   mean   miss   signify

1 The aim of the advertising campaign is to .... people to do more exercise.
2 By choosing fashionable brands, many users .... to show their sense of style.
3 The notion that each region of the brain has a separate mental function is now generally .... to be an oversimplification.
4 The speaker showed slides of brains of various species, in order to .... that all brains are symmetrical around a middle axis.
5 The authors use their opening chapter to .... that greater understanding of the brain is crucial.
6 The recent growth of service industries in some countries can be taken to .... that those nations now have a post-industrial economy.
7 Some children were playing football nearby, and I just .... being hit by the ball.

7 Would you like to have greater understanding of the causes of your own and other people's behaviour? Why, or why not?

Writing folder 8

Errors clinic

To achieve an IELTS Band 7, there should only be 'occasional inaccuracies' in your writing, and even for Band 6, you must show generally good control. Therefore, it is important to check both your answers carefully. This Writing folder deals with some typical errors made by IELTS candidates in spelling, word order and grammar, as shown by the *Cambridge Learner Corpus*.

Spelling

Double consonants

- Doubling can occur to differentiate the pronunciation of a preceding vowel, for example *later/latter*, so if you are unsure of the spelling, think how you would say the word aloud.
- Many English words that have double consonants near the beginning of the word come from Latin, and the double consonant is the result of a Latin prefix, for example *a*d*dress*, *o*p*pose*. Here are these patterns, together with some common IELTS spelling errors.

Latin prefix	English spelling	error	correct spelling
ad	abb, acc, add, aff, agg, all,	~~agressive~~	aggressive
	amm, ann, app, arr, ass, att	~~atracted~~	attracted
con	coll, comm, conn, corr	~~comercial~~	commercial
in	ill, imm, inn, irr	~~imigration~~	immigration
ob	occ, off, opp	~~oportunity~~	opportunity
sub	succ, suff, sugg, supp, surr	~~suported~~	supported

- However, many English words do not have double consonants in the first syllable.

1 Neatly cross out the extra letter in these errors made by IELTS candidates. One word is correctly spelled.

   0 rec¢ommend   3 wellfare   6 oppinion
   1 appologise   4 proffessional   7 tallented
   2 dissappear   5 different   8 refference

- When making comparative/superlative forms of adjectives, and adding -*ing* and -*ed* endings to verbs, remember that the final consonant may be doubled, as in *hot > hotter/hottest*, *begin > beginning*, *stop > stopped*. This usually occurs if the final consonant follows a short vowel.

Vowel combinations

2 Correct the spelling in these IELTS errors in a neat and legible way. If necessary, cross out the word and rewrite it in full. One word is correct.

   EXAMPLE: *extremely*

   0 ~~extreamly~~   3 beatiful   6 enormous
   1 acheived   4 belive   7 variety
   2 recieved   5 collegue   8 throughout

Missing letters

3 Errors commonly occur when a letter is silent, as in *dou*b*t*, or at the end of words. Insert the missing letter in these common IELTS errors, in the way shown.

   EXAMPLE: 0 ex[c]ellent   ex[c]iting

   1 enviroment   goverment
   2 tecnology   wich
   3 othewise   furthemore
   4 shoud   woud
   5 therefor   becaus
   6 approximatly   sincerly

Suffixes

4 Correct the spelling in these IELTS errors in a neat and legible way. If necessary, cross out the word and rewrite it in full.

1 hopefull	5 relevence
2 emptines	6 immediatley
3 expensiv	7 dramaticaly
4 successfull	8 predictablity

Word order

- Check your word order carefully, especially in questions or *wh-* clauses, or with adverbs. If you need to make a correction, try to do it neatly.

5 Correct the word order errors in these sentences, using one of the two methods below.

EXAMPLE: 0 *But what exactly ⟨happiness⟩is⟩?*

00 *Is it*
It is just a hoax or do you need to stop it happening again?

1 We always must look at the good side of everything that we do.
2 The spending slightly dropped to less than £10m.
3 The concept of the joint family exists rarely.
4 More flights will create certainly more noise.
5 In some families, parents give money to their children, but without any advice on how to carefully use it.
6 It seems that Japanese customs have been changing since around 1920 little by little.

6 Read this paragraph written by an IELTS candidate and correct the word order and spelling errors.

The isue of whether it is proper for children to work as under-aged workers is, in my opinion, not a streightforward one. I belive it can be a good experience as long as they are capable of doing the work. Most children come from poor families who do paid work. They work to help their parents to suport their lives, education or healt. These children will grow up as tough people mentally because they lern a lot of lessons about how humans live their lives. For example, they won't give up easily doing their jobs and they won't feel down so deeply when something dissapoints them. Furthemore, most of them become strong physically and they even may have fewer problems latter in their lives.

Grammar

Agreement

The *Cambridge Learner Corpus* shows that a lot of errors are made in this area. Check agreement in particular between:

- subject + verb (check both are singular/plural)
- pronoun + noun (check both are singular/plural)
- number + noun (a plural is needed with anything above 'one')
- after phrases such as *kind of* (+ singular), *one of* (+ plural noun + singular verb), *a number of* (+ plural noun + plural verb), *the number of* (+ plural noun + singular verb) etc.
- after *many* (+ plural)
- after *every/each* (+ singular)

7 Check agreement in these sentences written by IELTS candidates, making any corrections necessary.

1 On the plus side, if these development are getting better, the richer nations will benefit.
2 In other words, every children would get a technical education.
3 There are three reason for this.
4 Children does not read books, so they will never receive information in this way.
5 The number of Japanese tourist dropped for this reasons.
6 If they do not want to do this kind of jobs in the future, there is only one option.
7 In the hotel where he live everyone treats him well.
8 There are many thing that should be considered.
9 The other three nation spent nearly the same amount in this regard.
10 The other one is more surprising because it occurs in countries in which citizens has a very high income.

Advice

- Allow up to five minutes for checking your Part 1 answer. Do this before you start Part 2.
- Leave at least ten minutes at the end to check your Part 2 answer.
- Read through each answer twice.
- At the first reading, check everything makes sense and insert any missing information.
- At the second reading, check your answer more carefully, correcting within each sentence.

Topic review

1 Take turns to answer these questions with a partner, giving as much detail as possible.

    1 Are you prepared to put yourself in risky situations? Why, or why not?

    2 Do you think there will be significant changes to society in your lifetime?

    3 How do you react when faced with exciting choices?

    4 What hypothesis do some people have for the extinction of the dinosaurs?

    5 What are the pros and cons of belonging to a nuclear family?

    6 How big is the risk that an asteroid might hit the Earth one day?

Grammar

2 Read the text about extreme sports and complete each space with one word only.

Extreme sports **0** ....*such*........ as skydiving and bungee jumping are becoming more and more popular, along with **1** .... relatively new sport of 'BASE jumping'. BASE is an acronym **2** .... Building, Antenna, Span (bridge) and Earth (cliffs) – to put **3** .... another way, leaping from stationary objects with a parachute. In **4** .... short history, BASE jumping has already claimed the lives of around 50 people, mainly due **5** .... faulty parachutes.

Why do people take the enormous risks associated with **6** .... type of sport? It has **7** .... suggested that they feel the need to put **8** .... through some form of 'real' challenge, that **9** .... otherwise be missing in **10** .... lives. A minority of those from recent generations, **11** .... have grown up untroubled by global war, deliberately search out risky situations, or **12** .... it seems.

The jump-gone-wrong is a sad reminder that extreme can all too easily become too extreme.

3 Complete this paragraph using the verbs in brackets in an appropriate future form.

Many parts of the world are currently witnessing changes to the demographic profile of society and this trend **0** (continue) ....*is going to continue*...... for the foreseeable future, as people are living longer. People who are entering the job market now in their twenties **1** (spend) .... at least the next forty years working. When they retire, it is unlikely that the state **2** (award) .... them much of a pension, in spite of the fact that they **3** (work) .... all this time. For this reason, many people are choosing savings plans that, by the time they retire, **4** (earn) .... sufficient interest on maturity to provide them with additional funds.

Vocabulary

4 Complete each sentence with a noun from the box, including an article where necessary.

belief	danger	denial	~~failure~~	nature	perception	success

EXAMPLE: The lunar mission Apollo 13 seemed doomed to
............*failure*............ , but returned safely to Earth.

1 Some soldiers face .... throughout their working lives, yet seem untroubled by it.

2 The key to .... in business is to have both vision and flexibility.

3 There is still .... prevailing in society that the state will continue to provide adequate pensions and benefits.

4 The really incredible thing about .... is its diversity, with sometimes literally millions of species in a single habitat.

5 In the case of bereavement, the human mind's initial reaction is often to go into ....

6 The housing officer concerned clearly had .... that there was no genuine need for accommodation.

5 Decide which adjectives from the box are the most likely to collocate with each noun phrase. More than one answer may be possible.

acute	high	influential	overstretched	shrinking	unfair

adjective	noun phrase
....*overstretched, shrinking*....	health services
....	income distribution
....	labour shortages
....	living standards
....	market sector
....	taxation levels

6 Complete each second sentence so that it means the same as the first, using a verb from the box in the correct form.

~~affect~~	contribute	result	suffer	trigger

EXAMPLE: The devastation of Hurricane Katrina will have an effect on the world economy.

The world economy ...*will be affected*... by the devastation of Hurricane Katrina.

1 There is no doubt that global warming is leading to higher sea levels.
Higher sea levels are undoubtedly .... by global warming.

2 Serious air pollution has been caused in Malaysia by forest fires in Indonesia.
Forest fires in Indonesia .... in serious air pollution in Malaysia.

3 Rising oil prices have been responsible for operating difficulties in some businesses.
Some businesses .... from operating difficulties, due to rising oil prices.

4 One reason for increased life expectancy is better healthcare.
Better healthcare .... to increased life expectancy.

Style extra

7 Write a summary sentence for B–D, following the style of the example A. Include a phrase from each box and reword the information to make it more concise.

briefly   in a nutshell   in short
without going into detail

natural disasters
personality traits
private income
~~volcanic activity~~

EXAMPLE: **A** *In short, the Deccan Traps theory proposes that volcanic activity caused the end of the dinosaurs.*

A
The Deccan Traps theory makes the hypothesis that the lava, water vapour and greenhouse gases being ejected during eruptions caused global warming, which eventually led to the mass extinction of the dinosaurs.

B
An assessment of personal pensions, savings, revenue from rental properties and any additional earnings will dictate the extent to which the state will provide financial support for those over 65.

C
Earthquakes, eruptions, landslides, tsunami and floods may influence an individual's perception of the degree of risk he or she faces in their life.

D
Human beings differ in terms of how much embarrassment, anxiety, anger and insecurity they exhibit, not to mention the positive aspects of compassion, cheerfulness and love.

Migration

1 Why do animals leave one place for another, often travelling huge distances?

2 List possible explanations for how birds find their way during migration.

Reading

3 Skim this passage quickly, to check your ideas.

⏱ about 750 words

NAVIGATION TECHNIQUES IN BIRD MIGRATION

Birds are forced to migrate for a number of reasons, including seasonal climate cycles, a scarcity of food or of appropriate nesting sites. Established routes are followed, many involving
5 punishing distances over land and sea. The longest migration of any known animal is that of the Arctic tern, which travels more than 15,000 miles from north to south and back again.

What are some of the main 'cues' that research has
10 indicated birds use in order to navigate successfully during migration? As the question suggests, there is no single answer; Keeton (1972) concluded that bird navigation is characterised by 'considerable redundancy of information', whereby birds appear
15 to draw on more than one method. This would seem to be essential, given changeable weather conditions, the need to overfly a variable landscape and/or seascape, and the fact that some birds manage to navigate at night.

20 Rabol (1970; 1978) suggested that a bird is born with its migratory track imprinted as part of its DNA, but his ideas have been rejected by a number of experts, including Wiltschko and Wiltschko (1978), who suggest instead that navigation
25 techniques are an integral part of parenting. Of course, this does not account for the cuckoo, which does not remain with its parents (cuckoos lay their eggs in the nest of another bird).

There is no doubt that major topographical features,
30 such as hills and rivers, can provide birds with important landmarks. The fact that some birds, such as the swallow, return to the same nest year after year after a journey of thousands of miles suggests the ability to recognise key sites. Moreover, birds may use sight to orientate themselves in relation to 35 the sun, perhaps using its relative height in the sky to determine latitude. However, an experiment by Schlicte and Schmidt-Koenig (1972), whereby pigeons were fitted with frosted lenses, may indicate that sight is less important in birds than in humans, 40 for these birds could still use the sun for orientation.

It is thought that, unlike human eyes, birds' eyes can detect ultra-violet light in adverse weather conditions. Matthews (1951; 1953; 1955) suggested that birds use the sun's arc to establish longitude. 45 The sun appears to be used by a number of birds as a compass and they seem able to adjust their biological clock to compensate for shifting through time zones from east to west.

At night, the stars and moon provide an alternative 50 source of observable data for birds. There is evidence that some birds memorise constellations (for example, Emlen's work with indigo buntings in 1967 and Wallraff's 1969 experiment with caged ducks). If these constellations provide a reliable and 55 little-changing map in a clear night sky, the moon

4 **Read the passage again and answer questions 1–9.**

Questions 1 and 2

Choose the correct letter, ***A, B, C*** *or* ***D.***

1 According to Wiltschko and Wiltschko,
   A cuckoo behaviour supports a genetic explanation for navigation.
   B Rabol's ideas on imprinting are worthy of further investigation.
   C adult birds train their young to react to navigational cues.
   D more studies are needed on the role of parenting in navigation.

2 What does the text suggest about the role of sight in bird navigation?
   A Birds are unlikely to take notice of many physical landmarks.
   B It provides essential information for revisiting breeding locations.
   C Birds find it impossible to look directly at the sun when it is high.
   D It is without doubt the most important sense that a bird has.

Test spot

In an IELTS Reading matching task, it may help to highlight the options in the passage (for example, people's names), before you do the task. Remember that the information tested won't be given in the order in which it appears in the passage.

Questions 3–9

Look at the following statements about research and the list of people below.
Match each statement to the correct person or people.
Write the correct letter, ***A–J.***

3 proved that some birds navigate by the stars
4 raised the possibility of genetic programming
5 dismissed someone's ideas about disorientation
6 demonstrated that birds do not need perfect vision
7 argued that birds rely on a combination of cues
8 suggested that birds may use their sense of hearing to forecast bad weather
9 investigated the role of a sense of smell in bird navigation

List of People	
A Baker and Mather	F Papi
B Emlen	G Rabol
C Gould	H Schlicte and Schmidt-Koenig
D Keeton	I Walcott and Green
E Matthews	J Yodlowski et al

on the other hand is too random to be helpful, changing its position in the sky night after night.

Just as birds' vision is more sensitive than our own,
60 there is evidence to suggest that many birds can detect sounds outside our own range of hearing. Yodlowski et al (1977) discovered that homing pigeons were sensitive to sounds below 10 Hz, known as 'infra-sound', and could employ this for
65 orientation purposes and in the crucial early detection of severe thunderstorms, with a consequent adjustment of flight path.

Most birds don't have a good sense of smell, but fish-eaters such as petrels and shearwaters are significant
70 exceptions. These birds probably act on olfactory cues given that they only reach their nesting sites during the hours of darkness. However, this area of research is inconclusive: two experiments conducted by Papi (1972; 1978), where the olfactory nerve of pigeons
75 was cut, leading to a loss of navigation skills, gave inconsistent results; Baker and Mather (1982) regarded them as flawed, and suggested that the confusion may have been induced by the trauma of the experiments, or through loss of magnetic awareness.

80 Geomagnetism was suggested as a possible cue for bird navigation as early as 1859 and much research has been done in this area. The Earth's magnetic field is not of uniform intensity, being at its weakest at the equator; homing pigeons are thought to
85 exploit magnetic anomalies for orientation (Gould 1980). In earlier research, Walcott and Green (1974) fitted pigeons with electric caps to produce a magnetic field. Under overcast skies, reversing the magnetic field by reversing the electric current
90 caused the birds to fly in the opposite direction to their original course. This and other work suggests that magnetism does indeed play an important part in navigation for many birds.

Vocabulary Meaning groups

5 Add words from the passage within the meaning groups below. Build your vocabulary by recording new language in this way.

   1 Four adjectives similar to 'very important' (paragraphs 2, 3, 4, 7)
      essential, ...

   2 Two nouns connected with change or fluctuation (paragraphs 7, 9)
      ....

   3 Three adjectives describing unsatisfactory research (paragraph 8)
      ....

Speaking *Part 3*

1 Discuss these questions.

- Why do people emigrate to other countries?
- What issues are there to do with immigration today?
- What is your government's current policy towards immigration?
- How can migrants help a country's economy?

Listening

2 🎧 You are going to hear part of a lecture on the importance of Italian immigration in the development of Guelph, a city in Canada. Before you listen, read the notes opposite and decide what type of information is required in questions 1–9.

Complete the notes opposite. Write **NO MORE THAN TWO WORDS** *for each answer.*

ITALIAN MIGRANTS IN GUELPH FROM 1900

Reasons for leaving Italy

1 .... favoured northern industrialisation
Lack of work in the south – led to severe **2** ....

Destinations of those emigrating

- other parts of Europe
- South America, especially **3** ....
- North America

Examples of areas of work done by early migrants to Canada

4 .... (summer)
5 .... (winter)

Commercial development of Guelph

Subsidies made available for new **6** ....
Relocation of existing **7** .... companies.

The Italian-Canadian community

Grew up in **8** .... sector of Guelph
Still puts on an annual **9** .... every July

Style extra

3 The lecturer in the recording uses the common spoken expression *Of course* to indicate something that is obvious.

Of course this movement stopped altogether in 1939 with the onset of war.

In academic written English, an adverb, such as *naturally*, would be used here instead.

Make adverbs from the words in brackets to complete these sentences. Be careful with spelling. A negative prefix is needed in 2 and 3.

1 .... , many migrants missed their homeland. (understand)
2 Most migrants were .... keen to work hard in order to send money home. (doubt)
3 Guelph was .... a quiet backwater in the early twentieth century. (deny)

4 Another way of indicating something obvious is to use a short phrase. Fill in the missing words in these expressions.

1 It .... without saying that ...
2 It can be .... as read that ...
3 It is self- .... that ...

Grammar Relative clauses

5 Explain the change of meaning in sentences *a* and *b*. Sentence *a* contains a non-defining relative clause and sentence *b* a defining clause. What is the difference between these clauses? Which sentence suggests that *all* the men clung to their own culture?

a *The men, who were not yet official immigrants, clung to their own culture.*
b *The men who were not yet official immigrants clung to their own culture.*

G ⋯⟶ page 142

6 Use the prompts to write sentences containing either a defining or a non-defining relative clause, according to the meaning.

EXAMPLE: Many Italian men / came from both the north and the south / left to find jobs abroad.
Many Italian men, who came from both the north and the south, left to find jobs abroad. (non-defining)

1 Migration / had been happening for many years / stopped with the onset of war.
2 Many of the migrants / came to Canada / did casual work.

3 Many local businessmen / recognised the commercial opportunities of this 'new' workforce / applied for subsidies to develop new factories.
4 The migrants / were mostly men / often boarded together.
5 Migrants / arrived later / helped by those already there.
6 Those of the men / wanted to marry / often returned to Italy to find a bride.
7 The new culture / evolved / was based on Italian memories combined with the Canadian experience.
8 The Italian-Canadian community / has contributed a lot to Guelph / still thrives.

7 In which sentences in exercise 6 can you use *that* instead of *who*?

8 Underline the relative pronouns in these examples. Which one would you only use in formal English?

1 *Most of the members of the international club with whom I have discussed this are in favour of it.*
2 *The Italian-Canadian group, whose men and women had very different roles, established a stable community.*

9 Correct the errors that IELTS and other advanced level candidates have made with relative pronouns in these sentences. One sentence is correct.

1 The student who's work is not very good may give up studying.
2 I would like to propose two firms which advertisements I have seen in the local newspaper.
3 She was out with a group of people, among who the only one she knew was Charles.
4 We can learn from people whose cultures differ from ours.
5 People whom knowledge of computers is limited are obviously in a difficult situation.
6 One thing which has always concerned me is the huge amount of money that is paid to people whose have a job in sport.

Test folder 9

Classification

(Academic Reading, General Training Reading and Listening Modules)

You may be asked to classify several pieces of information from the passage, choosing among the same options (normally three) in each case. The options are all of the same type, for example, three time periods, or three opinions. They could be, for example, *before 1950 /after 1950 / both* or (in Reading Modules only) *satisfied / dissatisfied / neither*.

In the Listening Module the questions follow the order of information in the passage. In the Reading Modules they do not.

Reading

1   This passage is similar to Section 1 of General Training Reading, but slightly shorter, at about 225 words.

Advice

Reading Modules
- Skim the whole passage before you start working on any of the tasks.
- Read the instructions carefully and think about the meaning of the three options. Check what letters you should use for your answers: they may be A, B and C, or three other letters.
- Read the first question, and underline the key words. Find the relevant part of the passage. Read it carefully and consider all three options before choosing the correct one.
- Read the next question and find the relevant part of the passage. It might be *anywhere* in the passage.

Listening Module
- Use the time you are given to read the instructions carefully and think about the meaning of the three options. Check what letters you should use for your answers: they may be A, B and C, or three other letters.
- Listen for each answer in turn. Consider all three options before choosing your answer.
- Always give an answer – you won't lose any marks if it's wrong.

Museum of Immigration

The Museum of Immigration explores the stories of the more than nine million people who have migrated to Australia since 1788. It is located in the port where many of them arrived. The South Pier itself, where thousands of ships have docked, is recreated through photographs and some of the original documents recording new arrivals. The harbourmaster's house now forms part of the museum. It has been carefully restored and furnished to show what it was like to live there in the 19th century.

'Who and why?' is a virtual exhibition. You can read personal stories by immigrants, choosing by name or nationality. With just a click you can discover more about working and living conditions for new arrivals, or even search the records for your family. 'Journeys' features stories of how people have come to Australia – anything from a dangerous three-month sea voyage to a flight of a few hours. Listen as you wander round the museum, or maybe sit in the garden, designed as a tribute to the individuals and families who have immigrated to Australia.

The Bathurst Room is a specially designed, hands-on model room. Press a button, and watch an 18th century ship struggling through a rough sea. Press another, and miners labour to find gold. You can even dig for gold yourself!

Classify the following exhibitions.
Write ***I*** *if it is interactive*
     A *if it is purely audio*
     V *if it is purely visual*

1   Journeys   ....
2   Harbourmaster's house   ....
3   Bathurst Room   ....
4   South Pier   ....
5   Who and why?   ....

2 This passage is similar to those in the Academic Reading Module and Section 3 of the General Training Reading, but shorter at about 350 words.

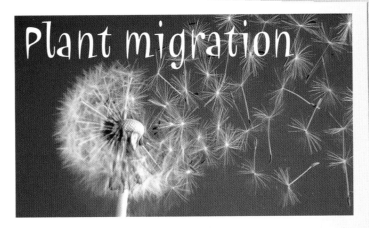

We generally think of plants as being rooted to the spot, but in fact they colonise new territory, most often through the dispersal of their seeds. This is important, because the seeds are more likely to grow if they are at a distance from the parent plant, not competing for nutrition and sunlight. Seeds are dispersed in a variety of ways.

The bird-cage plant forms a hollow sphere when it dies. This is blown across the plant's habitat, the deserts of the western USA. When the ball falls to earth, the seeds inside it fall out, and some of them will take root. The seeds of the broom are contained inside pods. Heated by the sun, the pods explode, hurling the seeds in all directions. The cotton that we use is the threads attached to the seeds of the cotton plant. These enable the seeds to travel long distances on the breeze.

Larger, heavier seeds require stronger carriers, who are attracted by the fruit encasing the seeds. When the seeds are fully developed, the fruit changes colour and smell to signal that it is now sweet enough to be eaten. The fruit of the durian tree of south-east Asia is eaten by squirrels and orang-utans. If the seed is swallowed whole, it will be carried away inside the animal's stomach and subsequently ejected, allowing the seed to grow in the new location.

In some plants, such as burdock, the seeds are attached to hooks. These catch the fur of passing animals, who carry the seeds away. Eventually the seeds fall, where they stand a chance of taking root. Coconut palms, on the other hand, produce their seeds inside a shell which floats on the surface of water, and can be carried hundreds of kilometres by the current. Coconut palms have colonised beaches throughout the tropics.

It is not only by dispersing their seeds that plants travel, however. The blackberry plant, for instance, produces stems which move at a speed of about five centimetres a day. When these touch the ground they put out roots, thus extending the plant's territory.

Classify the following plants as migrating by using

A sea or wind
B animals (including birds)
C neither

Write the correct letter, A, B, or C, after each plant.

1 coconut palm   ....
2 broom   ....
3 blackberry   ....
4 cotton   ....
5 burdock   ....
6 bird-cage plant ....
7 durian   ....

Listening

3 🎧 This passage is typical of Section 4 of the Listening Module.

What form of migration is characteristic of the following animals?

A annual return journey
B once-in-life return journey
C other

Write the correct letter, A, B or C after each animal.

1 whooper swans   ....
2 sockeye salmon   ....
3 micro-organisms   ....
4 grey whales   ....
5 European freshwater eels ....
6 ostriches   ....
7 locusts   ....
8 red-tailed hawks   ....
9 antelopes   ....
10 great gray owls   ....

The study of literature

A

B

C

1 Decide what point about books and reading is being made by the people above.

A *Reading is to the mind what exercise is to the body.* Sir Richard Steele (1672–1729)

B *When I get a little money, I buy books; and if any is left, I buy food and clothes.* Desiderius Erasmus (1465–1536)

C *I wonder whether what we are publishing now is worth cutting down trees to make paper for.* Richard Brautigan (1935–1984)

2 Describe reading habits in your country. Do people of all ages read books? Does this vary according to family background or socio-economic group?

Speaking *Part 3*

3 Now ask and answer these questions in pairs.

- Are books essential in the 21st century?
- Can the books we read tell us about real life?
- Is it possible to define literature?
- What benefits are gained from studying literature?

Reading

4 Read this passage within three minutes. Decide how far the writer is able to answer his own question.

⏱ about 800 words

WHAT IS LITERATURE?

If there is such a thing as literary theory, then it would seem obvious that there is something called literature which it is the theory of. There have been various attempts to define literature. You might define it as
5 'imaginative' writing in the sense of fiction – writing which is not literally true. But even the briefest reflection on what people include under the heading of literature suggests that this definition will not do: for example, along with the plays of Corneille and Racine,
10 French seventeenth-century literature includes Bossuet's funeral speeches, Madame de Sévigné's letters to her daughter and the philosophy of Descartes and Pascal.

A distinction between 'fact' and 'fiction', then, seems unlikely to get us very far, not least because the
15 distinction itself is often a questionable one. In the late sixteenth and early seventeenth centuries in England, the word 'novel' seems to have been used about both true and fictional events, and even news reports were neither clearly factual nor clearly fictional: our own
20 sharp discriminations between these categories simply did not apply. Moreover, if 'literature' includes much 'factual' writing, it also excludes quite a lot of fiction. A *Superman* comic and a Mills and Boon romantic novel are fictional but not generally regarded as literature. And
25 if literature is 'creative' or 'imaginative' writing, does this imply that history, philosophy and natural science are uncreative and unimaginative?

Perhaps one needs a different kind of approach altogether. Perhaps literature is definable not according
30 to whether it is fictional or 'imaginative', but because it uses language in peculiar ways. Literature transforms and intensifies ordinary language; it deviates systematically from everyday speech. If you approach me at a bus stop and murmur 'Thou still unravished
35 bride of quietness,' then I am instantly aware that I am in the presence of the literary. I know this because the texture, rhythm and resonance of your words are far removed from everyday language.

This, in effect, was the definition of the 'literary'
40 advanced by the Russian Formalists, who emerged in Russia in the years before the 1917 revolution, and flourished throughout the 1920s, until they were

effectively silenced by Stalinism. The Formalists saw literary language as a set of deviations from a norm, a kind of linguistic violence; but to spot a deviation implies being able to identify the norm from which it swerves. Moreover, the idea that there is a single 'normal' language, a common currency shared equally by all members of society, is an illusion. Any actual language consists of a highly complex range of discourses, differentiated according to class, region, gender, status and so on, which can by no means be neatly unified into a single homogeneous linguistic community. One person's norm may be another's deviation: the word 'ginnel' (meaning alleyway) may be poetic in one part of England but ordinary language in another. Even the most mundane text of the fifteenth century may sound 'poetic' to us today because of its archaism. Conversely, if everyone used phrases like 'unravished bride of quietness' in ordinary conversation, this kind of language might stop being poetic.

So, any belief that the study of literature is the study of a stable, well-definable entity – as entomology is the study of insects – can be abandoned. Literature, in the sense of a set of works of assured and unalterable value, distinguished by certain shared inherent properties, does not exist. The unquestioned 'great tradition' of the 'national literature' has to be recognized as a *construct*, fashioned by particular people for particular reasons at a certain time. There is no such thing as a literary work or tradition which is valuable *in itself*, regardless of what anyone might have said or come to say about it. 'Value' is a transitive term.

The fact that we always interpret literary works to some extent in the light of our own concerns might be one reason why certain works of literature seem to retain their value across the centuries. However, 'our' Homer is not identical with the Homer of the Middle Ages. All literary works, in other words, are 'rewritten', if only unconsciously, by the societies which read them; indeed, there is no reading of a work which is not also a 'rewriting'. No work, and no current evaluation of it, can simply be extended to new groups of people without being changed, perhaps almost unrecognizably, in the process; and this is one reason why what counts as literature is a notably unstable affair.

(line numbers: 45, 50, 55, 60, 65, 70, 75, 80, 85)

5 Do the following statements reflect the claims of the writer?

Write

YES *if the statement reflects the claims of the writer*

NO *if the statement contradicts the claims of the writer*

NOT GIVEN *if it is impossible to say what the writer thinks about this*

1 Some correspondence is considered to be a valid literary genre.
2 It was impossible to distinguish fact from fiction in late sixteenth-century news reports.
3 The stylistic features of a text often indicate whether it can be classified as literature.
4 The Russian Formalists should have been allowed to continue their work under Stalin.
5 People often interpret language that is old-fashioned as being literary.
6 Great works of literature are perceived in the same way through time.
7 In order to analyse a novel effectively, the reader needs to place it in its historical context.

Style extra

6 In this passage, the writer signals his disapproval in different ways. For example, the wording in lines 13–14 *seems unlikely to get us very far* shows that he sees the distinction between fact and fiction as *unhelpful*. Choose the adjective which best describes each underlined noun in 1–3, according to the meaning of the passage.

1 this <u>definition</u> will not do (line 8)
   this definition is untenable / misinformed
2 the <u>distinction</u> itself is often a questionable one (line 15)
   the distinction is untested / unworkable
3 the <u>idea</u> ... is an illusion (lines 47–49)
   the idea is improbable / invalid

7 Add a suitable negative prefix to these adjectives to form words showing disapproval. You can use some of these words in Writing folder 9.

1 creative
2 logical
3 rational
4 organised
5 sufficient

1 Have you ever done any translation to or from your own language? How easy is it to translate literature? What are the pros and cons of reading a novel in translation?

Listening

2 🎧 Listen to a conversation between a university tutor and two students of literature.

*Choose the correct letter, **A**, **B** or **C**.*

1 What does Anna feel about people who translate novels into their own language?
   A They can avoid using large dictionaries.
   B They are likely to produce a better product.
   C They may not pick up on everything important.

2 According to Anna, writers who translate the novels of other writers
   A have special priorities in terms of which features to preserve.
   B feel it is unacceptable to change the content in any way.
   C produce a translation that reflects their own writing style.

3 What does Gary mention as a problem in relation to reading Zola in translation?
   A the fact that there are so many translations to choose from
   B the way some of the spoken language has been translated
   C the lack of knowledge about nineteenth-century France

4 Why is Anna in favour of reading some literature in translation?
   A because it is easier than reading in the original language
   B because it offers relevant training for her future career
   C because it makes the study of literature much broader

Vocabulary Idiom and metaphor

3 Choose the correct meaning (a–e) for these phrases from the recording.

   1 have an edge on
   2 have a different agenda
   3 cause a storm
   4 have a false ring
   5 be a can of worms

   a make people react strongly
   b seem inauthentic
   c be better than
   d be complicated to deal with
   e see something in another way

4 🎧 Sometimes, idioms and metaphors are modified in use, often to give emphasis. Listen to some extracts from the recording again. What 'extra' words occur within the phrases?

5 Here are some related phrases to the ones in exercise 3. Complete the sentences by choosing a, b or c. Use a dictionary if necessary.

   1 This new product, the first in its field, represents real .... technology.
      a competitive edge b knife-edge c cutting edge

   2 The Scottish writer's latest play has .... the festival by storm.
      a taken b weathered c gone down at

   3 Things got off to a .... when the team leader resigned from the project almost immediately.
      a false modesty b false start c false move

   4 The journalist asked me several odd questions and I began to suspect he had a .... agenda.
      a busy b difficult c hidden

Grammar

Verbs followed by *wh-* clauses

6 Many verbs to do with thought and observation can be followed by a question word and clause, and this is particularly common in academic English. Explain how the meaning of *whether* differs from other question words by looking at these examples.

*I've been **considering how** literary translations should be approached.*

*Gary, could I just **check whether** this fits in with your current research?*

*Can you **clarify why** you're interested in this?*

G ⋯⫶ page 143

7 Complete these sentences from the *Cambridge Academic Corpus* with *how*, *why* or *whether*.

1 Such a historical program could explore .... and why certain features arise when they do.

2 Any or all of these reasons could explain .... Jacobs acted as he did.

3 The study examined .... there were any differences in identity status.

4 It is easy to grasp .... this explanation was unacceptable at the time.

5 In all of these cases, it was possible to determine .... or not a symptom truly existed.

6 The lines just quoted show .... Pascal conceives the problem.

7 We must try and understand .... Sartre never made any great attempt to assimilate Marxism.

8 It is not known .... there is any connection between the two incidents.

8 Choose the correct verb in these sentences from the *Cambridge Academic Corpus*. Note that all the verb options are commonly followed by question words, especially in academic English.

1 When *advised / asked / debated* why they had enrolled in the geometry class, 85% of the students saw it as essential.

2 It may be hard to *calculate / decide / wonder* whether this is a verb that has both transitive and intransitive senses.

3 The fact that considerable gains were to be made *informs / speculates / suggests* why the assets were seized.

4 We should now *estimate / observe / plan* how this theme is incorporated into the poem.

5 If we cannot *establish / notice / raise* which narrative is the 'primary' text, how can we *define / reflect / think* what is a 'secondary' or 'contemporary' source in relation to it?

6 It is important to *assess / imagine / realise* whether the migration of oil actually helped to generate these fractures.

7 Sterne's novel *arranges / demonstrates / notices* why so few grammarians of his time felt a major reform of writing would be accepted.

8 Some observers *checked / doubted / guessed* whether the peace treaty would ever be ratified.

9 Some phrasal verbs are used in academic English in a similar way. Match the sentence beginnings 1–5 with their endings a–e and join them using one of the phrasal verbs from the box with a suitable question word. Sometimes more than one phrasal verb is possible.

EXAMPLE: 1 d
These latest findings on glucose solutions should *bear out what* you discovered in the lab last week.

bear out	enlarge on	find out	weigh up	work out

1 These latest findings on glucose solutions should

2 Looking at the airline's questionnaires, please

3 From these historical trends, you can

4 Using the meeting transcripts, I'd like you to

5 To extend your history essay, you could

a was responsible for healthcare at the time.

b the next ice age is likely to occur.

c this policy affected the population as a whole.

d you discovered in the lab last week.

e ticket price or choice of destination is more important to its customers.

Writing folder 9

Task 2 Expressing disagreement

In the Task 2 essay, you may decide to disagree with the statement in the question. In academic English, it is very important to express disagreement cautiously and politely. In Task 2, you should present your argument clearly, using an impersonal and non-aggressive tone.

1   Read the task and tick possible reasons for disagreeing with the statement, choosing from the list and adding two ideas of your own.

Write about the following topic.

> **Television cannot replace the book as a learning tool, which is why children are less well educated today.**
> **To what extent do you agree or disagree with this statement?**

Give reasons for your answer and include any relevant examples from your own knowledge or experience.

Write at least 250 words.

- Television offers many educational programmes.
- Even soap operas can teach us about real life.
- TV documentaries show more than a book can.
- Children usually learn better from visual input.
- Many children don't read books but love television.
- Children are better educated than they used to be.
- ....
  ....
- ....
  ....

2   Read the answer below, ignoring the highlighted parts for the moment. Which of the reasons in exercise 1 are included?

In my opinion, each part of the statement is totally untrue. First I think television can replace the book as a learning tool and second, it is completely wrong to say that children are less well educated today. Now let me tell you why I think this.

Let's face it, kids enjoy television and they watch a great deal of it, so it is crazy to force them to read books if they have no wish to do so. There are some very good programmes on television, where you can learn loads of stuff, such as films about wildlife in remote places, and history programmes with real-life characters. These types of documentaries do more to educate a child than any book does, because they're more alive.

Why can't soap operas teach kids, too? When you watch a soap opera, you are seeing ordinary people dealing with difficult moments in their lives, and this can often help you to make your own decisions.

The second part of the statement is absolute rubbish. You really can't say that children aren't learning as much as before, particularly when schools have so many excellent things nowadays, like computers, electronic whiteboards and the Internet. My grandparents would have preferred today's high-tech learning thing to the boring textbooks they had. And what do you mean by 'educated' anyway? Apart from working on their school subjects, children today need to learn important things about real life, and books are useless for these survival things.

3 Choose the best qualifier in 1–4 below, in order to disagree cautiously and politely but at the same time avoid making the phrase sound informal. Then replace the words highlighted in yellow with your new phrases. More than one answer may be possible, but use each phrase once only.

1 is *kind of / somewhat / highly* questionable
2 appears *really / seriously / dreadfully* flawed
3 seems *rather / completely / 100%* dubious
4 makes *no / not one bit of / little* sense

4 Now rewrite the green highlighted parts to improve the tone by making it more impersonal and academic. Start with the words given and include the language indicated in the brackets.

1 *A number of reasons* (+ future passive: *give*) …
2 *It* (+ negative modal passive: *deny*) …
3 *… from which a great deal* (+ modal passive: *assimilate*) …
4 *… the subject* (+ passive: *bring*) *to life.*
5 *Young people* (+ modal passive: *inform*) …
6 *It is illogical to* (+ suitable reporting verb) …
7 *Moreover, it depends* (*what* + passive: *mean*) …
8 *… books are* (+ adjective with prefix *irr-*) …

5 In the final paragraph of the answer in exercise 2, the word *thing* is used four times. Replace it each time with one of the words below.

experiences   facilities   facts   issues

6 Look at the opening paragraph of the answer again and underline any phrases taken from the Task 2 statement. Rewrite these in your own words.

7 Write a conclusion for the essay in about 50 words. You should restate the writer's viewpoint but also try to introduce some balance or caution into the argument.

8 Now answer the task in exercise 1, following the advice opposite. You can of course choose to agree or disagree! Write at least 250 words.

Advice

- Read the task carefully.
- Underline key words and think of different ways of saying the same thing.
- Make a plan, putting each main point in a new paragraph.
- State your overall opinion in the introduction.
- If you disagree, express your disagreement cautiously, using qualifiers to soften your point of view.
- Develop and exemplify each of your main points.
- Restate your opinion in a conclusion.
- Leave enough time to check your answer for accuracy.

19·1 Earning a living

Speaking *Part 3*

1 With a partner or in small groups, discuss the following points.

- Describe the range of job opportunities in your country, for example small businesses and international companies.
- If you ran your own business, what would it be? Why?
- Make a list of things you think it's important to consider before setting up your own business.
- Speculate on possible developments in your country affecting the types of work available.

Useful language

independence	responsibility	working hours	social contact
shift work	manual work	job security	entrepreneur

Listening

2 You are going to hear a business consultant giving advice to people considering starting their own business. The recording is in two parts. Before you listen to each part, study the relevant questions carefully and think about possible answers. Remember to write the exact words you hear.

Questions 1–4
Complete the sentences below.
*Write **NO MORE THAN TWO WORDS** for each answer.*

1 One feature of running your own business is that it does not involve going through the normal process of ....

2 Having .... is very important when assessing your own suitability.

3 Seek .... opinions from friends and family.

4 Success is affected by your choice of .... and ....

Questions 5–7
*Choose **THREE** letters A–F.*
*Which **THREE** reasons are given for leaving a job and starting a business?*

A having difficulty getting a new job
B losing a job
C having a new boss
D being transferred to a different job or location
E being overlooked for promotion
F lacking a sense of achievement

Questions 8–14
Complete the table below.
*Write **NO MORE THAN TWO WORDS** for each answer.*

potential problem	comment
Inadequate 8	May need 9 .... from husband/wife
Excessive 10	Difficult to limit
High level of 11	Get support from family
Too many responsibilities	Assess your 12 .... and deal with any gaps
High chance of failure	Take only 13 .... risks
Over-reaction to failure	Use the 14 .... that you've made, to work out how to improve

Vocabulary Running a business

3 This account was written by Carol Henderson, who owns and runs a restaurant in London with her husband Daniel.

Look at the words in the box. If there are any that you don't understand, use an English–English dictionary. Skim the account to get an idea of what it is about, then read it again, completing it with words from the box. Think about both the meaning and the grammar, and make sure you copy the words correctly. Each word should be used no more than once. You won't need to use them all.

applicants	catering	chain	customers
CV	expenses	loss	management
profit	property	qualifications	
refurbishment	staff	suppliers	

Running our own restaurant

I've always enjoyed cookery, so when I was made redundant by the retailer that I worked for, I decided to change to the **1** .... industry. I successfully worked towards several **2** .... in Food Preparation, then gained experience by preparing food for parties and weddings.

Eventually, Daniel and I decided to set up our own small restaurant. We purchased a small **3** .... , which had previously been a bank, and carried out a complete **4** ....

There was plenty to do before we opened. For instance, we had to decide on the number of **5** .... we needed, and then advertise, interview the **6** .... who we shortlisted, appoint the people we thought were best, and provide training. It also took a long time to choose **7** .... who could provide the type of food we wanted, at a price we could afford.

So far the restaurant has been fairly successful. We're very pleased with the numbers of **8** .... we're getting and we've even started to make a **9** .... Our long-term plan now is to open a whole **10** .... of restaurants.

4 What do you think are the advantages and disadvantages of running your own business?

Pronunciation *Sounding interesting*

5 When you are speaking, it is of course important to sound interesting, and to help the listener to understand you.

🎧 You will hear each of these sentences (1–4) said twice. Which version sounds more interesting, and why? The statements in the box may help you.

> The pitch …
> The words …
> The stressed syllables …
> The word giving important information is at a high pitch level.

1 Many people would love to be their own boss, but have too many financial commitments to take the risk.
2 This at least is the conventional idea, although many people like this never start a business.
3 Another factor that can cause problems when you start to employ other people is the desire for power.
4 Don't try to control your staff so much that they can't work effectively.

6 🎧 Listen to a woman talking about the Part 2 topic in the box. Notice how she uses her voice to sound interesting.

> Describe your first day in a new job or at college.
>
> You should say:
>
>   what the job or course was
>   what you had expected before you started
>   what happened on the first day
>
> and explain how you felt at the end of the day.

7 With a partner, take turns to talk about the topic in the box. Make it sound as interesting as possible.

Reading

1 In small groups, read the attitudes towards work (A–F), and discuss how far you agree with them.

A The highest wages should be for doing jobs that few people are willing to do.
B People should be judged as human beings by how successful they are at work.
C People have a duty to society to work.
D People should be rewarded according to the value to society of the work they do.
E Money and promotion are the most effective ways of motivating people to work.
F Society should ensure that suitable work is available to meet people's needs.

2 Read the passage and answer the questions below. Remember that the attitudes mentioned are not necessarily the author's own attitude.

Questions 1–3
*Which **THREE** of the above attitudes towards work (**A–F**) are mentioned?*

⏱ about 650 words

The Historical Context of Attitudes to Work

Work, for much of the history of the human race, has been hard and degrading. But while it has always been recognised that work is necessary for the satisfaction of material needs, attitudes towards working hard – in the absence of
5 compulsion – have varied over the centuries.

Getting on for 3,000 years ago, the ancient Greeks regarded work as a curse. Philosophers such as Plato and Aristotle made it clear that the majority of men laboured so that the minority could engage in pure exercises of the mind – art,
10 philosophy and politics. According to Plato, 'Those who need to work must be willing to accept an inferior status.'

During the Middle Ages – from about 400 AD until 1400 AD – work was still perceived negatively, though with a positive attitude towards earnings which prevented one from being
15 reliant on the charity of others for the physical needs of life. Wealth was recognized as an opportunity to share with those who might be less fortunate, and work which produced wealth therefore became acceptable. However, any effort to accumulate excessive wealth was frowned upon. It was the
20 duty of a worker to remain in his class, passing on his family work from father to son.

With the Reformation, a period of religious and political upheaval in western Europe during the sixteenth century, came a new perspective on work. Two key religious leaders
25 who influenced the development of western culture during this period were Martin Luther and John Calvin, from Germany and France respectively.

Building on Luther's doctrines, John Calvin introduced a significant new attitude towards work. He taught that people's
30 daily life and deeds, and success in worldly endeavours, reflected their moral worth. Calvin believed that all men must work, even the rich. Men were not to wish for wealth, possessions, or easy living, but were to reinvest the profits of their labour into financing further ventures. Selection of an occupation and pursuing it to achieve the greatest profit 35 possible was considered a religious duty, even if that meant abandoning the family trade or profession. The key elements of these new beliefs about work – usually called the 'Protestant work ethic' – were hard work, punctuality, working for long-term (rather than immediate) benefits, and the great 40 importance of work.

In time, these attitudes became norms of Western culture. As the industrial revolution gathered pace in the nineteenth century, the idea of work as a religious obligation was replaced by the concept of public usefulness. Economists 45 warned of the poverty and decay that would befall the country if people failed to work hard, and moralists stressed the social duty of each person to be productive.

Now let us fast-forward to the present, to the information age which began in the 1980s. To a far greater degree than before, 50 work is now perceived as rewarding in itself. This work ethic stresses skill, challenge, autonomy, recognition, and the quality of work produced. Autonomy has been identified as a particularly important factor in job satisfaction. Motivation to work involves trust, caring, meaning, self-knowledge, 55 challenge, opportunity for personal growth, and dignity, instead of purely financial incentives. Workers seek control over their work – something lost with the mechanisation of the industrial age; and many contemporary jobs are conducive to meeting these needs. As a result, the work ethic has gained a personal 60 relevance not found in most occupations in the industrial age. Some studies have identified a decline in belief that hard work will create adequate benefits. This is a significant shift, because pay and 'getting ahead' were the primary incentives management used to encourage productivity during the 65 industrial age. To sum up, the contemporary work ethic places a positive moral value on doing a good job and is based on a belief that work has intrinsic value for its own sake.

Questions 4–10

Classify the following views as being those of

A Ancient Greece
B the Middle Ages
C John Calvin

Example: Wealth should not stop people from working.

Answer: C (*Calvin believed that all men must work, even the rich.*)

*Write the correct letter **A, B** or **C**.*

4 people should choose their occupation

5 work gives others freedom to carry out certain non-work activities

6 people should work hard

7 people who earn money should help others financially

8 work gives people a low position in society

9 a person's occupation should depend on the social position they are born into

10 people should use money they do not need to create more money

Questions 11–16

Complete the summary below.
*Choose **NO MORE THAN ONE WORD** from the passage for each answer.*

Test spot

Remember that the heading of a summary will help you to find the relevant part of the passage.

Work in the information age

Work is generally expected to be
11 .... for its own sake.
There is an emphasis on the benefits for the individual, and on the 12 ....
of his or her output. One of the major contributors to the enjoyment of work is
13 .... A number of factors, rather than money alone, create
14 .... In many jobs, workers are able to take
15 .... of what they do.
There has been a significant change in the main 16 .... that are effective in the workplace.

Grammar Noun phrases

3 The article is written in an academic style, using noun phrases – particularly ones containing abstract nouns – rather than verbs and adjectives. Find the noun phrases with the following meanings.

1 getting the material goods that are needed (paragraph 1)
2 not being forced to do something (paragraph 1)
3 seeing work in a new way (paragraph 4)
4 being useful to the public (paragraph 6)
5 being able to develop personal qualities (paragraph 7)
6 fewer people believing (paragraph 7)

G ···❖ page 143

4 Complete each *b* sentence with a noun phrase so that it means the same as the *a* sentence.

EXAMPLE: a The idea that work is worthwhile for its own sake developed relatively recently.

b The idea that work is worthwhile for its own sake is a *relatively recent development* ....

1 a One reason for the change in attitude towards work in the 16th century was that the population was expanding dramatically.

b One reason for the change in attitude towards work in the 16th century was the .... of the population.

2 a Industrialisation spread rapidly during the 19th century, resulting in many serious problems.

b The .... during the 19th century resulted in many serious problems.

3 a The industrial revolution made many more goods available.

b The industrial revolution greatly increased the ....

4 a Manual labour generally makes it difficult for people to be involved in deciding things.

b Manual labour generally allows minimal opportunity for ....

5 a In the late 20th century, people grew more aware of what they needed individually.

b The late 20th century saw a .... of ....

Speaking *Part 2*

5 With a partner, take turns to talk about this topic for one to two minutes. Try to use vocabulary from this unit.

> Describe what you regard as the ideal job.
>
> You should say:
>
>   what job it would be
>   why you consider it ideal
>   what other people think of somebody doing that job
>
> and explain how you would benefit from having that job.

Test folder 10

Summary completion

(Academic Reading, General Training Reading and Listening Modules)

A summary is usually of one part of the passage, but may be of the whole text.

In the Listening Module the questions follow the order of information in the passage. In the Reading Modules they may not.

The summary is worded differently from the passage, but the ideas are the same.

If you have to choose words from the passage, you will be told the maximum number for each answer.

If you have to choose words from a box, there will be more words than spaces, and they are usually different from ones in the passage.

Words must be spelt correctly to gain marks.

Advice

Reading Modules
- Skim the whole passage before you start working on any of the tasks.
- Read the instructions. If the answers come from the passage, check the maximum number of words for each space. Read the heading (if there is one) and the summary. Consider what information is likely to fit each space. Think about both the *meaning* and the *grammar*.
- Read the first gapped sentence. Find the relevant part of the passage – the heading will help you – and look for something that means the same. Find the words (in the passage or box) that fit the question. Copy them exactly. Continue with the next space.

Listening Module
- You will be given time to read the summary before you listen. Consider what information is likely to fit each space. Think about both the *meaning* and the *grammar*.
- Listen for each answer in turn. If you miss one, go on to the next question or you may miss that too.

All modules
- Check that your answers fit both the meaning and grammar, that the spelling is correct, and that you haven't written more than the maximum number of words.

Listening

1 🎧 This passage is similar to ones used in Section 4 of the Listening Module.

Complete the summary below.
*Write **NO MORE THAN TWO WORDS** for each answer.*

When companies are interviewing job applicants, one quality that they generally demand is personal initiative. This means that the person is a **1** .... , and understands his or her needs for
2 .... and experience. Recruiters prefer candidates to show a **3** .... in their job applications.

Another valuable quality is being able to deal with
4 .... without giving up. Candidates should feel positive about a **5** ....
They should be confident, and treat other people with
6 ....

They should base their questions in the interview on previous **7** .... It is useful to record the **8** .... that they can offer the employer. It is essential to be good at
9 .... in a variety of situations.

Reading

2 This passage is similar to ones used in the Academic Reading Module, though shorter, at about 625 words.

What is public relations?

What do you think public relations is? You may think it is about getting coverage in newspapers and magazines, on radio and television. It is, but not only that. You may think it is holding conferences, having a stand at an exhibition, making a video. Indeed, they may be part of it. You may think that public relations is about how organisations work out ways of causing the least offence to the environment and society, while still managing to stay in business. Or you may realise that all organisations depend to some degree upon other groups: suppliers, employees, government, civil servants, pressure groups, local authorities, customers, the media, the general public, even upon individuals.

These are some of the 'publics' that are the concern of anyone practising public relations. Every organisation enjoys, or suffers, relationships with its publics that continually affect the well-being of both parties. These relationships are not necessarily chosen. They exist whether you like it or not. Locate a new factory and it will have a surrounding community that may object to noise, smell, emissions, working hours, trucks. Politicians need to know about it; the local authority will have to give permission; environmental pressure groups may not like the product. Nowadays these publics cannot be ignored. Public relations is everything to do with an organisation's relationships and therefore with its reputation.

Public relations works at two levels. First, at the general level, everyone reads, watches or listens to the media. That forms the basis for their perception of what an organisation seems to be like. Clearly PR needs the media, but it is wary of it, mainly because of the fear that messages will be twisted.

The second level is people's own direct experience of an organisation. If you are an employee you will almost certainly know what the company you work for is really like and it may not be how their reputation is projected in the media. One of the reasons for the efforts companies make to improve internal relations is to avoid a contradiction between its public relations stance and what its employees say about it.

All organisations, whether commercial or not, have competing objectives. Companies try to increase their sales. A non-commercial organisation stands up for what it believes in – whether or not fighting heart disease is a better purpose than selling shoes or working for a greener future. Both types of organisation deploy their public relations resources to help them in the fight.

It is this partiality which lowers public relations practitioners in the esteem of journalists, business leaders and, to a lesser extent, the general public. The general public tends to follow the pattern that when you are familiar with a business sector, you are likely to think about it favourably. If you are unfamiliar with it, you think about it unfavourably. Within the media and even business, public relations is not always regarded very highly.

The feeling within the PR business is that neither journalists nor business leaders really understand what public relations is. This stems from the multiple nature of public relations.

As a strategic force it is often unseen. The part it plays in deciding the essence of a firm or product, in planning, and in the conscience of industry, is out of the public eye. The presentational aspects of public relations, especially the hype, the sound bites and the photo opportunities, are seen all the time and taken to be all that there is. Accusations of superficiality also arise when instead of tackling root causes, public relations experts are called on to cover up, distract attention, neutralise criticism. These are the notorious 'public relations exercises'.

The profession therefore has the task of demonstrating that good public relations is not shallow or cosmetic, but is fundamental to the well-being of organisations.

Questions 1–6

Complete the summary below.
*Choose **NO MORE THAN TWO WORDS** from the passage for each answer.*

What is included in public relations?

The field of public relations includes gaining
1 .... in the media,
organising 2 .... and
minimising 3 .... It is
above all concerned with relationships.
These have an impact on the
4 .... both of the
organisation and of its 'publics', for example,
if a company is considering a
5 .... It is these
relationships which affect an organisation's
6 ....

Questions 7–14

Complete the summary below using words from the box.

How do people see public relations?

People's 7 .... of an
organisation are based on what they are
exposed to in the media, and any contact
they may have had with it. PR is afraid of
8 .... by the media,
and organisations need to ensure
9 .... between PR
messages and the opinions of
10 ....

Organisations have 11 ....
that bring them into conflict with one another.
PR is used as a weapon, and so is
often criticised for its lack of
12 .... PR may be
misunderstood because of the
13 .... of its strategic role
in an organisation. It is also sometimes
condemned for 14 ....
when carrying out 'public relations exercises'.

aims	consistency	customers
distortion	impressions	invisibility
objectivity	opposition	rejection
shallowness	staff	

Speaking *Part 3*

1 In small groups, discuss these questions.

- How far do you agree with the idea that studying history can help countries to avoid repeating past mistakes?
- Could you comment on the suggestion that studying our own country's history can help us to understand present-day situations?
- How important do you consider it to study the history of other countries?

Reading

2 Skim the passage below, which is part of an article in which a historian explains why he thinks the study of history is important. As you read it, answer this question.

The writer's main point is that the study of history can help us to

A understand our own country's present situation.
B avoid repeating the mistakes of the past.
C put right the bad effects of past events.
D improve relations with other countries.

⏱ about 650 words

IN DEFENCE OF HISTORY

We live in an age when immense energies and resources are devoted to the falsification of the past, and it is therefore all the more important, in those places where the past can be researched and discussed freely and
5 objectively, to carry out this work to the limit of our abilities. It has been argued that complete objectivity is impossible, since scholars are human beings, with their own loyalties and biases. This is no doubt true, but does not affect the issue. To borrow an analogy, any surgeon
10 will admit that complete asepsis – that is, conditions in which there is absolutely no risk of infection – is also impossible, but one does not, for that reason, perform surgery in a sewer. There is no need to write or teach history in an intellectual sewer either.

We should have no illusions about this. While some of us 15 may prefer to forget history or to rewrite history to serve some present purpose, the facts of the past, as distinct from the record or perception of the past, cannot be changed. And the consequences of those facts cannot be averted by either ignorance or misrepresentation, whatever its motives. 20

In our own time there has been a considerable change in our perception of the scope, scale and content of history. In bygone times, it was considered sufficient if a country, a society, or a community concerned itself with its own history. In these days, when almost every action or policy 25 has a global dimension, we know better. We also have a broader and deeper idea of what makes up our own history.

The rapid changes of recent years have forced us – sometimes painfully – to realise that the world is a much more diverse place than we had previously thought. As well 30 as other countries and nations, there are also other cultures and civilisations, separated from us by differences far greater than those of nationality or even of language. In the modern world, we may find ourselves forced to deal with societies professing different religions, brought up on 35 different religious writings and literature, formed by different experiences, and valuing different aspirations. Not a few of our troubles at the present time spring from a failure to recognise or even see these differences, an inability to achieve some understanding of the ways of 40 what were once remote and alien societies. They are now no longer remote and they should not be alien.

Nor, for that matter, should we be alien to them. Between the various countries and cultures that make up this world, the forces of modernisation are creating, however 45 much we may resist it, a global community in which we are all in touch with, and dependent on, one another. Even within each country, modernisation is destroying the barriers that previously divided us into neatly segregated communities, each living its own life in its own way, 50 suffering minimal contacts with the outsider. All that is ending, and we must learn to live together. Unfortunately, intercommunication has not kept pace with interaction, and we are still deplorably ignorant of each other's ways, values and aspirations. 55

Ignorance is of course not the only problem. There are real differences, which must be recognised and accepted; real issues, which must be confronted and resolved. But even real differences and real problems are made worse by ignorance, and a host of difficulties may reasonably be 60 blamed on ignorance alone. Our education today should be concerned with how cultures around the world have developed in all their diversity; with the great ideas that inspire them and the texts in which those ideas are expressed, with the achievements they made possible, 65 and with the common heritage their followers and successors share.

History is the collective memory, the guiding experience of human society, and we still badly need that guidance.

3 Answer these questions. It is easiest to read one question at a time, find the relevant part of the passage and answer the question. They are in text order.

*Choose the correct letter, **A**, **B** or **C**.*

1 According to the first paragraph, surgeons and historians should
   A be sure of their own abilities before doing their work.
   B aim towards an ideal, even though it is unattainable.
   C try to cure the problems caused by past actions.

2 What is the main point that the writer makes in the second paragraph?
   A We are unable to prevent the past from affecting the present.
   B There can be no justification for ignoring the lessons of the past.
   C People sometimes refuse to accept the truth of some past events.

3 In the third paragraph, the writer claims that our need to know about other countries has changed because
   A our understanding of our own countries is as complete as it can be.
   B we need to discover how relationships between countries have evolved.
   C countries are affected much more by each other than they used to be.

4 What does the writer identify as a problem in the fourth paragraph?
   A lack of understanding of societies in other countries
   B the degree of difference between societies
   C the lack of a common language in which to communicate

5 One of the effects of 'the forces of modernisation' mentioned in the fifth paragraph is
   A the destruction of the essential values of some communities.
   B domination of small communities by larger ones.
   C a reduction in the isolation of communities inside a country.

6 In the sixth paragraph, the writer claims that education can
   A reduce the number and seriousness of problems between cultures.
   B help cultures to become more similar to each other.
   C put an end to conflict between cultures.

Vocabulary Word building

4 Decide what each of these words means in the passage. They are all often used in academic writing.

   1 *immense* (adjective, line 1)
      a extremely large in size or amount
      b carefully controlled

   2 *falsification* (noun, line 2)
      a proving that something is untrue
      b changing something in order to deceive

   3 *objectivity* (noun, line 6)
      a judgement based on facts and not opinions
      b opposition or disagreement

   4 *bias* (noun, line 8)
      a a weakness or limitation in one's abilities
      b a tendency to allow personal opinions to unfairly influence one's judgement

   5 *analogy* (noun, line 9)
      a a contrast
      b a comparison

   6 *to avert* (verb, line 19)
      a to prevent something bad from happening
      b to turn something bad into something good

5 Complete each sentence with a word related in form to the word in brackets. You might find an English–English dictionary useful.

   EXAMPLE: There are many instances of history being ...*falsified*.... for political reasons. (false)

   1 The study of history is of little value unless it is .... (bias)
   2 It is sometimes claimed that we can learn from past situations that are .... to ones in the present. (analogy)
   3 Historians sometimes have to deal with conflicting evidence, and .... cannot always be sure of their facts. (consequence)
   4 Our view of the society we live in is affected by how we .... its history. (perception)
   5 A .... of scandals eventually led to the collapse of the government. (successor)
   6 The availability of many old documents on the Internet has changed the study of history beyond .... (recognise)

6 Do you think it is possible to avoid bias when interpreting the past?

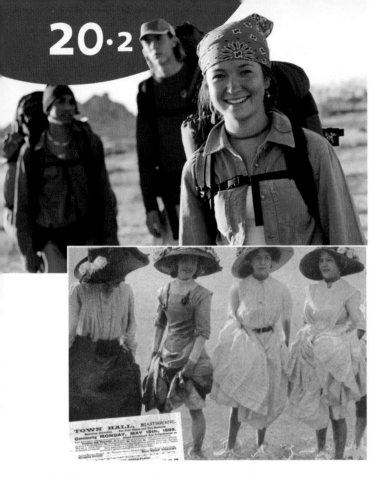

1 Do many people in your country go away on holiday? What types of holidays are popular?

Listening

2 You are going to hear part of a lecture about changes in the way British people take holidays. The lecture is in two parts. Before you listen to each part read the sentences or notes and think about the meaning of the missing words.

🎧 **Questions 1–7**
Complete the sentences below.
Write **NO MORE THAN TWO WORDS** for each answer.

1 In the 18th century the aristocracy thought the seaside was good for their ....
2 The aristocracy usually visited the seaside during the ....
3 The growth of seaside resorts during the mid 19th century was helped by the development of ....
4 In the mid 19th century people started going to seaside resorts for ....
5 In the 19th century, resorts tended to appeal to different ....
6 Some resorts attracted visitors by offering cheap ....
7 In the 1920s and 30s, ... recommended visits to the seaside.

🎧 **Questions 8–14**
Complete the notes below.
Write **NO MORE THAN THREE WORDS** for each answer.

Developments since 1948

1948 – new law giving workers **8** ....

1950s – large groups holidayed together, particularly workers from **9** .... centres in the north of England.

1960s – British seaside resorts lost their popularity because

- **10** .... planes went into service
- cheap **11** .... holidays were offered
- people wanted a **12** .... to show they had been abroad

Recently

- **13** .... make short breaks possible
- many young people travel abroad in a **14** .... between school and higher education.

Grammar Modal perfects

3 What does *could* mean in each of these sentences?

*Very few British people **could** swim in the 18th century. My luggage hasn't arrived – it **could** have been put on the wrong plane.*

G ┄┄┄┄➔ page 143

4 Rewrite each sentence, replacing everything that is underlined with a modal perfect.

EXAMPLE: It is impossible that people <u>found</u> it easy to travel before the coming of the railways.
*People **can't have found** it easy to travel before the coming of the railways.*

1 In the 1950s so many people went to the seaside at the same time that <u>they obviously wanted</u> to stay in crowds.
2 <u>I'm sure</u> the residents of quiet fishing villages <u>weren't</u> happy with the crowds of visitors.
3 Resorts that wanted to strengthen their tourist industry in the 1960s <u>needed to make</u> more effort <u>than they actually did</u> to compete with foreign resorts.
4 <u>It is possible that</u> British resorts <u>did not realise</u> how cheap holidays abroad would become.
5 <u>It was naïve of</u> people in the 18th century <u>to believe</u> that drinking seawater would cure any illness.
6 The popularity of holidays abroad <u>was perhaps encouraged</u> by a desire for a better life.

5 Here are some examples of errors that IELTS candidates have made with modal perfects. Correct the errors, making as few changes as possible.

1 The glass was broken, and I think that may caused by a cat!
2 He mustn't have thought enough about the consequences of his actions.
3 If I'd been there, you wouldn't had such a bad time.
4 The accident was very sad, but it can be prevented.
5 You must press the wrong button, because the lift went up instead of down.
6 It's your own fault you feel sick – you should didn't eat so much.
7 He said it took him two hours to walk here but it's only three kilometres, so it couldn't take so long.

Pronunciation *The 'long' pronunciation of vowels*

6 Look at these words where the stressed vowel (underlined) has its long pronunciation, and complete the pattern rules.

Each of the letters *a e i o u* represents two main pronunciations: the 'short' ones in *mad, let, bit, not, cut*, and the 'long' ones (long vowels and diphthongs) in *made, complete, bite, note, cute*.

Although there are exceptions, there are some regular patterns which will help you to pronounce many words correctly. (Note that vowels immediately followed by *r* normally have a different pronunciation.)

1 *safe, complete, ride, stone, amuse*
The vowel is followed by one consonant + silent
....

2 *safest, completed, rider, stony, amusing*
The word derives from a word in pattern 1, using a suffix (additional ending), particularly *-er, -est, -ed,* .... , ...

3 *creative, completion, final, social, solution*
The vowel is followed by one .... + an unstressed .... , such as *-ive, -ion, -ian, -al, -ial, -ous, -ious*.

7 In each set of words, circle the one that does *not* fit the given pattern.

Pattern 1: extreme, write, since, presume, June
Pattern 2: replaced, closest, icy, written, cuter
Pattern 3: spacious, fashion, region, conclusive, global

🎧 Listen and check that the words you have circled have short vowel pronunciations.

Speaking *Part 2*

8 With a partner, plan a short talk on this topic.

> Describe life in a particular period of history.
>
> You should say:
>
> which period you have chosen
> what were the benefits of life then
> what were the drawbacks of life then
>
> and explain whether you would like to have lived then.

Now give your talk to the rest of the class, one of you focusing on the benefits and the other on the drawbacks. Try to use modal perfects. At the end, everyone should vote on the best period to live in.

Some areas you might like to consider:
medicine   hygiene   working conditions
social relationships   homes   transport
clothing   education

9 All the answers to this quiz are given somewhere in this book.

HOW'S YOUR HISTORY?

1 Pangaea began to split apart around 200 million years ago. What was it?
2 What type of animal became extinct 65 million years ago?
3 Which musical instrument, whose name means 'sweet little goose', has existed for tens of thousands of years?
4 In which country were chopsticks invented?
5 What were first catalogued in the 2nd century BC, by the Greek Hipparchus?
6 In the 18th and 19th centuries, what new buildings in Britain led to many people moving from the countryside to towns?
7 What everyday product, manufactured by Pears, was among the first to be given a brand name?
8 What concept did Ebenezer Howard develop in the 1880s and 1890s?
9 What name is given to the rise in the birth rate in Australia and other countries between 1945 and the mid 1960s?
10 In 1957, plastic bags were introduced in the USA. What were they intended to wrap?

Writing folder 10

The Academic Writing Module

Advice

Before taking the test
- Time yourself writing 150 words on a topic that you are familiar with.
- Work out how long it takes you to write 250 words.
- Work out how many lines you use for 150 words and for 250 words.

Prepare
- Read the question and plan your answer.
- Re-read the question to make sure you have kept to the point.

Write
- Write your answer clearly and concisely.

Improve
- Check and improve your answer.
- Draw a line through anything you want to omit, e.g. ~~shows~~.
- Use numbers or an asterisk to show where you want to insert something, e.g. ①, *. Write the addition below your answer.
- Make sure your answer can be read easily, but don't waste time rewriting it.

Writing Task 1

- Spend 20 minutes on Task 1: it accounts for a third of the marks.
- Allow 5 minutes to prepare, 10 minutes to write, and 5 minutes to improve.
- You are given information in the form of a table, chart or diagram, and should present it in written form. Don't invent explanations or additional information.
- Give only the most important figures. They should be approximately correct: they don't need to be exactly right. Don't make any calculations.
- The key information can be presented concisely in an answer of about 150 words. If your answer is much longer (over about 200 words), it probably contains too much detail.

1 Read this task and answer the questions following it.

You should spend about 20 minutes on this task.

The charts below show what the history and engineering graduates of a particular university were doing six months after graduating. The figures cover a two-year period.
Summarise the information by selecting and reporting the main features, and make comparisons where relevant.

Write at least 150 words.

Destinations of graduates, six months after graduating

History graduates

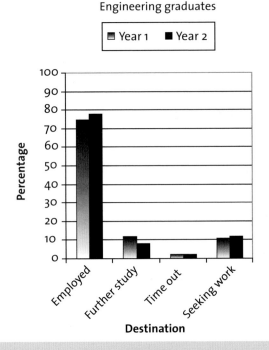

Engineering graduates

1 Underline the key words in the rubric.

2 What is the main comparison being made: subject, year or destination? Study how the bar charts are organised, including
   - the heading (e.g. *Destinations of graduates*)
   - the legend (the years)
   - the categories on the X-axis (the various destinations)
   - the values on the Y-axis (percentages).

3 What exactly do the bar charts show? Decide which three of the following pieces of information are shown by the charts.
   a About 63% of year 1's history graduates were employed.
   b More people studied engineering than history.
   c The number of historians was the same in years 1 and 2.
   d A greater proportion of historians than of engineers undertook further study.
   e Engineers were more likely to be seeking work than to be taking time out.
   f More historians than engineers took time out.

4 What is the most important information shown by the charts? Choose two of the following.
   a Historians were less likely to be seeking work than engineers.
   b A higher proportion of engineering graduates than of historians were employed.
   c The year-on-year changes in the figures were generally small.
   d Historians were more likely to go on to further study than engineers.

5 Which of these ways of organising your answer is likely to work best? This will be affected by the main comparison (1 above).
   a Go through the figures for history graduates, then those for engineering graduates.
   b Go through the figures for each year in turn.
   c Go through the four destinations, comparing the figures for historians and engineers.

6 Write brief notes for an outline of your answer.
   Introduction
      Topic: ....
      Summary: ....
   Comparison
      Employment: ....
      Further study: ....
      Time out: ....
      Seeking work: ....

7 Now write your answer.

Writing Task 2

- Spend 40 minutes on Task 2: it carries two thirds of the marks.
- Allow 10 minutes to prepare, 20 minutes to write, and 10 minutes to improve.
- You should consider a range of opinions, rather than only one point of view.
- If the question has two parts (as in the example below), make sure you answer both of them.
- If you have a lot to say, limit yourself to three or four points, to keep to about 250 words.
- When preparing, it may be easier to decide on your introduction after you have made notes.
- When writing, start with a short introduction.
- Deal with each opinion or main point in a separate paragraph.
- Finish with a short conclusion.
- Remember that you are being tested on your command of English, not on your knowledge, intelligence, or whether the examiner agrees with you.
- Give examples when you can. They don't have to be true!

2 Read this task, and write your answer.

You should spend about 40 minutes on this task.

Write about the following topic:
In many countries there is a shortage of suitable people for essential jobs.
What do you think are the causes of this problem and what measures could be taken to solve it?

Give reasons for your answer and include any relevant examples from your own knowledge or experience.

Write at least 250 words.

Units 17–20 Revision

Topic review

1 Compare and contrast the paired subjects below, giving as much information as possible.

   1 cars of the 1950s and of the present
   2 economic migrants and refugees
   3 job security and a high salary
   4 nature and nurture
   5 translations and original works
   6 you: at the beginning of this course and now

Grammar

2 Complete the second sentences so that they mean the same as the first, using a noun phrase.

   EXAMPLE: It is often difficult to decide when to expand a business.
   The .... *decision as to* .... when to expand a business is often a difficult one.

   1 With the advent of electronic publishing, translations of modern literature have become more widely available.
   Electronic publishing has increased .... translations of modern literature.

   2 People moved from the countryside to the towns in high numbers as a result of the industrial revolution.
   .... high numbers of people from the countryside to the towns resulted from the industrial revolution.

   3 Birds migrate seasonally to another location when food becomes scarce in a habitat.
   The scarcity of food in a habitat causes the .... birds to another location.

   4 The information age arrived, bringing changes in what people expected, as well as making them uncertain about the future.
   The .... the information age brought changes in .... , as well as .... the future.

3 Use a modal perfect of a verb in capitals to speculate about the following situations, using the ideas given in brackets and adding any necessary words. Decide whether it is possible to use both a simple and continuous form each time.

   EXAMPLE : The hardback edition of this book has gone out of print.
   REPLACE / SELL
   (paperback edition; poor sales)
   It could have been replaced by the paperback edition.
   It could have sold poorly. OR It could have been selling poorly.

   1 People in the 16th century lost their teeth early in life.
   HAVE / RECEIVE / DRINK
   (bad diet, little dental care, impure water)

   2 The number of tourists coming to London fell in late 2005.
   BE
   (cost, preference for other locations, threat of terrorism)

   3 A swallow migrated to the same nest three years running.
   USE / RECOGNISE
   (solar navigation, landmarks, sense of smell)

   4 Jenny didn't get the job she wanted.
   GIVE / BE / OFFER / SUFFER
   (Jenny: poor impression at interview, not decisive enough; the company: internal applicant, unforeseen cutbacks)

   5 Ryan received a low mark for his essay.
   BE / CONTAIN
   (poor organisation, irrelevance, too short)

4 Fill each space in this text with *how*, *whether* or *why*.

There are different approaches to the teaching of history in Britain, depending on **0** ......*whether*...... the target students are in primary, secondary or tertiary education. The history that features on the primary curriculum is largely project based and it is easy to see **1** .... For example, young children enjoy finding out **2** .... the Romans prepared their food, and **3** .... every native American lived in a 'tipi' or **4** .... , instead, some tribes used other types of living accommodation.

The history syllabus at secondary level used to focus largely on the superficial learning of dates and the events linked to them, rather than requiring students to debate **5** .... and **6** .... such events evolved. Nowadays, however, this rather unsatisfactory approach has been replaced by a more investigative style, where students explore the reasons **7** .... an event may have taken place, provided with at least some historical data.

However, it is only at tertiary level that students have the opportunity to delve into primary sources in any major way, when this is really **8** .... history should be approached.

Vocabulary

6 Use the definitions of words to do with work to complete the two word puzzles below. What are the horizontal words? Write a short definition for each one.

EXAMPLE: **0** a building or site used for business

1 a more important job within the same organisation (9)
2 a feeling that your position is safe and certain to continue (3, 8)
3 to be in charge of (a business) (3)
4 a way of working for a set period each day, for example in a factory (5, 4)
5 a small group of job applicants chosen from a larger group (5, 4)
6 all the people who are able to work in a country or area (6, 5)
7 an informal word for line manager (4)
8 the duties someone has in their job (16)
9 what causes a person to want to do something (10)
10 the money gained by a business once all costs have been deducted (6)

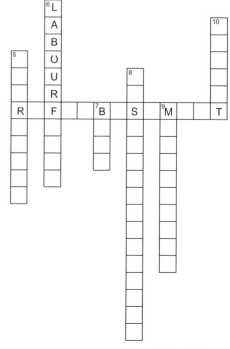

Style extra

5 Complete this tutor's evaluation of an essay with words formed from those in brackets. Sometimes you will need to use a negative prefix.

You have **0** (deny) ......*undeniably*...... done a great deal of appropriate research and your essay reads well. In your **1** (introduce) .... , you include some of the **2** (centre) .... issues you go on to discuss, but not all of them. This may be a simple **3** (see) .... on your part. I suggest you read this through again.

More **4** (worry) .... , the main premise of your work is, in my opinion, rather **5** (question) .... Perhaps you could go back to your original sources and check them **6** (care) .... I think you'll find that you have been **7** (inform) .... ! Have you been using material from the Internet **8** (occasion) .... ? If so, please be very sure of the **9** (valid) .... of any information you consult. Please make an early appointment to see me.

Grammar folder

Unit 1
Modality

The true modal verbs are *will, would, shall, should, can, could, may, might, must.* They have these grammatical characteristics:

1 In the negative they are followed by *not* or *n't*, e.g. *mustn't* (main verbs need a negative form of *to do*).
2 In questions they go before the subject, e.g. *Can you speak any foreign languages?* (main verbs need *to do*).
3 They have only one form: there is no infinitive, present or past participle, or *-s* ending.
4 They are followed by an infinitive without *to*.

There are also some verbs, referred to as semi-modals, which share certain characteristics of modals. These include *have (got) to, used to, ought to* and *need*.

Ability and inability: *can, can't, could, couldn't*

can, can't – present
Helen can speak three languages.
I can't understand what this writer means.

could, couldn't – past forms
If I could plan my essays more efficiently, they wouldn't take me so long.
When I was a child I could remember everything I read.
I couldn't understand why my essay only got a grade C.

To be able/unable to has a similar meaning.

Possibility: *may (not), might (not), can, could*
(and see GF Unit 10)

may (not), might (not), could
May and *might* are generally used to talk about something specific. *May* is usually slightly more sure than *might* or *could.*
Your computer may/might/could crash, so always back up your files.
Don't worry about the test – it may/might not be very hard.

Note that *couldn't* doesn't mean the same as *may/might not*.

can
Can is used for a more general, theoretical possibility.
Computers can crash. (= Computers sometimes crash.)

Strong obligation: *must, mustn't, have to,* (informal) *have got to*

must
Must refers to strong present and future obligations, imposed or accepted by the speaker. It also refers to laws and rules.
I must go home now and write an assignment.

have to / have got to
Have to / have got to refer to strong obligations in the present and future that are not imposed by the speaker. The speaker may be distancing him/herself from the obligation.
I have to read all these books by the end of the week. (My tutor says so.)
If in doubt whether to use *must* or *have to*, use *have to*.

had to
Had to refers to past and reported obligations.
I had to get up very early to go to school.
Our tutor said we had to be more careful when choosing topics.

Prohibition: *mustn't*

Mustn't means that something is forbidden, or that the speaker is saying what not to do.
When writing essays, you mustn't copy from the Internet.

Lack of obligation: *doesn't/don't have to*

Don't have to means that something isn't obligatory. Usually it's optional.
We don't have to attend the lecture as we've finished our essays.
At my school we didn't have to take any tests in the first year.

Note that the meanings of *mustn't* and *don't have to* are very different.

Weak obligation and weak prohibition: *should, shouldn't, ought to*

These are used to give advice, or say what would be a good thing to do, now or in the future.

- *Should* and *ought to* mean the same, but *should* is used much more often.
  You should spend / ought to spend more time studying and less time playing computer games.
- *Shouldn't* is used to give advice about what not to do. *Oughtn't to* is also possible, but is falling out of use.
  You shouldn't spend so much time playing computer games.

Necessity and lack of necessity: *need* as a main verb

Nowadays, *need* is mainly used as a main verb, forming the negative and questions with *to do*.
We didn't need to go to the seminar as it was for new students only.
Do you need to read any more books before you write your essay?

However *need* is still occasionally used as a modal verb, mostly in the negative, where the lack of necessity comes from the speaker:
You needn't come with me if you'd rather carry on studying.
This could also be expressed as
You don't need to come with me if you'd rather carry on studying.
For modal perfects, see GF Unit 20.

Unit 2
Perfect tenses

The past, present and future perfect tenses place a situation or action before a particular time. They are often used when clauses or sentences are not in chronological order. Compare these sentences:
Stephen played football for twenty years, and gave up last year. – This is in chronological order: he played then gave up. The past simple is used for both verbs.
Stephen gave up football last year. He had been playing for twenty years. – Here a past perfect tense is used to show that he played *before* he gave up.

Just, yet and *the first/only time* normally need a perfect tense.
Have you put your name down for the student games yet?
Last year was the first time I'd attended the student games.

Past perfect

The action/situation comes before a particular time in the past.
We won the championship last year – we'd only won it twice before.

Present perfect

This tense connects the past with the present.
Main meanings:
- an action/situation that started in the past and has continued to the present
  Sports of some sort have existed for thousands of years.
  I've never watched a rugby match.
- an action/situation that ended at an unspecified time in the past
  The only sport Joanne has ever played is table tennis.

- an action/situation that has caused a situation in the present.
  I've lost my trainers, so I can't go running.

Future perfect
The action/situation comes before a particular time in the future.
By the time the games start, at least twenty teams will have entered.

Perfect continuous tenses
These combine the meanings of the continuous and perfect tenses. They may emphasise a length of time, and may suggest that the action is temporary.
The players had been training for months and were very fit.
Next January Rachel will have been coaching the team for ten years.
Continuous tenses can only be used with verbs referring to a physical or mental action.

Present perfect continuous
Main meanings:
- actions which have lasted for some time and are likely to continue. Often a length of time is given.
  Some researchers have been developing software that can identify significant events in sport.
  I've been playing football since I was a child.
- actions which have lasted for some time and have just stopped. Usually no length of time is given.
  I've been watching the World Cup match on TV and now I'm going to have a cup of coffee.

Unit 3
Cleft sentences

Cleft sentences divide a sentence or clause into two sections, in order to highlight a particular part of it. This is particularly useful in written English, as it lacks the intonation and stress which are used to give prominence in speech.

It type: *it + to be* + key idea
This is the most common type of cleft sentence. From the sentence *Pear's created a brand in the nineteenth century because it hoped to increase sales*, it is possible to create several cleft sentences, each focusing on a different element (in **bold**):
*It was **Pear's** that created a brand in the nineteenth century because it hoped to increase sales.*
*It was **a brand** that Pear's created in the nineteenth century because it hoped to increase sales.*
*It was **in the nineteenth century** that Pear's created a brand because it hoped to increase sales.*
*It was **because it hoped to increase sales** that Pear's created a brand in the nineteenth century.*
The key idea often contrasts with something else, e.g. in the last example, it was for this reason and not another one.

The introductory part of a cleft sentence sometimes uses a modal verb + *to be*, e.g.
It must have been Pear's that created the first brand name.
It might be Procter & Gamble that makes the most washing powders.
When a pronoun is focused on, it is normally in the subject form, e.g.
Henry Ford invented the Model T Ford motor car. It was he who said, 'People can have it any colour – so long as it's black.'
In informal speech the object form (e.g. *him*) is often used.

What type: *What* clause as subject
This structure focuses attention on the part of the sentence that follows it. The first sentence in each pair uses a standard structure, while the second uses a *what* clause, to highlight the **bold** section.
You need a book about advertising.
*What you need is **a book about advertising**.*

I'm going to apply for a job in marketing.
*What I'm going to do is **(to) apply for a job in marketing**.*
Pear's created the first brand of soap.
*What Pear's did was **(to) create the first brand of soap**.*

Unit 4
Adverbial clauses

Adverbial clauses (like adverbs, such as *yesterday*, and adverbial phrases, such as *at the end of the week*) can add a large range of meanings to a sentence. They may begin or end a sentence.

These are the most common meanings of adverbial clauses, with some of the conjunctions that introduce them. The adverbial clauses are in **bold**.

Time *when, while, whenever, before, after, as, as soon as, once, now (that), since, until, till* (informal)
Time clauses use present tenses to refer to the future:
*Tell me **when you contact Jill**.*
This adverbial clause refers to when you should tell me. Compare *Tell me when you'll contact Jill.*
Here the *when* clause is not adverbial, it is the object: it refers to *what* I want you to tell me now.

Place *where, wherever*
*It's worth communicating with people, **wherever you meet them**.*

Cause and reason *because, as, since*
***Since nobody knew where she was**, nobody could help her.*

Purpose (what is hoped for as a result of the action) *so that, so* (informal)
*I shouted, **so (that) they would know I could see them**.*

Condition *if, unless, in case, on condition that, provided that, providing, as/so long as*
*You can explain the research project to our visitors **on condition that you don't use any jargon**.*
Like time clauses, conditionals use present tenses to refer to the future. The basic conditional structures are listed below. For variations using modal verbs, see GF Unit 8. The conditional clause states the condition which must be satisfied before the main clause may be true.
a   **Open conditional:** present tense in conditional clause, imperative in main clause.
    *Give me a call **if you need any help**.*
b   **Zero conditional:** present tense in conditional clause, present tense in main clause. This refers to something that is generally true.
    *Babies don't learn to speak **unless they hear other people speaking**.*
c   **First conditional:** present tense in conditional clause, *will* in main clause. This refers to something that may or may not happen in the future.
    *Your children will learn English very easily, **provided they play with English-speaking children**.*
d   **Second conditional:** past tense in conditional clause, *would* in main clause. This refers to something that isn't true now:
    *People would understand you more easily **if you spoke a little more slowly**.*
    Or it can refer to something in the future that is unlikely to happen:
    ***If everyone started learning the same foreign language**, we would all understand each other.*
e   **Third conditional:** past perfect tense in conditional clause, *would have done* in main clause. This refers to something that didn't happen in the past:
    *I spent so long on my mobile that I wouldn't have been surprised **if the battery had gone flat**.*

f Mixed conditionals: often past perfect tense in conditional clause (referring to something that didn't happen in the past), *would* in main clause (referring to something that isn't the case in the present or future):
If phones hadn't been invented, *it would be hard to keep in touch.*

Concession (contrast) See also GF Unit 6. *although, though* (informal), *even though, while, whilst* (formal), *whereas* (formal)
*Animals communicate, **although** they can't speak like human beings.*

Condition + contrast *even if, whether … or …*
Even if Roger phones us now, *it's too late to meet him this evening.*
(= I don't expect Roger to phone us now, but if he does …)
Whether I text them or email them, *I'll still have to wait for a reply.*

Manner *as if, as though*
*Dogs often behave **as if they can understand what people say.***

Unit 5
The passive

The passive is used to focus on a situation or action, and not on the agent – the person or process bringing it about. It is particularly common in academic English.
Usually the agent isn't stated. If it is, it is introduced by *by*.
The next meeting of the Carrier Bag Consortium will be held in London.
Billions of plastic bags are used by British consumers every year.

Formation of the passive

The passive is formed with the verb *to be* and the past participle of a transitive verb, e.g.

present simple	*It is made*
present continuous	*It is being made*
present perfect	*It has been made*
past simple	*It was made*
past continuous	*It was being made*
past perfect	*It had been made*
future simple	*It will be made*

It can also be formed with a modal + *be* + past participle:
It should be made
It might have been made

Compare these sentences:
A *The Irish Government introduced a tax on plastic bags in 2002.*
B *A tax on plastic bags was introduced by the Irish Government in 2002.*
In the active sentence, A, the agent (*The Irish Government*) is the subject of the sentence. What it introduced (*a tax on plastic bags*) is the object.
In the passive sentence, B, the object of the active sentence is the subject (*A tax on plastic bags*). The agent is a prepositional phrase introduced by *by* (*by the Irish Government*).

The passive + infinitive

Passive forms of verbs like *say, think, claim* are often followed by an infinitive, particularly in academic writing:
Plastic bags are sometimes claimed to be the worst form of pollution.

Non-finite passives

The infinitive and *-ing* form can be passive (in **bold**).
*Many people want the production of plastic bags **to be reduced.***
*Sea creatures risk **being harmed** by plastic bags.*

Unit 6
Concessive clauses

Concessive clauses (clauses of concession or contrast) imply a contrast between two circumstances: in the light of the circumstance in the concessive clause, the circumstance in the main clause is surprising. (See GF Unit 4.)

Conjunction + finite clause

Finite clauses are normally introduced by these conjunctions:
although, though (informal), *even though* (more emphatic), *while, whilst* (formal)
While they may not be able to analyse their pleasure, most people enjoy some form of music.

Whereas (formal) is mainly used to contrast two equivalent ideas, without implying that one is surprising:
Gamelan music relaxes me, whereas steel bands make me want to dance.

Condition + contrast *even if, whether … or …*
I listen to music all the time, even if I'm working. (= You wouldn't expect me to listen if I'm working, but I do.)

Other finite constructions:
Much as I would like to come to the concert, I'm really too busy.
(= Even though I would very much like to come to the concert …)
Strange as it may seem, that was the pianist's first public performance.
(= Even though it may seem very strange …)

Conjunction + verbless clause

The words in brackets can be omitted.
Although (he was) unable to read music, Keith could sing well.

Words that can be omitted are the subject and verb of the concessive clause, when the subject of the main clause is the same, and the verb is *to be*. This omission is most common in more formal or literary language.

Preposition + noun or *-ing* form *despite, in spite of*
Ticket sales for the concert were poor, in spite of all the publicity.
Despite trying really hard, I didn't enjoy the music Marian played me.

Unit 8
Modals in conditional sentences

For the basic conditional structures, see GF Unit 4.
Modal verbs can be used in main clauses as alternatives to *will* and *would*. Those listed below (and their negative forms) are the most common ones.
a Open conditional: modal verbs can't be used as imperatives.
b Zero conditional: *can, may, must*
  If someone is brought up in East Asia they may well be able to use chopsticks.
c First conditional: *can, may, might, must, should, shall*
  If you want some more food, you should ask for it politely.
d Second conditional: *might, could*
  If forks didn't exist, we might eat different types of food.
e Third conditional: modal perfects (see GF Unit 20), that is
  could, might, must (not *mustn't*), *can't* (not *can*) + *have done*
  He might not have eaten so much if he hadn't been very hungry.

Unit 9
Inversion

Inversion means that a verb comes before the subject of a sentence. It is most common in questions, but it also occurs in certain other structures.
In most forms of inversion, an auxiliary verb or *to be* comes before the subject, as in most questions.

After *so* when it stands for part of a sentence
The water supply failed, and so did food production.

After negative and degree adverbs

Certain adverbs and adverbial phrases can be moved to the beginning of the clause for emphasis. These are usually negative in meaning, or are adverbs of degree (e.g. *only, little*).
Not only did the water supply fail, but so did food production.
Under no circumstances will access to the ruins be allowed.
No sooner was the building finished than it was demolished.
Little do we know how much history lies beneath these new skyscrapers.

In third conditional clauses

This is fairly formal.
Had the city defences been repaired in time, the flood might have been prevented. (= If the city defences had been repaired in time …)

After place adverbs

When a place adverb or adverbial phrase is moved to the beginning of the sentence, the main verb can be placed before the subject if it is in a simple tense.
Here comes the next party of tourists.
Beyond the city boundaries lived a farming community.

Unit 10
Modal verbs of speculation and deduction

Certainty *must, can't* and *couldn't*

The interpretation of dreams must be one of the oldest human activities. (= I am sure that the interpretation of dreams is one of the oldest human activities.)
The certainty may be based on evidence, that is, the speaker may have reached that conclusion by a process of deduction.

Can't and *couldn't* mean the speaker is certain that something isn't true, maybe having considered evidence:
Dreaming about a forest can't/couldn't mean that I want to escape, because I'm very content with my life.

When speculating, we can use *may* (*not*), *might* (*not*) and *could* to talk about a specific possibility, and *can* for a more general, theoretical possibility. See GF Unit 1.

For modal perfects, see GF Unit 20.

Unit 11
Non-finite clauses

Non-finite clauses contain an infinitive (e.g. *to do*), present participle (*doing*) or past participle (*done*). The non-finite clauses in these examples are in **bold**.

As object: infinitive or present participle, depending on the verb that it follows.
*I hope **to see a glacier during my trip to Argentina.***
*I enjoy **listening to the sound of the waves.***

As subject, at the beginning of the sentence: present participle
***Preventing pollution of the lagoon** may not be easy.*

As subject, with *it* replacing the non-finite clause, which moves to the end of the sentence: infinitive
*It may not be easy **to prevent pollution of the lagoon.***
See Unit 7 Style extra, page 49.

As object, with *it* replacing the non-finite clause, which moves to the end of the sentence: infinitive
*The government is finding it hard **to persuade people to move away from the coast.***

As relative clause, with active meaning: present participle
*The talk is aimed at scientists **studying sea temperatures**.*

As relative clause, with passive meaning: past participle
*Measurements **taken over the last two centuries** show how the coastline has changed.*

As a form of relative clause: infinitive
*A good person **to consult about plate tectonics** is your professor.*
*The talk **to be given tomorrow** will be about the formation of mountains.*

As adverbial clause of purpose: infinitive
*A bridge has been constructed **to provide easy access to the island.***

Unit 12
Infinitives

Verbs have several infinitive forms. These can follow modal verbs (e.g. *must*) and certain main verbs (e.g. *want*), and are used in certain non-finite clauses (see GF Unit 11).
Major forms:
a ***(to) do*** – infinitive (active)
   *A good environment helps rats **(to) learn** quickly.*
   *An experiment was carried out **to investigate** how babies learn.*
b ***(to) be done*** – infinitive (passive)
   *More work needs **to be done** before we can describe the process.*
c ***(to) have done*** – perfect infinitive (active). Related to both the perfect tenses and to the past simple.
   *My dog seems **to have learnt** certain skills from his parents.* (= It seems that my dog learnt / has learnt …)
   *I'm sorry **to have missed** your presentation last week.* (= I'm sorry that I missed …)
   *I may **have finished** my research by next February.* (= It's possible that I will have finished …). NB *may finish* is also possible.
d ***(to) have been done*** – perfect infinitive (passive). Related to both the perfect tenses and to the past simple.
   *The rise in our average height seems **to have been caused** by better nutrition.* (= It seems that the rise in our average height was / has been caused …)
Continuous infinitives: related to continuous tenses, and only used with verbs that can be in those tenses. Mostly used after modal verbs.
e ***(to) be doing*** – continuous infinitive (active)
   *You must **be feeling** hungry.*
   *I would like **to be watching** TV instead of reading about genetics.*
f ***(to) have been doing*** – perfect continuous infinitive (active)
   *You should **have been working**, not having a good time!*
   *I seem **to have been studying** human social behaviour all my life.*

Unit 13
Talking about the future

There are many ways of talking about the future, usually reflecting the speaker's attitude. These are the main ones:

Will/'ll

● a decision or offer made at this moment
  I'll fetch my telescope so we can study the stars.
● a prediction; the most neutral way of referring to the future
  Rosetta will reach its destination in 2014.
● *Shall* can be used when the subject is *I* or *we*, particularly in questions, suggestions and offers when it comes before the subject.
  Shall we go and see the new film about the destruction of the Earth tomorrow?

Going to

● something already decided or (less often) arranged
  A new space probe is going to be launched next year.
● a future result of a present situation
  The recent rise in sea temperature means that violent storms are going to become more common.

Present continuous

● something already arranged or (less often) decided
  I'm being interviewed on the radio tomorrow about my research.

Present simple

This is less common than the structures above. It is used for
● a timetable, not usually involving the speaker
  Professor Wynn's lecture on asteroids starts at 3 p.m.
● time and conditional clauses introduced by *if, unless, when*, etc.
  I'll email you my map of the sky as soon as I get home.

Future continuous

- a temporary event in the future
  This time tomorrow I'll be sitting in the Planetarium.
- a future event that will happen as a matter of course, independently of the wishes or intention of anyone concerned
  I try to avoid Professor Swift, but I'll be seeing her next week.

Future perfect simple

- an event or situation that will be finished before a particular time in the future
  I'll have finished this project by Friday.

Future perfect continuous

- an event or situation that will be finished before a particular time in the future. It may emphasise a length of time, and may suggest that the action is temporary.
  By the time Rosetta reaches Churyumov-Gerasimenko, it will have been travelling for ten years.

Unit 14
Pronouns

Pronouns are words that replace nouns or noun phrases. Most of them can't follow *a* or *the*. There are several categories of pronouns, including personal (e.g. *I*, *him*), possessive (e.g. *our*, *ours*), negative (e.g. *nobody*, *nothing*), relative (e.g. *who*, *that*).

This, these, that, those

This and *these* refer to something near, and *that* and *those* refer to something distant.
These books used to belong to my grandmother. (The books are in front of me.)
Let's go and look more closely at that painting. (The painting is on the other side of the room.)

In a text, *this* can refer to something that comes earlier or later, and *that* normally refers to something earlier.
Several potato harvests failed. This/That is why many Irish people emigrated in the 1840s.
This is my proposal: to restrict our analysis to the last fifty years.

When referring back to an earlier noun phrase, these pronouns can be followed by *one* or *ones*. This is fairly informal.
Of all the histories of Australia I've read, I found this (one) the most interesting.

One, ones

These pronouns can follow *a*, *the*, etc. They replace singular and plural count nouns.
My home is far bigger than the one that my grandparents lived in.
There is sometimes tension between a village's established residents and new ones coming in from towns.

Each, everyone, everything

With *each*, it is clear from the context what is being referred to.
All these vegetables look very good, so I'd like some of each, please.
The government can't afford to provide a high standard of living for everyone.

Other, another, others

Other and *others* can follow *the*, *my*, etc. Although *other* and *another* normally go before a noun (e.g. *the other day*), all three words can be used to replace a noun phrase.
There were two main employers in the town: Armstrong's was one, and Jifford was the other.
Poor harvests were one reason for migrating, and lack of job opportunities was another.
The decline in the birth rate affects not only the young, but also others, who may find their state retirement pensions reduced.

Unit 16
Verb patterns

Verb patterns are one of the most complicated areas of English. Most verbs can be used in a number of possible patterns, and each verb has its own set of possibilities.

See also GF Unit 18, on verbs followed by *wh-* clauses.

The most common patterns (relevant verbs in **bold**):

a Intransitive verb (no object or complement)
  *A healthy child **grows** quickly.*
b Linking verb + noun phrase or adjective phrase as complement (subject and complement refer to the same person or thing)
  *Jeremy **became** a scientist.*
  *Small differences in personality can **grow** much greater in later life.*
c Transitive verb + noun phrase as object (subject and object refer to different people or things)
  *Rachel **met** a scientist.*
d Verb + finite clause
  *Many psychologists **believe** (that) health is related to personality.*
e Verb + infinitive
  *In my article I **attempted** to define the concept of personality.*
f Verb + object + *to* infinitive
  *Many psychologists **believe** certain aspects of personality to be innate.*
g Verb + object + bare infinitive
  *Recognition of a person **makes** electrical activity occur in our brains.*
h Verb + *-ing* form (including gerunds)
  *Would you **mind** explaining your experiment again, please?*
i Verb + object + *-ing* form (mostly with verbs of the senses)
  *Jeremy **heard** a scientist talking about childhood experiences.*
j Verb + indirect object + direct object
  *Jasmine **gave** her tutor a copy of her dissertation.*

Unit 17
Relative clauses

There are two types of relative clause:
Defining: gives essential information to identify what the noun refers to.
Birds which migrate are able to navigate extremely effectively.
The sentence is only about birds which migrate, and not all birds.

Non-defining: gives additional but non-essential information. If this information is omitted, it is still clear what exactly the noun refers to.
Arctic terns, which travel around 24,000 km a year, spend part of the year near Antarctica.
This sentence is about *all* Arctic terns.

As the examples show, commas are used in non-defining clauses, but not in defining clauses. It is important to use punctuation correctly in relative clauses, as inaccurate use can change the meaning of the sentence.
The company laid off its migrant workers who had come from Italy.
The company laid off its migrant workers, who had come from Italy.
In the first example only the migrant workers who had come from Italy lost their jobs – not migrant workers from other countries. In the second example, all the migrant workers had come from Italy, and they all lost their jobs.

Relative pronouns

In **defining relative clauses**, you can use:

- *who* or *that* when referring to people
  Men who/that migrated in order to make a living were often prepared to accept any available work.
- *which* or *that* when referring to things
  Migrants often had to accept jobs (which/that) local people refused to do.

The relative pronoun can be left out when it is the object of a clause, as in the second example above, where *which/that* stands for the object of *to do*. It must be included when it is the subject, as in *who/that migrated* in the first example above.

In **non-defining relative clauses**, you can use:
- *who* when referring to people
  Matthews, who published a number of articles in the 1950s, suggested that birds navigate by the sun.
- *which* when referring to things
  At yesterday's meeting, which focused on the labour shortage in the city, it was decided to advertise for workers abroad.
- *which* when referring to a whole clause
  *It has been observed that **birds follow major roads when flying**, which suggests that they can adapt their method of navigating.*
  Here *which* refers to the whole of the clause in **bold**.

whose
Whose is used to refer to people and – less often – things.
'The Life of Birds' is by David Attenborough, whose TV nature programmes were watched by millions.

whom
Whom is mostly used in fairly formal language. It can be the object in a clause, or follow a preposition.
The women whom migrants returned home to marry often had to move to a new country with their husbands.
It has been estimated that 60m Europeans emigrated to other continents between 1830 and 1930, most of whom went to North or South America.

where, when, why
These words can be used instead of a relative pronoun after appropriate nouns. It is possible to omit *when* and *why* in defining relative clauses, as in these examples:
The early twentieth century was the time (when) the first Italians moved to Guelph.
The lack of job opportunities in southern Italy was one reason (why) many men emigrated.

Unit 18
Verbs followed by *wh-* clauses

Clauses beginning with a *wh-* word or *how* can function in various ways within sentences:
As object: *I can't decide which translation of 'Hedda Gabler' I prefer.*
As subject: *How novelists get their inspiration is a mystery to me!*
Wh- clauses are based on questions, and mean that some information is unknown. Compare the certainty of a *that* clause with the uncertainty of a *wh-* clause:
I'm sure that this is the best translation.
I doubt whether this is the best translation.

Whether can usually be replaced with *if*:
I'm not sure whether/if this translation is worth buying.

Whether and *if* can be used with *or*, but *or* can't come immediately after *if*:
I'm not sure whether or not this translation is worth buying.
I'm not sure whether/if this translation is worth buying or not.

Many verbs, particularly ones used in academic writing, can be followed by *wh-* clauses.

Examples of sentences containing *wh-* clauses as objects:
It is not easy to explain why he stopped writing at such an early age.
We can see why Superman comics are so popular.
The opening chapter clearly demonstrates how the author regards her subject.
Asked whether/if his novel was autobiographical, the writer laughed off the question.
I'd like to read this book, but it's so expensive, I doubt whether/if I can afford it.

Unit 19
Noun phrases

In more formal English, nouns are often used in preference to related verbs:
*Some people have a **choice** of jobs.* (= Some people are able to choose their job.)
*Several **appointments** were made to the vacant positions.* (= Several people were appointed to the vacant positions.)

When there is no related noun, the *-ing* form of the verb can be used instead, though this is less common.
*His **being** a computer programmer impressed me.* (= He was a computer programmer, which impressed me.)

Transitive verb → noun/*-ing* form + *of*:
The restaurant was run successfully. It took up all our time. → ***The successful running of the restaurant** took up all our time.*
(A non-finite clause (see GF Unit 11) is another possibility here: *Running the restaurant successfully took up all our time.*)

Transitive verb with person or people → possessive + noun/*-ing* form, or noun/*-ing* form + *of*:
The company promoted the sales assistant. →
*The sales assistant celebrated **her promotion**.*
*Everyone celebrated **the sales assistant's promotion**.*
*Everyone celebrated **the promotion of the sales assistant**.*

Unit 20
Modal perfects

See also GF Unit 8, modals in conditional clauses, and GF Unit 12, infinitives.

Modal perfects – that is, modal verbs followed by the perfect infinitive *have done* – express the speaker's present opinion about an event, usually one in the past. The most commonly used modal verbs are *will, won't, would(n't), should(n't), could(n't), may (not), might (not), must, can't, ought to*.

Main meanings:

Possibility of a past event
Certainty, logical necessity:
It must have taken you a long time to write the history of the world.
Note that this certainty is an opinion: the meaning is different from *It took you a long time …*, which states a fact.

Possibility:
Sue hasn't arrived: she may/might/could have lost her way.
He may/might not have received my email.

Logical impossibility:
The author can't/couldn't have known about the latest research.

Criticising a past situation
Kathy should have read / ought to have read more background literature before writing her report.
The speaker is criticising Kathy for not reading much background literature.
The director of this film shouldn't have turned / oughtn't to have turned history into fiction.
The speaker is criticising the director for turning history into fiction. Note that *shouldn't have* is much more common than *oughtn't to have*.

Prediction
If we don't hurry, the seminar will have started by the time we arrive.
We'll be late for the seminar, but they won't have finished by the time we arrive.

Third conditional
I'd have chosen a different topic if you'd asked me to.
I wouldn't have chosen this topic if I'd found an easier one.

The following pages contain the answers to the exercises, sample answers for the writing tasks, and the recording scripts, which include underlining to show where the answers come. There are also useful additional notes and background information on the texts and topics. The *Map of Objective IELTS Advanced Student's Book* on pages 3–5 gives full details of the language and test skills covered in each unit. The *Content of the IELTS Test* on pages 6–7 provides information about the test, with links to the relevant Test folder or Writing folder. Good luck with your studies!

Unit 1

1.1 pages 8–9

1   The three statements show that there is a huge amount of information available nowadays. This means that you will need to be focused in your studies and know exactly how to find the most relevant material.

2   Terabytes are terrific – we are lucky to have so much information readily accessible to us, aren't we?

3   You can generally guess the meaning of compound nouns by thinking about the words that have formed them.

Answers
1 overkill   2 input   3 outcome   4 output   5 overwork

4   Uncountable nouns commonly cause errors – for example, many students wrongly add *-s* to them, as in 'informations'.

Answers
Overkill and *overwork* are both uncountable.
Outcome is countable.
Input and *output* vary: the uses shown in 2 and 4 are uncountable, but in the technical sense (computing, radio, etc.) it is possible to use both words countably.

5   Use an English–English dictionary if you don't know some of the words in the box.

Answers
1   overloaded: inundated, overwhelmed
2   tools: resources, means
3   inaccurate: biased, false
4   find: locate, retrieve
5   certain: sure, confident
6   journal: periodical, review
7   proficiently: efficiently, productively
8   assess: evaluate, judge

Here are some definitions for the four extra words:

critical (adjective)
describing something as bad or wrong *My sister is very critical of what I wear.*
very important *This is a critical decision for the company.*
extremely serious *Kevin is in hospital and his condition is said to be critical.*
giving opinions *The book is a critical study of Austen's novels.*

spine (noun)
backbone *I injured my spine several years ago.*
narrow part of a book, which is displayed on a shelf *The title is in large gold letters on the spine.*

support (noun)
agreement with an idea, group, etc. *There was plenty of support for his ideas at the meeting.*
help or encouragement *Janet is receiving financial support from the university.*
support (verb)
agree with ideas, views, etc. *Do you support the ban on foxhunting?*
help to show that something is true *Current research doesn't support his theory.*
hold the weight of *Is this ladder strong enough to support me?*
follow a team in sport *We both support Norwich City.*

virtually (adverb)
almost *The twins are virtually identical, but one has shorter hair than the other.*

6   All sections of the IELTS Listening Module are only heard once. The listening training in this unit is designed to build confidence and introduce some of the test formats to you. Concentrate as hard as you can while you are listening – you may want to close your eyes to achieve this.

The answers to the questions in exercise 6 will be heard on the recording (see text in italics in the recording script). The underlined words in Parts 2–4 relate to the answers to exercise 7.

Recording script

PART 1
Who are the three speakers? Why are they having a meeting together?
Mark: Hello, Dr Lucas.
Dr Lucas: Mark, welcome, and thanks for coming along to share your experience with us today as a final-year student. Can I introduce you to Jenny Boylan, who's in her first term here?
Mark: Hi, Jenny. And how are you enjoying university life?
Jenny: It's great, though I'm having a few problems on the study side …

Dr Lucas: Well, that's exactly why I've arranged for us all to be here this morning.

The older woman, Dr Lucas, has set up the meeting so that Jenny, a new student, can get some advice about studying from Mark, who is in his final year.

PART 2

What did Mark find difficult when he started at university? Was it the subject he was studying? Or something else?

Dr Lucas: Well, that's exactly why I've arranged for us all to be here this morning. Now Jenny, the first thing to say is – don't worry, many students feel a bit at sea with their study techniques to begin with. Isn't that right, Mark?

Mark: Definitely. When I started here, I found it so different from school. It wasn't that the subject itself was suddenly more challenging – I've always loved history and been confident in my field. But <u>at school I really only had to use a couple of core textbooks to find out what I needed, while here at uni I was presented with huge resources – the library, the Internet – with little idea of how to use them efficiently</u> …

Jenny: Exactly. The main problem I seem to have is time-wasting. I can spend a whole day in the library and come away feeling I haven't really scratched the surface.

Mark didn't find his subject, history, any more difficult. His problem at first was learning how to cope with much bigger reference sources than he had had to use at school.

PART 3

What two things does Mark suggest Jenny should do from now on when she's in the library?

Dr Lucas: Could you give us a concrete example of what you see as time-wasting, Jenny?

Jenny: Well, yesterday I had to do some background reading for an essay. I took down a big book from the shelves, thinking it would be useful – the title seemed to fit my essay topic – but it was hopeless! I sat there with it for nearly two hours, reading chapter after chapter, thinking that, eventually, I'd find what I needed. But it never happened.

Mark: OK, Jenny, first piece of advice: don't wander along the library shelves looking at book spines. Titles can be very misleading! You'll save time by putting yourself in front of a computer and <u>using the search tools to locate books – or articles – on your topic</u>. Didn't they explain this to you on the library tour at the start of term?

Jenny: Erm … I forgot to go.

Dr Lucas: OK, well make sure you fix up another tour immediately. They're still running them once a week, you know.

Mark: And another suggestion, Jenny, don't just rely on books. <u>You're likely to find much more up-to-date information in periodicals and journals</u>, you know.

Jenny: Right, I'll look for those, then.

Mark advises Jenny to use the library's electronic search tools. He also advises her to look for relevant articles in periodicals and journals, instead of only using books.

PART 4

Why does Dr Lucas warn Jenny about using the Internet as a source?

Jenny: And what do you both think about using the Internet?

Mark: Well, it isn't always used very productively. Sure, you can get lucky and find something really useful, but other days, you may retrieve virtually nothing. And perhaps even worse, sometimes you're totally inundated with possible material, and then you don't know where to start!

Dr Lucas: Mark's right, <u>I think you have to be extremely careful in this area, especially in assessing the accuracy of the facts themselves. You see, there are no quality controls on the Web. Information can become out-of-date, or may be false or biased to start with. Use it by all means, but always evaluate what you find.</u> You must be absolutely certain of all the sources you quote in essays.

Jenny: I've got a lot to learn, haven't I?

Dr Lucas: That's true, but we're here to support you. You shouldn't feel embarrassed about asking me for more help and advice, and Mark is willing to act as your student mentor, too.

Mark: In fact, why don't we go for a coffee now, then we can get to know each other a bit better …

Jenny: Thanks, I'd like that. And, er, thank you, Dr Lucas. It's been really helpful.

Dr Lucas: I'm pleased. Right, off you go then!

Dr Lucas explains to Jenny information on the Internet isn't always reliable, because it may be out-of-date, inaccurate or biased.

7 You will now hear Parts 2–4 again. Read the questions before you listen.

> **Answers** (relevant parts of the recording script above are underlined)
> 1 C 2 search tools 3 journals 4 B

8 Listen again with the recording script in front of you. Don't worry if you don't understand every word you hear – the important thing is to get the right answers!

9 These questions are typical of Part 1 of the IELTS Speaking Module. What information can you include? How long will your answers be? Can you add anything else? It's better to give an answer of two sentences than two words!

10

> **Answers**
> A 2 B 4 C 1 D 2 E 3 F 1 G 4 H 3

Recording script

A: I don't know … about ten hours I think.

B: Well, if you can afford to, it's obviously preferable to do nothing else apart from studying, but many students have to work as well, to support themselves. That's much harder.

C: To study in Britain.

D: A lot! I usually spend up to three hours each evening in the library and then I'm there all day again on Saturday. I always have Sundays off though, to play football. You need to relax sometimes.

E: For me, the most important thing is to improve my vocabulary. I must learn more words, especially ones that are important in academic English.

F: I'm planning to apply to a university in New Zealand next year, but I want to take the test first to see whether my level of English is high enough. I hope it will be!

G: It doesn't matter, you can do either.

H: Maybe grammar, or listening, or something like that.

11

1.2 pages 10–11

1 The questions introduce some of the ideas in the four reading texts. Think about your own approach to studying.

2 Read the Test spot first.
The four texts A–D have been written by students at British universities. Follow the instructions given on how to read the texts. The use of alternate red and blue in text A is designed to help you read the text in 'chunks', or groups of words. This is a more efficient way of reading. Text B highlights the most important words in the text and encourages you to 'skim' the text, moving your eyes more quickly across each line.

3 The four types of writer approach essay writing in very different ways. Think about your own technique – what works best for you?

Answers
1 C 2 B 3 D 4 A

4 The Grammar folder on pages 138–143 gives clear explanations of the grammar covered in each unit, with plenty of examples. The section for Unit 1 on page 138 explains the difference between modal and semi-modal verbs. Modal and semi-modal verbs are frequently used in academic texts, so it's important for you to be able to use them accurately.

Answers
1 could not c 2 must e 3 needed g 4 may a
5 mustn't d 6 have to e 7 might a 8 needn't h
9 can b 10 don't ... have to i 11 ought to f
12 should f

5

Answers
1 needn't / don't need to / don't have to 2 can't/cannot
3 must / has to 4 could/may/might 5 couldn't
6 had to / needed to 7 ought 8 mustn't / must not

6 Read the information on corpus data in the tinted box. All the authors of *Objective IELTS* have referred extensively to the *Cambridge Learner Corpus*, and this has given us a much clearer picture of what IELTS candidates can and can't do.

The sentences in exercise 6 come from the *Cambridge Academic Corpus*, part of the 300-million word *Cambridge International Corpus*. We have used the *Academic Corpus* to establish which structures and vocabulary are frequently used in academic English (both British and American). This corpus has also provided many of the examples in *Objective IELTS*.

Answers
In 1 and 2 the writer is unsure; in 3 and 4 the writer is certain.

Test folder 1

pages 12–13

Make sure you fully understand the notes and advice.

1 This reading passage comes from the website of a US university, and gives advice to students.

Answers
1 vii 2 v 3 ii 4 vi 5 xi 6 iii 7 x

2

Answers
1 iv 2 vii 3 ii

Unit 2

2.1 pages 14–15

1 The pictures show (A) an amateur cycling event in London, (B) a local game of snooker, (C) a javelin contestant at the 2004 Olympic Games, (D) a table tennis player from Singapore taking part in the women's singles quarter finals at the 2004 Olympic Games, (E) members of the Manchester United football team celebrating a goal, (F) Canada playing Australia at wheelchair basketball in the 2004 Paralympic Games; Canada won 70–53 to take the gold medal.

Suggested answers
A Cycling: an individual event, but a cyclist can be part of a team; amateur and professional (for example, the *Tour de France*); part of the triathlon event; usually outdoors, but indoor speed events take place in a velodrome.
B Snooker: a game between two people; amateur and professional; local, regional and national.
C Javelin: individual, but belonging to a team; often played at national or international level; an athletics (track and field) event; outdoors.
D Table tennis: an individual or team event, each side has one or two players (singles / doubles); local, national and international.
E Football: a team of 11 players; amateur and professional; local, national (league and cup) and international.
F Basketball: a team (five men / six women); amateur and professional; played indoors; local, national, international.

2

3 Remember to work out your reading speed in words per minute by timing yourself (your speed = 650 words divided by the time taken).

4 Look at the Advice given on page 12 in Test folder 1 before you do this Headings task.

Answers
1 x 2 v 3 viii 4 iii 5 vi 6 ii

5 The Style extra sections focus on the typical style of academic English, both written and spoken (for example, in lectures). Use similar language in your own writing.

Answers
1 d 2 g 3 b

6 Note that this grammar section focuses on the present and past perfect tenses, which are exemplified in the passage. The future perfect is dealt with in 13.2 (but is also mentioned in the Grammar folder for Unit 2).

Answers
Paragraph C (*They have decided*) Their research work is still continuing. If the text had said *They decided...*, the development work would have been in the past and completed.
Paragraph D (*what has happened*) This is a reference to recent time, in a time frame that is ongoing.

7

Answers
The past perfect is used to make it clear that an earlier time period is being referred to: the words *but then* signal a change from this earlier situation to the new direction taken by Carlo Colombo and his team.
The continuous form is used to focus on the duration of this state, i.e. football being an impossible challenge to developers.

8

Answers
1 has tested 2 Have you been doing 3 've/have been building 4 'd/had injured 5 have won / have been winning 6 had expected / had been expecting

2.2 pages 16–17

1 The pictures were taken at the World Student Games.

Possible answers
I used to take part in swimming competitions at school. My college football team plays in the national student league. I'd like to compete in an international student event – it would be an opportunity to travel and meet new friends.

2 Read the notes and predict the type of information needed.

Answers
1 two numbers and a word (month), or all numbers
2 number (price) 3 word(s) 4 word(s) (name)
5 word(s) (location) 6 word(s) (website address)

3

Answers (relevant parts of the recording script are underlined)
1 20–23 May 2 18 3 floor space 4 Hermica
5 University of Technology 6 www.sellgames.com

Recording script

John: Hello, Pirkko. I'm phoning to let you know that my college basketball team are very keen to come over to Finland to take part in the Tampere Student Games.

Pirkko: Well, that's great. We're hoping to make it a really special event this year, as it's the 80th anniversary of Finnish Student Sport!

John: Fantastic! We're all looking forward to coming. Let me just check – the games start on May 19th, right?

Pirkko: Oh, that was the provisional plan when you first contacted me, that they'd run from the 19th to the 23rd. But we've cut the programme by a day, <u>so now it'll begin on the 20th, still ending on the 23rd</u>. There's going to be an opening ceremony on the first evening.

John: We don't want to miss that, do we! And how much is the entry fee for the Games?

Pirkko: This year it's gone up from 16 to <u>18 euros a day per person</u>, I'm afraid, but you get a lot for that.

John: How do you mean?

Pirkko: Well, of course it covers the competition entrance, but you also get three meals a day and <u>even floor space if you want it</u> – we can't manage beds for everyone!

John: Sounds a bit basic to me. Can you recommend a hotel?

Pirkko: Well, Tampere is quite a big city, so there are a lot of hotels. The Homeland would be convenient if you come by train, or maybe you'd prefer <u>the Hermica, as it's offering a reduced rate for participants in the games</u>. It's spelt H-E-R-M-I-C-A. It's a very nice hotel.

John: And where is it exactly?

Pirkko: Well, that's the other good thing from your point of view. It's in the Hervanta district of Tampere, <u>near the University of Technology</u>.

John: And why is that good for us?

Pirkko: Because all the basketball matches are taking place near there.

John: Oh, I see.

Pirkko: Look, why don't I give you the website address, and then you can look up the programme and find out anything else you need to know.

John: Good idea. So, what is it?

Pirkko: OK, it's www dot sellgames – that's S-E-double L-G-A-M-E-S dot com.

John: Brilliant, I'll have a look now. Thanks, Pirkko.

Pirkko: See you soon, then. Bye, John.

4 Numbers are often tested in the IELTS Listening Module and, because everything is only heard once, you will need to be able to hear them without difficulty.

Answers
1 15th **2** 1940 **3** 9.13 **4** 6° **5** 19 **6** $\frac{1}{70}$

Recording script

Examples: It's the 80th anniversary of Finnish Student Sport! It's 18 euros a day.

1 Welcome to our 15th annual event.
2 No games were held in 1940, due to the war.
3 Please report to the track supervisor by 9.13.
4 The water temperature today is six degrees.
5 Approximately 19 per cent of runners have sponsorship.
6 In our questionnaire, less than a 70th of those asked played korfball.

5 Spell out the names and then play the recording to check your pronunciation. Remember to say 'double' where a letter is repeated (as in Serena Williams).

6 Try spelling the names of film stars or singers aloud. The more practice you get using English letters, the better!

7 Intensifying adverbs will be useful for both tasks in the IELTS Writing Module.

Answers
1 surprisingly **2** noticeably **3** extremely **4** bitterly
5 significantly **6** highly

8

Answers
1 closely related **2 highly** recommended
3 considerably worse **4 extremely** important
5 carefully considered / considered **carefully**
6 severely disturbed the ecosystem / disturbed the ecosystem **severely**

9 Think about each question and include as much information as you can.

Possible answers
- If you join a sports club, you will be able to go there whenever you want and make use of all its equipment. It's also a good place to make new friends.
- I think more sport should be taught in schools because children need to take exercise and have the chance to breathe fresh air.
- People get very excited watching their national team and many wave the national flag to support them. I think it's a way of identifying with your country and feeling proud to be one of its citizens.
- There's a saying that goes something like this: it doesn't matter if you win or lose, what's important is taking part. I agree with that, because you can get a lot of enjoyment from sport, whether you are good at it or not.

Writing folder 1
pages 18–19

The Writing folders show you the skills you need for the IELTS Writing Module and provide plenty of guided practice. Keep all your written work together and compare current work with earlier pieces – you'll notice how you've improved!

With the exception of Writing folder 1, *Objective IELTS Advanced* deals only with the Academic Writing Module tasks.

1

Answers
A is the GT task and B is the Academic task. Task B requires more use of argument (benefits / disadvantages).

2 These are only two examples of essay plans. Think what works best for you.

Answers
Mind map = Task B
Paragraph plan = Task A

3 See the paragraphed answer below. The sentence that has been crossed out in paragraph 2 is inappropriate (a personal comment in a more informal register). The deleted content in paragraph 3 is irrelevant to the task. The introduction and conclusion are too short: the introduction needs to make reference to the writer's opinion (which is given in the final sentence conclusion). The conclusion could summarise the argument and restate the opinion in another way.

Answer

How useful are sports players to our society? Do they earn too much money? This essay will discuss these questions.

If we consider the top sports players, it is true that they are paid huge salaries. For example, the footballer David Beckham earns millions with his club and then he is paid more money to endorse the products of various sports companies. ~~I wish I could earn a million dollars by wearing a pair of football boots!~~ Sportsmen tend to earn a lot more money than their female equivalents. In tennis, Martina Navratilova has won more titles than the greatest male players but her earnings are probably significantly less.

The most useful jobs in society are those that help people: doctors make people better when they are sick and teachers prepare a new generation for entry into society. Perhaps the most useful job of all is that of the firefighter, who saves lives and property on a regular basis. Yet firefighters are paid very little and often have to do a second job to earn enough money to live on. ~~Other people in society apart from sports players earn a lot of money. Some businessmen are millionaires.~~

Sport is undoubtedly one of our main forms of entertainment today. Even if people don't go to live matches, they watch sport on television, either broadcast live or the highlights afterwards.

However, this doesn't justify such large salaries, in my opinion.

Introduction rewritten

How useful are sports players to our society? Do they earn too much money? This essay will discuss these questions. In my own view, some sports stars do earn too much compared to other useful jobs in society. At the same time, because sport is prime entertainment, players can make demands on their employers, like film stars.

Conclusion rewritten

However, this doesn't justify such large salaries, in my opinion. Instead, we should reward the people who really matter in our society.

4 Only use a few rhetorical questions in an essay, because overuse would be unnatural.

Suggested answers
1 Why is so much sport broadcast today?
2 Is this really in the best interests of sport?
3 What are the effects of this on the players themselves?
4 How many tickets are sold at matches nowadays?
5 Can viewers cope with this sport overload?

5

Answer

Task B refers to growth in popularity, implying the need to write the essay within a time frame and/or compare and contrast today's situation with an earlier one, say ten years ago.

6

Answers

Reasons for growth of televised sport
2 Sport has become an important form of entertainment.
6 There are more TV channels than ten years ago.

Benefits
8 More people have developed an interest in sport.
7 Larger football clubs benefit financially from TV revenue.
4 Top players can ask for large salaries.

Disadvantages
3 Smaller clubs have suffered financial losses.
5 Fewer people attend live football matches nowadays.
1 Ticket prices have risen dramatically.

7 Remember that you must write at least 250 words, but it won't matter if you write more than this.

8

Sample answer

It is now possible to watch live sport on television on any day of the week, and the current amount of coverage will undoubtedly increase further in years to come. This is definitely having an impact on the live sports events themselves, and there are both benefits and drawbacks to this.

Why has there been such growth in televised sport? For one thing, with digital broadcasting, there are now many more TV channels than there were even ten years ago. Moreover, sport has become an important form of entertainment, appealing to both men and women.

What are the benefits of this state of affairs? One obvious advantage to the profession is the injection of capital provided by television companies. Larger football clubs benefit financially from TV revenue and the top players can command very large salaries. Less popular sports also receive money that can be invested in training and awareness-raising. Furthermore, there is a health benefit to some of the population, because through televised sport, more people have become interested in actually playing sport.

However, there are certain disadvantages to having so much sport on television. Considering football again, many smaller clubs have suffered financial losses recently, as they cannot compete with the larger ones. There has been a general decline in ticket sales, especially among smaller clubs. Fewer people attend live matches nowadays, preferring to watch from the comfort of their living room. What's more, ticket prices have risen dramatically.

To sum up, while televised sport has created many opportunities and benefited certain individuals and clubs enormously, it has also been responsible for changing the nature of live sports events for ever.
(273 words)

Unit 3

3.1 pages 20–21

1 The pictures show a nineteenth-century advertisement for Pears soap, a pair of Puma trainers (with the Ferrari logo on the heel) and the branded stud and label on a pair of Levi Strauss jeans. Think of some other well-known brands, and how you could answer the questions.

> **Possible answers**
> - I always buy the same brand of jeans, because they're the only ones I've found that fit me well.
> - I don't think it matters if other people know whether or not I buy a particular brand.
> - Lots of brands are very similar, so I don't look for particular brands of food or toothpaste, for instance.

2 Section 4 of the Listening Module is always a monologue and is delivered in an academic style – usually part of a lecture. Read the Test spot and underline key words before playing the recording.

> **Answers** (relevant parts of the recording script are underlined)
> 1 C   2 A
>
> 3 A   4 I   5 E   6 G   7 F   8 H   9 K

Recording script

Questions 1 and 2

Lecturer: At first sight, a bank account may seem very different from a laptop or a university, but what they have in common is that they're all products. Until relatively recently, the term tended to be restricted to manufactured goods, such as furniture or books, but now it's applied to virtually anything that's the focus of marketing activity; that is, activity to attract the attention of the general public, or perhaps companies. In terms of business, though, products are generally either manufactured goods, such as a laptop, or services, like bank accounts or training courses.

But because the purpose of the producer is to sell, pop singers, holiday resorts and so on can *also* be marketed as products – the purpose being to publicise that particular pop singer, etc. These days more and more people are even managing themselves as a product, for instance when applying for jobs.

Questions 3–9

Lecturer: In this analysis of products it's consumer goods that I'll focus on first. These are products that are manufactured and sold to members of the public – or consumers – rather than to companies.

Normally, with consumer goods, a number of manufacturers make similar products, and compete for sales. Levi Strauss has manufactured jeans since 1873, and until the early 1960s it was unusual in that it had virtually no competition. Since then, a lot of other manufacturers have entered the market. As a result, Levi's market share – that is, its percentage of all the pairs of jeans that are sold – has fallen dramatically.

Marketing is all about getting people to buy from you. One way of achieving this is by advertising, but another crucial element is the creation of brands. Until the late 19th century, it was simply *soap* that people bought, or a dress, or whatever. But then, manufacturers, including the soap maker Pears, began to realise that by giving their product its own name and advertising it to the general public, they could encourage purchasers to ask for *their* goods, and not those of a competitor. By the early 20th century, advertising was to be seen everywhere.

Brand names fall into two basic categories. Some manufacturers, like Microsoft, create a strong identification between the company and all its products by using the same name for both. Other companies use a variety of brand names: Procter & Gamble produces around 300 brands altogether, and it also sells several washing powders under different brand names, in order to maximise sales: Tide, Ariel and Daz are just three of these.

Often, companies manufacture a product line. Take the car manufacturer Ford, for instance. One of its cars, the Focus, is a product line consisting of closely related versions of one product, sold under the same brand name.

All the brands and products that a company produces make up its 'product mix': Ford specialises in one type of product – cars, while Yamaha has a much more diverse product mix, which includes motorcycles, musical instruments and electronic equipment.

Now let's turn briefly to retailers, such as the supermarket chain Tesco. Retailers are businesses which sell directly to consumers, usually in their stores – or retail outlets – but in some cases by mail order or through the Internet. They usually sell branded goods, which they've received from the manufacturer, but, like Tesco, they may also sell their own brands, which are normally goods that they buy from a manufacturer and sell under their own name. So, for example, alongside the Heinz brand of baked beans, Tesco also sells Tesco baked beans.

A brand doesn't just have a name, however: most have a logo which the company wants the public to associate with the brand. Coca Cola's logo, for example, is the distinctive way in which the name is written.

Now I just want to mention …

3 English words often occur in 'families', where related words that are either the same or different parts of speech are formed from various suffixes and prefixes. For example, the adjective *able* is related to other adjectives (*unable*, *disabled*), verbs (*enable*, *disable*) and nouns (*ability*, *disability*, *inability*). It's a good idea to keep a record of word families in your vocabulary notebook. Note: the *Cambridge Advanced Learner's Dictionary* contains a useful word families appendix.

Complete the table. Check your spelling carefully.

Answers

verbs	nouns	adjectives
produce	product, productivity, produce, production, producer	(un)productive
consume	consumer, consumption (*also* consumable, consumerism, consumerist)	(*also* consumable)
compete	competition, competitor (*also* competitiveness)	(un)competitive

4 Remember to think about the form needed in each sentence (which part of speech; singular or plural form).

Answers
1 consumers 2 unproductive 3 consumption
4 competitors 5 consume 6 competitive
7 produce/products

5 Mark the stressed syllables, following the example for style. Stress is usually marked in dictionaries in this way. Then play the recording and check your answers.

Answers
1 pro'ducer 2 'product 3 'produce 4 pro'duction
5 pro'ductive 6 produc'tivity 7 com'pete
8 com'petitor 9 com'petitive 10 compe'tition

6 Read the information about academic language and style given in Style extra. You will need to develop your academic writing in this way. The exercise will help you to become more aware of differences in style.

Answers
1 purchases; consumption 2 perceptions 3 recognition
4 reductions 5 deduction

7 Imagine a new line of clothing that you're going to launch. Make some notes, using vocabulary from the box. You might like to tell a friend about your ideas, record yourself, or write a short outline.

3.2 pages 22–23

1 Think about how pop groups might be formed. Then think about what the phrase *manufactured pop group* implies. Look at the picture of Hear'Say, an example of one such group.

2 Read the passage quickly, timing yourself. Choose the statement that best sums up the writer's main point.

Answer
B

3 Read the Test spot. This task type tests understanding of a writer's opinions or claims, while the *True / False / Not given* task focuses on facts. The *Not given* option is often the most difficult for candidates to decide on. Read the example, explanation and underlined sentence in the text (lines 4–6), which illustrates *Not given*.

Work through the statements, underlining relevant parts of the text in the same way.

Answers
1 NO — *branding would have been an alien concept to Leonardo da Vinci or Beethoven, or most other self-respecting artists and musicians, and one that the vast majority would have rejected.* (lines 9–16)
2 NOT GIVEN — The passage says *they performed in front of three judges* but nothing else is said about the judges.
3 NO — *all able to sing, dance* (lines 48–49)
4 NOT GIVEN — *As their licensing manager admitted, they were marketing the group before they even knew who was going to be in it.* (lines 75–78)
5 YES — *the quickest way to your customers' wallets is through their hearts* (lines 80–82)
6 NO — *the only brands which will succeed are those that make an emotional connection.* (lines 86–90)
7 NOT GIVEN — *this commercialisation of our private world breeds cynicism* (lines 97–100) but nothing is said about whether the public is concerned about this
8 YES — *Emotional exploitation ultimately generates a pessimism about human nature* (lines 103–105)

4 Read the explanation and examples of cleft sentences. They are particularly important in academic language.

Answers
1 fame can be manufactured
2 in a talent contest
3 because our emotions affect our behaviour
4 the group was marketed before it existed

5

Answers (and possible endings)
1 in the 19th century ... the 20th.
2 to increase their sales ... to reduce costs.
3 the use of brand names ... the manufacturing of products themselves.
4 low prices ... high quality.
5 the power of marketing ... their talent.

6 Read the Test spot. You will have the maximum opportunity to show your language range in this part of the Speaking Module, because it is a long turn.

Make brief notes. If you are stuck for ideas for a logo, look back at the companies on page 20. Talk for one to two minutes, either to a friend or recording yourself. Try to keep talking, even if you start to run out of ideas.

Test folder 2

pages 24–25

Make sure you fully understand the notes and advice.

1

Answers (evidence from the passage is given, but this is not part of the answer)		
1	NOT GIVEN	The movie *The African Queen* is mentioned as containing an early example, but there is no indication of who had the idea. (paragraph 2)
2	TRUE	*A set dresser might think of something to boost the level of credibility or realism of the story.* (paragraph 3)
3	FALSE	*A spokeswoman for the manufacturer said the company was not approached about the use of their product* (paragraph 3)
4	TRUE	*arranged product placement deals. The most common type is a simple exchange of the product for the placement … the cast and crew are provided with an ample supply of the company's products.* (paragraph 4)
5	NOT GIVEN	*Sometimes, a gift of the product isn't an appropriate form of compensation, so money powers the deal.* There is no indication of the film makers' preferences. (paragraph 5)
6	FALSE	*Before product placement really saw a surge in the mid 1980s, it was pretty much a do-it-yourself effort. Now there are entire agencies* (paragraph 6)
7	TRUE	*It's highly likely that you'll see one of the major soft drink companies represented.* (paragraph 7)

2

Answers		
1	YES	*all relative to any competitors.* (paragraph 1)
2	NOT GIVEN	*Your 'customer' may be a boss, friend or relative.* Your 'customers' are referred to in relation to you, not each other. (paragraph 2)
3	NO	*ideally you want to use those skills and talents that are highly valued by your 'customer' and that you enjoy using.* (paragraph 3)

4	YES	*These organizations have written or unspoken values and cultures that have a big impact on how we act.* (paragraph 4)
5	YES	*By finding the best 'position' to take relative to these competitors, we can make ourselves seen as not only different to them, but better.* (paragraph 5)
6	NOT GIVEN	The way we speak is not mentioned as part of the 'package' of our identity. (paragraph 6)
7	NO	*Personal Branding is not about being someone we aren't … It is simply about becoming the best 'You'.* (paragraph 7)

Unit 4

4.1 pages 26–27

1 The pictures show a waiter and customer communicating through sign language at the *Café Signes* in Paris; a woman displaying strong emotion through her facial expression; a social group of chimpanzees.

Think about the questions.

Suggested answers
Ways of communicating: television, radio, telephone, Internet chat rooms, email, letter; also gestures and body language, whistling
How animals and birds communicate: making sounds such as growling, hissing or calling, showing teeth, wagging tail, touching, opening or closing paw

2 Skim the passage, timing yourself as you read.

Suggested answers
Paragraph A: Most animals are able to communicate.
Paragraph B: Many primates use different sounds to communicate different meanings, and vervet monkeys use the largest number.
Paragraph C: Vervet monkeys are in danger when they search for food.
Paragraph D: Vervet monkeys make different sounds when they are in danger from different predators.
Paragraph E: Experiments show that vervets respond to warnings even when they are not in danger.
Paragraph F: Young vervets learn the calls and become more accurate as they grow up.
Paragraph G: Vervets can also understand warnings given by certain birds.

3 Read the Test spot, then complete the task, underlining key words as shown.

Answers		
1	E	*Experiments using recordings of the alarm calls when no predators are present show the same responses. The monkeys understand and respond to the call itself.* (lines 35–37)
2	C	*they climb down to search for food at ground level. Here they are far more exposed, and so at greater risk from predators.* (lines 20–22)

3 A *also with their owners: demanding food, asking to be let out, greeting them when they return home.* (lines 9–10)

4 D *it emits a loud barking call and the monkeys run into the trees ... the warning is a double-syllable cough. Other vervets respond by looking up into the air, then seeking shelter among the dense branches of trees or bushes ... a 'chutter' sound ... The monkeys stand up on two legs and look in the grass, then run to safety* (lines 24–33)

5 G *When a starling squeaks the warning 'danger in the air', nearby monkeys repeat it – translating it into their own term* (lines 51–54)

6 B *These sounds can be placed in three main categories: food calls, warnings of the presence of predators, and calls for help.* (lines 13–14)

7 D *(apparently from the noise made by a motorcycle engine that is getting a lot of fuel)* (lines 31–32)

8 B *The 'vocabulary' of most species amounts to only a handful of distinct sounds. However, the vervet monkeys of the Rift Valley in Kenya appear to have developed many more calls, each with its own meaning* (lines 14–17)

9 A *they are able to tell whether a sound is made by a parent or offspring, another member of their species, or a stranger.* (lines 5–6)

10 F *As they mature and gain experience, they begin to use the calls correctly.* (lines 46–47)

4 Think about the examples in brackets when deciding on your answers.

Answers
2 c 3 i 4 d 5 h 6 f 7 b 8 g 9 a

5

Answers
1 slang (= £ – pound sterling)
2 acronym (= National Aeronautics and Space Administration)
3 collocation
4 idiom (= in bad condition and likely to stop working soon)
5 jargon (in the field of linguistics)

6 These questions are typical of what an examiner might ask in Part 3. Think of the answers you might give, and extend what you say by giving reasons for your opinions or including examples to support your ideas.

4.2 pages 28–29

1 Think about accents in your own language.

2 Read the Test spot. Check that you understand all the words in the box (if not, use an English–English dictionary). Notice that they are all nouns. Read the summary and think about the spaces. Remember that you are unlikely to hear an exact word from the box providing the answer, so you must listen carefully to the meaning of what is said. Listen to the first part of the recording (questions 1–4) and complete the summary.

Then read the options A–D and questions 5–7. Listen to the second part of the recording and answer the questions.

Answers (relevant parts of the recording script are underlined)
1 conformity 2 status 3 norm 4 evaluation
5 D 6 B 7 C

Recording script

Questions 1–4

Lecturer: It's a striking feature of languages that different varieties acquire different social values. Any social group develops norms of behaviour, such as wearing certain styles of clothes, and members of the group are expected to conform to those norms. Since language is a form of behaviour, the group develops a distinct variety of language too, which helps to maintain and signal group identity. This variety comes to reflect the social status of its users: the higher this is, the greater the prestige of the variety of language.

Standard varieties of languages serve the needs of the national rather than the local community, and are associated with the goals and values of nations. People who use standard varieties tend to be well educated, so the standard is usually thought of as a model of correct language, and other varieties as incorrect.

All varieties of language reflect social relationships, and the judgements we make about language are often disguised *social* judgements. For instance, when parents tell their child off for using slang expressions, it's probably because they're afraid that other people will think the child is of lower status than they wish him or her to be considered.

Questions 5–7

Lecturer: In fact the English are very aware of social differences in accent, and can usually work out from it a person's region of origin, social standing and standard of education.

Accents are also classified aesthetically. In one experiment it was found that British people, who recognised where each accent came from, preferred rural accents to ones from British cities such as Birmingham or Liverpool. However, people from other countries, without that knowledge or the social attitudes that go with it, assessed the pleasantness of the accents differently.

Language is also a symbol of identity. People from a particular region, such as Yorkshire, in the north of England, may take pride in their local speech as part of their pride in their local culture, and may make an effort to retain their accent if they move to another part of the country.

Attitudes towards different varieties of language can be remarkably powerful. <u>In another piece of research, people listened to the same argument against capital punishment spoken with different accents.</u> Some accents were effective in changing people's views on this matter, while others weren't. Listeners were also asked to rate the quality of the argument. Generally, when the case was argued in an accent of high prestige, it was thought to be better argued than when presented in accents of lower prestige.

Clearly we need to be careful about how far our attitude to other people is affected by our reaction to their speech.

3 Think about these questions and make notes of key points.

4 Read the sentences and work out the function of each one. Refer to the Grammar folder on page 139 if you need help.

> **Answers**
> **1** place   **2** reason   **3** time   **4** condition   **5** purpose
> **6** concession

5

> **Answers**
> **1** so (that) – purpose   **2** Although – concession
> **3** Since – reason   **4** unless – condition   **5** while – time
> **6** Once – time

6

> **Answers**
> 1 **When** attempts were made to communicate with chimps in sign language, dramatic progress was claimed.
> 2 It was postulated that chimps would not be able to combine signs appropriately **unless** they understood at least some of the rules of human language.
> 3 A female chimpanzee, Washoe, was taught sign language **so (that)** she could communicate by using her hands.
> 4 **Although** at first her progress was slow, she learned 132 signs in just over four years and could combine them in short sentences.
> 5 Two more chimps, Moja and Pili, were taught to sign and made faster progress than Washoe **because** their training started when they were younger than she was.
> 6 Chimps have proved themselves able to communicate by using signs, **although** there is disagreement as to how far they understand the nature and grammatical rules of language. OR
> **Although** chimps have proved themselves able to communicate by using signs, there is disagreement as to how far they understand the nature and grammatical rules of language.

7 Work through the exercise. In each case, think of an adverbial clause that fits the meaning of the sentence.

> **Possible answers**
> **1** ... you are living in the country where that language is spoken.
> **2** ... animals are largely self-sufficient.
> **3** ... there are still many areas to be investigated.
> **4** ... research could be carried out on them.
> **5** ... it yields new information that is applicable to humans.

8

> **Answers**
>
> | /ɪ/ | /e/ | /ʌ/ | /ɒ/ | /iː/ |
> |---|---|---|---|---|
> | language sit wanted | instead set | come run | not quality | key receive see |
>
> | /ɑː/ | /eə/ | /ɪə/ | /əʊ/ | /aʊ/ |
> |---|---|---|---|---|
> | after heart laugh | air there | ear here | although no | found now |

Writing folder 2

pages 30–31

There are fewer marks available for Task 1 than for Task 2, so spend no more than 20 minutes on it.

1 The three graphs/charts show some common ways of presenting information visually.

> **Answers**
> **1** refers to B; **2** refers to C; **3** refers to A.
>
> **1** period   **2** vertical axis   **3** constant   **4** low
> **5** accounting for   **6** relative   **7** accounts for   **8** lowest
> **9** unit   **10** lines   **11** single   **12** horizontal axis
> **13** volumes   **14** high   **15** peaked

2 It is good to use a range of adverbs in Task 1 (exercises 2, 3, 4 and 5 focus on different types).

> **Answer**
> *Conversely* introduces contrasting information (**b**).

3

> **Answers**
> **1 c**   **2 a**

4

> **Answers**
> The intensifying adverbs are *significantly* and *dramatically* in description 1, and *considerably* in description 3. *Amazingly* would be inappropriate in all cases because it is too informal. *Noticeably* could replace *dramatically* or *considerably*. *Surprisingly* is inappropriate: in description 1 because the trends are not surprising, and in description 3 because we have insufficient information about the data to make that judgement.

5

> **Answer**
> *Approximately* (which is probably better than *roughly* in a neutral to formal piece of writing of this type).

6 Conclusion **b** is better. Conclusion **a** needs to be made less vague and should not repeat what has already been said.

7 Read the Advice given. For this practice task, aim to write at least 100 words (in the actual test, the minimum length for Task 1 is 150 words).

> **Sample answer**
> The bar chart shows relative percentage sales of four styles of trainers during a twelve-month period. In the first quarter, sales of the new 'Flying Boots' were fairly modest, only accounting for about 10% of sales. Sales volumes of the other three styles during the same period were similar, at approximately 30% each. Conversely, in the second quarter, sales of the new style doubled and the older style 'High rollers' performed less well. Sales of this style reached an all-time low in the third quarter, but recovered a little in the fourth quarter. Sales of the style 'Golden feet' continued to rise dramatically throughout the year, accounting for half of all sales in the fourth quarter, while sales of 'Zed runners' had dropped significantly by the year end.
> (128 words)

Units 1–4 Revision

pages 32–33

Each revision unit reviews the topics, grammar and vocabulary of the previous four units. The content of the Writing folders is practised and extended in the five *Writing workouts* at the back of the Workbook.

1 Work through the eight sentences, saying as much as you can about each one. Include examples from your personal experience.

2 The picture shows the hand-held PlayStation Portable (PSP).

> **Answers**
> 1 It 2 What 3 have 4 has 5 itself
> 6 may/might/could 7 to 8 may/might
> 9 although/but/though/yet 10 though

3

> **Answers**
> 1 a and b are incorrect:
>   a *Essays must have …*
>   b *Essays should be …*
> 2 a is incorrect: *have been training*
> 3 c is incorrect: *unless it is … OR if it isn't …*

4

> **Answers**
> 1 **surprisingly** poor 2 **considerably** bigger
> 3 **bitterly** disappointed 4 **increasingly** likely
> 5 **excessively** complicated 6 **widely** believed

5

> **Answers**
> 1 responsive 2 imitation/imitating 3 unpredictable
> 4 classification 5 consumption 6 inefficiency

6

> **Answers**
> 1 c 2 a 3 b

7

> **Answers**
> 1 collocation – Instead of wasting money as you do, why not put it in a bank?
> 2 acronym – FIFA has just released details about next year's championship.
> 3 idiom – You seem to have bitten the bullet regarding your workload.
> 4 proverb – Every cloud has a silver lining. ✓
> 5 idiom – What you said has really given me food for thought.
> 6 slang – Have you got any change for a quid?
> 7 collocation – This movie director is highly rated, you know.

8

> **Answers**
> 1 up until recently 2 Over the two-year period
> 3 In the meantime 4 shortly after that date
> 5 From time to time

Unit 5

5.1 pages 34–35

1 The pictures show everyday products made of plastic: a lunch box, plastic cups, sunglasses, a bottle of shampoo, a remote control, a CD, pens, a computer keyboard and mouse, and drinking straws, together with more unusual plastic products: a Polartec fleece jacket (made from recycled plastic) and Australian banknotes. Make a list of six plastic products that you use regularly and decide whether they could be made from other materials.

> **Possible answers**
> Mobile phone – only made of plastic
> Bottle of Coca Cola – also made of glass
> Plastic bags – can use brown paper sacks for shopping
> Plastic-coated wire – could also be coated with rubber
> DVD boxes – sometimes made of cardboard
> Mixing bowl in the kitchen – could be made of glass or metal

2 Think about the products in exercise 1.

> **Possible answers**
> *Cost:* It is probably cheaper to manufacture plastic bottles than glass ones although, with recycling, glass ones could be re-used. Rubber is probably a more expensive material to produce than plastic, too.
> *Weight:* Most plastic products are light to carry – for example, a mobile phone made of metal would be heavier.
> *Safety:* Glass bottles can shatter, and broken glass is dangerously sharp; plastic bottles don't usually break, they're more robust.
> *Versatility:* I never imagined clothes made of plastic! It is an extremely versatile material.

3 The notes will be used for the Speaking Part 2 task in exercise 8.

4 Use a dictionary if necessary to check understanding of the words in the box.

> **Answers**
> 1 conserve energy/resources   2 make healthier
> 3 resist corrosion   4 satisfy needs
> 5 operate efficiently/quietly   6 waste energy/resources
> 7 run quietly/efficiently   8 cut consumption

5 Read the Test spot and then predict possible answers in 1–5. Decide whether a space requires a number or word(s), and also think about part of speech and likely content.

> **Suggested answers**
> 1 nouns (two other factors apart from safety)
> 2 noun (something that could be harmed)
> 3 verb phrase (something positive/beneficial)
> 4 number (quantity of some kind, perhaps also given in kilos)
> 5 number (percentage or proportion)

Remember that you need to write between one and three words or a number. Write any numbers in figures not words (it is quicker to do this and you are less likely to make a mistake). Listen to the first part of the recording and answer questions 1–5.

Then read the table and predict answers to questions 6–10 before listening to the second part of the recording.

> **Answers** (relevant parts of the recording script are underlined)
> 1 performance (and) value
> 2 Meat
> 3 resist
> 4 3.74 kg/kilograms/kilos
> 5 50/fifty per cent / %
>
> 6 (the) sandwich bag
> 7 (the) bread industry
> 8 garbage/trash (accept *refuse* or *rubbish*)
> 9 1973
> 10 15/fifteen cents

Recording script

Questions 1–5

Lecturer: There are so many different types of plastic, and it's such a versatile material, that it's now used in thousands of ways, and we find it difficult to imagine living without it. Plastics are the choice for so many products featuring in different areas of our lives at the moment, from car parts to toy parts, from soft drink bottles to the refrigerators they're stored in. I believe that there are three main reasons why plastics have scored over other materials in satisfying the consumer's needs. <u>These are – safety, performance and, last but not least, value.</u>

Just consider the changes we've seen in the food retail business in recent years. The introduction of plastic bottles has meant that even an economy-size bottle of juice can easily be lifted – glass is much heavier, of course. And should you accidentally drop that bottle, it's far less likely to break. <u>Plastic wrap helps keep food fresh and free from contamination, which is particularly important with meat.</u> In each case, plastics help to make your life easier, healthier and, of course, safer.

Plastics also help you get maximum value from some of the high-cost items you need to buy. They ensure that cellphones and laptop computers really are light and easy to carry. <u>They help to make sure that major appliances like refrigerators and dishwashers will resist the corrosive effects of moisture and certain chemicals,</u> which guarantees they'll last longer. These appliances also operate more efficiently thanks to the use of plastics.

Food safety is of key importance to the consumer, and packaging such as heat-sealed plastic pouches and wraps means the resources that went into producing the food in the first place aren't wasted. It's the same thing once you get the food home, where resealable plastic containers keep your leftovers protected. In fact packaging experts have estimated that every kilo of plastic packaging can cut food waste by 3.74 kilos. That's a statistic that very few people are aware of.

Plastics also help to conserve energy in your home, lowering your heating – and cooling – bills by cutting electricity consumption. Indeed, plastic parts and insulation have helped to improve the energy efficiency of air conditioners by up to 50 percent since the 1970s. And these appliances run more quietly than earlier designs that used other materials.

In short, I believe plastics are a very good thing for the human race!

Questions 6–10

Lecturer: In the opinion of a growing number of environmental campaigners, the plastic bag is an unnecessary and damaging item that we should get rid of at all costs. This simple innovation, which was welcomed in the 1950s as an attractive modern material with many practical applications, is now seen by many as a major source of pollution.

1957 saw the launch of the sandwich bag, first produced and promoted in the USA as a good way of keeping lunchtime snacks fresh and clean. American companies quickly recognised the value of plastic bags, and, by 1966, the bread industry, for instance, used them for about one third of packaging.

But it wasn't just in the area of food packaging that the plastic bag was beginning to enjoy success. In 1969, the New York City Sanitation Department's 'New York City Experiment' showed how much cleaner, safer and quieter it was to use plastic bags in garbage collection, and the public soon started to line their metal trash cans with specially produced bags.

However, even in the late 1960s, people were still bringing home their shopping in baskets or brown paper sacks. The commercial production of plastic grocery bags didn't start until 1973, with the opening of the first manufacturing plant. The plastic carrier bag soon became an indispensable part of everyone's life, something that governments and campaigners worldwide are now trying to reverse. In 2002, for example, the Irish government introduced a new tax payable by consumers of fifteen cents a bag, which, in the two years following its introduction, raised 23 million euros for environmental projects. In the same year, the government of another country, Bangladesh, had to take a more drastic approach, banning the production of plastic bags and introducing an on-the-spot fine for using one. Since then, many governments have introduced similar measures and it now seems that the days of the plastic bag may indeed be numbered.

6   Notice how the speaker pauses before the last word in the list.

7   Practise saying sentences 1–5. Then listen to the recording to check your pronunciation.

Recording script

1   For the walk, you'll need to bring sandwiches, chocolate and, most importantly, plenty of water.

2   The product comes in four colours: red, green, blue and, unusually, purple.

3   During the experiment, you should monitor your temperature, pulse and, last but not least, heart rate.

4   In August, the weather will be a bit windy, dry and, without a doubt, sunny.

5   Plastics are used in computers, televisions and, naturally, mobile phones.

8   Read the Test spot. Look through the notes you made earlier and add any further ideas or examples from the recording.

9   Use some of the Useful language. Time yourself talking for one minute.

5.2 pages 36–37

1   The diary is about the accumulation of plastic bags at home.

2   The data given is for the UK. Write a paragraph describing the process. Then compare your answer with the suggested answer below.

> **Suggested answer**
> 150,000 tonnes of polyethylene are produced and from this, 9 billion bags are made per year. It is estimated that 7 billion of these are re-used for household rubbish, etc., while the remaining 2 billion are thrown into waste bins or become street litter. A tiny proportion of bags are recycled into heavy-duty plastic. Around 8 billion bags are buried in landfill sites every year, although 0.7 billion are incinerated to produce energy.

3   Read the passage quickly, timing yourself.

> **Answer**
> The writer thinks that plastic bags are not as serious a form of pollution as other plastic products (and other threats to the environment).

4   Read the Test spot and look at the underlining for 1. Underline key words and relevant parts of the passage in the same way for questions 2–8.

> **Answers**
> 1 wildlife   2 blown away   3 aesthetics
> 4 internal obstruction   5 plastic bottles   6 consumption
> 7 disposal   8 symbolic

5

> **Answers**
> 1 may be re-used (line 28)   2 may have been made (line 58)
> 3 being blown away (line 6), are being picked on (line 12),
>   being blamed (line 54)
> 4 is asked (line 17), are killed (line 40), are made out to be
>   (line 55)
> 5 have been carried (lines 27–28), have been ingested (line 36)
> 6 was set up (line 45)   7 to be affected (line 64)

6

> **Answers**
> 1 are seen   2 have been thrown away   3 may be used
> 4 is known   5 to be seen   6 has not been reduced

7   Try to use the phrases in a–e (*by far, not nearly as*, etc.) in
    your own writing.

> **Answers**
> 1 d   2 a   3 e   4 b   5 c

Test folder 3

pages 38–39

Make sure you fully understand the notes and advice.

Part 1

Read what is said about Part 1.

1   Read options **A–F**, and listen to the recording.

> **Answers**
> 1 C   2 F   3 A   4 E   5 D
> The third answer is, of course, the most suitable for Part 1
> of the test.

Recording script

1 **A:** What type of food do you enjoy most?
  B: Fruit.

2 **A:** Do you enjoy cooking?
  B: I don't eat much for breakfast or lunch. I usually have my
       main meal in the evening.

3 **A:** Why do some people avoid eating food they're not familiar
       with?
  B: I'm not altogether sure, but maybe they were brought up to
       eat only what they know is safe.

4 **A:** Do you have any plans affecting your work?
  B: I have plans, yes, certainly. I want to live in Canada or find a
       nice apartment. On the other hand, it's work too.

5 **A:** Do you think it's important to visit other countries?
  B: Hmm. Yes. (*long pause*) Maybe people should go abroad, so
       that they can compare that country with their own.

2   Think of suitable answers, and say them aloud.

> **Possible answers**
> 1   Some plastic goods are popular, such as children's toys. I
>   should think the main reasons are that they're colourful,
>   which attracts children, and cheap, which their parents
>   like.
> 2   It's very useful to be able to phone while you're
>   travelling on a train, for example. It saves time.
> 3   I think it's important for food to be packaged, for
>   reasons of hygiene. But the packaging should be kept to
>   a minimum.
> 4   Yes, we suffer a great deal from industrial pollution,
>   particularly in the big cities. And some people are
>   careless about litter, and just drop rubbish in the streets.
> 5   I always take my litter home with me, and try and
>   dispose of it in an environmentally friendly way.

Part 2

Read what is said about Part 2.

3   Read the card, then listen to the talk and the questions
    that follow it.

Recording script

Examiner: I'd like you to describe an occasion when you were
    pleased that an object was made of plastic.

Candidate: Right. Well, I'd like to tell you about a plastic fork. Once
    I was sitting in a motorway café, with a friend. We were on our
    way to see some other friends for the weekend, and it was quite a
    long drive, so we stopped to have a break. I was eating a cake,
    which was full of chocolate and cream. It was very tasty, but I
    was using a plastic fork that was quite small, and not very
    practical. I was annoyed that the café didn't supply metal ones.
        Anyway, we were sitting there chatting and eating, when a
    group of children and a couple of adults came into the café. The
    children were aged about seven or eight, and they were running
    around, chasing each other. The adults weren't doing anything to
    stop them, and I commented on this to my friend.
        Then, as they came past our table, one of the children pushed
    another one, who fell heavily against me, jerking my right arm
    across my body – and I was holding the fork in my right hand. The
    fork hit my left arm, scratched the inside of my elbow, and covered
    that part of my arm with chocolate and cream. Luckily the scratch
    wasn't serious, and when I'd washed my arm I was fine. But I was
    glad the fork was made of plastic. If it'd been metal, it would
    probably have broken the skin and made me bleed.

Examiner: Do you think anyone watching what happened felt the
    same way as you?

Candidate: They probably thought it was funny, but I hope they'd
    have been pleased that the fork didn't hurt me.

Examiner: On the whole, do you prefer plastic or more traditional
    materials?

Candidate: I usually prefer traditional materials, like wood or cloth,
    but sometimes it's better to have plastic!

4   Read the card and make some brief notes. Then give a
    talk, either to a friend or recording yourself.

Part 3

Read what is said about Part 3.

5   Read questions 1–3, then listen to the answers and assess them.

Recording script

Examiner: Could you describe how people use plastic credit cards?

Candidate: Yes, they are used instead of cash, to buy goods in shops, or pay bills. They can be used for paying online, too, when you just need to give the number on the card, and some other details.

Examiner: Can you contrast carrying credit cards with carrying cash?

Candidate: I think the biggest difference is that when you pay for something with a credit card you don't really feel that you are spending money. So the danger is that you spend far too much.

Examiner: Can you identify ways in which credit cards have changed our spending habits?

Candidate: When we see something we want, but can't afford it, in the past we generally saved up to buy it. But nowadays we're much more likely to buy it on credit card. So, as a result, a lot of people get into debt.

Questions 4–9

Think of how you could answer the questions, and speak aloud, perhaps recording yourself. Remember to develop your answers.

> **Possible answers**
> 4   One of the main reasons why people like using credit cards is that they can buy things that they can't afford.
> 5   Banks advertise a lot, both on TV and by sending junk mail to your home. Often you're told you won't need to start repaying a loan for six months or a year.
> 6   I think this would be difficult, but maybe the government should run an advertising campaign, emphasising the danger of getting heavily into debt.
> 7   I'm afraid that the people who borrow a lot will carry on doing that, and that fewer and fewer people will try to avoid getting into debt.
> 8   A lot more fruit and vegetables are imported than ten or twenty years ago, so we can buy the same things all year round, and not just when they're in season, in my own country.
> 9   I think it's good to have a choice, because it gives us opportunities to have a better lifestyle. On the other hand, we sometimes waste a lot of time trying to make up our minds.

Unit 6

6.1 pages 40–41

1   The pictures show different ways of listening to music, as well as different emotions: a happy crowd at the London Live 8 concert, audience involvement at a jazz club, and a person alone, relaxing outside with music on headphones.

> **Possible answers**
> Situations where you might hear music: in a supermarket, at a party, at a wedding, over the phone when holding for someone.
> 'Background music' (music played at low volume to create a positive atmosphere, for example in a shop) is generally irritating, but it can be relaxing at a swimming pool.

2   Several of these adjectives or their related nouns are in the passage.

> **Answers**
> 1   miserable (negative emotion)
> 2   elated (positive emotion)
> 3   hypnotised (neither positive nor negative)

3   The music is … .

> **Possible answers**
> A   light-hearted
> B   depressed
> C   optimistic

4

> **Answers**
> 1 A/C   2 B   3 A   4 B   5 C

5   Skim the passage, timing yourself.

> **Possible answer**
> The power of music

6   Answer questions 1–3 following the advice given in the Test spot.

> **Answers** (evidence from the passage is given, but this is not part of the answer)
> 1   B   *close to events of high emotion, your brain takes a 'recording'… a piece of music linked to an emotional event in your life may well bring it flooding back when you hear it again.* (lines 14–19)
> 2   A   *this is an 'iconic connection': when you listen to music, you make links to innate human vocalisations of excitement, depression, anger, and so on.* (lines 31–33)
> 3   D   *When musical surprises happen, emotional responses are guaranteed.* (lines 48–49)

7

> **Answers**
> 1   increasingly (line 6)
> 2   association(s) (line 13); associative (line 54)
> 3   unpredictable (line 19); predictions (line 47)
> 4   manipulation (line 26); manipulative (line 61)
> 5   universal (line 34)
> 6   recognisable (line 42)
> 7   reaction(s) (lines 53, 54)

8 scientifically (line 56)
9 effectively (line 62)
10 involving (line 65)

8 Write the families in your notebook. It is useful to learn certain words like this (first suggested in the notes for Unit 3).

9

Answers
1 and 3 are reporting the words or ideas of someone; 2 is marking the use of a word (because it is not meant literally).

10

Answers
said (line 1)   believes (line 11)   suggests (line 14)
points out (line 37)

11 The verbs *presume* and *suspect* indicate less certainty. Writing folder 3 practises reporting verbs.

Answers
said could be replaced by *claimed, considered, maintained* (the other verbs would alter the force of *said*, and we don't know how strongly Plato held to these words)
believes could be replaced by *argues, claims, considers, maintains*
suggests cannot be replaced by any of these verbs (*Research suggests ...*)
points out could be replaced by *emphasises*

6.2 pages 42–43

1 The pictures show an Indian sitar (left), an Australian aboriginal didgeridoo (centre), and an Indonesian gamelan orchestra (right).

Possible answers
I once went to an all-night concert at the London Proms with an Indian sitar player, a tabla player and someone playing an Indian wood flute. It was beautiful music, and the whole experience was very calming. When we came out of the concert, dawn was just breaking.
The sitar is definitely the hardest instrument of the three to play, in my opinion, because it has two sets of strings.

2 Read the Test spot and study the task. Listen to the example recording. Then listen to the rest of the recording and answer the questions.

Answers (relevant parts of the recording script are underlined)
1 C   **2** A   **3** B   **4** C   **5** B   **6** A   **7** C   **8** B

Recording script

Example

Hannah: Chris, we need to get on with planning our performance.
Chris: OK, Hannah. Are you happy with the pieces of music that we chose?
Hannah: Yes, they're fine.
Chris: Right. So we need to choose what should be happening during each piece. We'll be performing in the college theatre, so there's a good sound system for the recordings, we'll have the stage for the live action, and there'll be a giant screen at the back of the stage that the film and slides will be projected onto.
Hannah: Excellent.
Chris: Have you got the running order of the music we agreed on?
Hannah: Yes, here it is. The first piece is that exciting section from Tchaikovsky's *1812 Overture*. What do you think would go well with it?
Chris: How about one of us reading a really dramatic speech?
Hannah: But the music's very loud! It'd be impossible to hear any kind of speech, even if we shouted. <u>I think projecting a film of a firework display onto the screen would work better.</u>
Chris: Well, it would certainly get everyone's attention. OK, we'll do that.

Questions 1–8

Chris: What's next?
Hannah: The Balinese gamelan orchestra. It's a very delicate sound, as though the instruments are some distance away, and the sound is being carried by the wind.
Chris: How about if we stand on opposite sides of the stage and <u>say sentences that aren't connected, as though the audience is hearing snatches of different conversations,</u> blown by the wind?
Hannah: Mm, nice. … Then the mood changes, with a Jamaican steel band. That's very upbeat and exhilarating. I'd like us to do some tap dancing in a factory, surrounded by steel drums.
Chris: In a factory? <u>Film us there,</u> you mean? Yeah, good idea, I'll find out about possible locations.
Hannah: Next it's the Indian sitar music.
Chris: Mmm. I think we should have <u>someone on stage doing traditional Indian dancing.</u> In fact, I know just the person – Jayshree Begum. I'm sure she'd agree to do it!
Hannah: Perfect. OK, then the next piece of music is the South American pan pipes. Any ideas?
Chris: Mm, I could recite a South American poem.
Hannah: Or maybe we could have some pipes and mime playing them ourselves?
Chris: Isn't that too literal? I'd like to be a bit more imaginative.
Hannah: Mm, maybe you're right. <u>OK, we'll have the poem.</u> With you in a spotlight, and the rest of the stage in darkness.
Chris: Right. It's all beginning to take shape, isn't it?
Hannah: Yeah. Now the next piece is the slow part of Mahler's fifth symphony. I imagine this starting with the stage still in pitch darkness, then the lights come up very slowly, so the audience gradually realises there are people standing there, absolutely motionless.
Chris: Maybe lit from behind, so we're in silhouette.
Hannah: Lovely … <u>and then we start swaying, and doing very stylised, formal gestures, mostly with the arms.</u>
Chris: Oh, that sounds great. Right, what's next?
Hannah: The African band, you know, the one from Mali.

Chris: Ah yes, that'll be a complete contrast, really lively. It'll make people want to leap to their feet and fling themselves around. How about getting the audience to dance?

Hannah: What, suddenly shout out 'Everybody stand up and dance'? I don't think so! I'd rather we created a sense of place and endless time, with <u>slides of Mali</u>, showing the Sahara desert, Timbuktu, some of the ruins … each one dissolving into the next. It'd be a striking contrast with the music.

Chris: Mm. I still like the idea of audience participation.

Hannah: But it would be awfully embarrassing if we asked them to dance and they didn't!

Chris: Yeah, I suppose so. OK, we'll go with your idea.

Hannah: Right.

Chris: And the next section?

Hannah: That's the didgeridoo. As it's an Australian Aboriginal instrument, and so unusual, maybe we could show a film clip of it being played.

Chris: Or we could learn some traditional Aboriginal dancing.

Hannah: No time. … I know – how about a complete contrast, to make people sit up and think? <u>We could do a comedy sketch, standing quite still on opposite sides of the stage. If we get the timing right, we could fit the sound of the didgeridoo to the words.</u>

Chris: Hannah, that's an absolutely crazy idea! And I love it!

Hannah: Thank you. Well, the last piece is the electronic music by that German group Kraftwerk. That'd really lend itself to <u>a way-out gymnastics display</u>.

Chris: Maybe some film footage of the Olympic Games from years ago.

Hannah: Or we could ask the college gym team to perform on stage.

Chris: Yes, let's do that. After all, we want to involve a lot of people in this.

Hannah: OK, well there's plenty for us to do, isn't there, so …

3 Think which sounds are difficult for you.

4 Listen carefully to the recording.

> **Answers**
> **1** sit **2** said **3** run **4** song **5** not **6** gate **7** ear
> **8** now **9** heat **10** wrong **11** worth **12** show

Now listen to the next part of the recording and repeat the words in each pair.

5 Remember that you can check pronunciation in a dictionary.

6

> **Answer**
> **a** *While* introduces a time clause (*when* could be substituted).
> **b** *While* introduces a concessive clause (*although* could be substituted).

7 Read the tinted box and look at the Grammar folder on page 140 before you do exercises 8, 9 and 10.

> **Answers**
> **1** a **2** b

8

> **Answers**
> **1** f **2** d **3** b **4** a **5** c **6** e

9

> **Answers**
> 1 The music classes were satisfactory, despite the lack of individual tuition. OR The music classes were satisfactory, although there was not any individual tuition.
> 2 Nobody likes jazz more than I do, but in spite of / despite its promising title, this is a disappointing album. OR Nobody likes jazz more than I do, but although it has a promising title, this is a disappointing album.
> 3 The concert was supposed to last for at least an hour, whereas it was only forty minutes.
> 4 In spite of having played the trumpet for three years, I found this piece too difficult. OR Although I've been playing the trumpet for three years, I found this piece too difficult.
> 5 As can be seen from the chart, despite the fact that the USA has the highest percentage employed in this area, only 10% are women. OR As can be seen from the chart, although / even though / while the USA has the highest percentage employed in this area, only 10% are women.
> 6 There was a general feeling that in spite of / despite the friendly atmosphere, the entertainment was dull.
> 7 In conclusion, even though there are some advantages, the problems are too great. (Note that this sentence has been corrected by moving the second comma to the correct place.)
> 8 My daughter is not allowed to watch TV after 8.30 in spite of / despite the fact that some programmes would be interesting for her.

10

> **Suggested answers**
> 1 Although I love the band's earlier CDs, I'm not keen on their latest one.
> 2 With a guitar, the hand movement is downwards, whereas with a sitar, you also pull the strings.
> 3 Despite living in New York, the musician performs mainly in Europe.
> 4 Even though orchestral concerts involve many performers, not everybody / not every performer is needed throughout (the concert).
> 5 In spite of being over 100 years old, the song is still popular today. OR The song is still popular today, in spite of being over 100 years old.

11 Think about each question and make some notes. Try recording yourself talking about the questions and then listen to your answers. Think of ways to make improvements or say more.

Writing folder 3

pages 44–45

1

Suggested answers
1 Several people argued for a heavy fine to be imposed on people who fail to recycle glass and paper.
2 A few people suggested that recycling plastic is more expensive than burying it in landfill.
3 Someone claimed that if we were given separate containers, it would be easier for us to recycle different materials.
4 One person maintained that there is no need to recycle anything.

2 Try to use adverbs in reporting structures as an indicator of a widely held belief or view.

Suggested answers
1 The recycling of plastic is commonly/generally/widely believed to be too costly a process.
2 Air travel is now commonly/generally/widely seen as the biggest threat to the environment.
3 A new tax has been suggested on non-returnable bottles.
4 The latest international agreement is universally seen as insubstantial.
5 Excess supermarket packaging is commonly felt to be at the heart of the landfill problem.
6 Government measures on household recycling are reported to be imminent.

3

Answers
1 must be conserved   2 can be reduced
3 would be imposed   4 cannot be produced
5 might be offered

4

Sample answer
It is hard to deny the importance of recycling in the modern world. One has only to visit the nearest landfill site to understand the scale of the problem. Yet at the same time, recycling is not always the cheapest option. Nor is it the only issue with respect to the environment.

On the one hand, there is a lot that can be done in terms of household recycling. Kerbside collections of newspapers, bottles and cans trim the amount of rubbish that has to be consigned to landfill. Some councils even collect plastic bottles and recycle them, although it is commonly believed that the recycling of plastic is too costly a process.

Many people are lazy when it comes to recycling and opt to throw everything away instead of separating out materials to be recycled. To counteract this, fines or taxes may have to be introduced. A new tax has also been suggested on non-returnable bottles.

At the same time, there are other pollutants of our planet that have nothing to do with waste disposal. Air travel is now widely seen as the biggest threat to the environment and, unless higher taxes are put on aviation fuel, the situation will get worse. However, this kind of decision should be taken in an international forum, and it is vital that the world's largest nations (and heaviest users of fossil fuels) join this discussion.

It is to be hoped that our politicians will come together and agree a viable strategy for the world which will allow future generations to enjoy the beauty and diversity of our blue planet.
(266 words)

Unit 7

7.1 pages 46–47

1 The picture shows the International Space Station. Read the statements and decide how far you agree or disagree with them.

Background information
The International Space Station (ISS) is perhaps the largest and most complex international project in history. It has drawn on the scientific and technological resources of 16 countries: the USA, Canada, Japan, Russia, Brazil and 11 nations of the European Space Agency. It measures 108 by 88 metres and has a large number of solar panels, to provide power to its six laboratories.

2 Read the instructions and options **A–D**, then skim the passage, timing yourself. Decide which sentence best summarises the passage.

Answer
C

3 Look at questions 1–3 (options **A–F**). This task type is used in both the Reading and Listening Modules. Test folder 5 on pages 64–65 deals with all the multiple-choice tasks. Choose three (and only three!) answers, underlining the relevant parts of the passage.

Before continuing with questions 4–11, read the Test spot. Remember that the words must come from the passage and be correctly spelled.

4   Read the advertisement and write the relevant qualities beside questions 1–6. Then think about these qualities in relation to yourself.

5   Consider these qualities, and decide which are the five most important ones for an astronaut.

7.2 pages 48–49

1   Decide what you could say about travelling under water.

2   Read the instructions, questions 1–4 and options **A–F**, then listen to the first part of the lecture and answer the questions.

Read the Test spot. Then read options **A–H** and look carefully at the diagram before listening to the second part of the recording.

Recording script

Questions 1–4

Lecturer: There are two main types of device in which people can travel under water: diving bells, which are lowered and raised from the surface, and can't be propelled forwards, and submarines, which do have a means of propulsion.

It's possible that Alexander the Great descended into the sea in a diving bell 2,300 years ago, although this hasn't been proved, and some sort of submarine may also have existed in China not long afterwards.

The first workable submarine of recent times was designed and built in 1620 by a Dutch doctor living in London, Cornelius Van

Drebbel. This was a fully enclosed boat, propelled by the crew, who used oars, as in a normal rowing boat. The crew breathed air through tubes from the surface of the water. The submarine travelled along the River Thames for several hours, at a depth of over four metres.

Later in the seventeenth century, the British astronomer Edmund Halley patented a diving bell linked by pipes to barrels of air. Manned descents to depths of over 18 metres, lasting up to 90 minutes, proved that diving bells were practicable devices.

A number of experiments took place in the next two or three centuries, including one submarine in which the crew turned a hand crank to propel the vessel mechanically.

Jumping now to the 1930s, two United States explorers, William Beebe and Otis Barton, developed a bathysphere – which means 'deep sphere' – in which they dived to 922 metres. The bathysphere was just large enough for two people, and was raised and lowered from a ship by a steel cable. Electricity reached it along a power line from the mother ship, and the two men breathed oxygen from tanks fitted to the interior. They had a telephone link with the ship, and were broadcast on the radio all over the USA.

Questions 5–9

Lecturer: Nowadays we have submersibles that can withstand the immense water pressure far below the surface. One of these 'Deep Submergence Vehicles', as they're called, is Alvin, which has been in use since 1964. A typical dive lasts eight hours, and descends to 4,500 metres below sea level. Alvin is used for various scientific purposes, including, in 1985–86, surveying the wreck of the *Titanic*, the ocean liner that sank in the Atlantic in 1912.

The first thing you notice about Alvin is its bright red sail, displaying the name of the vessel. The sail is on top of the vehicle, at the front, and helps to maintain stability. Alvin is about seven metres long and just over 3.5 metres high, but only a small portion of that space is available for people. This is in the pressure sphere, which is located under the sail at the front of the vessel. With a diameter of about two metres, there's room for three people, but it's a tight squeeze. Usually there's a pilot and two scientists. From here they can look out in various directions, through four viewing ports.

Alvin carries a large number of instruments, including video and still cameras, mounted on the exterior at the front, along with lights for illuminating the ocean, as of course sunlight doesn't penetrate this far down. Usually there's a stowage basket mounted on a frame at the front, used to hold tools and scientific equipment.

Immediately under the sail is the hatch, which has a diameter of only 50 cm. This is the way into the vessel. On top of the sail there's a current meter, to measure the movement of the ocean.

Propulsion is provided by six electric thrusters, which make Alvin very manoeuvrable. Three of them are for forward and reverse movement, two for vertical motion, and a final thruster, right at the back of the vessel, turns the submersible round.

Now we'll turn to …

3   Read the explanation and examples, then work through the exercise (more than one wording may be possible). Note that sentences 2 and 4 are ungrammatical as they stand.

4 Think of ways of continuing the sentences.

5 Complete the table.

6 Play the recording and check your answers.

7 Read the questions and Useful language, and think about how you could answer the questions.

Test folder 4

pages 50–51

Make sure you fully understand the notes and advice.

1 Think about what the drawing shows. It is a ship of the type used by the Vikings of Scandinavia, over 1000 years ago. The Vikings reached North America, the Mediterranean and Russia in ships like this.

Skim the passage, then read questions 1–7 and the endings A–J. Underline and number the relevant part of the passage for each question.

Read the notes for questions 8–13, then complete them, finding the answers in the passage.

12	coins	*there was a demand for gold and other precious metals, some of which was turned into coins (paragraph 10)*
13	spices	*Probably even more prized at this time were spices, which were used for preserving and flavouring meats. (paragraph 11)*

2 The listening passage is part of a lecture. Read the box of words and the sentences. Make sure you understand the words in the box, and remember that they may not be the words that will be heard in the recording. Then complete the sentences as you listen to the recording.

Answers (relevant parts of the recording script are underlined)
1 fame 2 technology 3 knowledge 4 research
5 nationalism 6 endurance

Recording script

You will hear part of a lecture about the history of European exploration.
First you have some time to look at questions 1 to 6. (pause)
Now listen carefully and answer questions 1 to 6.
Lecturer: The explorations by Christopher Columbus and other Europeans during the 15th and 16th centuries showed a subtle difference from earlier journeys. A new element in the ethos of the time was <u>a thirst for glory and recognition of the individual</u>, which joined religion and riches as a major factor in exploration.

Regardless of the explorers' motives, those who crossed the oceans were able to navigate much more accurately than before, thanks to <u>the development of the quadrant and other instruments</u>, as well as a better understanding of the functioning of the magnetic compass. This, along with improvements in cartography, made voyages somewhat less dangerous.

During the 18th century there was a renewed emphasis on exploration for scientific purposes and <u>to improve the stock of information and understanding</u> that was available. European intellectuals became aware of their ignorance about certain aspects of the physical and natural world and were keen to do something about it. <u>Many ocean voyages were on vessels that were basically floating scientific laboratories.</u> They had trained scientists on board, as well as a vast array of equipment and skilled artists and draftsmen to make accurate records of the voyage.

<u>In the 20th century, countries competed to gain prestige.</u> With less and less land to discover and claim, there were races to the North Pole, the South Pole, Everest, the depths of the oceans, the moon and Mars.

The equivalent of exploration in the 21st century often has more to do with overcoming physical challenges than discovering the unknown: not simply to reach the peak of Everest, but to reach it alone, or without oxygen, or in the shortest possible time. Exploration has turned inwards: once we explored what is 'out there', <u>now we explore the limits of what we can withstand.</u>

Unit 8

8.1 pages 52–53

1 The pictures show food sold in the street, a smart, modern kitchen in a private home, and a father and son cooking food over a campfire.

Think about how you could answer these questions.

Possible answers
- In my family we generally take it in turns to cook, though I usually cook when we have people coming to dinner. I enjoy cooking when I've got some recipes to follow, and plenty of time to plan, but it's hard when I'm short of time.
- I don't think I could manage without labour-saving devices, particularly a dishwasher, because I hate washing up. But I sometimes buy gadgets that look interesting, then hardly ever use them.
- As people get busier and busier, I'm sure the emphasis will be on anything that saves time, like microwaves that just take a second to heat up a whole meal.

2 Skim the article and choose the answer.

Answer
C

3 Read the first Test spot. Remember that it is often possible to work out the meaning of unknown words from context, and that you don't need to understand every word in a passage. Work out suitable definitions for words 1–10 that fit the context of the passage.

Suggested answers
1 *combat* – verb: try to prevent something bad from happening or getting worse
2 *pooling* – verb: collecting and using together
3 *obsolete* – adjective: no longer in use
4 *address* – verb: deal with, try to solve
5 *granules* – noun: very small grain-like pieces of a substance
6 *suspended* – verb: hung
7 *dilemma* – noun: a situation in which a difficult choice has to be made
8 *sensors* – noun: devices to measure and record something
9 *incinerated* – verb: completely burned
10 *harness* – verb: control something, in order to use its power

4 Read the second Test spot before doing the task.

Answers (evidence from the passage is given, but this is not part of the answer)
1 H *The spoon can be connected to a computer and programmed to follow a certain recipe. ... it can warn at each stage ... if too much salt has been added. (lines 41–46)*

5 Read the tinted explanation about phrasal verbs with *up*. Remember that many phrasal verbs don't have an obvious meaning, as in **c** *make up*. These may need to be guessed from context.

> **Answers**
> 1 a 2 c 3 a 4 b 5 c 6 a 7 b

6

> **Answers**
> 1 c 2 b 3 e 4 a 5 d

8.2 pages 54–55

1 Consider how you could answer the questions.

> **Possible answers**
> - The traditional food of the country is becoming less and less popular because it takes a lot of effort to prepare. Nowadays more women go out to work and don't spend all day doing housework and cooking, so they often buy ready-cooked meals that just need to be heated up.
> - It's difficult to imagine the situation, but we'd have to eat food we could hold in our hands, so it'd be difficult to eat rice, and soup would be out of the question!

2 Read the Test spot. In IELTS, flow charts are sometimes a sequence of causes and effects, and sometimes (as here) chronological. Look at the first part of the flow chart and try to predict answers 1–7 before playing the first part of the recording.

Check that you understand the words in the box before continuing with the recording for questions 8–14 (use an English–English dictionary if necessary).

> **Answers** (relevant parts of the recording script are underlined)
> 1 shells 2 wood 3 meat 4 dining 5 fingers
> 6 gold 7 metals
>
> 8 affected 9 laughable 10 refined 11 curved
> 12 pointed 13 blunt 14 simple

Recording script

Questions 1–7

Lecturer: In Europe, knives have been used as weapons, tools, and eating utensils since prehistoric times, and spoons are equally ancient. In the early Stone Age, tens of thousands of years ago, it seems that in Southern Europe spoons were made of shells – evidence for this includes the fact that later the Greek and Latin words for a spoon come from the word for the shell of a snail. In Northern Europe wood was probably the most common material, and again there's linguistic evidence for this.

Though forks are much more recent, they trace their origins back over 2,000 years, to the Ancient Greeks. Their forks had two tines – they're the points that go into the food – and were designed to hold meat steady while it was carved and served. The tines allowed it to slide off easily.

By the 7th century, royal courts of the Middle East had begun to use forks at the table for dining. Forks became fairly common among the wealthy in Byzantium – modern Istanbul – and in the 11th century, they were introduced into Italy. The Italians, however, were slow to start using them.

During the Middle Ages – very roughly from the 9th or 10th century up to and including the 15th – Europeans used knives and their fingers for eating. Hosts didn't provide knives for their guests, and most people carried their own, in sheaths attached to their belts. These knives had pointed ends, and were used to spear food and raise it to the mouth.

Spoons of the Middle Ages were generally made of wood or horn, although royalty often had spoons made of gold, and other wealthy families might have silver ones. From about the 14th century, spoons made of brass, pewter and other metals became common. The use of pewter especially made spoons more affordable for ordinary people.

Questions 8–14

Lecturer: By the 16th century, forks were in everyday use in Italy, and in 1533 they were brought from Italy to France, when an Italian noblewoman married the future king of France. At first, using them was thought to be pretentious, and they were slow to catch on.

In the early 17th century, an Englishman named Thomas Coryate brought the first forks back to England after seeing them in Italy during his travels. The English, however, thought forks unnecessary, treated them with ridicule, and continued to use their hands. But slowly forks became fashionable among the wealthy. Small, slender-handled forks with two tines were used for sweet, sticky foods or for food which was likely to stain the fingers. By the middle of the 17th century, forks used solely for dining were luxuries, made of expensive materials. They indicated social status and sophistication, and were intended to impress guests.

Early table forks, like kitchen forks, had two fairly long, widely spaced tines, which ensured that meat wouldn't twist while it was being cut, but small pieces of food fell between the tines. In late-17th century France, larger forks with four tines were developed. Diners were now less likely to drop food, and as the tines were curved, forks served as a scoop, so people didn't have to constantly switch to a spoon while eating.

The fact that knives were still used as weapons always posed the threat of danger at the dinner table. However, once forks began to gain popular acceptance – forks being more efficient for spearing food – there was <u>no longer any need for a sharp tip at the end of a dinner knife. In 1669, the king of France declared knives like this illegal</u> on the street or at the dinner table, and he had all knife tips ground down, in order to reduce violence. Other design changes followed. Cutlers, who manufactured knives, began to make the blunt ends wider and rounder so that small pieces of food could be piled on the knife and carried to the mouth.

<u>The birth of blunt-tipped knives in Europe had a lasting effect on American dining etiquette.</u> At the beginning of the 18th century, very few forks were being imported to America. However <u>knives were being brought in and their tips became progressively blunter.</u> Because Americans had very few forks and no longer had sharp-tipped knives, they had to use spoons in place of forks. They would use the spoon to steady food as they cut, and then switch the spoon to the opposite hand in order to scoop up food to eat. This style of eating has continued to the present day, though with the fork replacing the spoon: many Americans cut their food, then lay the knife down and hold only the fork while they eat.

During the last hundred years or so, the ornamental styles of cutlery popular in previous centuries have <u>given way to much plainer designs</u>, and stainless steel has replaced many of the materials used earlier. Now there's a whole range of cutlery intended for different purposes in the kitchen or dining room – including different spoons for soup, dessert, tea, coffee; knives for main course, steak, grapefruit; forks for cake, main course, dessert. And the list grows longer as new specialised implements are invented.

3   Read the instructions and carry them out. Then decide how clear they are.

4   Read the information about the first conditional in the tinted box and complete the exercise.

> **Suggested answers**
> 1 should move 2 shouldn't 3 might; pull
> 4 can lift your dish 5 should ignore it
> 6 will be able to use; practise

5   Read the article. Notice the use of the second conditional in the second paragraph (*If switching to chopsticks forced people to eat more slowly, they might eat less*). Read the explanation above exercise 6.

6   Complete the summary using the modal verbs of your choice.

> **Possible answers**
> 1 would/might lose its point 2 would be tricky / wouldn't be easy 3 would/could be difficult
> 4 might/could poke 5 might eat 6 might not eat
> 7 would boom

7   Read the article.

8   Read the information on the third conditional above exercise 8 and complete the exercise.

> **Answers**
> 1 hadn't been cooked; might not have used
> 2 hadn't been put; wouldn't have been forced
> 3 might not have cut; hadn't been
> 4 hadn't been chopped; would have been needed
> 5 might have advised; had been

Writing folder 4
pages 56–57

1

> **Answers**
> The missing labels are:
> 1 upper section 2 lower section 3 outer compartment
> 4 inner compartment 5 watery gel 6 desiccant

2

> **Answers**
> 1 is twisted 2 causes 3 evaporates 4 is absorbed
> 5 prevents 6 can be cooled / is cooled / will be cooled

3   All the grammatical areas are included except for concessive clauses.

4

> **Answers**
> 1 involves 2 starts 3 goes on 4 stops

5   The three examples are: **propelling** (*the spaceship to its required height*); **providing** (*a shuttlecock effect*); **enabling** (*the craft to glide back to Earth*).

6

> **Sample answer**
> SpaceShipOne is a prototype spacecraft which can be sent up into space again and again. The craft is designed to be used in conjunction with White Knight, which is its launcher. When it is ready to be launched, SpaceShipOne is taken up to a height of approximately 15 km by White Knight. SpaceShipOne is then deployed by White Knight, which then glides back down to Earth. At this point, the booster rockets on SpaceShipOne are fired up, propelling the craft upwards to its required altitude of 100 km. When the craft is ready to re-enter the Earth's atmosphere, its wings can be tilted upwards. This provides an effect similar to that of a shuttlecock as it falls to the ground, holding the craft in the correct position for re-entry. After successful re-entry, the wings are tilted back to their normal position, enabling the craft to glide back safely to Earth.
> (150 words)

Units 5–8 Revision

pages 58–59

1 Give examples from your personal experience in your answers.

2

> **Answers**
> 1 despite having   2 Even though music is considered to   3 whereas in fact it is a material   4 While he performs

3

> **Answers**
> 1 d   2 g   3 h   4 f   5 k   6 c   7 e   8 j   9 b   10 i

4

> **Answers**
> 1 had contained; would/might have tasted
> 2 had lived; might/would have sung
> 3 had visited; would/might have found out
> 4 hadn't sailed; would have been called
> 5 hadn't been built; would have had to
> 6 hadn't been invented; wouldn't have been

5

> **Answers**
> 1 f   2 c   3 e   4 a   5 d   6 b

6

> **Answers**
> *Scientific processes*: contamination, corrosion, fuel
> *Moods*: carefree, elated, gloomy, sorrowful
> *Culinary equipment*: crockery, cutlery, microwave oven, refrigerator
> *Personal qualities*: brave, conscientious, decisive, disciplined, tolerant

7

> **Answers**
> 1 have always considered   2 conscientious   3 brave
> 4 decisive   5 tolerant   6 suspect   7 would/might argue
> 8 observed   9 is believed

Unit 9

9.1 pages 60–61

> **Background information**
> Venice and Shanghai have one thing in common: both cities are sinking. The rising sea level of the Adriatic is causing Venice to be seriously flooded on a regular basis, which is damaging the foundations of the buildings. A tidal barrier is under construction to protect the city. In Shanghai, the subsidence is due to its 'soft' ground, as the passage in 9.1 explains.

1 The pictures on page 60 show the cities of Venice and Shanghai. Think of ways to compare them.

> **Possible answers**
> *Architecture*: Venice has largely old buildings, some over 500 years old. Shanghai has undergone recent development and has many modern skyscrapers and high-rise accommodation.
> *Transportation*: Venice has a system of canals, so all transportation has to be on water, by public water-buses (*vaporetti*) and water-taxis; the traditional gondolas are mainly used by tourists these days. Shanghai has multi-lane roads, with heavy car use and some bicycles (a metro system is planned).
> *Demography*: Many of the people born in Venice are leaving and moving to other cities, as Venice becomes more and more dominated by tourism. Shanghai's population, on the other hand, is rapidly increasing, as it is a flourishing city with diverse employment prospects.

2 Read the task card. For the first listening, concentrate on the content (relevance) and register (formal/informal) of what the girl says.

> **Suggested answer**
> The initial parts to do with her family are irrelevant and have lost the candidate valuable time in which to show range. Her register is rather inconsistent, with some informal usage that should be avoided, for example: *OK, yeah, Well, really.*

Recording script

Candidate: OK, I'm going to talk to you about Venezia – that is to say, Venice – which my mother comes from originally. Her parents still live there but my mom moved away when she met my dad. He's from Puglia in the south of Italy. We all live in Bari, the main city there. OK, sorry, now I'm going to describe Venice. What can I say about Venice? It's … it's an old city and its infrastructure hasn't changed very much in hundreds of years – it's built on water, so instead of roads through the centre you have waterways, canals, and to get around you can either walk or take a boat. In … in Venice, there are public 'vaporetti' – those are the water buses which stop every so often to pick up passengers – and then there are lots of smaller water taxis, private boats and, of course, the beautiful gondolas which tourists love to take.

I feel … I feel very sad about Venice because it's a city that is … how can I put it? … it's losing its heart. Yeah, so so what I dislike about Venice is this: because so many people have moved away, more and more of the 'real' shops have closed down. By 'real' shops I mean bakers and other essential food shops, and it's true, every time I go back there, another one has gone. You know, it's really bad. If you walk through any part of Venice, nearly every shop you come across will be selling souvenirs, most of them rather tacky. I hate that. Well of course all year massive numbers of tourists visit Venice and I think it's a terrible problem because the city just becomes like … like Disneyland, yeah, it's true. To put it another way, it's not a living city any longer. Mm, I know tourists bring money to the city but they're killing it too, in a way.

It goes without saying that tourists come to Venice for the history, the buildings, the art. Venice looks so fantastic.

Obviously there are no high-rise buildings, and that makes the city unusual, but the canals make it unique. ... Most of the buildings in Venice are sinking. Right now there's a lot of construction work going on to strengthen the ... their foundations. There's terrible subsidence and the whole of Venice is sinking. It's really a big problem.

Examiner: Thank you.

3   Listen again and tick the words you hear.

Answers
All the words were in the recording, apart from *outskirts* and *rapid transit system*.
construction – the work of building or making something, especially buildings, bridges, etc.
foundations – the structures below the surface of the ground which support a building
infrastructure – the systems and services that ensure that a city, country or organisation operates effectively; for example, transport, power supply, rubbish collection
outskirts – areas that form the edge of a city or town
rapid transit system – a public network of fast trains serving a city
subsidence – when land or buildings sink to a lower level than before

---

4   Prepare your Part 2 notes, using the Useful language and any relevant vocabulary from the recording.

5   Skim the passage, timing yourself and underlining any unfamiliar words. Decide whether these words are important to the meaning of the passage – if they are, check their meaning in a dictionary.

6

Answers (evidence from the passage is given, but this is not part of the answer)
1   H   *There are now more than 4,000 buildings over 100 metres tall in Shanghai. That results in extremely severe ground settlement.* (lines 16–18)
2   C   *Among the planned solutions are a metro system, a huge motorway network and* (lines 23–25)
3   A   *an extraordinary skyscraper, emblematic of the successful mingling of western and eastern styles.* (lInes 31–33)
4   G   *boulevards are 12 lanes wide (and uncrossable), without any relationship to human scale, activity or urban life* (lines 50–52)
5   J   *Shanghai's character was being obliterated ... 'The market's rapid pace of wholesale importation of foreign imagery has resulted in a scary, perverse and at times ridiculous trend of turning modern cities into Disney-lands.'* (lines 53–58)
6   F   *'You have to make it attractive for people to leave and live in new cities nearby.'* (lines 66–67)

---

7   All the linking words and phrases occur as sentence openers in the passage.

Suggested answers
The first four linkers are all used to introduce examples/ reasons:
Other factors (line 21): provides further exemplification/ explanation
Alongside (line 40): signals a contrast (another type of building)
One ... another ... a third (lines 72–74), exemplifies and indicates that all three refer back to the same part of the passage (ten satellite towns)
Among (line 23): indicates that there are a number of (planned solutions) – *among* can only be used with three or more things, though these may be implied rather than specified (compare *among the most impressive*, line 29)
Worse yet (line 52): signals something even more serious (Shanghai's character is being obliterated)
Thus (line 76): refers back to the content of the previous paragraph (all of Wu Jiang's positive plans)

9.2 pages 62–63

1   Think about how you could answer this.

Possible answers
Many of the earliest cities or settlements were located beside water, which provided irrigation for agriculture. Natural resources such as water and fertile ground were important, and people also needed water for their livestock. Cities established near rivers became important trading centres. Other cities were built on higher ground in a defensive position, where invaders could be seen from a distance.

---

2   Read the summary and predict what is needed in questions 1–9.

Background information
Ur was an ancient city in southern Mesopotamia, located near the original mouth of the Euphrates and Tigris rivers on the Persian Gulf. Because of marine regression, the remains of Ur are now well inland in present-day Iraq, south of the Euphrates on its right bank.

Answers
1 year   2 number   3 noun – content word of some kind
4 verb   5 verb   6 noun   7 number   8 name or adjective relating to city   9 adjective relating to centre

---

Listen to the recording and write no more than one word or a number.

Answers (relevant parts of the recording script are underlined)
1 1934   2 5,500   3 animals   4 feed   5 trade   6 grain
7 80,000   8 Rainbow   9 religious

Recording script

Lecturer: One of the most important archaeological projects ever undertaken has to be that of the ancient Sumerian city of Ur, because it threw a great deal of light onto the previously dark past and expanded our knowledge in so many areas, from urban planning to the beginnings of writing. These excavations were a joint expedition between the British Museum and the University of Pennsylvania and were led by Leonard Woolley throughout, from 1922 until 1934.

From the extensive work of Woolley and his team, it was possible to establish that Ur was the very first city in the world, founded at least 5,500 years ago. Because Ur was strategically located close to the Euphrates River, there's no question that its first settlers would have been self-sufficient. Indeed, it was their development of irrigation and the domestication of animals that allowed a traditionally nomadic people to settle in one place with their livestock, knowing that they could depend on a regular source of food. However, away from the river banks, the environment was fairly arid and as Ur developed, it was no longer possible to grow enough to feed all its citizens – the soil simply wasn't fertile enough to support the level of production that the population required. For this reason, the people turned to trade. The inhabitants of Ur became highly skilled artisans and traded their goods for food and other resources.

The most flourishing period of Ur as a city was between 5,000 and 4,400 years ago, when it was an important cultural, religious and commercial centre. It was around 5,000 years ago that mankind's first writing system developed, stemming initially from the need to record the city's stocks of grain accurately.

Ur was not the largest city in the region at this time. While 4,700 years ago Ur had a population of 34,000 people, the trading centre Uruk, situated near the confluence of the Euphrates River and Iturungal Canal, had over 80,000 people, and extended over an area of 1,000 acres. Like any trading centre, Uruk had a diverse population, and was often referred to as 'The Rainbow City' for this reason. It was actually two cities: there was the newer trading centre, Kullab, on the bank of the Euphrates, and Eanna, the religious centre, which fronted the Iturungal Canal.

From about 4,400 years ago, Ur's power diminished but it rose again around 4,100 years ago. This started the period known as the Third Dynasty, when Ur-Nammu, the brother of King Utukhegal, established his kingship in Ur and its surroundings. Hardly had the Third Dynasty begun when it was brought to an abrupt end by invaders, who destroyed the city state and relegated Ur to being a backwater again.

3

Answers
1 archaeological   2 strategically   3 settlers   4 cultural
5 surroundings

4

Answers
The stylistic effect is to place emphasis on the fact that the Third Dynasty had only just begun when it came to an end.
Subjects:

1 Ur   2 I   3 a stone lion
The subject comes after the verb, or after an auxiliary such as *did* (as in example 2).

5 Read the information on pages 140–141 of the Grammar folder before doing the exercise.

Answers
1 No sooner had we got back to the hotel than Tom wanted to walk to the castle.
2 Seldom had I felt as safe as this walking around a city late at night.
3 Scarcely had they entered the office when the phone started ringing.
4 Hardly had the ticket price rise been implemented when it was announced that a further 5% increase would be imposed.

6

Possible answers
2 g Not only has the city of Bogotá got an excellent bus service, it also encourages the use of bicycles wherever possible.
3 a Not only do 10 million inhabitants live in the centre of Shanghai, a further 10 million live in its suburbs.
4 e Not only are there a lot of galleries in London, there are several museums too.
5 f Not only can high-rise buildings lack style and originality, they are sometimes poorly constructed as well.
6 b Not only was the ancient city of Ur built beside the Euphrates River, it was close to the Tigris as well.
7 d Not only does Siena offer visitors a historic centre, the countryside nearby is also very beautiful.

7

Answers
1 The train drivers are on strike and so are the bus drivers.
2 The Tokyo flight took off on time and so did the one to Taipei / the Taipei one.
3 Madrid has a metro and so does Bilbao.
4 I can take the metro and so can you.
5 John should walk to work and so should I.
6 Kiosks sell bus tickets and so do subway stations.

8

Answers
1 I hadn't been to Prague before and neither had Dominic. OR I hadn't been to Prague before, nor had Dominic.
2 The school can't provide parking spaces and neither can the sports centre. OR The school can't provide parking spaces, nor can the sports centre.
3 You won't be in time for the next train and neither will I. OR You won't be in time for the next train, nor will I.
4 Fortunately, the car wasn't damaged and neither was my bike. OR Fortunately, the car wasn't damaged, nor was my bike.

Test folder 5

pages 64–65

Make sure you fully understand the notes and advice.

1   Read questions 1–6, then choose your answers as you listen to the first part of the recording.

Then read questions 7–11 and listen to that section. Remember to choose *only* five answers.

Answers (relevant parts of the recording script are underlined)

1 A   **2** B   **3** B   **4** C   **5** A   **6** B

7–11 A, C, E, H, J (in any order)

Recording script

You will hear part of a lecture about the development of suburbs in the USA.

First you have some time to look at questions 1 to 6. (pause)

Now listen carefully and answer questions 1 to 6.

Lecturer: Today we're looking at how the suburbs of cities in the USA have developed since the middle of the twentieth century. But first, a little history.

Suburbs have existed in various forms since antiquity, when cities typically were walled and the villages outside them were inferior in size and status. However, the modern American notion of the quiet, unspoiled outskirts as a retreat for the wealthy city dweller is in evidence as early as the 6th century BC in Babylon. Further early evidence comes from Cicero, writing in the 1st century BC, who refers to *suburbani*, large country estates just outside Rome.

Throughout Europe, the distinction between the city and outlying districts tended to remain sharp through the Middle Ages and Renaissance. To accommodate a large influx of newcomers, city walls were expanded, or, as with London, towns adjacent to the overcrowded city were gradually annexed to it. Generally considered a less desirable location, the urban periphery was inhabited largely by the poor.

In England, the rich who owned weekend villas outside London gradually transferred their main residences there, and the middle class soon followed. By the mid 19th century, there was a marked preference for suburban living. Migration from the central city to the suburbs was encouraged by a succession of technological advances in transportation. Horse-drawn stagecoaches, railways, and the electric streetcar or trolley all enabled urban dwellers to commute longer distances than had previously been practical.

Now in Europe, unlike the United States, suburbs grew organically, as a response to human needs, and each suburb there generally has a centre, and often has a quite distinct quality from other suburbs. Since the mid-twentieth century, however, North America has seen a distinctive pattern of growth, called suburban sprawl – an almost endless spread of low-density housing without any distinct neighbourhood centres. This is an artificial system, conceived by architects, engineers and planners, and it's already showing itself to be unsustainable.

Unlike the traditional neighbourhood, sprawl is not healthy growth; it's essentially self-destructive. It consumes land at an alarming rate, while producing insurmountable traffic problems. As the ring of suburbia grows around most North American cities, so the void at the centre grows too. Business and people move to fresher locations on a new suburban edge, leaving behind deteriorating downtown neighbourhoods, which can only be revitalised with enormous effort.

Suburban sprawl came about as the direct result of a number of US federal policies. The most significant were the housing and loan programmes which, from the 1940s, provided mortgages to encourage home purchase. These mortgages were directed at new single-family suburban construction, discouraging the renovation of existing housing stock and the construction of higher-density housing. Simultaneously, a major highway programme, coupled with the neglect of mass transit, helped make automotive commuting affordable and convenient for the average citizen.

Before you hear the rest of the lecture you have some time to look at questions 7 to 11. (pause)

Now listen and answer questions 7 to 11.

Lecturer: Suburban sprawl actually tends to be very simple, consisting of just a few components which are normally kept strictly segregated from each other. One component is housing subdivisions, which are districts consisting only of residences. They're sometimes called villages, towns, or neighbourhoods by their developers, which is misleading, since those terms denote places which are not exclusively residential and which provide a richness of experience that is not available in a housing tract. Subdivisions can be identified as such by their contrived names, which tend toward the romantic, and often pay tribute to the natural or historic resource they have displaced: woodland, mills or ponds, maybe, that have been destroyed.

Another element, schools, have evolved dramatically in the past thirty or forty years. A comparison between the size of the car park and the size of the building is revealing: most are schools to which no child will ever walk. Pedestrian access is usually non-existent, and the spread of homes often makes school buses impractical, so the designs of schools in the new suburbs assume massive automotive transportation.

Other components, too, such as shopping areas and business parks, have their own separate locations. As a result, one of the most conspicuous components of sprawl consists of the endless roadways that are necessary to connect all these elements. Since each section of suburbia serves only one type of activity, and since daily life involves a wide variety of activities, the residents of suburbia spend an unprecedented amount of time and money moving from one place to the next. And as most of this motion takes place in singly occupied automobiles, even a sparsely populated area can generate the traffic of a much larger traditional town.

Now I'm going to examine the role …

2   Skim the passage, then answer each question in turn.

Answers (evidence from the passage is given, but this is not part of the answer)

1   B   *drawing on notions that were circulating at the time* (paragraph 1)

2   C   *the British countryside – now too often seen in a sentimental glow* (paragraph 2)

3   D   *far enough from existing cities to ensure that the land was bought at rock-bottom, depressed-agricultural, land values* (paragraph 3)

---

4 C *Garden cities would follow the same basic blueprint* (paragraph 4)

5 B *the garden city would reach its planned limit ... then, another would be started a short distance away. Thus, over time, there would develop a vast planned agglomeration, extending almost without limit* (paragraph 5)

Unit 10

10.1 pages 66–67

1 Think about your own experiences.

> **Possible answer**
> I don't dream very often, as far as I know! However, last night I did have a very vivid dream about staying in a hotel. I had lost my key and couldn't get back into my room. It was a very big hotel and I was running up and down flights of stairs looking for my key, feeling more and more confused. Then I woke up.

2 A *nightmare* is a very upsetting or frightening dream.

> **Possible answers**
> People who have more nightmares could have problems in their lives, or be psychologically disturbed.
> Dreaming may well contribute to our health and well-being, even if we don't recall the dreams later.

3 Read the headings and predict possible topics. Do the headings task (questions 1–6 only), following the advice given in the Test spot. Then work through the passage again to answer questions 7–13.

> **Answers**
> **1** iv **2** viii **3** v **4** vi **5** iii **6** ix
>
> | | | |
> |---|---|---|
> | **7** | NOT GIVEN | We don't know whether Brenda went ice-skating after the dream or not. (paragraph A and the first sentence of paragraph B) |
> | **8** | TRUE | *Those in favour ... argue that lucid dreams can ... inspire new ideas* (lines 17–20) |
> | **9** | NOT GIVEN | The text refers to the discovery of REM sleep 50 years ago and says it *opened up new avenues of sleep research*, but we don't know the relative importance of this research. (paragraph C) |
> | **10** | FALSE | *The 'NovaDreamer' ... emits a flashing light or sound cues* (lines 36–37) |
> | **11** | TRUE | *LaBerge claims that this increases the dreamer's chances of becoming lucid threefold* (lines 38–40) |
> | **12** | TRUE | *'It's a wish to control things out of their usual function and time. It is trying to redesign the mind in a way I don't think is necessarily helpful.'* (lines 55–57) |
> | **13** | FALSE | *At the moment, he's experimenting with ... in order to encourage seasoned lucid dreamers to have more of them.* (lines 62–66) |

4

> **Answers**
> **1** *inspire new ideas* – **b** does not collocate
> **2** *promote self-healing* (paragraph B), *promote a similar effect* (paragraph F) – all collocate
> **3** *strengthened the argument* – **c** does not collocate
> **4** *developed electronic devices* – **b** does not collocate
> **5** *Not everyone shares this enthusiasm* – all three collocate
> **6** *operates on a shoestring* – **a** does not collocate

5 Use an English–English dictionary to check meaning, and then decide on the more appropriate word in each pair.

> **Answers**
> **1** minor character **2** specialist **3** children **4** customer
> **5** manager

10.2 pages 68–69

1 The pictures show

A the painting *Tom Thumb and the Sleeping Giant* by Gustave Doré
B a blurred image of people rushing to work
C an Andean condor
D a rusty padlock on an old wooden door
E a road through the desert in Nevada, USA
F a set of clock faces
G an aerial view of a small island
H a fish called Lined Sweetlips in the Banda Sea, Indonesia

The pictures form part of the listening task, so think about what each picture might represent in a dream.

> **Possible answers**
> A dealing with a major problem
> B being alienated from society
> C feeling threatened
> D keeping something secret
> E suffering from a fixed routine
> F worrying about deadlines
> G being at peace with yourself
> H feeling trapped in some way

2 Read questions 1–4 and then listen to the relevant part of the recording.

Then do the same for questions 5–7.

> **Answers** (relevant parts of the recording script are underlined)
> **1** H **2** B **3** A **4** F
> **5** C **6** A **7** B

Recording script

Questions 1–4

Tutor: Right, first of all let's do a quick practical activity together. As you know, metaphor and symbols are important in the interpretation of dreams. Both Jung and Freud referred to symbolisation in their analysis. Now, there's not necessarily one right answer – these pictures are meant to act as a springboard for your own interpretations. So I'd like you to take turns to talk about a picture and suggest what each might represent in a dream. OK?

Carla: Fine. Shall I start?

Jason: Go for it, Carla.

Carla: Right, with this one, <u>I know Jung saw the sea as representing the unconscious, so perhaps something living in water like this exists in the unconscious. As it can move, it could be an insight or a new idea?</u>

Tutor: Well done. OK, Jason?

Jason: I had a dream a bit like this one! <u>I was following behind a group, trying to keep up. I remember feeling rather anxious about that. I guess it could represent today's competitive world ... or moving forward along life's path ... growing older, maybe? What's really interesting is that my dream had the same burnt colours as this.</u> Well, enough about me! Helen, your turn.

Helen: OK. This one is classic Jung, isn't it? <u>A larger-than-life character, who might be seen as threatening because of his size?</u> It might be some kind of problem that you have to deal with, a big one that you're really concerned about.

Tutor: He couldn't be seen as friendly, could he?

Helen: Protective! Maybe … no, I don't think so. Are you going to do one too?

Tutor: All right … well, here we have another classic symbol, don't we? The image has actually been used in the dream sequences of films by Bergman and Pasolini, two great directors. <u>In both films, there were no hands, maybe suggesting that time had run out.</u> So this one must be all about limits, pressure of deadlines, appointments, that sort of thing.

Questions 5–7

Tutor: OK, can you get out your notes about the case studies now? Helen, can you start? Summarise the dream and give us your interpretation. And, please, challenge each others' views, raise your own ideas.

Helen: Right, this dream is about climbing. A small group of people is trying to reach the top of a mountain – <u>they're nearly at the summit – but the dreamer gets separated from the others when the mist comes down. He stumbles around for a bit and then goes back down to the bottom,</u> where the sun comes out and he finds himself in the middle of a field of enormous white flowers.

Jason: A happy ending then?

Helen: Mm, not so sure. As I see it, getting split up from the rest of the party could be seen as exclusion, but it's his own decision to retrace his steps, isn't it? <u>Then he's surrounded by the flowers, which could mean that there's pressure on him to conform. But I think he rejects that.</u>

Jason: Yeah but the flower is basically a thing of beauty, a positive symbol. I think he's back in a comfort zone.

Tutor: OK, thanks Helen. Carla, let's hear yours next.

Carla: Well, it's the face-in-the-mirror dream. Woman looks into a mirror and sees a different face staring back at her. She's youthful and confident, but it's not a younger version of herself, it's

another person. She starts rubbing at the glass, and the face is still there, laughing now. <u>This is a crisis of identity – the dreamer may have experienced some problems recently, or could be full of regrets about her own life? The face in the mirror is young and happy – this could represent envy of others, perhaps.</u>

Tutor: And you all agree with that?

Jason: Well, mightn't it be something to do with a dual life – you know, presenting a different, more outgoing face to the outside world?

Tutor: Good. OK, Jason let's hear you now.

Jason: Er, I'm afraid I haven't done it.

Carla/Helen: Typical!

3

> **Answers**
> **a** certain (*must be*)
> **b** and **c** less certain, suggesting rather than affirming (*could/may/might*)
>
> **a** expressed to mean the opposite: *can't be*
> **b** with *couldn't*, the statement becomes certain – a refutation

4 A common error in using these modal verbs is to express the opposite meaning of *must be* as *mustn't be*, instead of the correct form, *can't be*. Note that *couldn't be* doesn't carry a past meaning – to talk about something in the past, the modal perfect *couldn't have been* is needed.

> **Answers**
> **1** could/may/might   **2** can't/couldn't
> **3** could/may/might   **4** can't   **5** must

5 Both examples are from the recording.

> **Answer**
> The speaker is fairly confident of being right in both examples, but wants to soften/hedge. Tag questions like these are a feature of spoken English and are too informal to be used in academic writing.

6 Use modal verbs in your answers.

> **Possible answers**
> **1** A dream about a forest could display a negative emotion, such as depression, and the need to escape from everyday life.
> **2** Books in dreams must symbolise wisdom and knowledge.
> **3** Might being involved in some form of accident in a dream suggest a state of anxiety?
> **4** Sitting on a wrong train couldn't represent making a wrong choice in life, could it?

7 Check you recognise the four phonetic symbols.

> **Answers**
> **1** /e/   **2** /juː/   **3** /ʌ/   **4** /iː/   **5** /e/   **6** /juː/   **7** /ʌ/
> **8** /iː/   **9** /e/

8 Think about how you will answer these questions. Maybe you could use modal verbs to speculate about some of them?

Possible answers
- In my opinion, dreams can reveal our innermost feelings, things that we don't want to think about.
- It's a complex question. I'm sure it must sometimes be helpful to have your dreams interpreted by a professional psychoanalyst, but equally it could be quite upsetting for the individual concerned.
- Might it be because we believe they could provide answers, even if we don't fully understand why we dream?
- Definitely. We are leading more pressurised lives and this means we suffer more psychological problems. I also think we understand psychology better than we did, say, a hundred years ago.
- It could be risky to do this, couldn't it? On the other hand, our inner selves are our true selves, rather than the masks we often choose to wear for other people, so we should attempt to discover them!
- Mightn't they both be equally important? There's the famous saying 'a healthy mind in a healthy body' and I think it's valid.

Writing folder 5

pages 70–71

1 Look back at the passage in 9.1 for ideas on city living.

2

Answer
B is the clearer answer because it is better organised and contains more exemplification to support the argument (though not all points are equally well exemplified – as exercise 3 reveals). The writer of B disagrees with the statement and states his/her opinion unambiguously in the opening paragraph, then goes on to exemplify each aspect in a new paragraph and finally includes a clear conclusion.

A, on the other hand, is rambling and contradictory, its paragraphs are disorganised, there is no introduction and the final sentence is unclear. Interestingly, as exercise 3 reveals, it has more points than B, but these are rarely developed or exemplified (apart from the information given on Bilbao).

3

Suggested answers
Live entertainment	A ✓ 2	B ✓ 3
Open spaces	A ✓ 1	B
Transport	A ✓ 3	B ✓ 3
Cultural benefits	A ✓ 1	B ✓ 2
Noise/crowds	A ✓ 1	B
Shopping	A ✓ 1	B ✓ 3
Architecture	A	B ✓ 2

4

Additions to table
Introducing / referring to a point	In terms of
Adding another related point	Another (obvious benefit) What is more
Contrasting previous information	At the same time However
Clarifying what has been said	In other words
Linking to the argument	... because of this Thus
Concluding / summarising	In short

5

Answers
city living: *urban living, lifestyle*
21st century: *contemporary, modern, nowadays*
stressful: *oppressive*
offers: *provides, support*
advantages: *benefits, opportunities*

6 There is no further sample answer. Answer B can be used for guidance.

Unit 11

11.1 pages 72–73

1 The quiz introduces many of the geographical terms that are practised in the unit.

Answers
1 the Grand Canyon, USA
2 the Great Rift Valley, stretches from Syria in the Middle East to Mozambique in East Africa
3 Dover Cliffs, on the south coast of England
4 the Mesopotamian Marshes, Iraq
5 Iguaçu Falls, on the borders of Brazil and Argentina
6 the Bay of Bengal, part of the Indian Ocean, bordered by India, Bangladesh, Myanmar (Burma)
7 the Gulf of Tonkin, bordered by Vietnam and China
8 Lake Chad, bordered by Chad, Niger, Nigeria, Cameroon

9 estuary 10 current 11 lagoon 12 glacier 13 canal
14 erosion 15 earthquake 16 drift

17 mountain 18 volcano 19 continent
20 sand and stones

2 Look at the instructions, the map, options **A–I** and the example. Play the recording for questions 1–5 and label the map as you listen. Next read questions 6–10 and play the second part of the recording, answering the questions as you listen. Finally study the second map and questions 11–15, and play the third part of the recording.

Answers (relevant parts of the recording script are underlined)

1 E **2** D **3** G **4** F **5** C

6 river **7** erosion **8** deposits **9** 250 **10** neck

11 A **12** B **13** G **14** I **15** C

Recording script

Questions 1–5

Lecturer: Today I'm going to talk about two natural features of the English coast, Spurn Head and Chesil Beach.

First, an explanation. A long, narrow accumulation of sand and/or stones, with one end joining the mainland, is called a 'spit', and Spurn Head is a good example of one. Spits are often created in sheltered areas where the waves aren't usually strong enough to wash the sand away, or where erosion further along the coast provides plenty of material.

If you look at the sketch map, you'll see how a spit is typically formed. In this example, the prevailing winds blow from the south west, creating a current flowing along the shore, known as 'longshore drift'. In this case it's moving roughly eastwards. The current carries sand or other material along the coast. At the turn in the coastline, the headland, larger stones are piled up on the sea bed in the sheltered water immediately to the east of it. This forms the beginning of the spit. As more and more stones and sand accumulate, the feature is extended eastwards.

The wind tends to pick up sand from the beach as it dries out, and carry it to the sheltered side of the spit to form dunes. These are stabilised as grasses begin to take root. Gentle, low-energy waves entering the sheltered area behind the spit deposit fine mud, creating an increasingly shallow area of salt marsh. This is regularly flooded by the tide, and large amounts of vegetation grow there. The marsh slowly fills the area of shallow sea that is now largely surrounded by the spit and the original coastline, which in this diagram lies to the north of the new spit.

Spits often form close to where a river widens into an estuary as it approaches the sea. However, the spit won't extend across the estuary if the river is too deep, or if the current of the river is strong enough to wash away any material deposited by longshore drift.

Questions 6–10

Lecturer: Now I'll go on to Spurn Head, which is a spit on the east coast of England. It's about five kilometres long, with the North Sea to the east, and the river Humber to the west and south, where the Humber reaches the sea.

Spurn Head consists of sand that has come from the soft land to the north west. The sea removes about six million tonnes of material from the cliffs each year, making them retreat one to two metres. This rapid erosion provides plenty of material for the spit. Longshore drift transports it southwards to Spurn Head, and deposits it there.

Records of the last thousand years show that the spit goes through a cycle of creation and destruction roughly every 250 years. What happens is that, as well as bringing material from further north, the sea moves sand along the peninsula towards the tip. This narrows the neck, and in time the sea breaches it. The tip is now isolated and is washed away, and then a new spit begins to take shape. The present spit is nearing the end of the cycle, and its narrowest point, which is only 50 metres wide, is in continual danger of being breached.

Questions 11–15

Lecturer: Now, let's look at another example of a spit. A striking feature of the south coast of England is Chesil Beach, which is almost 30 kilometres long and never more than 200 metres wide. It links the Isle of Portland to the mainland.

The beach probably began to develop ten or twelve thousand years ago, but the way it formed is uncertain. It consists of stones that are graduated in size. At the Portland end, they're as large as a large potato, while those at the opposite end are much finer, no bigger than a pea. The beach has created a shallow lagoon for much of its length, where it protects the River Fleet against the sea. The lagoon is rich in marine wildlife and birds.

The Isle of Portland itself is made of limestone, and footprints of dinosaurs have been found in it. A great many London buildings, including St Paul's Cathedral, are made of Portland stone. Stone has been *quarried* for hundreds of years, but it was first *mined* in 2002, in the west of the island, not far from Chesil Beach. In places the stone is above a softer material, which the sea is eroding. This has led to the formation of some collapsed caves along the south-east coast of the island, close to the southern tip.

A harbour has been constructed by enclosing the bay between the mainland and the Isle of Portland, with Chesil Beach forming its western boundary.

3 Read the task and Useful language. Spend no more than one minute making some brief notes. Try to use relevant words from the quiz. Then talk (perhaps recording yourself) for between one and two minutes.

11.2 pages 74–75

1 Think about the questions, speculating on possible answers if you don't know. The answers will be found in the reading passage.

2 Skim the passage for the answers to the questions in exercise 1. Remember to time yourself as you read.

Answers
- Because South America and Africa used to be joined (lines 30–33).
- The island of Spitzbergen (also known as Svalbard) used to be much further south, near the Equator (lines 41–44).
- No – volcanoes and earthquakes are linked to plate tectonics and tend to occur at plate boundaries (lines 60–67).

---

3 Look at the map of Pangaea and try to identify the present-day continents.

> **Answers**
> **1** North America   **2** South America   **3** Asia   **4** Europe
> **5** Africa   **6** Indian subcontinent   **7** Australia
> **8** Antarctica

4 Read the Test spot and follow the advice given for short-answer questions when answering questions 1–6.

For questions 7–12, it may help you to underline relevant parts of the passage.

> **Answers** (evidence from the passage is given, but this is not part of the answer)
> **1** earthquakes and floods   **2** (a) supercontinent
> **3** fossils   **4** climate change   **5** plates
> **6** mountain ranges
>
> **7** E *After Wegener's death in 1930, new evidence from ocean floor exploration and other studies rekindled interest in his theory* (lines 55–57)
> **8** C *indications that there were once glaciers in regions of South Africa led to the conclusion that this land must once have been situated much further away from the tropics. ... the occurrence of coal – the product of ancient temperate or tropical forests – in Spitzbergen, an island that is now close to the North Pole.* (lines 38–44)
> **9** D *A fatal weakness in Wegener's theory was that it could not satisfactorily answer ... what kind of forces could be strong enough to move such large masses of solid rock over such great distances?* (lines 50–54)
> **10** B *it was physically impossible for most of these creatures to have swum or have been transported across the vast ocean.* (lines 28–30)
> **11** D *his proposal was not well received, even though it seemed to agree with the scientific information available at the time.* (lines 48–50)
> **12** E *The theory states that the Earth's outermost layer is fragmented into a dozen or more plates of various sizes that are moving relative to one another as they ride on top of hotter, more mobile material.* (lines 60–63)

5 Read the explanation above exercise 5, then work through the exercise. You will find more information in the Grammar folder on page 141.

> **Answers**
> **1** A meteorologist <u>working in Germany</u> wrote two articles about continental drift.
> **2** <u>Finding similar fossils on both sides of the Atlantic</u> was strong evidence of continental drift.
> **3** Wegener was intrigued by fossils <u>found in South America and Africa</u>.
> **4** It is impossible <u>for coal to form in a cold climate</u>.

6

> **Answers**
> **1** sentences 1 and 3   **2** sentences 2 and 4   **3** sentence 0

7

> **Answers**
> **1** active   **2** passive   **3** *-ing*   **4** infinitive

8

> **Answers**
> **1** proposed   **2** Comparing   **3** moving   **4** to accept
> **5** revolutionising

Test folder 6

pages 76–77

Make sure you fully understand the notes and advice. The advice applies to labelling all visuals – there is no significant difference between diagrams and maps.

1 Study the map and try to work out what it shows, then read questions 1–7. Each answer is a letter. Answer the questions as you listen.

> **Answers** (relevant parts of the recording script are underlined)
> **1** G   **2** H   **3** J   **4** B   **5** D   **6** F   **7** E

Recording script

You will hear a hotel owner describing some interesting walks to a guest in the hotel.
First you have some time to look at questions 1 to 7. (pause)
Now listen carefully and answer questions 1 to 7.
Woman: Is this your first visit to the area?
Man: Yes. I'm planning to do a lot of walking while I'm here. Are there any walks you'd recommend?
Woman: Oh, it's very nice for walking around here. <u>If you turn right out of the door of the guest house and follow the road, it'll take you to the lighthouse. You can't miss it – it's close to the road, right on the headland. There's a footpath near it, just before the road turns left. You should go along the path to the edge of the cliffs, down the steps, and turn left, so you're going back along the beach towards the headland, and if you're lucky, you might find some fossils at the bottom of the cliffs.</u>
Man: Do many people find them?
Woman: Well, not so many these days, to be honest. But you never know.
Man: I read that there are some caves in the cliffs as well.
Woman: That's right, but you'll have to go south along the beach for those. <u>They're at the nearest part of the cliffs to where we are, just where the land starts curving round.</u> But they get cut off by the tide, so be very careful.
Man: Yes, I will be.
Woman: Another nice walk is on the north side of the estuary. <u>If you turn left from here, and go along the road as far as the crossroads, instead of continuing along the road, take the footpath that runs parallel with it. That'll take you across the river, then you can turn right onto another path. The stream is very shallow, and there are stepping stones across it, so you'll be able to cross without much trouble. Then you'll come to the salt</u>

marsh. Keep to the river bank, or you might have difficulty walking. Beyond that there are sand dunes and a beach, and the islands just offshore.

Man: Is it possible to row to the islands?

Woman: Yes, there's a place to hire boats in the village. <u>Visitors aren't allowed to land on the island that's furthest from the shore, so as not to disturb the birds</u>, but you can go to the others. In fact they get plenty of birds too. The southernmost island is covered with wild flowers at this time of year. And <u>there are the remains of an ancient fortress on the island that's right in the estuary</u>.

Man: OK, well thanks very much. I'll go out for a couple of hours now.

Woman: Enjoy yourself, and I'll see you later.

2   Read the advice relating to the Reading Modules, then look at the diagram. Read the passage and write your answers, making sure you write no more than two words from the passage for each answer.

Answers		
1	continental slope	*Its seaward edge is marked by the continental slope, which is considerably steeper. This adjoins the continental rise* (paragraph 1)
2	axial rift	*In the centre of the ridge, at the highest point away from land, there is a trenchlike feature called the axial rift.* (paragraph 2)
3	continental shelf	*Seaward from the coast there is usually a gently sloping area called the continental shelf... off the coast of Africa, for instance, it is relatively narrow* (paragraph 1)
4	abyssal plain	*the continental rise, an almost vertical area running down to the abyssal plain* (paragraph 1)
5	ocean ridge	*The South Atlantic is divided into two major areas by an ocean ridge ... It sometimes breaks the ocean surface as islands* (paragraph 2)

Unit 12

12.1 pages 78–79

1   The picture shows Mary J Blige, an American singer. Think about how you could answer the question.

Background information
The singing career of Mary J Blige began in 1991 and she continues to produce successful CDs today. She grew up in Yonkers, New York, a very deprived area. Her natural singing talent won through and she soon landed her first recording contract. The emotional honesty in her songs reflects the great traditions of blues and soul, and she has won many awards for her music.

2   Read the article quickly, timing yourself. Remember your target of 300 words per minute by the end of the course! Make notes on the writer's view.

Answer
The writer's view is that nature and nurture are both involved in most skills, and influence each other. For example, to be a good singer we need to be born with the physical capabilities, but we also need to learn how to use them.

3   Work through questions 1–10. Only questions 1–6 follow the order of the article.

Answers (evidence from the passage is given, but this is not part of the answer)

1	NO	*genes and environment are not independent. They influence each other greatly, and their effects can almost never be disentangled.* (lines 15–17)
2	YES	*Newborn babies respond favourably with lower heart and respiration rates to having people nearby. So we are 'naturally' driven to live in social groups* (lines 30–32)
3	NO	*your height is a combination of your genes and various external factors.* (lines 44–45)
4	NOT GIVEN	The writer does not compare the effects of living conditions on people and on rats, simply suggesting that living conditions have some effect on both: *It is always dangerous to extrapolate from animals to humans ... this experiment shows that environmental factors can produce very different outcomes from similar genetic materials.* (lines 51–54)
5	YES	*Your ... likes and dislikes ... are an inseparable combination of your genes and the experiences you have had growing up.* (lines 56–58)
6	YES	*the either/or choice ... limit our ability to solve the problems we face today.* (lines 63–65)

7 B **8** A **9** C **10** B

4   Think about how you could answer these questions.

5   Read the information about the grammar of phrasal verbs before doing the exercise.

Answers
1 switching on   **2** hit on   **3** to lay on   **4** decided on
5 take on   **6** to check up on   **7** to call on

6

Answer
The particle can follow the object in sentences 1, 3 and 5.

Answers
Various pronouns are possible. Note their position in relation to the particle.
1 Before switching it on
2 Some scientists have hit on it
3 The university is going to lay it/one on
4 Have you decided on it
5 we must take one on
6 We need to check up on him
7 to call on him

12.2 pages 80–81

1 The pictures show a pair of great egrets building a nest, a yellow warbler singing and a female blackbird feeding its young.

Think about how you could answer the questions. Use the modal verbs *could, might, may, must, couldn't* to speculate about the answers.

Possible answers
1 building nests (both), laying eggs (females), singing or displaying feathers to attract females (males), finding food for their young (both), defending their young (both), defending their territory (both)
2 Some are learned and some are innate – the listening passage deals with this.
3 Generally yes, but in some circumstances they may learn the song of a different species.
4 No – also mynahs, starlings, mockingbirds and others.

---

2 Read the Test spot, then study questions 1–7 and play the first part of the recording and answer the questions. Afterwards read questions 8–12 and think about possible answers, then play the second part of the recording.

Answers (relevant parts of the recording script are underlined)
1–3 (in any order): identify food, migrate, build nests

4 F **5** D **6** C **7** E

8 Australia **9** electrical brain activity **10** 60/sixty days
11 dialects **12** buses

Recording script

Questions 1–7

Interviewer: The more we discover about the behaviour of birds, the more impressive it seems. But do they learn what to do, or is it somehow in their genes? Here in the studio is animal behaviour specialist Jenny Johnson to tell us. Jenny.

Jenny: Thank you. Much of what birds know is innate, or instinctive, programmed into their genes. <u>They're born knowing how to identify food</u> – and remember that what one species eats may be poisonous to another, so it's important to get it right. In the spring, when the days grow longer, the increased light alters hormone levels in birds' blood, triggering several essential

changes in behaviour. For one thing, <u>the alteration makes them migrate at the right time</u>, so that they reach their nesting sites at the right time for the next stage in their life cycle. <u>They're also programmed to build nests</u>, with different species producing very different styles of nests. So these are things that birds are programmed to do at certain times.

Interviewer: And what about the sounds that different species of birds make: are they also innate?

Jenny: Yes and no. <u>Some species are genetically programmed to produce particular sounds, and don't need to learn them. Every dove coos, even if it doesn't hear other doves doing it.</u> The same is true of nearly all birds' hunger and danger signals, which are among the 20 or so simple calls that are used to communicate certain messages.

Interviewer: Does this apply to birdsong, too?

Jenny: Birdsong seems to be a combination of genetic programming and learning. Some species are born with the ability to learn to sing, but not with the song itself, so it's different from cooing. <u>Normally a chick – that's a young bird – hears the songs of lots of species while it's growing up, but the chick always picks out and learns the correct song for its own species.</u> That's what it's been programmed to do. But <u>if a bird is reared in isolation, so that it doesn't hear other birds of any species, the song it sings will be a rudimentary version of the normal song.</u> The programming isn't enough for it to sing the song in full. And interestingly, <u>if a chick is brought up among birds of a different species, it learns their song</u> – even if it can hear its own species singing around it.

Questions 8–12

Interviewer: Do we know anything about the learning process?

Jenny: Well, one bird that's been studied a great deal is the <u>zebra finch, a small, colourful bird that originates in Australia</u> and has black and white stripes on its tail, like a zebra. Just as we have to hear language when we're babies in order to learn to speak, zebra finches need to hear song early in life to be able to produce it. To become fluent in their song, they also need to practise it repeatedly, and in fact one study found <u>evidence that they practise in their sleep: electrical brain activity goes on which is similar to the brain activity when they're awake and singing!</u>

Interviewer: That sounds like an efficient use of their time! Is there any time limit on when a bird can learn to sing?

Jenny: Normally a male zebra finch develops a version of the adult's song when it's at least 20 days old, and will have more or less learned the song by the age of 35 days. Practising it means that <u>it masters the song by around 60 days</u>, and if it hasn't heard any zebra finches singing by then, it won't learn the song at all. After the age of 90 days, when the bird is fully mature, its song won't change.

Interviewer: And do all individual birds of the same species sing exactly the same song?

Jenny: No, they don't. For some species, <u>small differences can develop, which over generations become different dialects</u>, just as with human languages. This is often the case with birds that imitate others. Marsh warblers, for instance, spend the winter in Africa, and can mimic the calls of over 70 bird species. These will be other birds living in the same region, so each male warbler's song indicates which part of Africa he winters in.

A few species, like starlings and mynahs, imitate sounds that aren't birdsong, and incorporate them into their own individual songs. Some starlings have been known to mimic sheep. <u>In Oxford they mimic buses.</u> But the Australian lyrebird seems to be the bird world's best mimic: it can imitate 12 other birds, car engines, car alarms – even chainsaws cutting down trees!

Interviewer: Jenny, thank you.

Jenny: Thank you.

3   Read the tinted box. Then complete the **b** sentences.

> **Answers**
> 1 to have occurred   2 to have finished
> 3 to have been doing   4 to be warning   5 to be caused
> 6 to have been studied

4   Play the recording, and repeat the infinitives. Be careful to stress only the main verbs.

5   It can be difficult to understand a talk or lecture if the speaker is not presenting the ideas clearly enough. Read the paragraph and decide on the main point.

> **Answer**
> B

6

> **Possible answers**
> 1   Power stations are built in remote places where there is a great deal of wildlife.
> 2   Farmland is treated with pesticide, which kills insects and young birds.
> 3   Birds come to the land around power stations for shelter, knowing that weeds grow there, no pesticides are used, and they will not be disturbed or shot.
> 4   The land around power stations is protected, like miniature nature reserves or game parks.
> 5   Once a bird learns that it will be safe here, it returns.
> 6   Weeds are removed from gardens, but here they are allowed to grow, and they attract butterflies and other insects.

7   Think about what you have read and heard in this unit about birds, and decide what you could say about them.

Writing folder 6
pages 82–83

1   The graphs here and commentary in exercise 2 come from a research project tracking climate change.

2

> **Answers**
> 1 False   2 True   3 True   4 False

3

> **Answers**
> | | | |
> |---|---|---|
> | wet | wetter | wettest |
> | dry | drier | driest |
> | rapid | more rapid | (the) most rapid |
> | gradual | more gradual | (the) most gradual |

4

> **Possible answers**
> 1 practically   2 not quite/entirely the same   3 somewhat
> 4 considerably

5

> **Sample answer**
> The graphs provide climatic information for Cape Town and Upington in South Africa. The red and blue lines plot average maximum and minimum monthly temperatures, while the orange bars show average rainfall. From the line graphs it can be seen that there is less fluctuation in temperature in Cape Town than in Upington, where maximum temperatures reach over 35 degrees C in January (the highest temperatures in Cape Town are well below 30 degrees C). Both places are at their coolest in June and July. In Upington, temperatures rise steeply again through August and September, whereas in Cape Town, the increase is more gradual.
>
> Upington is much wetter than Cape Town outside the months of June to September. March is the wettest month in Upington, with an average rainfall of around 180 millimetres. In contrast, Cape Town has hardly any rain in the period November to March. Its peak rainfall is in June, when it receives approximately 100 millimetres.
> (159 words)

Units 9–12 Revision
pages 84–85

1   The pictures show the Helford Estuary in Cornwall and the Regent's Canal in Little Venice, London. Try to produce long sentences, comparing the two subjects and giving examples to support your ideas.

2

> **Answers**
> 1   Not only was New Orleans hit by a severe hurricane but (it was also hit) by disastrous flooding as well.
> 2   Hardly had we checked into our hotel on the bay when we were taken on yet another boat trip.
> 3   No sooner do babies learn to crawl than they start walking.
> 4   Not only are there genetic factors to consider but there are also environmental ones.
> 5   Little did I think that I would be visiting the city of Rosario for work.
> 6   Not until the following night did the torrential rain ease up.

3

> **Answers**
> 1 to be doing   2 to be investigated
> 3 to have been contacted   4 to have dealt with
> 5 to have been building up   6 to have been established
> 7 to be monitored   8 to have been caused

4

> **Possible answers**
> 1 ... may possibly be vulnerable to flooding.
> 2 ... could be the reason for its poor diet.
> 3 ... might be that you ate a lot of cheese late last night.

5

> **Suggested answer**
> Yesterday I **had a discussion with** the **managing director** of the company Dreams-U-Like, Dr Janet Stephenson. I believe she **has a PhD in** psychology and she seems to know her **field. Additionally**, a **specialist** in dream analysis, Barry Whitehead, is doing some **consultancy work** for her. We should **investigate Mr Whitehead's reputation**, as he **might be able to assist us as well**. Dr Stephenson claims that he is **impressive with clients**, and gives good **presentations**. What **views do you have on the matter?**

6

> **Answers**
> 1 touches on; had expanded on   2 haven't decided on
> 3 is passed on   4 hit on   5 was brought on

7

> **Answers**
> *Across*
> 1 gulf   4 lake   6 construction   9 Rift   11 skyscraper
> 12 erosion   13 dune
> *Down*
> 1 glacier   2 infrastructure   3 spit   4 lagoon
> 5 earthquake   7 cliff   8 outskirts   10 ground

Unit 13

13.1 pages 86–87

1   The picture is an artist's impression of the meteor impact on Earth which may have caused the extinction of the dinosaurs 65 million years ago (the passage deals with this and other theories).

> **Possible answer**
> Dinosaurs could have become extinct because of severe climate change, which removed their source of food.

2   These terms come up in the reading passage.

> **Suggested answer**
> A catastrophist would believe in a sudden, devastating effect, whereas a gradualist would argue that the dinosaurs died out over a longer period of time.

3   Skim the passage, timing yourself.

4   Read the Test spot and complete the summary following the advice given.

> **Answers**
> 1 crater   2 debris   3 eradication   4 biodiversity
> 5 incident   6 dispute   7 proof   8 duration
> 9 conditions   10 coincidence   11 quantities
> 12 arguments

5   The passage originally appeared in the *New Scientist*, a popular science magazine, and has quite a light-hearted tone. In academic texts, the tone should be more serious.

> **Answers**
> Rewritten sentences:
> This catastrophic event is the **most commonly held explanation** for why dinosaurs **became extinct** 65 million years ago, but **is the theory tenable?**
> On one side are the 'catastrophists', who **claim** the impact **led to the extinction** of the majority of life on Earth ...
> ... scientists may finally be able to **establish** exactly what happened ...
> Geologists (**most of whom** are catastrophists, **naturally**) are **waiting eagerly** to analyse the core.
> Secondly, **other factors apart from** meteors were **contributing to an unstable environment**.

6   The language of cause and result is very important in academic writing, for most subjects.

> **Answers**
> 1 outcomes/effects   2 were caused; led   3 resulted
> 4 was responsible   5 caused; as a result
> 6 contributed/led   7 trigger/cause   8 explanation

13.2 pages 62–63

1   The quiz introduces some of the more technical language in the listening task. Check you understand all the vocabulary.

> **Answers**
> 1 True
> 2 False – an asteroid is different. It is made of rock.
> 3 False – their orbits are elliptical or oval.
> 4 False – although the comet's nucleus consists mainly of water, carbon dioxide, ammonia and methane in their icy states, there is also dust mixed in.
> 5 True – the tails of comets are created as they get warmer (from the sun).
> 6 False – it also contains gases.

2   Read the sentences and predict possible answers before listening to the recording.

> **Answers** (relevant parts of the recording script are underlined)
> 1 chaser   2 launch rocket   3 Earth   4 belt   5 August
> 6 mapping   7 crust   8 gas; dust   9 oceans

Recording script

Lecturer: OK, everyone, let's start. Today, I'm going to be talking to you about the European Space Agency mission Rosetta, more popularly known as the 'comet chaser'. The aim of the mission is to orbit, and eventually land on, a small comet in our solar system. This is something that clearly has never been done before.

Actually, the ESA had a bit of bad luck. Rosetta was originally going to be launched in 2003 but the mission had to be postponed due to a malfunction of the launch rocket. This in turn meant that the ESA had to find another comet, because the one they first chose, called 46P/ Wirtanen, will have travelled far beyond Rosetta's flight path by now!

Rosetta was launched on March 2nd 2004 and will be tracking a comet known as Churyumov-Gerasimenko … let's call it C-G for short during this lecture. Under the revised flight plan, Rosetta will make one flyby of Mars and three of the Earth before heading for C-G. This circuitous route will enable Rosetta to make two excursions into the main asteroid belt before its rendezvous with our fast-moving cosmic iceberg in August 2014.

Rosetta will slow down and go into orbit around C-G and from an altitude of just a few kilometres, its cameras will be able to map the entire surface of the comet at high resolution. This mapping exercise will enable a safe landing site to be selected and, once this has been done, the Rosetta lander will separate from the orbiter and slowly descend to the icy surface. If everything goes according to plan, the lander will anchor itself to C-G's crust and begin a detailed survey of its surroundings.

Over a period of several weeks, data from the nine instruments on the lander will be sent back to Earth via the Rosetta orbiter. The lander will dispatch close-up pictures of the comet's nucleus, drill into the dark organic crust, and sample the primordial ices and gases. Meanwhile, the orbiter will have been transmitting radio signals through the nucleus to the lander, in order to analyse the internal structure of the comet.

The orbiter will monitor the changes that take place in the comet as it hurtles on its way towards our Sun. As the comet is increasingly warmed, bright jets will appear, creating distinctive fails, as gas and dust are ejected into space. In fact, C-G is probably a much better choice of comet than the original one, in that it typically becomes much more active than Wirtanen does as it approaches the Sun. Scientists certainly won't get bored studying this comet!

The enormous amount of data that will be returned during Rosetta's voyage is likely to change our understanding of comets fundamentally. In addition, it will provide new insights into such basic mysteries as the formation of our oceans and even the origins of life. Thirdly, it is expected that Rosetta will give scientists vital insights about how to respond should there ever be a comet on a collision course with our planet.

OK, so that's the Rosetta mission, which will terminate in December 2015. Try to find out more about it over the next few weeks. Why not check out the official website …

3 Mark the main stress as you listen, following the example as a model.

> **Answers**
> 'actually   'basically   'certainly   e'ventually
> funda'mentally   'hopefully   in'creasingly   i'nitially
> o'riginally   'typically

4 Note that not all the adverbs from exercise 3 were used in the recording.

Recording script

1 Actually, the ESA had a bit of bad luck.

2 Scientists certainly won't get bored studying this comet!

3 The aim of the mission is to orbit and eventually land on a small comet in our solar system.

4 The enormous amount of data that will be returned during Rosetta's voyage is likely to change our understanding of comets fundamentally.

5 As the comet is increasingly warmed, bright jets will appear …

6 Rosetta was originally going to be launched in 2003 …

7 It typically becomes much more active than Wirtanen does as it approaches the Sun.

5 Check your pronunciation and stress once you have done the exercise.

> **Answers**
> 1 actually   2 originally   3 eventually   4 Typically
> 5 certainly

6

> **Answers**
> 1 b   2 d   3 c   4 a   5 e

7 Read the Grammar folder on page 142 before doing this exercise.

> **Answers**
> 1 will have been travelling
> 2 won't reach
> 3 will be approaching
> 4 will cause
> 5 will be formed
> 6 will take / will be taking
> 7 will be found
> 8 will terminate / will be terminated
> 9 will have passed
> 10 will be making

8 The notes in B are unfinished, because the time allowed had come to an end!

> **Answer**
> A is the more useful (follows the advice given in the Test spot).

9 Aim to talk for the full two minutes.

Test folder 7

1   Make sure you fully understand the notes and advice. Look at the picture and make sure you know what a crater is (it is a round hole in the earth, made by an impact or explosion, or the hole inside a volcano).

2   Read the instructions, options **A–I** and questions 1–6. Make sure you understand the options. Listen to the example, then answer the questions as you listen to the rest of the recording.

> **Answers** (relevant parts of the recording script are underlined)
> **1** B   **2** G   **3** F   **4** D   **5** I   **6** H

Recording script

You will hear part of a lecture about meteorites, and about some craters they have created on Earth.
First you have some time to look at questions 1 to 6. (pause)
Now listen carefully and answer questions 1 to 6.

Lecturer: For thousands of years, people have been fascinated by streaks of light flashing across the night sky. These 'shooting stars' are actually tiny grains of dust from space that burn up in Earth's atmosphere before reaching the ground. But hundreds of times a year, a rock called a meteorite survives the fiery trip from space and lands on Earth. The vast majority are pieces of asteroids, the small rocky bodies that orbit the Sun.

One November morning in 1492, a young boy saw a large stone plummet from the sky and land near the town of Ensisheim in Alsace, France. This fall is the earliest one witnessed in the Western world from which meteorite samples have been preserved. Immediately after it fell, people began chipping off pieces as souvenirs, and fragments of the Ensisheim meteorite can be found in museum collections all over the world.

When the Krasnojarsk meteorite was found in 1749, no one believed that rocks came from space. But a German physicist analysed this meteorite's unusual mixture of stone and iron, and began to convince sceptics that meteorites did indeed originate far from Earth.

Antarctica is an ideal place to find meteorites because the dark specimens are easy to see against the snow and ice. As the ice sheets move, they push older ice to the surface. Powerful winds remove the ice, exposing the meteorites buried underneath.

The largest meteorite on display in any museum is a 34-ton piece of iron that's just part of a much larger meteorite, called Cape York. This landed in Greenland thousands of years ago, before any people lived there. Cape York originally weighed around 200 tons before it broke apart in the atmosphere.

In 1947, people in eastern Siberia saw a huge fireball that exploded as it streaked across the sky, bursting into tens of thousands of fragments that made cracking and roaring noises as they fell to Earth. These iron fragments crashed into thick woodland, tearing apart and uprooting many of the trees, and creating thousands of craters.

Although countless meteorites have crashed onto the planet, most of the craters that they left have been erased or hidden by natural forces. Only about 200 meteorite-impact craters have been found, of various sizes. Vredefort Crater, in South Africa, is a ring of mountains with a diameter of 300 kilometres, which seems to be a record.

One of Earth's largest intact meteorite craters, Wolf Creek Crater, was long known only to the local population of native Australians. Their legend describes a rainbow snake that emerged from the crater and formed a nearby watercourse as it slithered away. In 1947, oil company geologists spotted the stunning crater during an airplane survey of some of Australia's most remote desert.

Now let's consider what we can learn from meteorites.

2   Skim the passage. Then read the instructions, examples, questions 1–9 and list of people. Scanning the passage for the people is quicker than looking for the information contained in the questions. Make sure you understand why B is the answer to question 7. Then find the answers to the remaining questions.

> **Answers** (evidence from the passage is given, but this is not part of the answer)
> **1** E   *William Herschel at first believed that there were other galaxies besides the Milky Way … However he later came round to the view that the universe consisted solely of the Milky Way system (paragraph 2)*
> **2** K   *He built an antenna to try to locate the origin of this noise, and found to his surprise that it arose from the Milky Way. (paragraph 4)*
> **3** I   *Shapley arrived at a size about three times too great. (paragraph 3)*
> **4** C   *When Galileo first turned his telescope on the sky, in 1609, he found proof that, as Pythagoras had suggested, the Milky Way indeed consisted of innumerable stars. (paragraph 1)*
> **5** L   *Hey had discovered radio emission from the sun. (paragraph 4)*
> **6** D   *The idea that the Milky Way is a vast disc-shaped aggregation of stars comprising all the stars seen by the naked eye or with a telescope was first put forward by Thomas Wright (paragraph 2)*
> **7** B   (example)
> **8** H   *the role of interstellar dust, which Edward Barnard was beginning to uncover. (paragraph 3)*
> **9** F   *William Herschel at first believed that there were other galaxies besides the Milky Way, a theory that had been advanced earlier by Christopher Wren. (paragraph 2)*

Unit 14

14.1 pages 92–93

1   The pictures show grandparents spending time with their grandchildren.

> **Possible answer**
> The charts show that there will be more elderly people in Australia in the future, which has implications for government expenditure on healthcare and social services.

2 Spend between two and three minutes reading the passage. A *baby boom* is a period of time when there is a large increase in the number of babies born.

3 The information for questions 1–5 occurs in the first half of the passage.

Answers
1 C *In 2031, if not before, 27% of all Australians of voting age … will be aged 65 or older.* (lines 24–26)
2 A *In 1961, the total fertility rate in Australia peaked at 3.6 babies per woman.* (lines 8–9)
3 B *Between 2011 and 2031 … . During this period, the population aged 65 and over is projected to grow from 3 to 5 million.* (lines 15–19)
4 C *By 2031, … . In the years immediately beyond this, baby boomers are projected to swell the population aged 85 and over from 612,000 to 1.1 million.* (lines 19–23)
5 B *the potential labour force is expected to expand at a slower rate from 2011* (lines 32–34)
6 structural ageing **7** income support **8** (competing) demands **9** (potential) burden **10** (likely) stimulus

4 The nouns and noun phrases are explained below.

Answers
1 *living standards*: the amount of wealth and comfort (accommodation, possessions, etc.) people have in a particular society
2 *labour shortages*: a lack of people available to work
3 *social expenditure*: the money spent by government at a national or local level to provide care and facilities for citizens in need
4 *standard of living*: (see 1)
5 *role(s)*: the position or purpose of a person or organisation
6 *market sector*: a defined part of the population that is targetted commercially

5 The adjectives used are given in italics.

Answers
1 *enhanced* living standards
2 *serious* labour shortages
3 *associated* social expenditure
4 *acceptable* standard of living
5 *respective* roles
6 *influential* market sector

6

Answers
1 rising (living standards)
2 acute (labour shortages)
3 related (social expenditure)
4 satisfactory (standard of living)
5 corresponding (roles)
6 powerful (market sector)

7

Answers
1 *enhanced* – opposite: declining
2 *serious* – opposite: negligible
3 *associated* – opposite: unconnected
4 *acceptable* – opposite: inadequate
5 (no opposite)
6 *influential* – opposite: ineffectual

8 Think about your own answers to these questions.

Possible answers
- Many couples are choosing to have smaller families. In addition, birth control is more readily available than it used to be.
- It puts an added burden on the state in terms of providing social care.
- Ideally, but this would cost a great deal of money, especially given an ageing population.
- It is highly likely that people will retire later and, in fact, the government in my country is currently considering this.
- Young people can learn many things from their grandparents, because they have so much more experience of the world. Grandparents often provide a better example of moral values, for example.
- Longevity is due to a combination of better diet, advances in modern medicine and perhaps less personal risk than previously.

9 Try to use similar language to what you hear in the recording. A positive effect on the examiner can be achieved by starting your sentences in different ways.

Recording script

Examiner: OK, let's continue our discussion of changes in society. Can you explain why the birth rate is falling in many countries?

Candidate: Well, of course I'm not an expert, but there are probably several reasons for this decline. Often, both people in a relationship are working, so it's hard for them to bring up large families … mm they are choosing not to, in other words. Also, I read somewhere that there may be an environmental issue … that pollution is causing couples to be less fertile. I think that's a real possibility.

Examiner: And … what impact does an ageing population have on society?

Candidate: It has many implications. First, older people usually need more support … I don't just mean healthcare, but also social support, you know, like entertainment, to give them a better quality of life, to stop them feeling lonely. Secondly, because there are fewer younger people working and paying taxes, it means that there is a question mark over resources, how much the state can provide.

Examiner: Do you think the state should provide completely free care for the elderly?

Candidate: Yes, I do, in theory, but as I said earlier, in practice there may be not enough money to do that. People are going to have to save for their old age, I guess.

Examiner: And in the future, will working people have to retire at a later age than they currently do?

Candidate: Um … I suppose so, yes. Actually, I don't think there is anything wrong with that. I mean if you want to go on working, you're healthy and your brain is still sharp, you have a lot to offer, all that experience and knowledge …

Examiner: And, more generally, what can young people learn from their grandparents and great-grandparents?

Candidate: Oh, many, many things! Sometimes we complain that old people don't understand us, but they have seen a lot, experienced many different things. So they can give us advice on life … and speaking personally, my grandmother is a really good listener too. I talk to her about many things I wouldn't ever discuss with my parents …

Examiner: Why are people generally living longer nowadays, in your opinion?

Candidate: It must be down to healthcare, good hospitals, and a better diet as well. That's crucial, you know, what you eat.

Examiner: Thank you.

14.2 pages 94–95

1 The pictures show (left) a modern residential estate of detached houses with garages and (right) a photo from the 1940s of terraced housing in a residential street close to a power station.

> **Possible answer**
> Nowadays, many people are living in better housing than they were when my grandparents were children. More people have cars today, as well as other consumer goods which weren't available then, such as colour televisions, computers and mobile phones.

2 Study options **A–G** and questions 1–5 before playing the first part of the recording. Check your answers to 1–5 before reading the questions for 6–10 and playing the second part of the recording.

> **Answers** (relevant parts of the recording script are underlined)
> 1 F 2 B 3 E 4 C 5 G
>
> 6 A 7 C 8 C 9 B 10 B

Recording script

Questions 1–5

Lecturer: In this course we'll be looking at some of the causes of social change around the world, and we'll have one or two examples of each. In this brief introduction, though, I'll use the UK to illustrate some of the great variety of changes that occur.

Social change may come about as a result of physical conditions, such as drought, flooding or crop failure. The Irish potato famine of the 1840s led vast numbers of individuals and whole families to emigrate from rural areas of Ireland to cities, particularly in Britain and the USA. As is usually the case, those who went away were the most active and ambitious, and by losing those people, many rural Irish communities subsequently stagnated.

Immigrants usually make a massive contribution to the culture of the receiving country, and Britain has benefited a great deal from this over the centuries. Some groups, like the French protestants of the 17th century, have become assimilated into the dominant culture. It's too early to predict the long-term effects of some recent waves of immigration to Britain, although newcomers from some parts of Asia, particularly China, Vietnam, India, Pakistan and Bangladesh, have had a remarkable impact on national eating habits in the UK.

Contact with other communities doesn't only come about through immigration. As a result of the massive increase in air travel in recent years, many people have adopted customs that they first encountered abroad, such as drinking wine, or sitting in pavement cafés. This reflects a change from previous generations, who knew little of behaviour outside their immediate neighbourhood, let alone in other countries.

Political factors can lead to considerable social change, and probably the most significant for Britain was the First World War of 1914 to '18. This did a great deal to allow women to catch up with men in terms of political power, job opportunities and individual freedom.

Questions 6–10

Lecturer: Britain has had a fair degree of political stability for several hundred years. As a result, political factors have played a relatively minor role in social change, compared with many other countries, and economic factors have been far more important.

I now want to look briefly at how economic factors influenced one major change – the movement of millions of people from the countryside into urban areas during the late 18th century and throughout the 19th. New methods of production meant that, for the first time, most items were manufactured in big factories, instead of in people's homes, and these required a large number of workers living nearby – remember there was little public transport and no cars. However, the massive expansion of cities in the 19th century brought with it many problems, including poor health, road congestion and substandard housing.

Just to give you an idea of how one change can lead to a succession of others, the need for a better-educated workforce resulted in education becoming compulsory in the late 19th century. This was a factor in weakening the ties of extended families and the wider community, and establishing the nuclear family – that is, one consisting of husband, wife and children – as the main operating unit of society. And, as a consequence, the roles of husband and wife changed quite significantly.

At the beginning of the 19th century, only a quarter of the population of Britain lived in urban areas. By the 1970s, that figure had become three quarters. Since then, though, the flow into towns has to some extent been reversed, with many people moving from urban to rural areas. Unlike traditional village dwellers, though, a lot of the new residents work in towns, and almost all of them depend on towns for their shopping, education and entertainment. This has obviously had an impact on social structure and life in villages, which I'll come back to later.

Although towns have often been blamed for having an alienating effect on their residents, this certainly isn't always the case. Most big towns contain 'urban villages', that is, small areas with a settled community linked in a network of relationships. Many urban villages used to exist in areas of poor housing, and were destroyed by slum clearance programmes, in which people were moved to new housing estates at a distance, but now there's evidence of urban villages in both poor and more affluent areas.

Now let's turn to …

3 It can be useful to signal how you are going to deal with a topic in your writing, as this gives the reader a clearer idea of both content and coverage.

Answers
1 a 2 c 3 a 4 a 5 b 6 c 7 b

4

Answers
1 *each*: cause of social change
2 *those*: individuals and whole families
3 *this*: the massive contribution of immigrants to the culture of the receiving country
4 *these*: big factories
5 *others*: changes
6 *one*: a family

5 Read the information on page 142 of the Grammar folder before doing the exercise.

Answers
Rewritten essay extract:
Today's students have to deal with a number of problems. **These** include an acute shortage of affordable accommodation and rising debt. To supplement their finances, students are often forced to work long hours and **this** will more often than not affect the quality of their college work. Even if the students manage to get a good degree, **they** then face declining job prospects, **which** are particularly poor for **those** in arts and humanities.

6

Answers
1 … small ones
2 … 8 million of them/these
3 … the individuals themselves
4 … makes her
5 Some claim … others disagree
6 … which was more than
7 For those who …

Writing folder 7

pages 96–97

1 It is important to write in a *consistently* appropriate style and tone.

Answers
Appropriate features: impersonal style, neutral to formal language, serious tone

2

Answers
Aggressive tone
which I find totally ridiculous (line 2)
You really should not (lines 2–3)

Colloquial and informal language
folks (line 5)
we're all gonna be even older (line 7)
cost a packet (line 11)
forking out for (line 12)
Do you think we'll all have to slave away until we're 90? (lines 15–16)
fewer babies on the scene (line 17)
kids (line 19)
our planet is already packed out (line 20)
Come on, it won't be that bad! (line 30)

Humorous style
Apart from leading to huge sales of false teeth and walking sticks (lines 8–9)

3

Suggested answers
Second paragraph:
folks = people
we're all gonna be even older = (the population is) projected to continue ageing
cost a packet = result in increased expenditure
forking out for = funding / contributing to

Third paragraph:
fewer babies on the scene = (a) declining birth rate / lower fertility
kids = children
slave away = remain in the job market / continue to be employed
(our planet is already) packed out = overpopulated

4 Use some of the language in exercise 3 when you rewrite the paragraphs.

Answer
Rewritten paragraphs 2 and 3:
It is true without a doubt that people are living longer, due to a healthier diet, rising living standards and better medical treatment. Indeed, the population is projected to continue ageing. What will be the main issues of having a larger percentage of older people in our society? First and foremost, it will result in increased expenditure in terms of looking after the elderly and funding their pension payments. Such an imbalance in the population will place an added burden on younger people, through higher taxation levels and more substantial family commitments. It is highly likely that people in their 60s and 70s will be forced to remain in the job market, given the current statistics.

As for a declining birth rate, that certainly seems to be the case in my country at the moment. However, governments should not be encouraging people to have larger numbers of children, because the planet is already overpopulated.

5 The original opening paragraph contains some rather aggressive language, which would have a negative effect on the examiner. Remember that the opening paragraph in particular needs to make a good impression on the examiner.

> **Answers**
> **1** impossible **2** provided **3** questionable **4** actually
> **5** cannot be denied **6** will be required

6 Think about the examiner comments written in red and then write a final sentence for the fourth paragraph.

> **Possible answer**
> Society has always had to face change and ours is no exception, but any reform should be viewed positively rather than be seen as problematic or threatening.

7

> **Sample answer**
> While it cannot be denied that in certain sectors of the job market there are currently fewer openings for graduates, the situation regarding employment prospects is a complex one, which varies across the world. Demographic trends need to be considered, along with new areas of work. In certain types of employment, some growth can be demonstrated. What is certainly true is that higher education will have to adapt to reflect the changing requirements of industry and modern society.
>
> Firstly, because of declining birth rates, fewer young people are entering the job market and this will eventually reduce unemployment among the skilled workforce. In some parts of the world, the 21st century is bringing a shift away from traditional manufacturing towards more service-oriented work, often with less predictable working hours.
>
> Some sectors are experiencing a healthy demand for new recruits. In biotechnology, for example, there are many opportunities, although here graduates are usually expected to continue studying beyond a first degree to doctorate level. Academic institutions may therefore need to seek increased funding for postgraduate research, particularly for the science faculties.
>
> It could perhaps be argued that universities should adjust the balance of their programmes, reducing the number of graduates produced in areas such as media studies and the arts in favour of more science and maths graduates, who are more likely to find immediate work. However, society as a whole will continue to benefit from a mix of well-educated people, so these disciplines and others should be maintained. The next twenty years will see great changes in both the workplace and education, but this should be regarded as an opportunity in itself, rather than a problem for society.
> (278 words)

Unit 15

15.1 pages 98–99

1 The pictures show the extreme sport of potholing and the daily – but also risky – situation of cycling in heavy traffic. Make a list of everyday risks.

> **Possible answers**
> Taking part in dangerous sports
> Crossing the road in busy traffic
> Travelling by car or public transport
> Using knives or electrical appliances in the home
> Eating prepared food that may be contaminated
> Walking on slippery icy paths
> Living in an earthquake zone

2 Skim the passage, timing yourself. Think about your personal reaction to it.

3 Read the notes for questions 1–10 and think about the part of speech needed in each gap. Complete the exercise, remembering to write one- or two-word answers. Check your answers to questions 1–10 before dealing with questions 11–15. Underline the relevant parts of each paragraph or write down line numbers as you answer questions 11–15.

> **Answers**
> **1** unwillingness — *unwillingness to measure consequences. (line 2)*
> **2** obesity — *we refuse to let our kids walk to school and instead trigger obesity (lines 6–7)*
> **3** fatalities — *The resulting growth in road traffic probably resulted in five additional fatalities (lines 13–14)*
> **4** injuries — *protective aids, such as body armour, lead to more injuries (lines 28–29)*
> **5** random — *rare random events … it is the random nature of the event that poses the feeling of threat. (lines 39–42)*
> **6** human error — *because they are natural, they are beyond control – unlike accidents caused by human error. In such cases, the relative rarity of the event provides psychological reinforcement for risk denial (lines 44–47)*
> **7** sport — *do so in the name of sport … The attraction of such activities is the fact that they involve risk. (lines 53–55)*
> **8** early detection / early warning — *reports … have forced scientific risk assessment to adopt a role as early warning indicators … scientific studies contribute to the early detection of lurking danger (lines 58–62)*

9 emotional distortions — *components that people use as yardsticks for perceiving and evaluating risks. There are also the emotional distortions mentioned above. (lines 68–70)*

10 officials — *should officials take these into account ... or try to change them by providing more information? (lines 71–74)*

11 G *People take risks in order to test their own strength and to triumph over natural forces. (lines 55–57)*

12 E *the likelihood of its occurrence is extremely low. A look at the perception of rare random events shows, however, that probability plays hardly any role at all in how people perceive danger: it is the random nature of the event that poses the feeling of threat. (lines 38–42)*

13 B *an immediate slowdown was ordered on 500 sections of suspect track. Frustrated by delays, a third of rail passengers switched to the roads, where the accident rate per kilometre is 12 times that of rail. The resulting growth in road traffic probably resulted in five additional fatalities – compared with only six caused by broken rails over the last 30 years. (lines 10–15)*

14 F *the relative rarity of the event provides psychological reinforcement for risk denial (lines 46–47)*

15 C *no one foresaw the consequences of people changing their behaviour once they were securely belted up – driving faster and more recklessly. Similarly, sports researchers have found that protective aids, such as body armour, lead to more injuries because players take greater risks. (lines 25–29)*

4 Think about this question, particularly considering intonation, volume, speed and pitch.

Answers
happy or enthusiastic: speech is usually relatively loud and fast, with wide variation in pitch
sad or bored: speech is usually relatively quiet and slow, with little variation in pitch – fairly monotonous

5 Read **a–e** then play the recording.

Answers
1 d   2 b   3 a   4 c   5 e

Recording script

1 A: Is it time to go?
  B: Yes. *[falling intonation]*

2 A: Excuse me.
  B: Yes? *[rising intonation]*

3 A: Did you enjoy the film?
  B: Yes. *[fall-rise]*

4 A: Would you like some chocolate?
  B: Yes! *[rise-fall]*

5 A: Could you spare me a few minutes, please?
  B: Yes. *[level intonation]*

6 Play the recording again and choose from patterns **f–j**.

Answers
1 i   2 f   3 g   4 j   5 h

7 Play the recording and compare the two answers. The benefits of using intonation to sound interested include: sounding more natural, being more effective if giving a talk and sounding more polite in reply to a speaker.

Answer
He sounds more interested the second time.

Recording script

(the script is the same both times)
Examiner: Could you describe any risks that you take in your hobbies?
Candidate: Yes, I've got a passion for potholing, which means climbing down into underground caves and trying to make your way through them. There's always a risk of losing your balance and falling, or even of getting lost, if you explore a cave system that you're not familiar with.

8 Read the questions and Useful language and answer the questions, perhaps recording yourself.

Possible answers
- I tend to be fairly cautious, and assess risks before doing something, though I usually ignore the dangers of everyday activities.
- If you thought about the risks every time you travelled, you'd never go anywhere. So I think it's better to ignore them, except when there's an obvious danger, like overcrowding on a boat or bus.
- On the whole people don't like power stations, because of the pollution they cause or, in the case of nuclear power stations, the possibility that an accident would be very serious. On the other hand, there isn't much support for alternatives like wind farms, because some people don't like the way they look.

15.2 pages 100–101

1 Think about different types of class.

Possible answers
Lecture, seminar, workshop, one-to-one tutorial, laboratory session

2 Read the options and example. Listen to the recording, paying particular attention to the example. Complete the exercise.

Answers (relevant parts of the recording script are underlined)
1 C   2 B   3 A   4 A   5 B

Recording script

Lecturer: OK, thank you all for your suggestions for the study days on philosophy at the end of the month. These are the ones I've chosen for the six sessions.

We'll tackle three topics on each day. On the first day, which is a Thursday, we'll start with language, and the question of whether speakers of different languages see the world in different ways. <u>I'll spend the first half hour giving you an overview of the main theories, and then we'll divide into discussion groups.</u>

Next there'll be time for you to consider the law: to be more specific, the question 'Is it ever right to break the law?' <u>For this, could you form yourselves into teams of four or five? I'll give each team a different case study. Then you can go off anywhere you like for an hour, to discuss the case without any interference from me.</u> I'd like you to plan a short presentation on it, which you'll give when we all come together afterwards.

<u>Also for Thursday I've chosen 'Political ideologies',</u> considered from a philosophical point of view. Professor Robertson has agreed to produce a handout summarising his views, which I'd like you to read in advance so <u>we'll have a starting point for discussion.</u>

Several of you were interested in the application of philosophy to medicine, so <u>on Friday we'll begin with a session on what it means when doctors say they 'know' the cause of an illness. Susan Harris, of the School of Medicine, will put forward her views on this,</u> and after she's finished she'll give you a handout of questions to discuss in small groups.

Then we'll go on to the question 'What is time?' <u>Barry Clark, one of our PhD students, will give an introduction to this rather heavyweight subject. He'll have to leave immediately afterwards,</u> so we won't have any discussion or questions until after he's gone, when I'll take over from Barry.

And we'll end on a perhaps slightly lighter note, with a look at 'The philosophy of coincidence'. No lecture for this – you'll need to think in advance about what coincidences are, and <u>I'll begin the discussion by asking some of you to put forward your ideas.</u> I'll give you a couple of references so you can read up on the topic beforehand.

3 Check your understanding of *coincidence* – an occasion when two or more similar things happen at the same time, especially in a way that is unlikely or surprising. Decide on factors from **A–F** and think about your own experiences of coincidences.

> **Answers**
> A, C, E, F

4 Match coincidences 1–3 to options **A–C** in exercise 5.

> **Answers**
> 1 B 2 A 3 C

5 Read questions 1–5 before playing the recording.

> **Answers** (relevant parts of the recording script are underlined)
> 1 B 2 A 3 C 4 A 5 B

Recording script

Tutor: OK. Now we've been considering some of the factors that affect how we understand and interpret the world around us, and today we're going to look at coincidences. Could someone come up with a definition?

Student 1: It's when two or more similar things happen at around the same time, and seem to be connected, but there isn't any obvious explanation.

Student 2: And people think it's surprising, or significant.

Tutor: OK, that'll do to start. Let's have a few examples.

Student 3: There's the birthday coincidence.

Tutor: Uh-huh?

Student 3: Well, if you have a class of 20 or 30 children, people are amazed if two of them have the same birthday.

Tutor: And how significant is it if that happens?

Student 3: Not at all. Because <u>with only 23 children, there's a one in two chance that any two of them will share a birthday.</u>

Student 1: <u>Most people think you need a far larger number of children.</u>

Student 3: Of course it's far less likely that two particular children will have the same birthday, or that any two will share a particular birthday.

Tutor: Right. Another example?

Student 2: What about people who correctly predict the result of a football match for five consecutive weeks, to try to persuade you to buy the computer program they claim to be using?

Student 3: That's impressive!

Student 1: And their predictions are correct?

Student 2: They certainly are.

Student 1: Ah, then they've probably also sent out other predictions, which were wrong.

Student 2: Exactly. They start by writing to a number of people, and divide them into three groups: they tell one group that one team will win, tell another group that the other team will win, and tell the third group that the result will be a draw. The second week they only write to the people who'd received the correct prediction, and again divide them into three groups. And so on, for five weeks. The people who receive all five correct forecasts are very impressed of course, but <u>they don't know that, for every person who gets five correct predictions, 242 don't!</u>

Student 3: It seems very impressive when you only know part of what's happened.

Student 1: Then there are the apparent coincidences in fortune telling or astrology.

Tutor: Go on.

Student 1: Well astrologers describe someone's personality when they don't know the person, only the pattern of stars when they were born. Lots of people believe them, but <u>they generally forget about the statements that aren't true, and only remember the ones that are.</u>

Student 3: So in this case people are selecting evidence and seeing a pattern which doesn't exist.

Tutor: Yes – which we often do.

Student 1: And sometimes people may miss a pattern that really does exist. For instance, the higher the number of ice creams that are sold, the more attacks there are by sharks on people swimming in the sea. It's not that sharks get more dangerous because people are eating ice cream! <u>The reason is that a rise in hot weather has led to both.</u>

Tutor: Yes. Then there's the interesting case of a woman who won an American lottery twice within four months.

Student 3: Gosh!

Student 2: Lucky woman!

Tutor: How likely do you think that is?

Student 1: Must be one chance in millions.

Tutor: According to some of the early newspaper reports, the chances of such a coincidence happening were one in 17 trillion. But then two statisticians at Harvard University calculated that, with millions of people regularly buying lottery tickets in America, <u>the odds of such an event happening to someone somewhere were only about 1 in 30</u> – not that amazing after all.

6 Read the explanation about abstract nouns before doing the exercise.

> **Answers**
> In the first sentence of each pair, the noun is countable, and refers to one instance.
> In the second sentence of each pair, the noun is uncountable, and refers to the concept in general.

7

> **Answers**
> **a** uncountable
> **b** countable

8 Work through the exercise, referring to exercise 7 to help you.

> **Answers**
> **1** a **2** a **3** – **4** an **5** a **6** – **7** – **8** a **9** a **10** –

9

> **Answers**
> **1** acceptance **2** existence **3** consideration **4** thought
> **5** certainty **6** suspicion

10 Think of any experiences of this type that you have had.

> **Possible answer**
> When I was a child I went to my brother's room in the middle of the night and told him my mother was cleaning my bedroom. Maybe I'd dreamt she was going to, but I still believed it, even though I was awake.

Test folder 8

pages 102–103

Make sure you fully understand the notes and advice.

Think about what the two drawings show. You will be able to answer in more detail when you have read the passage.

> **Possible answer**
> The first shows a group of demoralised, unemployed people; the second shows people being honoured in a civic ceremony.

Read the notes and skim the passage, then read the instructions, paragraph A and the questions. Make sure you understand why A is the answer to question 4. Read each of the other paragraphs in turn, and work out which piece of information each paragraph refers to. Then decide which groups of people the two drawings show.

> **Answers** (evidence from the passage is given, but this is not part of the answer)
> **1** E *unemployment, like sickness and accidents, hits unexpectedly, irrespective of the victim's merits*
> **2** B *they were faced with the horrible dilemma of letting the unemployed starve, or destroying their moral character*
> **3** G *The councillors held a civic ceremony, at which the governor of the region presented the first insurance cheques. There were speeches, photographs, and cheering.*
> **4** A *example*
> **5** F *The latter had been resentfully regarded as snoopers, because of their somewhat aggressive way of making their demands. The former, however, having no moral lesson to teach but simply a business transaction to carry out, treated their clients with business-like courtesy*
> **6** C *To make sure these payments were not taken for granted, however, they decided that the 'relief' would be made so difficult and humiliating to obtain that there would be no temptation for anyone to go through the process unless it was absolutely necessary. Further, the moral disapproval of the community would be turned upon the recipients of the money*
> **7** D *When they permitted themselves a rare luxury, such as going to the cinema, their neighbours who still had jobs looked at them sourly*
> **8** E *He then suggested that if the work that these unemployed people had done for the community could be regarded as a form of 'insurance premium', payments now made to them could be regarded as 'insurance claims'.*
> **9** D *to the surprise and disappointment of the councillors it also led to quarrels, unhappy homes, class hatred and crime.*

The drawing on the left shows unemployed people from town A. The drawing on the right shows unemployed people from town B.

Unit 16

16.1 pages 104–105

1   The pictures show a men's tennis champion holding up his trophy to the crowd and a highly stressed woman giving a press conference. Think about your personal reactions to the situations in the bullet points.

Possible answers
- I enjoy meeting new people, so I feel quite excited when I know I'm going to.
- It rather depends why it's happening. If it's because of something I've chosen to do, like speaking in a seminar, it doesn't worry me, but if somebody else focuses everyone's attention on me, it can be quite stressful.
- I'd like to think that I'd keep cool in a crisis, but I suspect that, if people around me were panicking, I would panic too.
- I remember once not being able to find my passport, when I was due to go abroad later that day. It was pretty stressful, but I worked out how to get a replacement passport, and I was still able to leave on time.
- I have to admit that I'm quite competitive, so I love winning, whether it's a matter of luck or skill. So winning a competition makes me feel very happy.
- If I'm in a position to help someone in need, I usually try to do so – it's fairly instinctive, so I don't really think about whether I should help them or not – I just do.

2   Spend no more than one minute making notes and then talk for between one and two minutes, perhaps recording yourself.

3   Skim the passage for its general meaning, timing yourself. Then read the list of headings and complete questions 1–6. Remember that you should take *all* the key words in a heading into account when choosing your answers. So, for example, with heading **ix**, the paragraph will mention not just personality (which is mentioned in a number of paragraphs), but will talk about the influence people's *lives* have on their personality.

When answering questions 7–13, it may be helpful to underline the relevant parts of the passage.

Answers (evidence from the passage is given, but this is not part of the answer)
1   ix   for example, *personality differences that might have been very slight at birth become dramatic in later adulthood.*
2   iii   for example, *These dispositions come partly from the expression of inherent features of the nervous system, and partly from learning.*
3   vi   for example, *Yet we now know that this is not the case.*
4   v   for example, *Personality measures turn out to be good predictors of your health, how happy you typically are – even your taste in paintings.*
5   i   for example, *Deliberate rational strategies can be used to override intuitive patterns of response*

6   vii   for example, *The dominant approach is to think of the space of possible personalities as being defined by a number of dimensions.*
7   YES   *different people respond in quite remarkably different ways even when faced with roughly the same circumstances. Alan ..., whilst Beth ...* (paragraph A)
8   NOT GIVEN   The passage states *personality seems to become stronger as we get older ... personality differences that might have been very slight at birth become dramatic in later adulthood* (paragraph B) but there is no mention of analysing our personalities.
9   NO   *Nervousness, for example, might be a factor of temperament* (paragraph C)
10 NOT GIVEN   *The discovery that temperamental differences are real is one of the major findings of contemporary psychology.* (paragraph D) It is not claimed that this discovery has affected subsequent research.
11 YES   *their personalities are more similar to those of their blood relatives than to the ones they grew up with* (paragraph E)
12 YES   *The slower, rational, deliberate systems show less variation in output from person to person* (paragraph F)
13 NO   *Virtually all theories agree on two of the main dimensions ... However they differ on how many additional ones they recognise.* (paragraph G)

4

Answers
1   respond   2   determined   3   consequences   4   inherent
5   dilemma   6   manifests

5

Possible answer
It is of very little use, because people's behaviour varies a great deal in different situations. For example, someone may be reserved in some situations but not in others. Our personalities are far too complex to be summed up in two or three words. In addition, expecting someone always to be helpful or selfish, for example, may put pressure on them to be helpful or selfish when they want to behave differently: it is sometimes easier to do what other people expect you to do than to behave differently.

16.2 pages 106–107

1   Make sure you understand the adjectives used as headings, using an English–English dictionary if necessary. Then complete the table. Note that two adjectives appear twice (*special* and *distinct*); the different meanings are illustrated in these sentences:

Special
You'll need special tyres on your car for driving in snow. (specific)
We knew at once that the singer had a special talent for opera. (striking)
Distinct
This word has three distinct meanings. (different)
There's a distinct smell of garlic – have you been cooking? (striking)

Answers

vital	specific	complex	different	striking
crucial	certain	complicated	dissimilar	distinct
essential	particular	intricate	distinct	exceptional
indispensable	special	involved	diverse	extraordinary
key			unlike	remarkable
				special
				unusual

---

2 Notice the picture of the trombone at the bottom of the page (this musical instrument is mentioned in the recording). Read the questions then listen to the recording.

Answers (relevant parts of the recording script are underlined)
1 C   2 A   3 B   4 B   5 B   6 C

Recording script

Lecturer: Recognition is one of the mind's most vital skills, and we use it daily in everything from the simplest to the most complex of tasks. And at the moment when we recognise something, electrical activity takes place inside our brains.

Our faculty for recognition can break down, however. Someone suffering the brain disorder agnosia will look at an item – a cup, perhaps – and have no idea what it is. Agnosia tends to be very specific: one sufferer may be unable to recognise faces, while another has difficulty with man-made objects. Such disorders can result from localised damage to a specific area in the brain, suggesting that we use different parts of it to store items of different kinds. This would explain the variation in the symptoms of agnosia.

It appears, in fact, that the brain stores and categorises things not according to their appearance or function, but by our individual relationship with them. A musical instrument, such as a trombone, can be seen, felt, played or heard. Each quality of an item seems to be stored in a separate region of the brain, in what are sometimes called 'recognition units'. So a musical instrument would have several units: its shape would be remembered in our visual areas, the word in our vocabulary area, touch in the touch area, and its sound in our hearing area. Someone who has never touched a trombone, though, wouldn't have a touch recognition unit.

Each region of the brain may contain the recognition units of objects that seem very different, but they're together because they share the particular quality that concerns that region. So our trombone might sit in the same bit of the brain as a drinking straw – or a pencil, if we suck them – because they're all non-food items that we put in our mouths. When we think of a trombone, all of our separate trombone recognition units are drawn together from their separate storage regions and united, to give us what we recognise as a trombone. So it seems that our own individual experiences create the geography of our brains, and that in turn affects our behaviour.

Faces occupy a special category of our recognition faculties – and brain scans show heightened activity in these areas not only when we *see* faces, but even when we *imagine* seeing them. One reason is that humans are social animals. We live as we've always lived, in groups, and our survival depends on our ability to communicate with others of our own species. So we've evolved with special brain wiring for face recognition – even a newborn baby will orientate itself towards objects that resemble faces, like a balloon with eyes, nose and mouth drawn on it.

Why is it that we forget one person's face yet remember another – even though neither face might be particularly striking? The recognition unit of a face stays active if we have seen or imagined that person frequently, but this doesn't necessarily require a strong stimulus: that person may stay in our memory if we often see someone else who resembles them. But if we neither see nor think about a person for a long time, the facial recognition unit we have for them falls into disuse, and we may not recognise them if we see them again.

Our reactions to faces involve strong emotions. When we meet someone for the first time, we may decide, without any evidence, that they look trustworthy, perhaps, or threatening. This irrational response happens because when we see someone, we check whether or not we know them, and this activity uses two pathways within the brain, one conscious, the other unconscious. Through the latter we can relive an emotional reaction we have had to someone who merely looks slightly like the person we are meeting for the first time.

The conscious pathway works more slowly, and enables us to work out, for instance, whose face we're looking at, and how we should behave towards them. The unconscious pathway is faster, and goes through one of the brain's centres of emotion. If we meet a person whose face slightly resembles someone we feared and hated in the past, for example, we briefly experience again our feelings towards that original figure. It's this emotional memory that gives us an almost instantaneous first impression of the person we're meeting.

3 Match the sentences with the grammatical description and read the information in the tinted box about verb patterns in academic writing.

Answers
1 c   2 e   3 a   4 b   5 d

---

4 Complete the exercise, referring to exercise 3 if necessary.

Answers
1 d   2 c   3 g   4 a   5 e   6 b   7 f

---

5 Correct the grammatical errors, keeping as close as possible to the original.

> **Answers**
> 1 Life forced them to work and (**to**) **grow up** before their time.
> 2 I am an outgoing person. I like talking to customers to make them **feel** comfortable.
> 3 Nowadays, people seem **to have** a better material life than before.
> 4 It is very good to let children **do** some paid work.
> 5 *correct*
> 6 Nowadays, lack of money **makes people spend** too much time working.
> 7 A good education enables them **to get** jobs in the future.
> 8 I would like to suggest (**that**) **you build** a small storeroom outside the house.
> 9 *correct*
> 10 I **want our newspaper** to help me to solve this problem.

6 The verbs in the box are often used in academic writing. This exercise will help you to become familiar with their meaning and how to use them grammatically.

> **Answers**
> 1 encourage 2 intend/mean 3 considered
> 4 demonstrate 5 argue/contend 6 mean/signify
> 7 missed

7 Consider possible answers to this question.

> **Possible answers**
> Yes, I think if I understood better why I behave as I do, it would help me to avoid doing things I regret later. OR No, on the whole it might make people less interesting and unpredictable if we knew how they were likely to behave in every situation.

Writing folder 8

pages 108–109

It is very important for you to check your written work carefully. There is further practice in the Workbook (Writing Workout 4).

1

> **Answers**
> 1 apologise 2 disappear 3 welfare 4 professional
> 5 *correct* 6 opinion 7 talented 8 preference

2

> **Answers**
> 1 achieved 2 received 3 beautiful 4 believe
> 5 colleague 6 enormous 7 *correct* 8 throughout

3

> **Answers**
> 1 n environment   government
> 2 h technology   which
> 3 r otherwise   furthermore
> 4 l should   would
> 5 e therefore   because
> 6 e approximately sincerely

4

> **Answers**
> 1 hopeful 2 emptiness 3 expensive 4 successful
> 5 relevance 6 immediately 7 dramatically
> 8 predictability

5

> **Answers**
> 1 We **must always** look at the good side of everything that we do.
> 2 Then the spending **dropped slightly** to less than £10m.
> 3 The concept of the joint family **rarely exists**.
> 4 More flights will **certainly create** more noise.
> 5 In some families, parents give money to their children, but without any advice on how to **use it carefully**.
> 6 It seems that Japanese customs have been **changing little by little** since around 1920.

6

> **Answer**
> *Corrected paragraph:*
> The **issue** of whether it is proper for children to work as under-aged workers is, in my opinion, not a **straightforward** one. I **believe** it can be a good experience as long as they are capable of doing the work. Most **children who do paid work** come from poor families. They work to help their parents to **support** their lives, education or **health**. These children will grow up as **mentally tough** people because they **learn** a lot of lessons about how humans live their lives. For example, they won't **give up doing their jobs easily** and they won't **feel so deeply down** when something **disappoints** them. **Furthermore,** most of them become **physically strong** and they **may even have** fewer problems **later** in their lives.

7

> **Answers**
> 1 On the plus side, if these **developments** are getting better, the richer nations will benefit.
> 2 In other words, every **child** would get a technical education.
> 3 There are three **reasons** for this.
> 4 Children **do** not read books, so they will never receive information in this way.

5 The number of Japanese tourists dropped for **this reason / these reasons**.

6 If they do not want to do this kind of **job** in the future, there is only one option.

7 In the hotel where he **lives** everyone treats him well.

8 There are many **things** that should be considered.

9 The other three **nations** spent nearly the same amount in this regard.

10 The other one is more surprising because it occurs in countries in which citizens **have** a very high income.

Units 13–16 Revision

pages 110–111

1 Answer each question in detail, giving examples to support your ideas.

2 The picture shows a group of skydivers leaving their aircraft.

> **Answers**
> **1** the **2** for/of **3** it **4** its **5** to **6** this/that **7** been
> **8** themselves **9** would **10** their **11** who **12** so

3

> **Answers**
> **1** will be spending / will spend
> **2** will award
> **3** will have worked / will have been working
> **4** will have earned

4

> **Answers**
> **1** danger **2** success **3** a/the belief/perception
> **4** nature **5** denial **6** a/the perception/belief

5

> **Answers**
> **1** unfair income distribution **2** acute labour shortages
> **3** high living standards **4** influential, shrinking market
> sector **5** high, unfair taxation levels

6

> **Answers**
> **1** being triggered **2** have resulted **3** have suffered
> **4** has contributed

7 The basic aim here is to end up with a more concise style, with the secondary aim of finding 'umbrella' noun phrases that can replace lists of specifics.

> **Possible answers**
> **B** In a nutshell, an assessment of private income will define the extent of state support of the over 65s.
> **C** Without going into detail, natural disasters may influence an individual's perception of risk.
> **D** Briefly, human beings differ in their personality traits, both positive and negative.

Unit 17

17.1 pages 112–113

1 The picture shows the mass migration of African wildebeest.

> **Possible answer**
> Animals may migrate because of food shortages, severe climate change, or in order to move to a breeding area.

> **Background information**
> Every April, approximately 1.5 million wildebeest and 200,000 zebra and gazelle undertake a perilous journey of nearly 3,000 kilometres, tracked by predators such as lions and cheetahs. Their migration from the Serengeti plains to the hills of Kenya's Masai Mara is driven by the scarcity of food and water. An estimated 400,000 wildebeest calves are born on the plains between late January and March, and they too make the annual journey in search of rain-ripened grass.

2 The passage will outline different navigation techniques.

3 Skim the passage, aiming to read it within 2 minutes 30 seconds. The picture is of snow geese in migration.

4 Read the Test spot regarding the matching task before answering questions 3–9.

> **Answers** (evidence from the passage is given, but this is not part of the answer)
> **1** C *navigation techniques are an integral part of parenting.* (lines 24–25)
> **2** B *The fact that some birds ... return to the same nest year after year ... suggests the ability to recognise key sites.* (lines 31–34)
> **3** B *some birds memorise constellations (for example, Emlen's work with indigo buntings)* (lines 52–53)
> **4** G *Rabol suggested that a bird is born with its migratory track imprinted as part of its DNA* (lines 20–22)
> **5** A *two experiments ... where the olfactory nerve of pigeons was cut, leading to a loss of navigation skills ... Baker and Mather regarded them as flawed* (lines 73–77)
> **6** H *an experiment by Schlicte and Schmidt-Koenig ... may indicate that sight is less important in birds than in humans* (lines 37–40)
> **7** D *Keeton (1972) concluded that bird navigation is characterised by 'considerable redundancy of information', whereby birds appear to draw on more than one method.* (lines 12–15)

8 J *Yodlowski et al (1977) discovered that homing pigeons were sensitive to sounds below 10 Hz ... and could employ this ... in the crucial early detection of severe thunderstorms* (lines 62–66)

9 F *two experiments conducted by Papi ..., where the olfactory nerve of pigeons was cut, leading to a loss of navigation skills* (lines 73–75)

5 Try to use a range of vocabulary in your writing, rather than relying on 'simple' language. For example, it is better to include a word like *essential* instead of repeating *very important*.

Answers
1 integral, key, crucial   2 adjustment, anomalies
3 inconclusive, inconsistent, flawed

17.2 pages 114–115

1 The pictures show the arrival of Italian immigrants in New York (top and bottom left), an acupuncturist with a patient (top right), and a group of migrant workers harvesting and packing green peppers in California, USA (bottom right). Check that you understand the meanings of *emigrate, immigration, immigrant, migrant*:

emigrate – to leave a country permanently and go and live in another one

immigration – the process of coming to live in a different country

immigrant – someone who is living permanently in a country other than their own by birth

migrant – a person who travels to find temporary work, such as seasonal fruit picking

Think about your answers to these Part 3 questions.

Possible answers
- People often emigrate in search of a better life for themselves or their families, for example because of enhanced employment prospects, a better standard of living or a more favourable home environment.
- If a country already has high unemployment, immigration can cause dissatisfaction and even civil unrest, in that immigrants are taking jobs that its citizens might do.
- My government is currently reshaping its policy on immigration. I believe that a certain quota of asylum seekers are permitted to enter, as well as professionally qualified people where there are skill shortages.
- Migrants often do the jobs that others don't want to do, and also bring skills that may be in short supply, for example in the nursing profession.

---

2 Read the notes and predict the type of information needed in questions 1–9 before listening to the recording.

Answers (relevant parts of the recording script are underlined)
1 Government (policy)   2 poverty   3 Argentina
4 railroad/railway construction   5 manual labouring
6 factories   7 manufacturing   8 East-End/east-end
9 (Italian) festival

Recording script

Lecturer: OK, the photo I'm showing you now is of a group of factory workers in Guelph. It was taken in 1933, when migrants were still coming over from Italy to Canada in search of work. Of course this movement stopped altogether in 1939 with the onset of war.

In order to understand why Italians came to Canada, you need to understand why they left Italy. In the late nineteenth century, Italy was divided into three regions – the north, the south, and a central region which included the capital, Rome, and the Vatican. The recently industrialised north was much more prosperous than the rest of the country. This state of affairs was influenced by government policy, which encouraged northern growth at the expense of the agricultural south, where work was in very short supply, with consequent extreme poverty.

This regional disparity led to animosity between Italians of the north and those in the south, and by the turn of the century many Italian men from both the north and the south were leaving to seek seasonal employment elsewhere in Europe, in South America – notably Argentina – and North America. They hoped to earn enough in a few months to enable them to return home, but this usually proved to be an impossible dream.

In the very early days, most of the migrants who came to Canada worked outdoors in the summer, doing things like railroad construction. Many of them often travelled across the whole country in one season. In the winter, when this type of work wasn't available, migrants mostly went to urban centres like Toronto, where they picked up casual work, for instance manual labouring.

The first Italians came to Guelph in the early 1900s. The city at that time was a small, quiet town and local businessmen felt frustrated by this, knowing that slow growth was limiting their own prosperity. They believed that Guelph's commercial growth had to be more actively encouraged, specifically by promoting industry and creating a large industrial working class. The city started to subsidise the development of factories, and land was made available to accommodate new enterprises. Guelph also became the new home for many established manufacturing firms, and by 1911, the population had doubled. Thousands of workers were taken on, many of whom were Italian migrants.

Until this time, male migration had predominated – the men often boarded together, and found jobs and accommodation for those who came after them. The men, who were not yet official immigrants, clung to their own culture. Eventually, many were able to send for their families, or returned to Italy to find a suitable bride, and in time, as the next generation of children was born in Canada, a new culture evolved, still based on Italian memories but combined with the more immediate Canadian experience. The Italian-Canadian ethnic group, whose men and women had very different roles, established a stable and respectable community in the East-End sector of Guelph. Today, it is still an active and thriving community, hosting an annual Italian festival in July.

3 The phrases *Of course* and *Of course not* are mainly appropriate to spoken English. The Style extra section focuses on written ways of signalling something that is obvious.

> **Answers**
> 1 Understandably 2 undoubtedly/doubtless
> 3 undeniably

4

> **Answers**
> 1 goes 2 taken 3 evident

5

> **Answer**
> Sentence **a** contains a non-defining relative clause, with the clause giving additional information about the subject (the men). It tells us that all the men clung to their own culture. Sentence **b** contains a defining clause and here, there is a change of meaning: it suggests that only those men who were not official immigrants clung to their own culture, but tells us nothing about other men.

6 Read the relevant section in the Grammar folder on pages 142–143 before doing the exercise.

> **Answers**
> 1 Migration, which had been happening for many years, stopped with the onset of war. (non-defining)
> 2 Many of the migrants who came to Canada did casual work. (defining)
> 3 Many local businessmen, who recognised the commercial opportunities of this 'new' workforce, applied for subsidies to develop new factories. (non-defining)
> 4 The migrants, who were mostly men, often boarded together. (non-defining)
> 5 Migrants who arrived later were helped by those already there. (defining)
> 6 Those of the men who wanted to marry often returned to Italy to find a bride. (defining)
> 7 The new culture which evolved was based on Italian memories combined with the Canadian experience. (defining)
> 8 The Italian-Canadian community, which has contributed a lot to Guelph, still thrives. (non-defining)

7 The pronoun *that* can only be used in defining relative clauses.

> **Answers**
> *That* can be used in sentences 2, 5, 6 and 7.

8

> **Answer**
> The relative pronouns are *whom* and *whose*. The pronoun *whom* is only used in formal English – an informal equivalent sentence would normally omit the pronoun: *Most of the people (who) I have discussed this with are in favour of it.*

9

> **Answers**
> 1 The student, **whose** work is not very good, may give up studying.
> 2 I would like to propose two firms **whose** advertisements I have seen in the local newspaper.
> 3 She was out with a group of people, among **whom** the only one she knew was Charles.
> 4 *correct*
> 5 People **whose** knowledge of computers is limited are obviously in a difficult situation.
> 6 One thing which has always concerned me is the huge amount of money that is paid to people **who/that** have a job in sport.

Test folder 9

pages 116–117

Make sure you fully understand the notes and advice.

1 Read the notes, skim the passage, then read the three options and the questions. Make sure you understand the options, and notice that you need to write I, A or V as the answers. Complete the exercise.

> **Answers** (evidence from the passage is given, but this is not part of the answer)
> 1 A *Listen as you wander round the museum* (paragraph 2)
> 2 V *The harbourmaster's house now forms part of the museum. It has been carefully restored and furnished to show what it was like to live there in the 19th century.* (paragraph 1)
> 3 I *The Bathurst Room is a specially designed, hands-on model room. Press a button, and watch an 18th-century ship struggling through a rough sea. Press another, and miners labour to find gold.* (paragraph 3)
> 4 V *The South Pier itself, where thousands of ships have docked, is recreated through photographs and some of the original documents recording new arrivals.* (paragraph 1)
> 5 I *'Who and why?' is a virtual exhibition. You can read personal stories by immigrants, choosing by name or nationality. With just a click you can discover more about working and living conditions for new arrivals, or even search the records for your family.* (paragraph 2)

2 Think about what the photograph shows and what result this has.

> **Possible answers**
> The photograph shows the seeds of a dandelion being blown by the wind.
> As a result, some of the seeds will grow at a distance from the parent plant.

Skim the passage, then read the instructions, options and questions. Answer the questions.

> **Answers** (evidence from the passage is given, but this is not part of the answer)
> 1 A *floats on the surface of water, and can be carried hundreds of kilometres by the current.* (paragraph 4)
> 2 C *Heated by the sun, the pods explode, hurling the seeds in all directions.* (paragraph 2)
> 3 C *The blackberry plant, for instance, produces stems which move at a speed of about five centimetres a day. When these touch the ground they put out roots* (paragraph 5)
> 4 A *These enable the seeds to travel long distances on the breeze.* (paragraph 2)
> 5 B *In some plants, such as burdock, the seeds are attached to hooks. These catch the fur of passing animals, who carry the seeds away.* (paragraph 4)
> 6 A *This is blown across the plant's habitat* (paragraph 2)
> 7 B *The fruit of the durian tree of south-east Asia is eaten by squirrels and orang-utans. If the seed is swallowed whole, it will be carried away inside the animal's stomach and subsequently ejected, allowing the seed to grow in the new location.* (paragraph 3)

3 Read the rubric, question, three options (**A–C**) and questions (1–10). Make sure you understand the options. You can still answer the questions if you don't know the particular types of animals in the questions. You are unlikely to have as many as ten questions in a matching task in the Listening Module.

> **Answers** (relevant parts of the recording script are underlined)
> **1** A **2** B **3** A **4** A **5** B **6** C **7** C **8** A **9** A **10** C

Recording script

You will hear part of a lecture about animal migration.
First you have some time to look at questions 1 to 10. (pause)
Now listen carefully and answer questions 1 to 10.

Lecturer: Today I'm going to talk about animal migration, which is the seasonal or periodic movement of animals, including birds, fish and insects. This movement takes place in response to changes in climate or in the availability of food, or it can be to ensure reproduction.

Migration most commonly, though not always, involves movement from one area to another and then back again. This is called 'round-trip', or 'return', migration, and it may be seasonal, as in the spring and autumn migrations of many species of birds. Whooper swans, for instance, nest and breed in sub-Arctic

habitats, and every autumn around 7,000 birds fly 800 km from Iceland to Britain, to spend the winter there. They reach a speed of over 90 km an hour, and in good weather conditions can reach Scotland in under 13 hours. With the arrival of spring, they return to Iceland.

In some species the migration may require a lifetime to complete. Like other species of Pacific salmon, sockeye salmon are born in freshwater streams, travel to ocean waters, and then return to the stream where they were born. Here they breed before dying. Unlike some Atlantic salmon, which may repeat the cycle several times, Pacific salmon make the round trip only once.

Migration occurs in a wide range of animals, from micro-organisms in freshwater lakes, which shift seasonally from deep to shallow water as a result of temperature changes, to whales. Grey whales make a round trip of 20,000 km each year. They have their young in the warm, shallow lagoons off the Pacific coast of Mexico. Then in the late spring they travel north along the coast of North America to the Arctic, where they feed during the summer. They return south in the autumn.

European freshwater eels are thought to breed in the Sargasso Sea, a calm area of the Atlantic Ocean north of the West Indies and east of Florida and Bermuda. The young eels are slowly carried eastwards by the Gulf Stream, and various physiological changes occur, which will enable the eels to live in freshwater rivers and lakes in Europe. After a number of years they return to the Sargasso Sea to produce the next generation, and the parent eels then die.

In addition to round-trip migration, some migrations are nomadic in nature. This is where movement is irregular, and depends on temporary local conditions. For example, ostriches, the large flightless birds that live on the plains of central and eastern Africa, move in response to varying local conditions of food and climate. In these migrations, the animals follow no regular route and don't return to any one place.

Migratory locusts of Africa and Asia exhibit one-way migration to new sites. When their populations peak and food becomes scarce, enormous masses of locusts move to new areas, almost blackening the sky as they pass overhead.

Migration based on the availability of food is often dictated by seasonal climate change. As the cold settles in, North American red-tailed hawks, for instance, can no longer find the small rodents and birds that they normally eat. This scarcity prompts the birds to fly south to warmer areas, like Mexico, to find a more abundant food source, and they follow this pattern each year.

Plant-eating mammals, such as antelopes, typically graze in herds, which can quickly eat all the grass in an area. In the summer, the grass regrows quickly, but in winter, it doesn't, forcing these herds to travel to find fresh food supplies. When spring brings new growth, the herds move back to the areas where they found food the previous summer.

Great grey owls are birds whose migration is very variable, perhaps occurring one year, and then not again for several years. The number of individuals taking part also fluctuates enormously.

Unit 18

18.1 pages 118–119

Background information
Sir Richard Steele (1672–1729) was an Irish essayist, dramatist, journalist and politician, whose real name was Isaac Bickerstaff.
Desiderius Erasmus (probably 1465–1536) was a Dutch humanist who lived in various European cities including Paris, Basel, Louvain and Cambridge (where he was Professor of Divinity and Greek). His Colloquia, originally written in Latin, paved the way for the ideas of Martin Luther and the Reformation.
Richard Brautigan (1935–1984) was an American novelist, short-story writer and poet, whose most famous book, Trout Fishing in America, was written in 1967.

1

Suggested answers
Physical exercise keeps you fit, while reading keeps you mentally alert.
Books are more important to me than food or clothes.
Modern writing is of questionable quality.

2

Possible answers
Some people of all ages read books in my country, though I would say that the majority don't buy books. I don't think socio-economic groups have much bearing on our modern reluctance to read books – most people prefer to watch television.

3

Possible answers
- I believe books are certainly less important than they were, especially now that we have the Internet as a research tool. However, they are essential to me and I have quite a large collection of novels and short stories!
- Some books written in the past can inform the reader about how life was lived at a particular time. Contemporary fiction may show us a lifestyle that is different to our own.
- I'm not sure, but I think literature comprises novels, poetry, plays and short stories. I suppose there's also a question about 'good' and 'bad' literature – can a poorly written, blockbuster novel be described as 'literature'?
- As a reader of literature, you become more knowledgeable and more articulate too. I also think that your own writing can benefit from studying literature extensively.

4

Background information
The reading passage is taken from *Literary Theory: An Introduction* by Terry Eagleton, which was published in 1983 and remains an essential reference book at university level.

Take exactly three minutes to read the passage quickly and decide how far the writer is able to answer his own question.

Answer
Throughout the text the writer raises possible answers to the title question, only to dismiss each of them.

5

Answers (evidence from the passage is given, but this is not part of the answer)

1 YES — *French seventeenth-century literature includes … Madame de Sévigné's letters to her daughter* (lines 10–12)
2 NO — *… even news reports were neither clearly factual nor clearly fictional* (lines 18–19)
3 YES — *Perhaps literature is definable not according to whether it is fictional or 'imaginative', but because it uses language in peculiar ways.* (lines 29–31)
4 NOT GIVEN — The passage only talks about the Formalists being *effectively silenced by Stalinism* (lines 42–43), with no opinion expressed.
5 YES — *Even the most mundane text of the fifteenth century may sound 'poetic' to us today because of its archaism.* (lines 57–59)
6 NO — *The unquestioned 'great tradition' of the 'national literature' has to be recognized as a construct, fashioned by particular people for particular reasons at a certain time.* (lines 67–70)
7 NOT GIVEN — In the final paragraph, the writer is considering how the interpretation of literary works inevitably changes over time, as the reader's ideas are shaped by current context.

6

In academic writing, disapproval must be indicated tactfully and politely.

Answers
1 untenable 2 unworkable 3 invalid

7

Answers
1 **un**creative 2 **il**logical 3 **ir**rational
4 **dis**organised/**un**organised 5 **in**sufficient

18.2 pages 114–115

1 Think about these questions. Some of the issues will come up in the recording.

> **Possible answers**
> I've translated some letters and a business report into my own language from Spanish.
>
> I've never translated literature, but I think it must be harder to translate successfully than, say, business or academic language, because of the nuance and style.
>
> I don't think it's desirable to read anything in translation, but unless you know a foreign language well, you just have to! The benefit of reading something in translation is that you can read more widely than you otherwise would be able to.

2 Study the questions before playing the recording.

> **Answers** (relevant parts of the recording script are underlined)
> 1 B   2 A   3 B   4 C

Recording script

Tutor: Right, sit down both of you. Now, Anna, you've prepared some questions for us to discuss today, haven't you?

Anna: Yes, I've been considering how literary translations should be approached.

Tutor: Ah, yes, a very interesting area. Gary, could I just check whether this fits in with your current research?

Gary: Yeah, definitely. Funnily enough I've been reading the French writer Emile Zola in translation recently.

Tutor: Good.

Anna: Right, well my first question relates to the translator: should a novel's translator have the original or the target language as their mother tongue?

Tutor: And that's a good place to start. So, what's your view, Anna?

Anna: I should start by saying the obvious: that every translator needs to have a very good knowledge of the foreign language they're translating to or from. It's not enough to rely on even the largest of dictionaries, because they don't always help with literary nuance. <u>For me, it's preferable for the translator to be a native speaker of the end translation's language because then I think that work will read more naturally in its own right.</u>

Gary: I take your point, Anna, but isn't there then a risk of the translator missing – or misunderstanding – something crucial in the source text?

Anna: I think that's always a danger with translations, whatever the nationality of the translator.

Tutor: There are good and bad translations, after all.

Anna: Exactly. Er, another question I wanted to raise is this. Do novelists make better translators of fiction than other people?

Tutor: That's another great question! Can you clarify why you're interested in this? Have you read any novels translated by other writers?

Anna: Yes, I was thinking of one particular series published in Italy actually, which includes Calvino's translation of the French writer Queneau. The Argentinian writer Borges is translated in the same series.

Tutor: OK, so based on this reading, how would you answer your question?

Anna: On the evidence of those titles, I'd say yes, <u>writers have a real edge on other translators. In the one done by Calvino, for example, there seemed to be much more attention to the original writer's style, plus a genuine attempt to recreate it in the new language.</u> That's important, surely, but many translators seem to have a rather different agenda, in that they are trying above all to represent the content faithfully.

Tutor: Gary, do you have anything to add here? Or another question to air, perhaps?

Gary: Well, to the best of my knowledge, I've never read a translation prepared by another author, so I can't really comment, although it does seem logical for one writer to be able to translate the work of another more … sympathetically. Moving on, … in relation to the nineteenth-century writing of Zola, where lots of translations of the same titles exist, <u>I know there is a lot of debate in terms of how the speech of that time has been rendered in translation. Many of Zola's books featured Parisian slang of the period in a radical new way, and it appears that that is difficult to capture.</u>

Anna: Impossible! I know that an English translation of one of his books resorted to London Cockney slang, which caused quite a storm on publication, but that has a totally false ring coming from the mouths of French characters, and it also seems rather dated nowadays.

Gary: But that's going to be a problem with any translation, isn't it? I mean language changes all the time, so should you translate a 1950s novel into the language of today, or is that a crime in itself because it takes the work out of its historical context?

Anna: Literary translation is one big can of worms! I can say to you now that I have no intention of becoming a translator myself, ever! However, – and this is my final question – isn't a compromise text better than having no text in translation at all? <u>We can't learn every single language, so we will always need translations, or be restricted to the literature written in our own language, which seems a very narrow way of approaching the subject to me.</u>

Tutor: Well done, both of you. Now, can you write up some of your ideas on this for me by next Wednesday? I'd like to …

3

> **Answers**
> 1 c   2 e   3 a   4 b   5 d

4 Idioms and metaphors are often modified for emphasis by the addition of 'extra' words, as in this example, which was said by the British Home Secretary, Charles Clarke, after the London bombings in July 2005: *We are looking for a small number of very evil needles in a very large haystack.*

> **Answers**
> 1 real   2 rather   3 quite   4 totally   5 one big

Recording script

Anna: They have a real edge on the others.

Anna: Many translators seem to have a rather different agenda.

Anna: and I know that an English translation of one of his books resorted to London Cockney slang, which caused quite a storm on publication, ...

Anna: ... but that has a totally false ring coming from the mouths of French characters.

Anna: Literary translation is one big can of worms!

5

> **Answers**
> 1 c   2 a   3 b   4 c

6

> **Answer**
> *Whether* has a similar meaning to *if* and its use indicates that there are different answers or outcomes involved. The words *or not* sometimes follow later in the *wh-* clause, and this meaning is generally understood even if it is not stated. (*Let me know whether you're coming.* = if you're coming or not)

7 Read the section in the Grammar folder on page 143 before doing the exercise.

> **Answers**
> 1 how   2 why   3 whether   4 why   5 whether   6 how
> 7 why   8 whether

8

> **Answers**
> 1 asked   2 decide   3 suggests   4 observe
> 5 establish; define   6 assess   7 demonstrates
> 8 doubted

9 More than one answer may be possible.

> **Possible answers**
> 2 e Looking at the airline's questionnaires, please **weigh up whether** ticket price or choice of destination is more important to its customers.
> 3 b From these historical trends, you can **work out when** the next ice age is likely to occur.
> 4 a Using the meeting transcripts, I'd like you to **find out who** was responsible for healthcare at the time.
> 5 c To extend your essay, you could **enlarge on how** this policy affected the population as a whole.

Writing folder 9

pages 122–23

1 In academic writing it is important to disagree cautiously and politely. Think of two more ideas.

> **Possible answers**
> Books are relatively inexpensive, so should be freely available in schools.
> Television programmes often have content that is unsuitable for children.

2 Read the sample answer, which includes all the ideas in exercise 1 apart from: Children usually learn better from visual input.

3 In the sample answer, disagreement is not expressed politely! Using qualifiers is one way of sounding more cautious and polite.

> **Answers**
> 1 somewhat   2 seriously   3 rather   4 little
>
> **Possible replacement answers**
> is totally untrue   > seems rather dubious
> is completely wrong   > is somewhat questionable
> is crazy   > makes little sense
> is absolute rubbish   > appears seriously flawed

4

> **Possible answers**
> 1 A number of reasons will be given in this essay.
> 2 It cannot be denied that children enjoy television ...
> 3 ... from which a great deal can be assimilated ...
> 4 ... the subject is brought to life.
> 5 Young people can be informed by soap operas, as well.
> 6 It is illogical to claim...
> 7 Moreover, it depends what is meant by 'less well educated'.
> 8 ... books are irrelevant ...

5 Remember to vary the language you use, rather than repeat the same word.

> **Answers**
> excellent facilities
> learning experience
> important facts
> survival issues

6 It is better to avoid using language from the task wherever possible.

> **Suggested answers**
> *replace the book as a learning tool*
>   > be used as an alternative educational medium to the book
> *children are less well educated today*
>   > nowadays, children have less knowledge than previously

7

8

Sample answer
The statement is somewhat questionable, as it seems to imply that the role of television in education is exactly the same as that of the book, which is clearly not the case. Moreover, children are undoubtedly better educated today than they were in the past, and this is largely thanks to the availability of multi-media learning resources such as television and the Internet.

Research has shown that many children learn better from visual input, such as that provided by television. There are many educational programmes on television and even 'entertainment' can provide some form of educational stimulus.

Furthermore, it cannot be denied that children today are happy to watch television but may need encouragement to read a book. Therefore, they should be offered programmes with educational value, from which they can learn more about the world around them. Many documentaries include interesting footage of events that a child living in a city might never see – take the migration of the African wildebeest, for example. In this way, television can add a great deal to a child's experience and knowledge of the world.

Naturally, there will always be a place for the printed book, which is a relatively inexpensive medium of learning material. That said, many books are not readily available, although the Internet now provides many books online that were once out of print. In the final analysis, educational institutions should take advantage of all appropriate resources, including television, in order to stimulate a child's imagination and thirst for learning.
(250 words)

Unit 19

19.1 pages 124–125

1 The pictures show workers assembling bikes, and two operators at a call centre. Make some notes about a comparison of the two jobs (for example, factory/workshop setting and telecom/computer setting; manual work and service industry). Then consider possible answers to the questions, using some of the Useful language.

Possible answers
- Most businesses are very small, with only a handful of employees. The majority of them are shops or offer services. There are some large companies, like manufacturers of cars or fridges, but in the last few years quite a number of foreign companies have moved into the country, and are competing with them, and some local businesses are struggling.
- I'd love to offer a service for busy people, where somebody would do all the things the customers don't have time for, like shopping, cleaning and looking after pets.
- I think the most important thing is to decide what you're really interested in, and whether you'd enjoy doing it as a job. For instance, I love cooking, but I would hate to be a chef and have to cook for dozens of people every day. It's also essential to decide on a realistic income to aim for.
- One possibility is that manufacturing will decline, and the demand for services will grow. I think, too, that fewer people will be employed in agriculture.

2 Read questions 1–7, then listen to the first part of the recording. Afterwards read questions 8–14 and listen to the second part of the recording.

Answers (relevant parts of the recording script are underlined)
1 selection 2 self-knowledge 3 objective
4 product; market

5, 6, 7 B, E, F (in any order)

8 income 9 funds 10 (working) hours 11 stress
12 skills 13 calculated 14 mistakes

Recording script

Questions 1–7

Consultant: As a way of earning a living, running your own business has two distinctive features. <u>The first is that you don't go through the usual selection procedure</u>; you're not competing against other applicants, or facing psychological tests or cunning interview questions to test your suitability for the job. <u>You're the sole judge of your fitness to start and run your own business.</u> <u>This puts a very heavy responsibility on your self-knowledge</u>, because not everyone is suited to this type of work. You can also learn about yourself from the opinion of colleagues, friends or family, but this carries the risk of emotional problems. They may feel under pressure to give a favourable opinion for fear of offending you. <u>Unless you can expect an objective view, it's better not to ask them at all.</u>

The second unusual characteristic of setting up on your own is that you decide what type of business it is and who you'll be selling to. If your business is well run, it stands a good chance of succeeding. In practice, however, <u>you can make success more likely by selecting your product and market carefully.</u> Although you may be able to create a demand for what you have to sell, it's much easier if that demand already exists.

While many people dream of setting up their own business, not so many actually do so. Some, of course, are entrepreneurs from the start, starting a business without ever working for another organisation. Others, who have been employed, are sometimes pushed into making the change by external circumstances, such as <u>being sacked or made redundant</u>. They may have been thinking about becoming self-employed for years, but been too comfortable to do anything about it. It also often happens that <u>someone is confident of being appointed to a more senior position within their organisation, and another person is chosen instead</u>. This can have a very demoralising effect, and even destroy the satisfaction the person gained from their work. A third reason is <u>when someone begins to feel that they've got nothing to show for the years they've been working</u>. This may be triggered by reaching a particular age, such as 40, or by seeing friends or colleagues as being more successful.

Questions 8–14

Consultant: When you're considering whether or not to start your own business, you need to make a realistic assessment of what it involves, particularly while you're getting established. Your business life is unlikely to be easy.

At the outset, and perhaps for some time, <u>you may find you can't draw as much income from your business as you'd like</u>. It can be very helpful if your husband or wife is earning <u>so that they can provide the funds you need to live on</u>.

While you might think you can choose when to work, in practice <u>you'll probably find you have far longer working hours than you'd like</u>. This is almost unavoidable. If your business isn't going well, you'll have problems to overcome; and even if it's successful, you may want to make as much money as possible in case things start going wrong!

<u>Running your own business can lead to a great deal of stress</u>, particularly if you allow the business to overwhelm you. Talk to your family about your work, and ask for their support, so that you're not facing the problems alone.

You'll need to be a salesperson, technical expert, accountant and administrator, all in one. <u>Be honest about your skills. If you can identify your weaknesses</u>, consider being trained or try to afford expert assistance.

Failure is very likely if you take a major gamble; but if you only want to pursue low-risk ventures you may be short of ideas to follow up. <u>The best chance of success comes from calculated risks</u> which allow you to make a sound estimate of the likely outcome.

Founding and controlling a successful business can yield a tremendous sense of achievement, but there may be failures. If there are, you must be able to accept failure without finding the effect devastating, and <u>improve your future performance by drawing all the lessons possible from your mistakes</u> – if indeed you've made any.

You're probably wondering whether it's such a good idea to start your own business, but now I'll go on to some of the rewards.

3   Make sure you understand the words in the box, then complete the exercise.

> **Answers**
> **1** catering   **2** qualifications   **3** property
> **4** refurbishment   **5** staff   **6** applicants   **7** suppliers
> **8** customers   **9** profit   **10** chain

4   Make some notes on the topic, using your own ideas as well as some mentioned in the listening passage and in exercise 3.

> **Possible answers**
> Advantages include the freedom to carry out your own ideas, perhaps being able to take time off whenever you want to, feeling committed to your work because it's your own choice.
> Disadvantages include the difficulty of taking time off if there's nobody else to do the work, the lack of a regular income, having to do everything from marketing to finance.

5   Remind yourself of the benefits of sounding interesting (this was introduced in Unit 15). Read what is in the box and then play the recording.

> **Possible answers**
> **1** Version **b** is better; for example, the pitch is more varied, the words linked more smoothly and the stressed syllables are more regular.
> **2** Version **a** is better; for example, the words are linked more smoothly and the stressed syllables are more regular.
> **3** Version **a** is better; for example, the pitch is more varied and 'another' is at a high pitch level to signal the new topic.
> **4** Version **b** is better; for example, the words are linked more smoothly and the stressed syllables are more regular.

6   You are now going to hear a model Part 2 topic. As you listen, make notes on what makes the woman sound interesting.

> **Possible answer**
> She uses a wide pitch range; she varies the speed and uses pauses for dramatic effect; she varies the volume; she shows her feelings, for instance by laughing.

Recording script

Woman: When I was 14, I got a job delivering newspapers to people's homes. I had to arrive at the paper shop at six o'clock every morning, take the newspapers for my round, and cycle off and deliver them. And I needed to be at school before nine.

I'd applied for the job because I wanted to earn some money. I hadn't thought much about what was involved, but I was sure there'd be nothing to it.

But I was wrong! In most homes, the newspaper had to be pushed through the letterbox in the front door. And it was sometimes a struggle to find the right front door. A lot of them weren't numbered, some letterboxes were at ground level, or not in the door at all, and several were so small it took ages to get the newspapers through. And there was another problem: dogs jumping up at the letterbox and trying to bite my fingers!

I just about managed to get to school on time, but I was so exhausted that I almost fell asleep during a maths lesson. I decided not to go back the next morning, but then I thought of the money I could earn, so I changed my mind. Luckily it was much easier from then on.

7   Quickly make a few notes on the topic, then speak for one to two minutes. If possible, record yourself then listen to how interesting you sound.

19.2 pages 126–127

1   The pictures show a cleaner in an office block and a surgeon and other medical staff carrying out an operation. Think about how you could compare the jobs.

> **Possible answers**
> Cleaning is unskilled work and is usually poorly paid and of low status. It may involve working early in the morning or late at night. Medical work is highly skilled and may be well paid and of high status, though this varies from country to country. A surgeon has far more responsibility than a cleaner, because there is always the risk of the patient dying.

Look at the attitudes **A–F**, and think about your own reaction to each one.

2   Try doing the task as a timed test activity. There are more questions than there would be in the IELTS test, so allow yourself 25 minutes.

> **Answers** (evidence from the passage is given, but this is not part of the answer)
> 1–3 B, C, E (in any order)
>   B *John Calvin introduced a significant new attitude towards work. He taught that people's daily life and deeds, and success in worldly endeavours, reflected their moral worth.* (lines 28–31)
>   C *the idea of work as a religious obligation was replaced by the concept of public usefulness. Economists warned of the poverty and decay that would befall the country if people failed to work hard, and moralists stressed the social duty of each person to be productive.* (lines 44–48)
>   E *pay and 'getting ahead' were the primary incentives management used to encourage productivity during the industrial age.* (lines 64–66)
> 4 C *Selection of an occupation ... was considered a religious duty* (lines 34–36)
> 5 A *the majority of men laboured so that the minority could engage in pure exercises of the mind – art, philosophy and politics.* (lines 8–10)
> 6 C *pursuing it to achieve the greatest profit possible was considered a religious duty ... The key elements of these new beliefs about work – usually called the 'Protestant work ethic' – were hard work ... and the great importance of work.* (lines 37–41)
> 7 B *Wealth was recognized as an opportunity to share with those who might be less fortunate* (lines 16–17)

> 8 A *'Those who need to work must be willing to accept an inferior status.'* (lines 10–11)
> 9 B *It was the duty of a worker to remain in his class, passing on his family work from father to son.* (lines 19–21)
> 10 C *Men ... were to reinvest the profits of their labour into financing further ventures.* (lines 32–34)
> 11 rewarding (line 51) 12 quality (line 52)
> 13 autonomy (line 53) 14 motivation (line 54)
> 15 control (line 57) 16 incentives (line 64)

3   This is an example of a noun phrase: *the history of the human race.* Find other noun phrases in the passage meaning the same as 1–6.

> **Answers**
> 1 the satisfaction of material needs (line 3)
> 2 the absence of compulsion (lines 4–5)
> 3 a new perspective on work (line 24)
> 4 public usefulness (line 45)
> 5 opportunity for personal growth (line 56)
> 6 a decline in belief (line 62)

For more information see the Grammar folder, page 143.

4

> **Answers**
> 1 dramatic expansion
> 2 rapid spread of industrialisation
> 3 availability of goods
> 4 involvement in decision making
> 5 growing awareness; individual needs

5   Spend one minute making notes and then speak for up to two minutes, perhaps recording yourself.

Test folder 10
pages 128–129

Make sure you fully understand the notes and advice.

1   Think about what is shown in the photograph (the woman is interviewing the man for a job). Read the summary and think about what word classes and meanings might fit each space. Complete the summary as you listen.

> **Answers** (relevant parts of the recording are underlined)
> 1 self-starter 2 training 3 focus 4 pressure
> 5 challenge 6 respect 7 research 8 skills
> 9 communication

Recording script

You will hear a careers adviser talking to a group of students about applying for jobs.

First you have some time to look at questions 1 to 9. (pause)

Now listen carefully and answer questions 1 to 9.

Adviser: Now I know that many of you are applying for jobs at the moment, so here's some advice on maximising your chances of success. If you've been invited to a job interview – particularly if it's your first – you're probably delighted that you've got that far. But you may be wondering how recruiters make their choice. They want to appoint the best person for the job, but how do they decide? Sometimes it's difficult to know exactly what they're looking for in an ideal candidate, so let me tell you what generally impresses interviewers.

One important area is personal initiative. This covers a range of skills, competencies and qualities, and includes things like being a self-starter – that is, not waiting to be told everything, but making an effort to find out for yourself, asking questions, doing tasks that need to be done and which are within your capabilities.

Initiative also involves showing a potential employer that you've identified your professional goals and have worked out how to achieve them: both the training and the hands-on experience that you want within the organisation. Most recruiters will be uneasy if you've applied for jobs as varied as an accountant, a teacher and a sales executive: they'll suspect that you lack the necessary focus, and they won't expect you to be interested enough in the work, or determined enough to succeed.

Recruiters generally want someone who won't give up. In most jobs these days people are working under pressure, and you need to be able to handle it. As the saying goes, 'If you can't stand the heat, get out of the kitchen.' Recruiters are normally interested in someone who's enthusiastic about getting involved, so you should show that you welcome a challenge. They also look for confident individuals who are adaptable and flexible.

The ability to project the right image is a must-have skill for most employers. This means always behaving in a professional way, and having respect for people, whether these are colleagues, customers or suppliers. And this needs to be maintained even in difficult situations. And always make sure you promote a positive image both of yourself and of the organisation.

If applicants haven't bothered to find out before the interview about the organisation they're applying to, it suggests that they aren't really interested in working there, so it pays to do some research. Then, in the interview itself, you can ask questions that both impress the recruiters and give you the information you need.

Job applicants very often undersell what they're capable of doing, and this may be because they've failed to review their experience so far. It's a worthwhile exercise to compile a list of your skills and how you developed them. Then, when you get to an interview, you'll have plenty of examples to refer to.

You may be the perfect candidate, but you need to let others know about it. It's really important that one of your strengths is communication. You need to be able to put your point across in a discussion, take on board what other people are saying and respond appropriately. Being at ease and able to chat with others on an everyday level is a valuable aspect of this, too.

I hope this is making you think about how to prepare for an interview and also how to behave …

2   Read the notes and skim the passage, then read questions 1–6 and complete the summary. This will take you to the end of the second paragraph (*reputation*).

For questions 7–14, the title of the summary gives a clue to which part of the passage the answers will be found in – beginning *Public relations* and referring to people's perception of what an organisation seems to be like. Note that the words in the box do not necessarily appear in the passage. Read the rest of the passage, beginning at *Public relations*, and complete questions 7–14.

Answers

1 coverage   **2** conferences   **3** offence   **4** well-being
5 new factory   **6** reputation

7 impressions	*everyone reads, watches or listens to the media. That forms the basis for their perception of what an organisation seems to be like.* (paragraph 3)
8 distortion	*Clearly PR needs the media, but it is wary of it, mainly because of the fear that messages will be twisted.* (paragraph 3)
9 consistency	*One of the reasons for the efforts companies make to improve internal relations is to avoid a contradiction* (paragraph 4)
10 staff	*between its public relations stance and what its employees say about it.* (paragraph 4)
11 aims	*All organisations, whether commercial or not, have competing objectives.* (paragraph 5)
12 objectivity	*It is this partiality which lowers public relations practitioners in the esteem of journalists, business leaders and, to a lesser extent, the general public.* (paragraph 6)
13 invisibility	*As a strategic force it is often unseen.* (paragraph 8)
14 shallowness	*Accusations of superficiality also arise* (paragraph 8)

Unit 20

20.1 pages 130–131

1   The picture shows ruins at the ancient city of Ephesus, in Turkey. Consider how you might answer the questions. Some answers are given in the reading passage.

Possible answers

● I think it's very important to know the results of past policies, so that governments don't make the same mistakes. We need to study history to gain this knowledge.

● It seems to me that most aspects of present-day life have been affected by past events. Conflicts that go back for years can't be solved without understanding why the communities involved feel as they do about each other.

- Just as I believe studying our own country's history helps us to understand our lives better, I think we need to know about other countries' histories, to get some insight into their present-day situations.

2 Skim the passage, timing yourself. Answer the global question.

> **Answer**
> D

3 Work through the multiple-choice questions. It may be helpful to underline the relevant parts of the passage.

> **Answers** (evidence from the passage is given, but this is not part of the answer)
> 1 B *complete asepsis … is also impossible, but one does not, for that reason, perform surgery in a sewer. There is no need to write or teach history in an intellectual sewer either. (lines 10–14)*
> 2 A *And the consequences of those facts cannot be averted by either ignorance or misrepresentation (lines 19–20)*
> 3 C *In bygone times, it was considered sufficient if a country, a society, or a community concerned itself with its own history. In these days, when almost every action or policy has a global dimension, we know better. (lines 23–26)*
> 4 A *Not a few of our troubles at the present time spring from a failure to recognise or even see these differences (lines 38–39)*
> 5 C *Even within each country, modernisation is destroying the barriers that previously divided us into neatly segregated communities, each living its own life in its own way, suffering minimal contacts with the outsider. (lines 48–51)*
> 6 A *But even real differences and real problems are made worse by ignorance, and a host of difficulties may reasonably be blamed on ignorance alone. (lines 58–61)*

4

> **Answers**
> 1 a 2 b 3 a 4 b 5 b 6 a

5 This exercise will help you to use words from the passage and from exercise 4.

> **Answers**
> 1 unbiased 2 analogous 3 consequently 4 perceive
> 5 succession 6 recognition

6 Think about how you might answer this question.

> **Possible answer**
> It is very difficult to avoid bias altogether, particularly if we grow up in a society that assumes its own version of history is the only possible interpretation. However, it is important to do one's best to be objective.

20.2 pages 132–133

1 The pictures show modern backpackers and some 19th-century women at the seaside. Consider how you would answer the questions.

> **Possible answers**
> It depends a lot on how much money people have. Some can't afford to go away at all, others visit their families, but those with plenty of money go abroad several times a year. Skiing holidays are very popular in the winter, and beach holidays in the summer, but more and more young people are spending six months or a year travelling round the world.

2 Look at questions 1–7 and predict the answers, then listen to the first part of the recording. Then do the same for questions 8–14.

> **Answers** (relevant parts of the recording script are underlined)
> 1 health 2 winter 3 (the) railways 4 entertainment
> 5 (social) classes 6 accommodation 7 doctors
>
> 8 paid holidays 9 industrial 10 jet 11 package
> 12 suntan 13 low-cost airlines 14 gap year

Recording script

Questions 1–7

Lecturer: Today in our survey of the social history of Britain we're going to be looking at the seaside holiday, and I'll start with a brief overview. Nowhere in the country is more than about 150 km from the sea, but for centuries the sea was the preserve of shipping. It wasn't associated with leisure, even for those people who could afford to travel for pleasure.

Britain's annual seaside ritual began in the 18th century with the new aristocratic fashion for sea bathing. Hardly anyone could swim in those days, and the main attraction of the seaside was the benefits of seawater and sea air for the health. Submersion in the ice-cold waves, followed by a glass of seawater mixed with milk or honey, was thought to cure all illnesses, so the aristocracy came in the winter. This fashion was soon followed by other people with money.

In the mid 19th century seaside resorts expanded rapidly as railways were constructed connecting industrial towns with the coast. Far more people were now able to travel to the seaside, and sleepy coastal villages were transformed into booming seaside towns. They were no longer primarily regarded as health resorts, but as entertainment centres, and people generally went there in the summer.

The holidaymakers were mostly middle class, as they were the only people who could afford the expensive train fares and seaside accommodation. But by the end of the 19th century, working-class families were also flocking to the coast from the industrial towns and cities. 19th-century seaside resorts attracted distinct social classes and their reputation as either upmarket or downmarket became part of the national folklore, continuing into the 20th century and even to some extent today. Resorts that catered for the mass market laid on popular entertainments and provided inexpensive accommodation to entice people to stay longer, as many working-class families could only afford day trips to the seaside.

In the 1920s and 30s seaside holidays boomed as never before, as doctors began to stress the importance of fresh air, exercise and sunlight. This was because the poor state of the nation's health had become a major concern.

Questions 8–14

Lecturer: From the late 19th century onwards, more and more workers had time off work with pay, but the trend was given new impetus in 1948, when Parliament passed an Act guaranteeing paid holidays. Soon, two-thirds of manual workers were having a fortnight off each year, and the majority of working-class families had enough money to stay away for a week or two. Most chose to go to the same resort that they had previously visited on their day trips: usually the closest to where they lived. In fact, many returned year after year to the same accommodation. Group holidays, involving extended families, streets or even whole towns, were still the norm. Entire communities went on holiday together, especially when the major employers in northern industrial towns closed down for a week or two in the summer.

The success story of British seaside resorts ended in the 1960s. One factor was the new jet aircraft, which brought travel to Spain or the Greek islands within reach of far more people. Then, too, the ever-expanding international tourist industry organised flights and accommodation covered by a single, fairly low payment: this was the birth of the package holiday. Sunshine replaced the sea as the main holiday attraction, and an annual foreign holiday, with a suntan to prove it, was now taken for granted as part of modern life.

With the even greater affluence of the last few years, it's no longer unusual to take two or more holidays a year: maybe a long-haul flight to Thailand, Australia or the USA, plus a winter skiing holiday in Bulgaria, Andorra or Canada. And in between, there may well be weekend breaks abroad, as the growth of low-cost airlines has meant that a flight to Spain or Italy can be cheaper than a much shorter train journey within Britain.

Another change is that, instead of the large groups of the past, the trend is for families to holiday by themselves. Many older teenage children and young people go on independent holidays with friends rather than their relations. And another trend is for school-leavers not to go straight on to higher education, but to take what's called a 'gap year' first, spending time in Australia, perhaps, or travelling round the world.

It's all a far cry from the seaside holidays in Britain of the past. Now, let's go on to …

3

Answers
could swim = were able to swim (an ability in the past; *could* is the past tense of *can*)
could have been put = the speaker now thinks it is possible that this happened in the past

4 Refer to the Grammar folder on page 143 before doing the exercise. Remember that modal perfects are frequently used in academic English.

Answers
1 … they **must have wanted** to stay in crowds.
2 The residents of quiet fishing villages **can't/couldn't have been** happy …
3 … **should have made** more effort to compete with foreign resorts.
4 British resorts **may/might not have realised** how cheap …
5 People in the 19th century **shouldn't have believed** that …
6 The popularity of holidays abroad **may/might/could have been encouraged** by …

5 Correct the errors in the tenses. In each case you should use a modal perfect.

Answers
1 The glass was broken, and I think that **may have been caused** by a cat!
2 He **can't have thought** enough about the consequences of his actions.
3 If I'd been there, you **wouldn't have had** such a bad time.
4 The accident was very sad, but it **could have been** prevented.
5 You **must have pressed** the wrong button, because the lift went up instead of down.
6 It's your own fault you feel sick – you **shouldn't have eaten** so much.
7 He said it took him two hours to walk here but it's only three kilometres, so it **can't/couldn't have taken** so long.

6 Remember that the long pronunciation of vowels is the same as the name of the letter (a, e, i, o, u). Complete rules 1–3.

Answers
1 e   2 *-ing, -y*   3 consonant + suffix/ending

7 Decide on the odd one out. Then play the recording and listen for the odd one out in each set – the word with a short vowel.

Answers
All the vowels are long except:
Pattern 1: *since* (the vowel is followed by *two* consonants)
Pattern 2: *written* (the ending *-en* is not included in the list)
Pattern 3: *fashion* (the vowel is followed by *two* consonants)

8 Spend no more than a minute making brief notes for your talk, then speak for one to two minutes, perhaps recording yourself. Make sure you sound interesting!

9 Try and answer the quiz from memory. If you can't remember an answer, try and find the relevant unit and find the answer.

> **Answers** (the relevant section of the book is given)
> 1 a supercontinent (11.2)
> 2 dinosaurs (13.1)
> 3 the ocarina (Revision Units 5–8)
> 4 China (8.2)
> 5 the stars (Test folder 7)
> 6 factories (14.2)
> 7 soap (3.1)
> 8 the garden city (Test folder 5)
> 9 the baby boom (14.1)
> 10 sandwiches (for lunch) (5.1)

Writing folder 10

pages 134–135

Task 1

> **Answers**
> 1 The charts below show what the history and engineering graduates of a particular university were doing six months after graduating. The figures cover a two-year period. Summarise the information by selecting and reporting the main features, and make comparisons where relevant.
> 2 The main comparison is by subject, i.e. the similarities and differences between history and engineering graduates.
> 3 Sentences a, d and e are correct. There is no indication of the numbers of graduates, so the bar charts do not show b, c or f. They may or may not be true.
> 4 All four statements are true, but b and d contain the most important information because they deal with the largest categories.
> 5 Because the charts compare students by subject, c would be the most efficient way of making the comparison.
> 6 Suggested notes:
> **Introduction**
> Topic: destinations of university's history and engineering students six months after graduating
> Summary: majority in both groups employed
> **Comparison**
> Employment: higher proportion of engineering graduates than historians
> Further study: higher proportion of historians than engineers
> Time out: higher proportion of historians than engineers
> Seeking work: smallest category for historians; engineers more likely to seek work than take time out
> 7 **Sample answer**
> These two charts, covering a two-year period, show the destinations of a university's history and engineering graduates, six months after graduating. In both groups, the majority were employed, and the changes from year 1 to year 2 in all categories were broadly similar.
>
> One significant difference was that engineers were more likely than historians to be working. From 63% in year 1, the figure for historians rose modestly to 67%, while the corresponding figures for engineers were 75% and almost 80%.
>
> On the other hand, a higher proportion of historians than engineers went on to further study: in year 1 this category accounted for 27% of historians against only 12% of engineers, with both figures dropping slightly the following year.
>
> In both years, 7% of history graduates took time out, a higher proportion than those seeking work. The reverse was true for engineers: 2% took time out, while just over 10% were seeking work.
>
> The charts show that the engineers were more likely to be employed or seeking employment than the historians. (172 words)

Task 2

> **Sample answer**
> Many countries have a staff shortage in medicine and other fields requiring a great deal of training. At the same time, there may be a lack of unskilled and semi-skilled workers, like cleaners or drivers.
>
> The gap in skilled professions is partly due to time and money: the training for a nurse or doctor takes several years and is very expensive. Future needs cannot be predicted very accurately, so it is hard to ensure that enough people are trained. Many individuals and countries simply cannot afford the training.
>
> Some governments have tackled this problem by determining what subjects students should study. This ensures that enough lawyers, teachers, and so on are trained. One drawback, however, is that it ignores differences in people's motivation and aptitude, and may mean that someone who might have been an excellent dentist has become a mediocre accountant instead.
>
> A shortage may also result from variation in the cost of living. In my country, very few public sector employees, such as police officers, can afford accommodation in the most affluent regions, resulting in ever-increasing staff shortages in those areas. The problem can be alleviated, though only to a limited extent, by subsidising housing for certain workers.
>
> As the level of education rises, fewer people are willing to take on menial work such as refuse collection. The unpleasantness of such work could be recognised through high wages, although this would require a transformation of the country's economy.
>
> To conclude, shortages are probably inevitable, although the fields and geographical areas where they occur are likely to change from time to time. (263 words)

Units 17–20 Revision

pages 136–137

1 Try to compare and contrast the subjects in detail, giving examples to support your ideas.

2

> **Answers**
> 1 the availability of
> 2 The movement of
> 3 seasonal migration of
> 4 arrival of; people's expectations; uncertainty about

3

> **Suggested answers**
> 1 They could have had a bad diet. They could have received / been receiving little dental care. They could have been drinking impure water.
> 2 The fall could have been because of cost. It could have been down to a preference for other locations. It could have been due to the increased threat of terrorism.
> 3 The bird could have used / been using solar navigation. It could have recognised / been recognising landmarks during flight. It could have used its sense of smell to find its way.
> 4 Jenny could have given a poor impression at the interview. Jenny may not have been decisive enough. The company could have offered the job to an internal applicant. The company could have suffered / been suffering unforeseen cutbacks.
> 5 Ryan's essay could have been poorly organised. It could have contained irrelevance. It could have been too short.

4

> **Answers**
> 1 why 2 how 3 whether 4 whether 5 why/how
> 6 how/why 7 why 8 how

5

> **Answers**
> 1 introduction 2 central 3 oversight 4 worryingly
> 5 questionable 6 carefully 7 misinformed
> 8 occasionally 9 validity

6

> **Answers**
> 1 promotion 2 job security 3 run 4 shift work
> 5 short list 6 labour force 7 boss 8 responsibilities
> 9 motivation 10 profit

Acknowledgements

The authors would like to express their gratitude to Alyson Maskell for her many constructive suggestions and meticulous attention to detail. Thanks also go to Annabel Marriott at Cambridge University Press for her enthusiasm and careful project management, and to Stephanie White at Kamae Design for her creative design solutions.

The authors and publishers would like to thank the teachers and consultants who commented on the material:

Singapore: Rosanna Maiolo; Taiwan: Daniel Sansoni; United Arab Emirates: Belinda Hayes; UK: Jan Farndale, Mike Gutteridge; Clare West.

The authors and publishers are grateful to the following for permission to reproduce copyright material. It has not always been possible to identify the sources of all the material used or to contact the copyright holders and in such cases the publishers would welcome information **from the copyright owners**.
Apologies are expressed for any omissions.

p. 10–11: Adapted extract from 'Writing at University' by Crème and Lea © 2003. Reproduced by kind permission of Open University Press/McGraw-Hill Publishing Company; p. 13: Rachel Liddle for the adapted article 'Waking the Brain' from *The Guardian* 23 July 2003. © Rachel Liddle; p. 14: *New Scientist* for the adapted article 'Let software catch the game for you' by James Randerson, 3 July 2004, pp. 36–37: adapted article 'Battle of the Bag' by Caroline Williams, 11 September 2004, p. 40: adapted article 'The power of Music' 29 November 2003, p. 56: diagram 'The self-cooling drink can', 24 April 2004, p. 57: diagram 'SpaceshipOne', 18 September 2004, p. 86: adapted article 'Killer Blow' by Kate Ravilious, 4 May 2002. © New Scientist; p. 22: *The Guardian* for adapted article 'Hearts for Sale' by Madeleine Bunting, 9 April 2001, p. 52: 'Chips with everything' by Ian Sample, 5 February 2004, p. 60: 'Where Blade runner meets Las Vegas' by Stuart Jeffries, 8 November 2004. © Guardian Newspapers Limited; p. 25: Adapted text 'Building a Personal Brand Identity' by Chuck Pettis. Copyright 2003, BrandSolutions Inc. All Rights Reserved. For information on branding visit BrandSolutions at www.brand.com; p. 28: Open University Press for adapted text for Listening exercise 'Language variation and English' by David Stringer, p. 101: adapted text 'Language and Social Reality' by Geoffrey Esland, p. 104: 'Personality. A User's Guide', by Daniel Nettle. © Open University Press; p. 46: NASA for adapted text 'Why do we explore space?' taken from the website http://adc.gsfc.nasa.gov, © NASA; p. 50–51: ThinkQuest Oracle for text 'Why Explore?', taken from the website www.thinkquest.org © ThinkQuest Oracle Help Us Help; pp. 54–55: California Academy of Sciences for adapted text 'History of Eating Utensils' by Debra McPherson, 1998 (www.calacademy.org/research/anthropology/utensil/index.html. Reprinted by permission of California Academy of Sciences, San Francisco, CA; p. 54: AsiaRecipe.com for 'How to use chopsticks' taken from http://AsiaRecipe.com; p. 64: Columbia University Press for adapted text for Listening exercise 'History of suburbs' from *Columbia Encyclopedia*. Reprinted by permission of Columbia University Press; p. 64: Farrar, Straus & Giroux and SLL/Sterling Lord Literistic for adapted text for Listening exercise 'What is Sprawl and why' from *Suburban Nation*. Copyright © 2000 by Andres Duany, Elizabeth Plater-Zybeck & Jess Speck. Reprinted by permission of North Point Press, a division of Farrar, Straus and Giroux LLC and SLL/Sterling Lord Literistic, Inc; pp. 66–67: *Pittsburg Post Gazette* for adapted article 'Lucid Dreams say they can learn skills, cure ills' by Virginia Linn, 11 December 2003. © Pittsburg Post Gazette; pp. 74–75: US Geological Survey for adapted text and map 'Historical Survey', taken from the website http://pubs.usgs.gov. © US Geological Survey; p. 77: Blackwell Publishing Ltd for illustration 'The floor of the South Atlantic Ocean' from *The Nature of the Environment*, by Andrew Goudie. Used by permission of Blackwell Publishing Ltd; p. 82: Carbon Dioxide and Information Analysis Center for adapted text 'Global and hemispheric temperature anomalies' taken from the website http://cdiac.esd.ornl.gov/trends/jonescru/joneshtml. © Jones, et al and The US Department of Energy, CDIAC; p. 82: John Wiley & Sons, Australia for the graphs 'Water shortage in South Africa' from the Jacaranda Project Worksheet www.jacaonline.com.au/downloads/sose/2004-11-africa.pdf. © 2004. Reproduced by permission of John Wiley & Sons Australia; p. 90: The American Museum of Natural History for the adapted text for the listening exercise 'What if you could catch a falling star' taken from the website www.amnh.org. Used by permission of the American Museum of Natural History, New York City; p. 91: Michael Rowan-Robinson for the adapted text 'Milky Way' from *Universe*; p. 92: The Australian Bureau of Statistics for adapted text 'Australian Social Trends 1999' taken from the website www.abas.gov.au. ABS data is used with permission from the Australian Bureau of Statistics; p. 98: Peter Fraser Dunlop for the adapted text 'Risk taking is good for you' from *The Guardian*, 15 July 2004, by Vivienne Parry. Reprinted by permission of PFD on behalf of Vivienne Parry; p. 102: Harcourt Inc for adapted text 'A story of two towns' taken from *Language and Thought in Action* by S I Hayakawa and Basil H Pillard, copyright 1939, renewed 1967. Reprinted with permission by Harcourt Inc; p. 130: American Philosophical Society for the adapted text from *The Proceedings of the American Philosophical Society, Volume 143 no 4*. Adapted with permission.

CDROM

Section 1 Reading: Palgrave Macmillan for the adapted text from *The Future of Brands* by Rita Clifton and Esther Maughan. Copyright © 2000 Macmillan Press Ltd. Reproduced with permission of Palgrave Macmillan; Section 2 Reading: WGBH Media Library for adapted text 'Birth of an Expedition' by Peter Tyson from the website for the Nova program *Into the Abyss*. From the WGBH Educational Foundation. Copyright © 2000 WGBH/Boston; Section 3 Reading: Professor Steven Rose for the adapted text 'Natural Conclusion' from The Guardian, 19 April 2003, © Professor Steven Rose; Section 4 Reading: *The Daily Telegraph* for adapted article 'Don't think about it, sleep on it' by Raj Persaud, 6 September 2005 and for Section 5 Reading: adapted article 'The right place for a flirting flatfish' by Roger Highfield, 27 August 2003, © Telegraph Group Limited; Section 6 Listening: 'Monitoring the pulse of Mount Vesuvius' by Elisabeth Pain. Taken from the website www.nextwave.sciencemag.org. 12 August 2005. Adapted with permission. © 2005 AAAS; Section 7 Listening: BBC.co.uk for the adapted extract 'The rise of the Victorian Middle Class' by Dr Donna Loftus, taken from the website www.bbc.co.uk/history/society_culture/society/middle_class. Used by permission of BBC.co.uk; Section 8 Listening: The Scottish Enterprise for adapted text 'Taking risks for Growth' 29 September 2004, taken from the website www.scottishbusiness.women.com. Used by kind permission; Section 10 Listening: SCRE Centre for adapted text 'As we see it' by Hendry, Shucksmith and Love, taken from http://www.scre.ac.uk/rie/n1143hendry.html. Used by permission of the SCRE Centre, University of Glasgow.

The publishers are grateful to the following for permission to include photographs, logos and other illustrative material:

Key: l = left, r = right, t = top, c = centre, b = bottom, u = upper, l = lower

Action Plus/©Chris Barry p. 16 (b); Image courtesy of The Advertising Archives p. 20 (l); Alamy/©Atmosphere Picture Library p. 84 (l), /©Jan Caudron/Anaklasis p. 125, /©colinspics p. 14 (tc), /©Jeremy Hoare p. 106 (r), /©Images of Africa Photobank p. 72 (tr), /©Neil McAllister p. 94 (l), /©VIEW Pictures Ltd p. 71; Bridgeman Art Library/©Museo Archeologico Nazionale, Naples, Italy, Giraudon p. 59, /Sir Richard Steele (1672-1729) (engraving) (b/w photo), English School, (18th century) / Private Collection p. 118 (tl); CORBIS/©Bettmann p. 114 (bl), /©John Farmar; Ecoscene p. 72 (br), /©Fine Art Photographic Library p. 68 (tc), /©Owen Franken p. 72 (tc), /©Jose Fuste Raga pp. 60 (r), 61, /©Eric and David Hosking 80 (r), /©Hulton-Deutsch Collection p. 94 (r), /©Yang Liu p. 26 (tr), /©Mary Ann McDonald p. 26 (br), /©Christine Osborne p. 42 (r), /©Tim Pannell p. 120 (r), /©Louie Psihoyos pp. 45, 124 (l), /©Roger Ressmeyer p. 118 (b), /©George Shelley p. 114 (tr), /©Stapleton Collection p. 118 (tr), /©Mark L Stephenson p. 68 (tl); ©Mary Evans Picture Library p. 114 (tl); Getty Images/AFP/©PAUL BARKER p. 14 (bc), /AFP/©LIU JIN p. 52 (l), /AFP/©ERIK VIKTOR p. 88 (b), /©Brian Bahr p. 14 (br), /©Matt Cardy p. 40 (l), /©Michael Crabtree p. 124 (r), /Robert Harding World Imagery/Louise Murray p. 60 (l), /Robert Harding World Imagery/John Henry Claude Wilson p. 42 (l), /©Dave Hogan p. 22, /The Image Bank/Peter Adams p. 68 (tr), /The Image Bank/Peter Dazeley p. 92 (l), /The Image Bank/Jump Run Productions p. 110, /The Image Bank/Anup Shah p. 112 (t), /The Image Bank/Paul Thomas p. 123, /The Image Bank/David Trood Pictures p. 52 (r), /The Image Bank/Adrian Weinbrecht p. 54, /©Robert Laberge p. 14 (bl), /©Andy Lyons p. 14 (tr), /©David Mcnew p. 114 (br), /©Ralph Orlowski p. 20 (c), /Photodisc/Amanda Clement p. 68 (cr), /Photodisc/Malcolm Fife p. 81, /Photographers Choice/Jean Luc Morales p. 40 (r), /Stone/Bruce Ayres pp. 104 (t), 126 (r), /Stone/Mary Kate Denny p. 43, /Stone/John & Eliza Forder p. 98 (l), /Stone/Paul Harris 84 (r), /Stone/World Perspectives p. 46, /Stone/Ed Pritchard p. 98 (r), /Stone/Steven Rothfeld p. 120 (l), /Stone/Paul Souders p. 42 (c), /Justin Sullivan pp. 20 (r), 32, /©Chung Sung-Jun p. 16 (t), /Taxi/Ken Chernus p. 132 (t), /Taxi/Harvey Lloyd pp. 72 (tl), 130, /Taxi/Chip Simons p. 104 (b), /Taxi/Steve Smith p. 68 (wc), /Taxi/Arthur Tilley p. 92 (r); Heritage Images/Ann Ronan Picture Library p. 132 (b); The Kobal Collection/©TOUCHSTONE PICTURES p. 48; NHPA/©Bill Coster p. 112 (b), /©B Jones & M Shimlock p. 68 (br); OSF/Photolibrary.com/©Mike Birkhead p. 26 (bl), /©Mauritius Die Bildagentur Gmbh p. 128, /©Mark Jones p. 68 (uc); Red Cover/©Johnny Bouchier p. 52 (c); Redferns/©Bob Willoughby p. 40 (c); Rex Features/©PAUL COOPER p. 26 (tl), /©FRANCOIS DURAND p. 78, /©c.20thC.Fox/Everett p. 24, /©Lehtikuva OY p. 126 (l), /©RESO p. 68 (bl), /©SIPA PRESS p. 36, /©Richard Young p. 14 (tl); Science Photo Library p. 106 (l), /©Lynwood Chase p. 117, /©John Chumack p. 88 (t), /©Bernhard Edmaier p. 90, /©C.K. Lorenz p. 80 (l), /©University of Cambridge Collection of Air Photographs p. 72 (bl), /©Jim Zipp p. 80 (c).

The following pictures were taken for Cambridge University Press on Commission: Gareth Boden pp. 34 (t, b), 38

Freelance picture research by Hilary Fletcher

The publishers are grateful to the following illustrators:

Mark Draisey: pp. 11, 12, 100, 101, 102; Kamae Design: pp. 36, 48, 54, 56, 57, 58, 62 (b), 65, 73, 74, 75, 76, 77, 82, 83, 92; Valeryia Steadman: pp. 8, 66; Laszlo Veres: pp. 50, 62 (t), 86, 136, 137

The publishers are grateful to the following contributors:

Alyson Maskell: editorial work
Hilary Fletcher: photographic direction, picture research
James Richardson: audio recordings